IN THE SHADOW OF THE WALL

IN THE SHADOW
OF THE WALL

*The Life and Death
of Jerusalem's Maghrebi Quarter,
1187–1967*

VINCENT LEMIRE

TRANSLATED BY JANE KUNTZ

STANFORD UNIVERSITY PRESS
Stanford, California

Stanford University Press
Stanford, California

A previous version of this work was published in French in 2019 under the title *Au pied du Mur: Vie et mort du quartier maghrébin de Jerusalem (1187–1967)* [In the Shadow of the Wall: Life and Death of Jerusalem's Maghrebi Quarter (1197–1967)] © 2022, Éditions du Seuil.

This book has been published with the support of the Centre national du livre.

Printed in the United States of America on acid-free, archival-quality paper

Library of Congress Cataloging-in-Publication Data
Names: Lemire, Vincent, 1973- author.
Title: In the shadow of the wall : the life and death of Jerusalem's Maghrebi
    Quarter, 1187-1967 / Vincent Lemire ; translated by Jane Kuntz.
Other titles: Au pied du mur. English
Description: Stanford, California : Stanford University Press, [2023] |
    Originally published in French under the title: Au pied du Mur. | Includes
    bibliographical references and index.
Identifiers: LCCN 2022046052 (print) | LCCN 2022046053 (ebook)
    | ISBN 9781503615397 (cloth) | ISBN 9781503634206 (paperback) |
    ISBN 9781503634213 (epub)
Subjects: LCSH: North Africans—Jerusalem—History. | Jewish-Arab
    relations—History. | Maghrebi Quarter (Jerusalem)—History. |
    Jerusalem—Ethnic relations—History.
Classification: LCC DS109.8.M32 L46 2023 (print) | LCC DS109.8.M32
    (ebook) | DDC 305.892/7610569442—dc23/eng/20220927
LC record available at https://lccn.loc.gov/2022046052
LC ebook record available at https://lccn.loc.gov/2022046053

Cover design: George Kirkpatrick
Cover photo: Unknown photographer, tinted by the designer, *The Dome of the Rock and the Western Temple Wall, Jerusalem*, between 1898–1946,
Courtesy of the Library of Congress, G. Eric and Edith Matson Photograph Collection.
Typeset by Elliott Beard in Garamond Premier Pro 10.75/15

To Marie,
for life

We need history, for we require refreshment. A pause to rest our conscience, that the possibility of a conscience might endure—not only the locus of thought but of practical reason, giving full license for action.

Patrick Boucheron, What History Can Do:
Inaugural Lesson delivered at the Collège de France
on 17 December 2015. *Paris: Fayard, 2016.*

CONTENTS

IN THE SHADOW OF THE WALL

INTRODUCTION

A PLACE FOR HISTORY

There are places for history that tend to favor the face-to-face
meeting of past and present, by examining documents and
events differently, by seeking to hinge what has disappeared
on what appears.

Arlette Farge, Des lieux pour
l'histoire. *Paris: Le Seuil, 1997*

Saturday, 14 February 2004: Jerusalem is under a blanket of snow, as is often
the case in winter in this mountain town, perched at an altitude of nearly eight
hundred meters. Three days earlier—late Wednesday morning, 11 February—a
5.2 earthquake has shaken the region, causing some damage in Jericho, Jerusalem, and Bethlehem. But again, that's nothing out of the ordinary in a region
regularly hit by seismic events, sometimes of far greater magnitude.[1] On this
Saturday, braving the cold and snow, a few women are gathered in prayer before
the Western Wall, within the perimeter set aside for women, right at the foot
of the talus that borders the plaza at the southern end. By chance, there are no
tourists on the embankment above the talus which leads to the Maghrebi Gate,
the only access route authorized for non-Muslims to reach the Temple Mount,
or Haram al-Sharif. The weather is indeed hardly conducive to strolling; it has
been raining and snowing profusely for several days. Everything is quiet; only
the praying and chanting can be heard, while other sounds are muffled by the

snow that covers the entire landscape and gives an impression of a harmonious, cohesive, and peaceful space.

Suddenly, without warning, the talus collapses on itself, triggering the blacktop layer to cave in. Huge blocks of stone roll down into the middle of the prayer area, overturning tables and chairs, and fortunately causing no casualties. The rockslide immediately uncovers numerous vestiges, sections of wall, foundations, vaults and pilasters, demonstrably old and until now concealed by the backfill that has just collapsed. So far, none of this is particularly newsworthy, for as we know, a "land slippage" is nearly always accompanied by a "time slippage": the Holy City, time and again destroyed and rebuilt, sits atop a multitude of overlaid archaeological layers, and when the land subsides, it brings to light chronological strata for all to see, like an open-air stratigraphic cut. But in this case, it is not an episode of biblical history or crusader legend that this accident has suddenly exposed, but a history far more recent and in many ways more combustible: that of the Maghrebi Quarter where, since the Middle Ages, there once lived several hundred inhabitants originating from Morocco, Algeria, and Tunisia—a historical neighborhood of Jerusalem that was destroyed within a few hours in June 1967, in the aftermath of the Six-Day War.

The unearthing of these vestiges was bound to rekindle the buried memory of the vanished neighborhood, as evidenced by these excerpts from the preliminary report released on 12 March 2007 by a UNESCO mission sent to the site by the World Heritage Committee to assess the impact of this collapse:

> The pathway leading from the Western Wall Plaza to the Maghrebi Gate of the Haram es-Sharif is what remains of the Maghrebi Quarter, demolished by Israel in the aftermath of the six-day war of June 1967. [. . .] In the early 1970s, after the demolition of the Maghrebi Quarter, support walls were built on the northern and southern sides of the pathway, while a concrete structure was built over it to allow the construction of the pavement and the erection of a protective canopy. Since that time, the pathway has been the main access to the Haram es-Sharif for visitors and for the Israeli police and, since 2004, for Jewish worshippers accompanied by the Israeli police. [. . .] In February 2004, weakened by heavy rain and snow, the northern wall of the pathway collapsed, thus creating risks for the users. The collapse of the wall exposed the vaults of the underlying structures.[2]

Further on in the report, the UNESCO experts pointed out that the issue was referred to the World Heritage Committee by the officials of the Jordanian Waqfs, who considered the excavations undertaken by the Israeli authorities at the foot of the collapsed talus to be illegal under international law. If the affair escalated to this point, it is because it reawakened the trauma of the inhabitants' expulsion and the demolition of the quarter, as explicitly noted by the Jordanians: "The Waqf stated that the entire area of the former Maghrebi Quarter and the pathway are its property and that, since 1967, it had requested the return of the keys of the Maghrebi Gate, to no avail. [. . .] The Waqf fears that the archaeological excavations will destroy the last remains of the Maghrebi Quarter." The UNESCO experts conveyed their concern and demanded that the Israeli government "stop immediately the archaeological excavations," in the conclusion of the report sent by their director-general to the secretary-general of the United Nations, Ban Ki-moon.[3]

Since then, the "Maghrebi Ramp" affair has become one of the recurrent points of contention between Israel and UNESCO, as the Arab members of the organization step up resolutions intended to remind all members of the "Islamic" character of this perimeter and to protect heritage deemed "endangered"—going so far as to trigger the unilateral withdrawal of the United States and Israel from UNESCO in late 2018.[4] Beyond the complex geopolitical context in which it unfolded, the affair can be analyzed as symptomatic of a dramatic *return of the repressed*: the Maghrebi ramp, described in the 2007 report as "what remains of the Maghrebi Quarter," functioned as a "memory keeper" allowing remembrance to reemerge like an intruder nearly fifty years after it was formed, when the ramp accidentally gave way.[5] Just as a butte preserves the memory of ancient geomorphic formations abraded over time by erosion, the Maghrebi ramp indicated by its very presence that something had existed *before*, in place of today's spacious Western Wall Plaza (figure 1).[6] In fact, this talus, partly backfilled at the time of the neighborhood's demolition in June 1967, was the last vestige of a vanished history, terraced and deliberately forgotten after the Six-Day War.

Although the Maghrebi Quarter of Jerusalem is effectively a "persistent stigma," there is no denying that it is also a fragile and paradoxical *remembrance*, precisely because it is deprived of an established and instituted *memory*.[7] The quarter is a buried remembrance, unformulated, unexpressed,

FIGURE I. **View of the Maghrebi Quarter, looking northeast, early 1920s. Source: ©
Matson Photograph Collection, Library of Congress.**

unelaborated. It belongs to what clinical psychology calls "unspoken" or
"denial," and what we might call more commonly a "memory lapse." Surprisingly, it turns out that the 1967 destruction is unknown to most visitors
to the Holy City, and no exhaustive history of the Maghrebi Quarter has
yet been published.[8] Even though it was located at the very heart of the old
city, amid the most sacred sanctuaries of the three monotheistic religions,
a focal point of observers and diplomats the world over—or perhaps more
to the point, *because* of all that—the history of this bit of the city, from its
origins to its disappearance, has never been given the thorough *longue durée*
examination it deserves. Although it has been logically obliterated by Israeli
historiography, it is also worth mentioning that this history has not earned
a place in the Palestinian national narrative either, unlike the *nabka* of 1948,
the pivotal feature of Palestinian national identity.[9] Undoubtedly because it
lies largely outside the narrow scope of national identities, it makes sense that
the Maghrebi Quarter of Jerusalem would remain even today one of the blind
spots of the region's historiography, including in works devoted entirely to

the 1967 Six-Day War.[10] In order to grasp what is at stake in this history, this initial surprise must be a starting point that at first leaves us incredulous, but which we must locate at the core of our analysis: Why has the history of the Maghrebi Quarter of Jerusalem never been written?

In the Shadow of a Party Wall: Situation and Location

One reason why the history has gone unwritten is undoubtedly that it takes place in a complex space-time that is particularly tricky to untangle, and because it has been obscured by the shadow cast by the singularly cumbersome "party wall." The Maghrebi Quarter was indeed located quite concretely "up against the Wall," at the foot of the Western Wall (Kotel ha-Maaravi in Hebrew), kept as holy since the late Middle Ages by the Jewish communities of Jerusalem and considered today the central holy place of Judaism.[11] Given that the wall's imposing Herodian stonework is a vestige of the second Temple, destroyed by the emperor Titus's Roman troops in the year 70 CE, we must immediately add that, from the vantage of religious representations, the history of the Maghrebi Quarter is situated not only "in the shadow of the Wall" but also in the shadow of the Temple, which makes this history all the more thorny and challenging (figure 2). It is literally "immured" in this head-to-head confrontation of stone with the Temple's imposing party wall, and therefore must first be rescued from this stifling proximity, at least *temporarily*, by taking a crucial step back.

Even if it is obvious that the fate of the Maghrebi Quarter was increasingly bound up with that of the Western Wall starting in the early twentieth century, when the sanctuary was becoming a focal point for certain figures of the Zionist movement, it is nevertheless true that its history did begin *before* that time, and that it was not always so tightly bound to that of its famous party wall. To enable a history of the Maghrebi Quarter that is unencumbered and open, the quarter must necessarily be repositioned in the *longue durée*, to loosen the teleological grip forged by its tragic destiny when it was finally razed during the night of 10 to 11 June 1967 to make way for an expansive plaza in front of the Western Wall, now more monumentalized than ever (figure 3). As in Greek tragedy, it is the death of the Maghrebi Quarter that in the end absorbed the meaning of its life: its disappearance is what finally reduced to silence the story

FIGURE 2. View of the Maghrebi Quarter, looking east, early 1930s. Source: © Matson Photograph Collection, Library of Congress.

of its very existence. And the few rare studies published on the subject speak solely of its destruction. It is therefore against this imperative, at once tragic and teleological, that a genuine *history* of the Maghrebi Quarter, of its life and death, must be constructed.[12]

This history begins in 1187, when Saladin (Salah ad-Din), victorious conqueror of Jerusalem, launched an ambitious policy to repopulate and reurbanize the Holy City, particularly in its southern outskirts, largely abandoned during the Crusades era.[13] In the late twelfth century—with help from one of his closest lieutenants, the Sufi mystic of Andalusian heritage Sidi Abu Madyan, and at the instigation of his eldest son, al-Afdal Ali—Saladin had an array of religious endowments established, whose purpose was to welcome, house, and care for pilgrims of Maghrebi origin. This gesture of generosity, well suited to the imperial ambition of the prestigious founder of the Ayyubid dynasty, was matched by the construction of a new oratory on the Haram al-Sharif intended for Maghrebi pilgrims, as well as a Koranic school or madrassa devoted to the teaching of Maliki law, the dominant school of jurisprudence in the Maghreb. Nothing was unprecedented here, since Jerusalem has always

FIGURE 3. **Wreckage of the Maghrebi Quarter, June 1967. Source: © Marylin Silver-tone, Magnum.**

been rebuilt and repopulated by the contribution of exogenous populations wishing to settle as close as possible to monotheism's sacred sanctuaries. What is more surprising is that this assembly of waqfs (religious endowments) was still functioning in the Ottoman era, the British Mandate, and the Jordanian period . . . and right up to the moment when the quarter was demolished in June 1967.

Over nearly eight centuries, despite the vagaries and ravages of time, these endowments that soon merged under the prestigious banner of Sidi Abu Madyan performed the function corresponding to their founder's intent: in the early 1960s, the Abu Madyan stewards were still distributing bread and meals to the inhabitants of the quarter during Ramadan, donating warm clothing and coal in winter, paying burial costs for the neediest among them, purchasing lamp oil for lighting the mosque, and paying the regular salary of an employee in charge of maintenance. Meanwhile, Moroccan, Algerian, and Tunisian pilgrims kept coming in greater and greater numbers as transport modernized and allowed for a more convenient stopover in Jerusalem on the way to or from Mecca. The Waqf Abu Madyan, was effectively perpetuated.

Not only did it resist the ravages of time and the onslaught of challengers; it *persisted*. It achieved what it set out to do, and what its founders intended it to do: last and endure. This long-term history, open to the winds of empires, migrations, and the Mediterranean, deserves to be narrated and interrogated, with recourse to the *longue durée* as a constituent part of its truth—for "territorial constructions are above all consolidated time," to quote Marcel Roncayolo's felicitous phrase.[14]

A Discipline in the Shadow of the Wall: Sources and Methods

If the history of the Maghrebi Quarter has yet to be written, it is undoubtedly because of how long it has remained in the shadow of the Western Wall, but also because it is a particularly emotive and painful history, one that has pinned history as a discipline "up against the wall," summoned to simultaneously mobilize all its heuristic and ethical standards: tact, composure, and method. That is first because this history immediately runs the risk of being drowned in the toponymical controversy over what to call the Wall. As the "Wailing Wall" or "Wall of Tears," according to Christian tradition, it is believed to bear witness to Jewish sorrow at the destruction of the Temple in the year 70. As Kotel ha-Maaravi, or the "Western Wall," it has been venerated by the Jews since the sixteenth century as a vestige of the second Temple of Jerusalem. As "al-Buraq" for the Muslims, it commemorates the nighttime journey of Muhammad, who is believed to have tethered his winged horse (al-Buraq) at this site before praying with the prophets of the ancient alliance (figure 4).

Myth versus myth, memory versus memory, religious tradition versus religious tradition: even within the halls of UNESCO, the controversy focused on the Wall's *verticality* and its toponymy, erasing along the way the *horizontal* history, both urban and civic, of the Maghrebi Quarter that had once spread at its feet.[15] To make such a history possible, a simple but categorical methodological principle must be adhered to: historians are not in the business of purveying proof of authenticity, and they must resolutely refuse this function so often foisted upon them, particularly in Jerusalem. On the presumption that "collective memory is essentially a reconstruction of the past," and that it unceasingly adapts "the image of earlier facts to beliefs and spiritual needs of the present," to cite Maurice Halbwachs's robust warning, the historical discipline

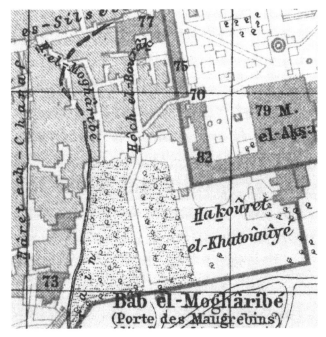

FIGURE 4. The "Hôch el-Bourâk" and the "Harat el-Moghâribe," circa 1890. Source: Baedeker Guide, map of Jerusalem, 1893.

must not compromise itself *within* these vying memories, but must still take charge of them in its own way, from a fully assumed *outside* position, making these processes of memory-building objects of history in their own right.[16]

It is fascinating, for example, if not to say mind-boggling, to compare the traditionally agreed-upon etymology of the place name "Kotel ha-Maaravi"— the Western Wall as the ultimate vestige of the second Temple, located on the western side, a tradition certified in certain rabbinical *midrashim* since the fifth century CE but pinpointed at that location only in the middle of the sixteenth century—with the one posited in the early 1950s by the Islamic scholar Louis Massignon. Having observed that the first settled communities of Muslim Maghrebis in this perimeter (in the late twelfth century) precede by three centuries the Jews' assigning of sanctuary status to this portion of the wall (in the sixteenth century), he suggests that the place name perhaps originally designated the "Wall of the Westerners" or the "Wall of the Maghrebis," since the term "Maghrebi" ("Maaravim" in Hebrew) does indeed mean "Westerners," as seen from the Middle Eastern perspective, especially since certain sources seem to indicate that this sanctification of the Wall corresponds in time with the arrival in Jerusalem of "maaravim" Jews expelled from Spain in the late fifteenth century.[17] History as a discipline would stand to gain little by attempting to settle this controversy. Rather, it should confine itself to stating that only the way a place is used can truly provide the basis for legitimizing any appropriation. But controversy can provide food for thought, to better understand the degree to which the persistence of Maghrebis in Jerusalem can also undoubtedly be explained by the paradoxical power of this *Western* Islam nestled in the heart of the holy places of the East.

Recognition of this entanglement of memories also contributes to understanding why the issue has become increasingly displaced and elusive in the contemporary era: "Western" Muslim pilgrims settled at the foot of a "Western" wall made a sanctuary by communities of "Western" Jews, dislodged in 1967 by the rise of the Zionist project. There is a kind of Larsen effect in this story, a feedback loop that literally *disorients* our contemporary representations; and this is perhaps also what has rendered it inaudible, illegible, and in a certain way therefore invisible. To disentangle this saturated memory loop, we have to get back to the fundamentals of the discipline and recall that the processes of memory construction and legitimizing are not the product of discursive or ideological strategies alone, but also of much more concrete and embodied procedures: legal action, real estate investment, and day-to-day grassroots social welfare. The history of the Maghrebi Quarter and its long persistence are precisely products of these strictly history-related analytical categories.[18]

This compendium of actions has left traces in a disparate and scattered set of archival holdings, a feature that may well provide a further explanation, of a purely operational order, as to why no one to date had attempted a synthesis of the the Maghrebi Quarter's history. Long concealed within the recesses of miscellaneous documentation, this history today can only be one of *disclosure*—a diachronic narrative, but also the history of the single-minded quest for its scattered archives, sometimes nonexistent, often all but inaccessible. To achieve this, we cannot make do with the mere factual information contained within; sustained attention must also be devoted to the documents' form and materiality, their locality, and the context of their production, circulation, and conservation—all of which bears witness to the many transnational connections that weave together this quarter's history, but also to the strictly heuristic issues of this "piecemeal" history, so often disjointed and thwarted, but a history "nevertheless," partly hobbled by the always significant gaps in its documentation (figure 5).[19] Displaying this documentary archipelago does "allow for a glimpse" into the historian's craft, but it must not impede the emergence of narrative flow and historical chronology. I will therefore endeavor to organize this reconstitution respecting whenever possible the sequencing of documentation as it emerges or evades discovery, to weave together the chronicle of the Maghrebi Quarter of Jerusalem and that of its archives.

Let us attempt a brief sequential overview. The local waqf archives housed at Abu-Dis in East Jerusalem tell an "Islamic" story of the Maghrebi Quarter, and testify to the endowment's judicial foundation since its medieval origins, but also to the consistent effort to adhere to its initial objectives. The Ottoman archives, housed in Istanbul, are a reminder that control of religious

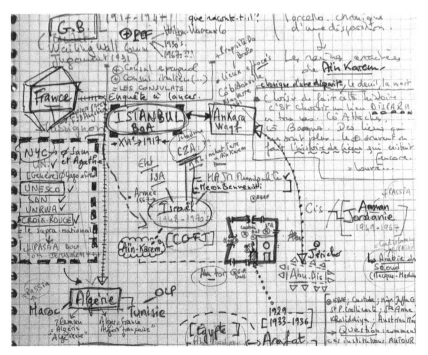

FIGURE 5. **A documentary archipelago. Excerpt from "Maghrebi Quarter" research notes, 2016. Source: © Vincent Lemire.**

endowments was a fundamental leveraging tool in the service of the imperial government, particularly in a strategic city like Jerusalem, at the center of mid-nineteenth-century power dynamics: stewards were appointed or dismissed, accounts were approved or rejected, petitions submitted by the quarter's inhabitants were carefully reviewed. And in the end, an imperial history of the Maghrebi Quarter begins to take shape. The archives of the Jerusalem municipality for the years 1890 to 1910 demonstrate, in turn, that the neighborhood was well integrated into the rest of the city; that it was well maintained, well lit, and regularly cleaned; and that it enjoyed the same modernization efforts that were observable in the rest of the city at that time.[20] All these archival holdings have to be patiently collected and connected to arrive at an overall vision of the history of the Maghrebi Quarter of Jerusalem from its origins until the early twentieth century, because each contains an irreducible measure of its truth, and because this documentary dispersal is itself inherent to its history.

Microcosm, Macrocosm: Minor and Major Histories

The scatteredness of the documentation grows more pronounced when, starting in the early twentieth century, the "minor history" of the Maghrebi Quarter comes to intersect with a multitude of "major histories" whose archival imprint is far more resounding; and it becomes difficult to sort out the *microcosm* (Maghrebi Quarter) from the *macrocosm* (general historical context) among the available data. The Central Zionist Archives, located in West Jerusalem, preserve evidence of various attempts to purchase the Maghrebi Quarter starting in the early twentieth century and during World War I, and certain correspondence produced in Germany recalls both the German history of the Zionist movement and the historic opportunity that the alliance between the Reich and the Ottoman Empire represented at the time of the Great War. In the archives of the League of Nations housed in Geneva, but also in the personal archives of former officials of the British Mandate, it is in 1929 that the history of the quarter reemerges against the background of bloody confrontations where access to the Western Wall by Jewish worshippers was at stake.

In 1948 the first Arab-Israeli war deprived the Waqf Abu Madyan and the inhabitants of the Maghrebi Quarter of their main source of income. The village of Ein Karem, which for centuries had regularly earned agricultural and property royalties for the endowment, ended up west of the green line, in Israel, at the time of the cease-fire. France, as the prevailing colonial power in the Maghreb, now found itself "up against the wall" and believed it discerned a kind of genuine "historic opportunity" in this new situation: the French diplomatic archives, preserved at La Courneuve and Nantes, testify to the geopolitical stakes that the Maghrebi Quarter represented in the 1950s for the Quai d'Orsay (the French Foreign Ministry), ever concerned not only to reassert France's role as powerful protector of the Holy Places in Jerusalem, but also to use the defense of the Maghrebi Quarter as a tool of soft power intended to legitimize its sovereignty over Morocco, Tunisia, and Algeria.[21]

The colonial archives of French Algeria, preserved at the National Overseas Archives at Aix-en-Provence, coupled with the personal archives of Louis Massignon, provide evidence of both the intellectual genesis of this attempt at "imperial protection," and the increasingly blatant contradictions encountered by the Government General of Algeria, which was subsidizing the inhabitants of Algerian origin in Jerusalem while coordinating the struggle against those fighting for independence in Algeria.[22] This French sequence of the Maghrebi Quarter's history, until now totally overlooked, represents at any rate an extraordinary opportunity for the historian, for this "colonial reactivation" of the Waqf Abu Madyan produced intense documentation in the form of legal documents, political reports, and social research, which together give quite a comprehensive picture of the neighborhood and its inhabitants a few years before its destruction. The royal archives in Rabat preserve a few traces of appeals to the Moroccan king's private funds to subsidize his pilgrim-subjects living in Jerusalem during that same period. Because it served as a laboratory and testing ground for various political and geopolitical strategies, the microcosm of the Maghrebi Quarter has thus proved to be an excellent observation post of Middle Eastern and Mediterranean history.

The timing of the neighborhood's demolition represents the ultimate heuristic and methodological hurdle. It is at the moment of its *disappearance* that the Maghrebi Quarter made its *appearance* in the historiography, as if its history were beginning at the precise moment in which it was ending, by crossing paths with the "major history" of the Arab-Israeli conflict in the hours following the end of the Six-Day War. This first contradiction concealed a second one, no less astonishing: if the destruction of the Maghrebi Quarter, during the night of 10 to 11 June 1967, had occasionally been recounted, it had never yet been *documented*. This is explained in part by the operational specificity of this kind of "fait accompli" hidden from public view, akin in this case to veritable spoils of war, which consequently leaves no paper trail in the official archives. But a further, more tangible explanation involves a disdain among most historians working on armed conflicts toward technical admin-istrative archives, which they deem of little use for writing the "major history" of political decisions or their military applications.

Yet the destruction of the Maghrebi Quarter provides a way out of this methodological impasse. If the military archives remain largely silent on this event, the administrative archives documenting the logistical preparation of the demolition reveal its strictly *political* whys and wherefores. To understand how such an operation could have been undertaken in such short order and ultimately with such "stealth," I had to explore the technical series of the Israeli municipal archives in Jerusalem, which give a highly detailed account of the operation's logistics, but also of the reparations procedures set up afterward to mitigate any negative fallout. These reparations dossiers, comparable to post-mortem inventories, illuminate with extraordinary and invaluable precision the daily life of the inhabitants of the Maghrebi Quarter on the eve of its demoli-tion. Other archival sources, notably those of the Red Cross and Red Crescent, provide complementary data on what had become of these inhabitants by the mid-1970s, when their trajectories were diffracted after the place of their former collective existence was gone. The microhistory of the Maghrebi Quarter sheds light not only on the larger history of the Middle East and the Mediterranean, but on history as such, as a method and a discipline.[23]

Many Trajectories, One Itinerary

The history of the Maghrebi Quarter of Jerusalem thus contains a multitude of histories. Because it takes place at the intersection of several temporalities and several territories, because it intercuts different scales of space and time, and because it enfolds several historical trajectories, several worlds, and hori-zons, it offers an invaluable vantage point of the history of Jerusalem, a "world city" open to the winds, so challenging to encompass in its entirety and in the *longue durée*.[24] It is a *Mediterranean* history first of all—a history of migrations, pilgrimages, and expatriations; of poor pilgrims and settled refugees; and of sponsors and benefactors, mindful to leave something behind in the city of prophets and the Last Judgment. Saladin and Abu Madyan are among these sponsors and benefactors: one was a glorious conqueror born in Tikrit in Iraq and buried in Damascus, the other a famous Sufi mystic born in Seville in Andalusia and buried in Tlemcen in Algeria. Both left their mark at the heart of Jerusalem by establishing a Maghrebi home that was still active nearly eight centuries later. Next, the history is *colonial*, since the Maghrebi Quarter was kept alive by a succession of agents of French colonial power before being demolished and wiped off the map by Israeli conquerors, its very presence materializing the inconsistencies of the Zionist project and the ambiguities of "return" to a territory already so densely inhabited and administered.[25] And finally, the history is one of the *Arab-Israeli conflict*, from the first attempt at purchasing the neighborhood by officials of the Zionist movement all the way up to the Six-Day War. It includes the riots of 1929; the residence of the young Yasser Arafat in one of the neighborhood houses in the early 1930s; and the first Arab-Israeli war of 1948, which deprived the endowment of its chief source of property revenue.[26]

Do all these trajectories merge into one *history*? Just because they intersect in the same place, do they add up to a set of cohesive meanings? Like Georges Pérec in his *Espèces d'espaces* (*Species of Spaces and Other Places*, 1974), we have reasons to doubt this, recalling that spaces are neither homogenous nor even "isotropic," meaning that their properties are not identical depending on one's vantage point.[27] But we can also consider, again with Georges Pérec but this time in *La vie mode d'emploi* (*Life: A User's Manual*, 1978), that "pieces of space"—an apartment building, a public garden, a street, or a neighborhood—have a life unto themselves, a coherence and a persistence, and that these "fragments of the world" can refocus our gaze and serve as observatories for understanding and deciphering, to be precise, worlds far more vast and elusive.[28] In the specific case of the Maghrebi Quarter of Jerusalem, this gambit of taking the case study approach has the advantage of feeding into a refreshed history of Jerusalem: a genuine urban, civil history attentive to the materiality of places and the people living there, to their singular trajectories and day-to-day living conditions, a history that does not reduce the Holy City to shadow theater—intellectual debate, a battleground, or a field of operations—but which endeavors to *situate* and *embody* the balance of power and the tipping points (figure 6).

To match up these different trajectories without going astray, I needed to choose an itinerary; and for that, I needed to build a timeline. Even if certain structuring factors of the neighborhood's life would appear predisposed to *continuity*, it was my job to locate the major *breaks* that necessarily mark forks in the road, turning points, and changes of pace, all of which point to a radical *before* and *after*. In the history of the Maghrebi Quarter of Jerusalem, 1948 and 1967 are the two pivotal dates that divide the narrative into three large chronological sequences, and which organize the text you are about to read.

Prior to 1948, despite contingencies, rivalries, and conflicts, the Waqf Abu Madyan managed somehow to function in accordance with the wishes of its founders, thereby preserving the neighborhood's way of life. But importantly, it managed to do so while remaining relatively autonomous when it came to finances and decision making. In the prologue to this book, to outline the en-

FIGURE 6. **Aerial view of the Maghrebi Quarter, looking north, 1931.** Source: © Matson Photograph Collection, Library of Congress.

dowment's legal framework, I will first analyze its "Islamic history" by studying the *waqfiya* text of 1320, on which the stewards and judges base their decisions when evaluating the rights and duties of the various protagonists. In chapter 1, the imperial Ottoman context emerges as a long period of consolidation for the endowment during which its activities were strengthened and the scope of its involvement broadened, as evidenced in particular by the analysis of its accounts ledgers and a deep dive into the municipal archives of that era. Between the World Wars I and II, the Waqf Abu Madyan had to confront new challengers and a less favorable political context, but at the time of the July 1927 earthquake it still managed to maintain its preparedness level and to ensure the upkeep of its properties in the Maghrebi Quarter, as we will see in chapter 2.

In 1948, the loss of land royalties from the rich Ein Karem farmlands tilted the history of the Maghrebi Quarter toward an entirely new horizon. Now under the tutelage of the French Consulate General in Jerusalem, it was integrated into the "Muslim policy" of a waning colonial empire, and forever relinquished its managerial autonomy (chapter 3). By 1955, the worsening situation in Algeria and the special alliance between France and Israel gradually impeded the historic prospects opened up a few years earlier, especially since the Jordanian administration was unwilling to accommodate this supranational enclave implanted right in the middle of the old city of Jerusalem (chapter 4). All in all, if this "French history" of the Maghrebi Quarter of Jerusalem appears to historians as a short-lived hiatus, it must have represented for those who experienced it a "potential history"—one that, though never fulfilled, has to be understood in its own time frame if we are to fully comprehend all its ambiguities.[29]

As of 1967, the history of the Maghrebi Quarter correlates directly with Israeli history; the conditions of its destruction (chapter 5) and the way in which the repercussions of that destruction were handled (chapter 6) are emblematic of the paradoxes of Israeli democracy, mindful to respect certain rules and procedures while at the same time embracing a "facts on the ground" policy as soon as a historic opportunity arises. From this perspective, the demolition of the Maghrebi Quarter compels us to reconsider the historic turning point that the Six-Day War represented in the history of Zionism and of Israel. Until now, we tended to shift the effective impact of this turning point to the late 1970s, as if only the rise to power of the right (1977) had created the conditions for the flourishing of a new religious Zionism, more on the offensive and less respectful of the rules of international law. The conditions of the Maghrebi Quarter's destruction demonstrate, however, that a certain messianic rapture had taken hold of the country and its administration in the hours immediately following the 1967 victory, even if close analysis of the documentation also reveals debates and disagreements between the army, the civilian government, and the Jerusalem municipality during this same time.

Beyond the mishaps, contingencies, and unforeseen circumstances, these different trajectories do effectively merge into a *history*, and therefore an itinerary. This history is that of the Maghrebi Quarter, but it is also that of Jerusalem, Israel, Palestine, and the Mediterranean. It is the history of the gradual shift from the age of empires to the age of nations, from supranational structures and sovereignties to nation-states and national sovereignties.[30] The inhabitants of the Maghrebi Quarter of Jerusalem were "orphans of empire" on several counts: they were orphans of the French colonial empire, but also more broadly of the fallen Islamic empires, for a brief time protected by the last gasp of French colonial ambition before being trapped by the rise of the Israeli national project. It is likely no coincidence that the last documents I was able to collect pertaining to the former inhabitants of the Maghrebi Quarter come from UNESCO and the UN Relief and Works Agency for Palestine Refugees in the Near East (UNRWA), the Red Crescent, and the Red Cross. Dislodged from their former living place, uprooted and displaced, having sought refuge in Silwan, Nablus, Jericho, or Amman, these "orphans of empire" were placed under the responsibility of the international community.

PROLOGUE

THE LEGAL FOUNDATION OF A
JERUSALEM NEIGHBORHOOD

THE FOUNDING ACT OF THE WAQF ABU MADYAN

> There is very little on the history of the Mughrabi neigh-
> borhood. This is also true of the monumental essays bearing
> the titles *Mamluk Jerusalem* and *Ottoman Jerusalem*, which
> contain only partial and insignificant information on the
> neighborhood. It is customary to think that the residents of
> the Mughrabi neighborhood were of lowly social status. There
> is almost no information on the public or religious structures
> that were in their neighborhood.
>
> Yuval Baruch, *"The Real Story,"* Israel
> Antiquities Authority, *2017.*

The founding act that constitutes the legal cornerstone of the Maghrebi
Quarter was drafted in Jerusalem, in Arabic, by the great-grandson of Sidi
Abu Madyan Shu'ayb on the twenty-ninth day of the month of Ramadan in
the year 720 according to the Hijiri calendar, or on Sunday 2 November 1320
by the Gregorian calendar.[1] The Waqf Abu Madyan is not the oldest waqf established for the benefit of the Maghrebi Quarter, since the waqf founded by
the son of Saladin, al-Afdal Ali, dates back to 1193. But it is certainly the best
documented, the most richly funded, and the one that would ensure most of
the quarter's income until 1967. This is why all the waqfs set up in the Maghrebi

Quarter before and after the 1193 waqf would eventually accrete to it and come under the stewardship of the Waqf Abu Madyan officials, all subsumed under that name. There are two versions of this waqfiya or founding act that can be deemed legally authentic, the locations of which are equally significant. The first version is found in the registries of the Islamic Tribunal of Jerusalem (Sijillât Mahkamah Shar'iyya).[2] These archives were for a long time preserved on the grounds of the Haram al-Sharif, where the tribunal assembled until the early Mandate period,[3] then kept on Salah ad-Din Street during the Jordanian period, and then transferred in 1983 to Abu-Dis, in the suburbs of East Jerusalem, since security conditions in the city center were no longer adequate.[4] These registries, an invaluable trove of information on the social and economic history of Jerusalem, almost uninterruptedly cover the period from 1529 to the late 1970s. They account for all aspects of daily life in Jerusalem since, at least until the 1920s, the tribunal's jurisdiction included criminal, civil, and commercial proceedings for all communities of the city.[5] In the 1980s, at the same time as they were being transferred to Abu-Dis, the registries were also being microfilmed, producing three copies found today at the University An-Najah in Nablus, at the University of Amman in Jordan, and at the University of Haifa in Israel.[6] The second version of the *waqfiya* deemed authentic from the legal and administrative standpoint is located today in Ankara (figure 7), in the archives of the General Division of Religious Endowment, transferred in 1936 from Istanbul as part of the takeover of religious endowments by the new Turkish Republic. The archives themselves were constituted on the basis of the former archives of the Ottoman Ministry of Religious Endowments, founded in 1826.[7]

Two French translations of the 1320 waqfiya are available today: the one produced by Louis Massignon in 1949 and published in the *Revue des études islamiques* (REI) in 1951;[8] and the one produced by the Tribunal of Jerusalem on 17 June 1902 (10 Rabii al-akhir 1320), for which a typed copy from the early 1950s is found in the archives of the French Consulate of Jerusalem transferred to Nantes.[9] The two translations do not differ in content, but are quite different in form. The one produced by a clerk at the Jerusalem tribunal in 1902 is tight, straightforward, at times elliptical: a simple, functional legal document meant to summarize as succinctly as possible the endowment's legally operational features, meant for a user who needs no commentary on how the document

VGMA. 583.27.20-1

FIGURE 7. **Founding deed of the Abu Madyan waqf.** Source: © VGMA, 583-27-20.

fits into its religious context. The one produced by the Islamic scholar and orientalist Louis Massignon is longer, more expressive, sometimes a bit over-blown, and at any rate more explicit, intended for a reader interested in the document's religious and cultural references. I will be following Massignon's more historically robust version, while noting in passing the variants that seem significant in comparison to the 1902 version. The structure of the text echoes the elements typical of a founding act of an Islamic endowment: initial address, identity of the donor, description of the fixed assets, identification of the beneficiaries, rules of administration and stewardship, final reminder of the inviolability and inalienability of the fixed property assets, date of the act, and concluding prayer.[10]

The Donor: A Descendant of the Illustrious Sidi Abu Madyan

The identification of the donor is not worded exactly the same in the two versions. The tribunal's translation is unencumbered by historical accuracy. The surnames are simply strung together one after the other: "The present is a precise and legal act of bequest drawn up by the servant of God of whom he asks forgiveness, the philosopher, Sheikh Imam and pious hermit Abu Madyan Shu'ayb Ben Sayidna el Sheikh Saleh wiseman and soldier of the Faith Abu Abdallah Muhammad Ben el Sheikh el Imam, benediction of Muslims worthy of God Abu Madyan Shu'ayb."[11] It is hard to recognize who is who in this brief litany of names, lineages, and attributes, especially once one knows that the celebrated Sufi mystic Sidi Abu Madyan died in 1197, well before the legal authentication of this founding act (1320).[12] In the translation submitted by Massignon, we understand technically that the donor is not Abu Madyan himself, but one of his great-grandsons, who received from his famous ancestor the assets he is preparing to secure for endowment:

> This is an act stating the constitution of a valid and lawful waqf, the formal and permissible establishment of a habous by the humble servant of God of whom he awaits forgiveness and remission of his sins, the Sheikh Imam, the wise, the honorable, the scrupulous, the ascetic, the submissive, the eminent, the model Abu Madyan Shu'ayb son of our lord the Sheikh, the virtuous (Salih), the wise, the devout, the soldier of the Faith Abu-Abdallah Muham-

mad, son of the Sheikh Imam, the blessing upon Muslims, the assertion of
God, the survivor of the primal virtuous generation Abu Madyan Shu'ayb, the
Maghrebi (of origin), the Maliki (rite), may God be generous with his blessings
upon him in time and space. . . .

Massignon is addressing French readers accustomed to the Maghrebi term
habous to designate a waqf. He translates at length the virtues of the donor; he
specifies that he is "Maghrebi (of origin) and "Maliki (of rite)" and especially
indicates that the donor is indeed "the survivor of the primal virtuous generation Abu Madyan Shu'ayb"—in other words, that he is a direct descendant
of the patron saint of Tlemcen.[13] The founding text, thus translated by Massignon, is consistent with the biography of Sidi Abu Madyan Shu'ayb as it was
set down in tradition: born in Andalusia in the region of Seville around 1126,
he studied in Fez and Tlemcen before leaving on a pilgrimage to Mecca, where
he met the famous Sufi poet of Iranian origin Abdal Qadir al-Gilani. On his
way back from Mecca, he joined the armies of Saladin in Palestine and took
part in the battle at Hattin against the Crusaders (1187), where he is said to
have lost his left hand.[14] After the conquest of Jerusalem, Saladin bequeathed
to him the lands of the village of Ein Karem, and at the same time put his son
al-Afdal Ali in charge of reurbanizing the perimeter of the future Maghrebi
Quarter, to the south of the Holy City.[15] After his return to the Maghreb, Abu
Madyan lived and taught in Béjaïa (Algeria), then in Marrakesh, and finally in
Tlemcen, where he died in 1197. He was buried in al-Ubbad, a little village on
the outskirts of Tlemcen, which is still today a pilgrimage site, an important
center of Sufi piety, and a central feature of Algerian cultural heritage.[16] The
lands bequeathed by the descendant of Abu Madyan in 1320 thus originate in
the reconquest of Jerusalem by Saladin a little over a century earlier, a reconquest followed by a comprehensive strategy to repopulate the Holy City and
to permanently settle a sizable Maghrebi community in its southern part.[17]
This concurrency is confirmed by another endowment, created in 1193 for the
benefit of Maghrebi jurists of the Maliki rite by al-Afdal Ali, the eldest son
of Saladin, then sovereign prince of Damascus and Jerusalem (figure 8).[18] The
memory of this endowment is reported by the historian Mujir ad-Din three
centuries later:

The Afdaliyeh Madrassa: once known as El Qobbeh (the Cupola), in the Maghrebi Quarter. It is a waqf of El Malek el Afdal Nur ad-Din Abu-Hassan Ali, son of El Malek Salah-ed-Din, may God cloak him in mercy! He bequeathed it to the Maliki jurisconsults of Jerusalem. He also constituted as a waqf the Maghrebi Quarter for the benefit of the Maghrebi community, irrespective of origin, for both men and women. The donation took place at the time when the prince al-Afdal reigned over Damascus, to which Jerusalem was joined. Nevertheless, since the title deeds of these two endowments were not found, a protocol was drawn up establishing the waqf status for each property; the contents of the deed were certified before the judicial authorities (Mahkamah), after the death of the founder."[19]

In this passage, Mujir ad-Din, a native of Jerusalem who presided over the Islamic Tribunal for three decades (1486–1516), speaks from experience and is not especially surprised that centuries-old founding acts may have been mislaid; he relies on tradition to attest to the existence of the endowments and takes care to certify them in writing ex post facto to avoid any future challenge.[20] This interplay of founding and refounding, which ends up embedding

FIGURE 8. **Dome of the Afdaliyya Madrassa (circled), circa 1910. Source: © EBAF.**

different traditions into one and the same judicial corpus, is quite typical of the system of Islamic endowments, which provides that an original and often prestigious founding allows other donations of lesser importance to accrete to it, thereby benefiting from the stature—and hopefully the long-lastingness—of the original structure. We should note that there is no contradiction, but rather complementarity, between the waqf established by al-Afdal Ali and the Waqf Abu Madyan. The first has to do with the *terrain* or the perimeter of the quarter, granted for the benefit of the Maghrebis, while the second gradually aggregates and enhances the *buildings* erected there.[21] Another endowment contemporary to this same era, created by Umar al-Mujarrad al-Maghrebi in 1303, followed this same logic of accretion and complementarity by yielding to the community three houses of the Maghrebi Quarter, one of which comprised no fewer than ten rooms.[22] What matters for us to remember, at any rate, is that the Waqf Abu Madyan was founded in the early fourteenth century by a descendant of the prestigious Sufi mystic Sidi Abu Madyan, based upon an original bequest by Saladin in the late twelfth century, and that it was precisely this Waqf Abu Madyan—thanks to its generous allocation—that lent its name to the whole array of religious endowments, whether preexisting or subsequently accreted to it (figure 9).

The Maghrebis of Jerusalem, in any case, seem very early to have enjoyed a reputation in Jerusalem, thanks notably to their participation in the reconquest of the Holy City. In 1206 the great Andalusian mystic Ibn Arabi traveled to Jerusalem and noted that "the Maghrebis enjoy excellent repute in this city, because they accomplished marvels in the defense of Muslims."[23] Correspondingly, the prestige of Jerusalem and its Malaki school of law grew continuously among Maghrebi and Andalusian intellectuals, as evidenced by the many travel narratives that praise the "spiritual merits of Jerusalem" (*fada'il al-Quds*) and which emphasize the importance of stopping there before continuing to Mecca or Medina, in order to wear the special garment there that symbolizes entry into a state of "consecration" (*ihram*) on the pilgrimage route. Muhammad al-Abdari al-Hayhi al-Maghribi, qadi (judge) of Marrakesh, in 1289; Ibn Battuta, native of Tangiers, in 1325 and again in 1348; Khaled Ibn Issa al-Balawi, native of Almeria, in 1337; Ibn Khaldun, native of Seville, in 1400; Abdallah al-Ayashi, native of Fez, in 1663; Muhammad Ibn Uthman al-Maknasi, native of Meknès, in 1785—all these travelers, famous to varying degrees, describe

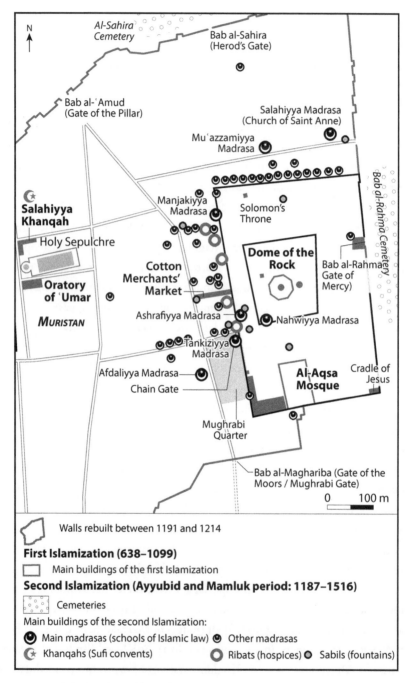

N
↑

Al-Sahira Cemetery

Bab al-Sahira (Herod's Gate)

Bab al-'Amud (Gate of the Pillar)

Salahiyya Madrasa (Church of Saint Anne)

Mu'azzamiyya Madrasa

Bab al-Rahma Cemetery

Salahiyya Khanqah

Manjakiyya Madrasa

Solomon's Throne

Holy Sepulchre

Cotton Merchants' Market

Dome of the Rock

Bab al-Rahma (Gate of Mercy)

Oratory of 'Umar

MURISTAN

Ashrafiyya Madrasa

Nahwiyya Madrasa

Tankiziyya Madrasa

Afdaliyya Madrasa

Al-Aqsa Mosque

Cradle of Jesus

Chain Gate

Mughrabi Quarter

Bab al-Maghariba (Gate of the Moors / Mughrabi Gate)

0   100 m

Walls rebuilt between 1191 and 1214

First Islamization (638–1099)

Main buildings of the first Islamization

Second Islamization (Ayyubid and Mamluk period: 1187–1516)

Cemeteries

Main buildings of the second Islamization:

Main madrasas (schools of Islamic law)   Other madrasas

Khanqahs (Sufi convents)   Ribats (hospices)   Sabils (fountains)

FIGURE 9. The Islamic foundations of Jerusalem during the Ayyubid and Mamluk periods, 1187–1516. Source: © Dario Ingiusto.

Jerusalem as an indispensable stage in the "quest for knowledge." They speak of their rich exchanges with the ulemas of the Holy City, and testify to the vitality of the Sufi movement within the Maghrebi community which by then was firmly established in the city. All relate the experience of praying in the mosque of the Maghrebis, built at the southwest corner of the Haram al-Sharif, adjacent to the Maghrebi Gate, which connects the sanctuary to its eponymous neighborhood.[24]

Some of the travelers also describe their encounters with Maghrebi dignitaries who had risen to the highest judicial or religious functions: Muhammad al-Nafati, cadi of Jerusalem in the 1660s, or Muhammad al-Tayeb al-Taflani al-Maghribi, mufti of Jerusalem in the 1750s.[25] The Maghrebi rulers were not to be outdone, and also took part in spiritual and intellectual exchanges which also had a political dimension. In 1344 the Moroccan Merinid Sultan Abu al-Hassan Ali Abdelhaq bequeathed to the al-Aqsa Mosque a splendid Koran in thirty volumes, written on gazelle-skin parchment in a saffron-based ink. This masterwork of Maghrebi calligraphy, produced in triplicate, was sent to Mecca, Medina, and Jerusalem. Only the Jerusalem copy has survived; it is a treasure of the Islamic Museum, which occupies the former building of the Mosque of the Maghrebis on the Haram al-Sharif.[26] A few years earlier, in 1339, this same Sultan Abu al-Hassan Ali Abdelhaq had ordered the construction of the "Sidi Abu Madyan" mosque near Tlemcen, in the vicinity of the tomb of the prestigious Sufi mystic. The Waqf Abu Madyan, hardly an isolated phenomenon, was on the contrary the pivot of a whole array of spiritual and material connections, woven over the *longue durée* between the Maghreb and Jerusalem.

The Bequest: The Rich Countryside of Ein Karem and the Pilgrim House

After this identification of the benefactor, the founding act of 1320 goes on to identify and localize the bequest itself: the assets that comprise the waqf, starting with the most significant, the rich lands of Ein Karem:

> A village known by the name of Ein Karem, one of the villages adjacent to Jerusalem. This village includes farmed and fallow lands, both cultivated and abandoned, slopes and plains, unproductive bare rock, buildings in ruins,

farm houses, buildings in good repair with their surrounding fields, a little garden, pomegranate trees and other kinds irrigated with water from springs on the property, olive trees of a "rumi" or western variety, carob trees, fig trees, sessile oaks, qiqebs (hardwoods). This village is bounded on all sides: to the south by the great Maliha (salt pan); to the north by properties belonging to Ein-Kaout, Qalunya, Harash, Sataf and Zawiya el-Bakhtyari; to the west by Ein Esheshqqaq, and to the east by properties belonging to the Maliha and to Beit Mazmil. This village is established as a waqf, with all attendant rights, appurtenances, fields, cultivated lands, threshing floors, loamy earth, with freshwater springs on location, prairies, planted trees, disused wells, vineyards, in a word, with all rights relating thereto, both within and without. However, the mosque, house of God, the path and the cemetery intended for use by Muslims, are not included in the present waqf.[27]

This description of the Ein Karem countryside matches what we know of this village, nestled in a fertile valley some five kilometers below and west of Jerusalem, and renowned for its rich soil and plentiful freshwater springs (figure 10). In his monograph on Jerusalem and its vicinity in the nineteenth century, the Israeli geographer Yehoshua Ben-Arieh writes that Ein Karem is "the most important village west of Jerusalem."[28] Today it still provides a destination for walks and outings, and is enjoyed for its cool temperatures, terraced farmland, gardens, vegetable farming, and orchards (figure 11).[29] It is indeed bounded to the south, as the 1320 text indicates, by "Maliha" (or "Malha," today in the southern suburbs of Jerusalem), then to the southeast by Beit Safafa and to the southwest by Bittir. To the north it is bounded by the localities of Qalunya, Sataf, and Deir Yassin, and to the west also by the lands of Sataf; to the east by the northern boundary of the Malha; and then on the way to Jerusalem by the Orthodox Monastery of the Cross.[30]

The abundance of freshwater springs has contributed to the valley's reputation and to its connection with numerous Biblical traditions linked to the theme of baptism.[31] In Byzantine times, in the context of setting the stations of the "Liturgy of Jerusalem," the village was identified as the site of the "Visitation," when Mary was visited by her cousin Elizabeth while both were pregnant, one with Jesus and the other with St. John the Baptist—the founding encounter that would later reunite the two cousins around the inaugural motif of baptism.[32] The springs and the vineyards planted on the terraced slopes

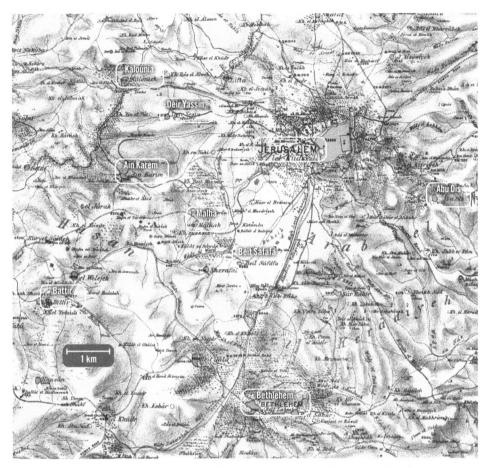

FIGURE 10. Vicinity of Jerusalem and Ein Karem. Source: © Palestine Exploration Fund, map of western Palestine, 1880.

FIGURE II. **Gardens of Ein Karem, circa 1920. Source: © Matson Photograph Collection, Library of Congress.**

account for the name given to the village, Ein Karem ("spring of the vine" in Hebrew), and the New Testament tradition of the "Visitation" explains why travel narratives of the modern era frequently report the place name "Ein Sitti Meriam" ("Mary's spring" in Arabic) for one of the village watering holes.[33] We note that the founding text takes care to mention the "loamy earth" and to name the many "irrigated trees" present in this countryside (pomegranate, olive, carob, fig, and oak), to attest to the village's wealth and guarantee regular income for the waqf as established. We also note that no legal limit or constraint is cited, since the "[whole] village is established as a waqf, with all attendant rights," and that, as is customary, only the mosque (as "house of God"), the path, and the cemetery escape the endowment's ownership.

The text next identifies a second property asset constituted as waqf, "in Jerusalem at the place called *Kantarat* (bridge) Om-el-Banat, at the Haram's Bab el-Silsileh. This building includes an *iwan* (a kind of protected entrance), two rooms, a courtyard, and a toilet. Beneath this building is a storage area and a cellar (*qabw*)."[34] Louis Massignon indicates that this building corresponds in all likelihood to one of the quarter's two zawiyas, the other being situated in the largest of the three houses bequeathed in 1303 by al-Mujarrad, higher up and at the northwest corner of the quarter. The structure of this part of the text, listing the assets involved in the bequest, makes it possible to describe the financial and functional structure of the religious endowment. It typically rests on two pillars. The Ein Karem properties, situated outside the city walls, constitute the "active" pillar of the endowment, its main source of income. The zawiyas, located in Jerusalem proper on the edge of the Haram al-Sharif, represent its "passive" pillar, its main expenditure line, intended to host and care for Maghrebis in Jerusalem. What we have here is a "public" or "charitable" waqf (*waqf khayri*) and not a "private" or "family" waqf (*waqf ahli*), since its revenue is intended for public welfare and not for the benefit of the founder's descendants.[35]

The Beneficiaries: Maghrebis—Transient or Resident in Jerusalem

Further on, the text provides an exact list of the endowment beneficiaries, based on an expansive definition of the term "Maghreb," which designates here all the Islamic regions west of Egypt:[36]

> The abovementioned grantor established his waqf for the benefit of Maghrebis residing in Jerusalem, the Holy City, and of those among the Maghrebis who might come to this city, whatever their qualities, professions, their sex, age, and social condition. Let no one who raises any objection whatsoever against them claim to take part in the benefits of this endowment. They shall enjoy this benefit directly by living in Jerusalem or by levying rents or land tenancy, or by reaping benefits of whatever nature. They shall be allowed to parcel out the lands (and farm them directly) or lease them for sharecropping (*muqâsama wa muzâra'a*). The endowment's benefits shall be devoted by priority to new arrivals, to the neediest, and to those whose circumstances are the most burdensome."[37]

The endowment was thus intended to meet the needs of Maghrebis residing in or visiting Jerusalem: both pilgrims passing through the Holy City for short stays, and families of Maghrebi origin who lived there permanently and might need relief. We will see in later documents that striking a balance between these two categories of beneficiaries was challenging, as the boundaries between them were fluid and each status could prove temporary, since families who came on pilgrimage could extend their stays by a few months before settling permanently, adding along the way the suffix "al-Maghrebi" to their surname to recall their origin and confirm their rights to endowment benefits.

The text does specify, however, that the "new arrivals" were to receive priority over the settled families when it came to benefits. Massignon would reiterate this detail time and again in the 1950s when it came to confirming the mandate to provide hospitality and relief to those he called "voluntary expatriates" of the pilgrimage, to better highlight that, in his view, historically "the right to asylum [. . .] is precisely at the core of the waqfs of the holy places of Islam."[38] The text goes on to specify which kinds of benefits the recipients will "be entitled to," between those who "will dwell" in the zawiya, those who will farm the Ein Karem land themselves, and those who will share "rents or land tenancy"—thus reflecting the difference in needs between an ailing pilgrim in need of care, a homeless family seeking shelter, and visitors who require only temporary assistance. At any rate, for this endowment as for so many others, it was obviously the potential to parcel out, sharecrop, and lease the land that would result in the gradual loss of control of this hereditament, even though the endowment's legal framework theoretically prohibited any divestiture to third parties.

After identifying the endowment's beneficiaries, the text specifies that the administrator will be required to satisfactorily maintain the property, to "enforce repairs, constructions or improvements deemed necessary,"[39] "so as to ensure the conservation of the endowment's assets and to increase its revenues."[40] The text then goes on to mention four specific expenditure items consistent with its mandate. First, the endowment's administrator must "purchase bread and distribute it during the three months of Rajab, Sha'ban and Ramadan, to Maghrebis recently arrived in Jerusalem or already residing there [. . .] at the rate of two loaves for each man and each woman. At the time these distributions are taking place, after the *asser* [afternoon] prayer, the assistants will recite from the Koran seven times the *Fatiha* and three times the *Ikhlas* (sincerity) and the two surahs of protection (surah 12–14)." Second, "a meal [will be] served on the feast days of Eid el Fitr (which concludes the Ramadan fasting period), of the Sacrifice and of the birthday of the Prophet, to needy Maghrebis."

Third, "the administrator of the foundation will supply all those in need coming from western North Africa and living in the zawiya with funds to purchase a new garment out of 'bard' to protect them from the cold." Finally, "if a Maghrebi were to die penniless, the cost of his funeral and shroud would be paid out of the endowment's revenues." The four specific actions detailed in the text refer to the basic needs of the beneficiaries identified earlier, since they involve hosting, feeding, clothing, and, if need be, burying the transient pilgrims or the "voluntary exiles" who may have chosen to stay on longer within the holy places. All the structuring elements of a holy Islamic endowment designed as "permanent charitable almsgiving" are included here.[41] What would become a subject of debate and questioning, of course, was the proportion of the budget to be allocated to expenditures involving investment in and restoration of properties, on the one hand, and operating expenses and recurring charitable actions (bread, meals, clothing, funerals) on the other. Here again, the Waqf Abu Madyan was representative of a set of problems common to many Islamic endowments when faced with this same choice.

The text's conclusion ordinarily aims to seal the rights and prerogatives inherent to the waqf and to preclude any possibility of deterrence from its objectives, for "it comprises no stipulation liable to result in its annulment or to cancel its effects." It is "perpetual, sacred," and entails "no rift." To make sure there will be no rift, it is first provided that the stewardship of the endowment will be entrusted to "the one person from among the Maghrebis residing in Jerusalem who would be the most clear-sighted."[42] Next, using conventional wording, the eventual infringers are warned in ample detail against what they risk:

> Neither the government nor the governed, nor any authority exercising absolute power, shall be enabled to modify the present waqf, or annul it, ignore it, criticize it, or issue complaints against certain of its provisions, attempt to annul it wholly or partially whether conspicuously or by instigation, or as a result of a judicial decision, a consultation, or a subtle ruse that cannot escape the notice of God who sees what escapes our vision and what hearts conceal. Whosoever shall commit such deeds or abet those who do so will be answerable before God [. . .] on the day when each soul will answer for [. . .] the good and bad deeds he has committed."[43]

These formulations aim to ensure the strictly "sacred" character of the fixed assets and their inalienability, specifying that they "can be subject neither to sale, nor donation, nor pledge, nor any pecuniary transaction, nor exchange nor usurpation. No one shall appropriate it for himself if he believes in God and the Last Judgment, and believes that these properties belong to God Almighty." To prevent the tenants of these *awaqaf* properties from assuming virtual ownership of the properties because of the duration granted on the lease, it is provided that "leasing of the village can in no case extend beyond a period of two years" and that "the lease cannot be renewed until the first has expired."[44] We will see that this stipulation would be increasingly infringed over time and, as one can imagine, would be frequently contested by farmers of the leased land. This guarantee of inalienability of an endowment's assets, at any rate, was to be the basis for its durability and even its everlastingness, as was the case for *pro anima* monastic donations in the context of Western Christendom.[45]

The eschatological dimension of the act of giving is addressed in the text by a few striking phrases aimed at countering common wisdom and making the passage of time an additional guarantee rather than a risk: "However long the time may be, it shall not alter this endowment; however differing the ages may be, they shall not weaken its scope. Quite the contrary, every era shall but further confirm it, every instant shall consolidate and strengthen it ever more, unto eternity, until God shall inherit the earth and all it comprises. For surely He is the best of heirs."[46] Wishful thinking? Most probably, in the strictest sense. But these lines must be read for what they are: both an aggregate of conventional formulas and the mark of an authentic way of thinking about history, time, and the apocalypse in Islamic culture.[47] Most especially, they would be, for six centuries, the judicial tools that would allow judges to preserve the endowment as best they could against attempts at appropriation, alienation, and usurpation, provided that the complaints were filed and these judges could take up the issue.

I

IN THE EMPIRE OF THE SULTANS

STEWARDSHIP AND CONSOLIDATION
DURING THE OTTOMAN ERA

During the summer of 1949, one Mr. Pierrestiger, an official of the French Consulate of Jerusalem, was tasked by the consul René Neuville with assembling documentary evidence that would consolidate the legal bases of the Waqf Abu Madyan. To this end, he visited the archives of Jerusalem's Islamic tribunal, transcribed the documents he deemed most important, and then placed his selections into a blue cardboard folder labeled "Documents and Translations" and a beige subfolder on which he wrote "Translations—Incomplete."[1] His compilation was indeed incomplete, as evidenced by the typed lists he produced for clarity's sake the way a historian would draw up an inventory of sources. Today these documents are housed in the diplomatic archives of Nantes, within a collection repatriated from the French Consulate (in 1978 for the period 1840–1944, and between 1983 and 1998 for the period 1948–77).[2] The first list is titled "List of documents relating to the Waqf Abu Madyan of Ein Karem," and includes ten items. It begins with the 1320 waqfiya and proceeds to a certain number of "Rulings of the Sharia Tribunal," mostly dating from the late nineteenth and early twentieth centuries, which confirm "the authenticity of the waqf" amid various conflicts or challenges with its Ein Karem tenants.[3]

Another list, slipped into the same file, gives an idea as to how the endowment's stewardship was implemented (figure 12). It is titled "State of documents found at the home of the late Hajj al-Arabi al-Moghrabi, mutewalli [steward] of Maghrebi waqfs in Jerusalem, and entrusted to Hajj Bashir Effendi al-Moghrabi al-Husseini, appointed after him as *mutewalli* of the aforementioned waqfs."[4] It includes fifty-two items, is handwritten in Arabic, and then translated and typed out in French. It bears no date, making it necessary to consult the salary ledgers housed in the imperial archives of Istanbul, which indicate that on 11 November 1900, following the death of "Hajj 'Arabi ibn Halife bin Kasem al-Konstantini al-Moghrabi," the endowment's administration was handed over to "Hajj Bashir Effendi al-Moghrabi."[5] This list thus dates to late 1900 and includes deletions and marginalia that nearly always concerns problems of dating the documents.[6] The first document on the list is the waqfiya instituted by Umar al-Muarrad al-Maghrebi in 1303; and the last document is, as one would expect, the decree "designating Hajj al-Arabi mutewalli of the aforementioned waqf dated 22 Moharram 1302 (1884)"—sixteen years before his death, in that case.[7]

An overview of the other documents reveals that they were all produced between 1705 and 1837 and that most of them involve landholdings or real estate properties in addition to the original endowments ("a house in the Armenian quarter" in 1809, a house "in the Blacksmiths' quarter" in 1813, "a mill in the Maghrebi quarter" in 1839, "fields of prickly pear" in 1861, a "fourth of an olive grove in Lydda" in 1837, property rights located in Nazareth in 1791, 1793, and 1857 . . .).[8] Note that these are lesser donations than the initial bequests of the medieval period. We also observe that these later additions are increasingly endowments of a private or "family" nature (*waqf ahli*), which accrete to the public or "charitable" (*waqf kahyri*) initial endowments. The Waqf Abu Madyan is once again emblematic of a general historical trend: the flourishing of private endowments whose purpose was to ensure the transfer of a family endowment while benefiting from the stewardship structure of a reputable public endowment.[9] The 1949 data collection was indeed incomplete, as confirmed by a publication recently drawn from the archives of the Islamic Tribunal of Jerusalem, which tabulates some sixty documents having to do with the Maghrebi Quarter during the Ottoman period. Nevertheless, the content of these documents is no different from those collected by the consular official: additions of secondary donations on behalf of the Waqf Abu Madyan,

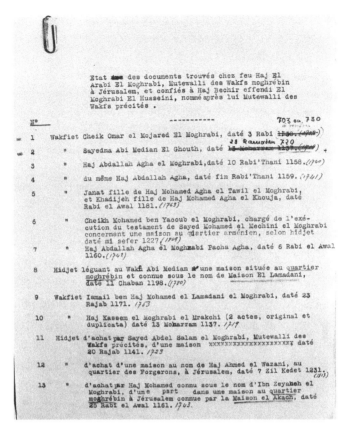

Etat des documents trouvés chez feu Haj El
Arabi El Moghrabi, Mutewalli des Wakfs moghrébin
à Jérusalem, et confiés à Haj Bechir effendi El
Moghrabi El Husseini, nommé après lui Mutewalli des
Wakfs précités .

—————— 703 ou 730

Nº

1   Wakfiet Cheik Omar el Mojared El Moghrabi, daté 3 Rabi 1130. (1718)
                                        23 Ramadan 730
2   "   Sayedna Abi Median El Ghouth, daté 13 Moharram 1137. (1724) +
3   "   Haj Abdallah Agha el Moghrabi,daté 10 Rabi'Thani 1158. (1745)
4   "   du même Haj Abdallah Agha, daté fin Rabi'Thani 1159. (1746)
5   "   Janat fille de Haj Mohamed Agha el Tawil el Moghrabi,
            et Khadijeh fille de Haj Mohamed Agha el Khouja, daté
            Rabi el Awal 1181. (1767)
6   "   Cheikh Mohamed ben Yacoub el Moghrabi, chargé de l'exé-
            cution du testament de Sayed Mohamed el Mechini el Moghrabi
            concernant une maison au quartier arménien, selon hidjet
            daté mi sefer 1227 (1812)
7   "   Haj Abdallah Agha el Moghrabi Pacha Agha, daté 6 Rabi el Awal
            1160. (1747)
8   Hidjet léguant au Wakf Abi Median d'une maison située au quartier
            moghrébin et connue sous le nom de Maison El Lamadani,
            daté 11 Chaban 1198. (1780)
9   Wakfiet Ismail ben Haj Mohamed el Lamadani el Moghrabi, daté 23
            Rajab 1171. 1757
10   "   Haj Kassem el Moghrabi el Mrakchi (2 actes, original et
            duplicata) daté 13 Moharram 1137. 1729
11 Hidjet d'achat par Sayed Abdel Salam el Moghrabi, Mutewalli des
            Wakfs précités, d'une maison xxxxxxxxxxxxxxxxxxxxx daté
            20 Rajab 1141. 1723
12   "   d'achat d'une maison au nom de Haj Ahmed el Wazani, au
            quartier des Forgerons, à Jérusalem, daté 7 Zil Kedet 1231. (1815)
13   "   d'achat par Haj Mohamed connu sous le nom d'Ibn Zeyaneh el
            Moghrabi, d'une part dans une maison au quartier
            moghrébin à Jérusalem connue par la Maison el Akach, daté
            25 Rabi el Awal 1161. 1743

FIGURE 12. "State of Documents Found at the Home of the Late Hajj al-Arabi al-Moghrabi, Mutewalli of Maghrebi waqfs of Jerusalem," November 1900. Source: © CADN, Jerusalem, 294 PO/2, 37/1.

purchase of orchards and cultivated wastelands (*hakura*), deposit notices, rental contracts, recovery proceedings, repair of a dilapidated mill, and so on. In other words, routine management of a charitable foundation financed by revenue from its real estate assets.[10]

One final list, slipped into the folder compiled by the French consular official in 1949, is worth highlighting for it summarizes the donations accreted over time to the Waqf Abu Madyan, and helps to demonstrate that latter donations ultimately constituted a sizable assemblage of landholdings and properties in various quarters of Jerusalem and outside the Holy City. It is titled "List of Maghrebi waqf properties in Palestine":

Village of Ein Karem; Maghrebi quarter; Zawiya of the Maghrebis; Seven shops in Bab el-Silsileh; Six shops in the Jewish Quarter; Two houses in the Jewish quarter; A house in Daraj el-Tabouneh; A house in the Armenian Quarter; Two houses in Bab el-Silsileh; A house in the Sa'dieh Quarter reverting to the guardians of the Koran; A house in Bab Hutta; A stable in Bab Hutta; A house in the Christian Quarter; Two shops near the prickly pear fields; Three plots of land near Maghrebi Gate; A tract of land at Ras el Amud in Silwan; Three property shares of a piece of land located near Birket Es-Sultan, outside Jaffa Gate; An olive grove in Lydda; Four shops in Gaza, in the el-Daraj quarter; A house near the Muslim orphanage; Half a house near Suq el-Hosr, Jaouneh quarter.[11]

It is noteworthy that the three original properties are listed first: Ein Karem, the Maghrebi Quarter, and the Zawiya of the Maghrebis, respectively established as a waqf by al-Afdal Ali in 1193, by Umar al-Mujarrad al-Maghribi in 1303, and by a descendant of Abu Madyan in 1320. These three endowments clearly made up the essential core, in both property and financial terms, of what the stewards would gradually consolidate under the generic term of "Waqf Abu Madyan." They also constituted the historical foundation, and one might even say "identity" base, since they grouped together three properties that were the most visibly identified as belonging to the Jerusalem maghrebis: the village of Ein Karem, the Maghrebi Quarter, and the zawiya of the same name. The properties subsequently added were hardly negligible, but were of lesser importance, less overtly identified and intended only to earn supplementary rental income for the endowment: shops, residential houses, a stable, orchards (mostly located south of the quarter, below the zawiya al-Katunya, the location of today's Davidson archaeological park and the vestiges of Umayyad palaces), and a few plots of land outside the walls (Silwan, Birket es-Sultan) or in other towns in Palestine (Lydda/Lod, Gaza), undoubtedly the result of the scattering of certain Maghrebi families.

Not unlike myself, the consular official in 1949 seemed a bit confused and was trying to get his bearings. So at the end of his dossier he attached a road map of Palestine ("Survey of Palestine—Motor Map—1/500,000th") published in 1938, at the bottom of which he handwrote the caption "Location of the Maghrebi *wakoufs*," and upon which he drew black squares on Jerusalem, Ein Karem, Gaza, Lydda, Ramleh, and Nazareth. The squares are not all the same size: those of Jerusalem and Ein Karem are markedly larger than the ones for Gaza, Lydda, Ramleh. and Nazareth. In the upper left the map features an insert of the old city of Jerusalem and its immediate vicinity, on which the official has drawn eight red dots: at Bab Hutta; at Bab el-Silsileh; in the Christian Quarter; in al-Wad Street; in the Jewish Quarter; in the Armenian Quarter; along the edge of the Sultan's Pool; and at Silwan. On the back of the map the consular official paper-clipped a little sketch of the Maghrebi Quarter's location, drawn by Massignon, most probably when he was translating the waqfiya in 1949–50 (figure 13). This drawing speaks to how hard it must have been to reconstitute the site with any precision: Massignon notes in the upper left: "Ask Neuville for exact map of Waqf Abu Madyan." He colors in green what he identifies as "the zawiya," but adds a large question mark right next to it, again with the same green pencil. Further south, he identifies a small segment of the Western Wall as the "Wailing Wall" and, still further south, all the way to the ramp above, he identifies the largest segment of this same wall as being the "Buraq."[12]

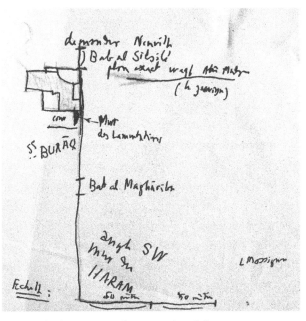

FIGURE 13. **The Maghrebi Quarter, location sketch by Louis Massignon. Source:** © CADN, Jerusalem, 294 PO/2, 37/1.

Facing Challenges by the People of Ein Karem:
Contestation and Consolidation

In the documentary dossier put together in 1949, three sets pertaining to the Ottoman period drew my attention: the first dated 1693, the second 1696, and the third, the 1800s. These three sets testify to how the Waqf Abu Madyan was consolidated in the seventeenth and eighteenth centuries, and how its stewards managed to assert their rights when challenged by the people of Ein Karem. The first document is a ruling by the Jerusalem tribunal dated 18 October 1693 (17 Safar 1105) "acknowledging the existence of the Waqf Abu Madyan in Ein Karem and authorizing the steward of the waqf to take charge of the mosque," against a plaintiff (Sheikh Abd-el-Kader, son of Hajj Abd-el-Aziz al-Maghribi) who claimed he retained the office of mosque steward, which was purportedly "bequeathed to him by his father."[13] This document demonstrates that contemporary jurisprudence defined in broad terms the scope of the waqf, since, as we recall, the mosque was theoretically excluded. The judge does reiterate that "the entire village of Ein Karem and all its realty assets make up the waqf of Sidi Abu Madyan instituted for Maghrebis, except for the mosque," but says that, "since the mosque is located in the village and does not possess a waqf" of its own, he authorizes the administrator of the Waqf Abu Madyan (Hajj Muhammad, son of Hajj Hussein El-Bakry) to "appoint an imam and to pay him 4 piasters yearly out of the income from the Ein Karem landholdings," and to "repair and construct whatever is deemed necessary for the mosque [. . .], especially given that the income from the waqf landholdings can afford these expenses."[14] The endowment was thus soundly enough established by the late seventeenth century to be entrusted with the stewardship of the Ein Karem mosque, even though the founding text would appear to have excluded it.

Three years later, a further ruling from the same tribunal, dated 6 November 1696 (10 Rabi'ul Akhar), reaffirmed the endowment's soundness, this time with regard to how the agricultural revenues were to be shared.[15] We see the same administrator, Hajj Muhammad El-Bakry, accuse the village sheikhs of Ein Karem of assessing the wheat and barley harvest "before measuring it" concretely, which has led to a "fraudulent" estimate of the share owed to the waqf, the actual harvest having turned out to be more plentiful than forecast. The Jerusalem judge "opened the Sultanic ledger, and there he found written that the share owed to the waqf Maghrebi sirs [. . .] is of one third." He declared that the defendants "had admitted to setting the waqf's share of wheat and barley prior to measuring the harvest," and demanded accordingly that the wrong suffered by the waqf was to be righted by the defendants, "consistent with their confessions."[16] This document is essential, for it depicts an actively engaged administrator capable of outsmarting the tenant farmers on Ein Karem's properties and obtaining swift reparations by drawing upon the endowment's legal framework. It also shows that the Waqf Abu Madyan, like all religious endowments of the same type, required monitoring and continuous "legal maintenance" if it was to remain profitable; otherwise, the natural slope of history would bend toward a gradual encroachment of assets and revenues by their tenants and keepers.[17] Finally, this document helps us gauge what a financial catastrophe the loss of Ein Karem in 1948 would represent for the Maghrebis of Jerusalem.

The third batch of documents relates to court proceedings between 1805 and 1807 in which the waqf administrator successfully sues for debt recovery, once more against the villagers of Ein Karem, but this time with the backing of Istanbul and the governor of Damascus. On 7 May 1805, a *firman* (decree) is sent to the governor of Jerusalem, Yahia Bey, informing him that "the steward of the Sidi Waqf Abu Madyan has complained to us that certain inhabitants of Ein Karem are refusing to pay what they owe the waqf."[18] Back in Istanbul, the Ottoman government enjoins its representative in Jerusalem to "imprison all those who owe anything to the waqf and [to] release them only once they have paid." On 9 October 1806, the governor writes "to the sheikhs and inhabitants of Ein Karem" to demand payment of the money owed, failing which "it is His Excellency who shall pay in your stead, but he will require than you reimburse him in quadruplicate. Have pity on yourselves, then. You have been warned, do as ordered."[19] The *wali* of Damascus, the immediate superior of the governor of Jerusalem, also intervenes in this sequence of events, for on 25 October 1807 he reports that "after successfully collecting from the inhabitants of Ein Karem all arrears and outstanding debts, dating back fifteen years, for the Waqf Sidi Abu Madyan, we have ordered the steward of the waqf to have the zawiya of the waqf restored."[20]

What follows is more surprising, for it features a renowned imperial endowment in Jerusalem, the Haseki Sultan hospice, founded in 1552 by the wife of Suleiman the Magnificent: "If there should be funds remaining after all the expenditures deemed necessary for this work and for the needs of the waqf, it should purchase bread for the Takiat Haseki Sultan located in Jerusalem, and set aside a certain sum to purchase bread to be distributed among the Maghrebis of Jerusalem." The signature on this document may provide a hint: "Hajj Muhammad Agha Abu Zarria Moghrabi Bey, wali of Damascus." The wali of Damascus, a high-ranking official on the organizational chart of provincial Ottoman administration,[21] is clearly of Maghrebi origin, which might explain why he got so involved in this matter.[22] At any rate, though this debt recovery operation proved successful in the end, it did require considerable leveraging by the Ottoman state, from Istanbul to Jerusalem by way of Damascus—a sign of the importance of the endowment from the imperial administration's perspective, but also of the persistent problem of effectively collecting the leasing fees.[23] Like all such judicial episodes, this new sequence can be analyzed as a sign of the endowment's "juridical resilience," but also as proof of the structural precariousness of this kind of religious institution, comparable to that of feudal power in Europe in the late Middle Ages, which constantly ran the risk of being "forgotten by its subjects" and required constant reminders of "its power's legacy" when confronted by peasants who, for their part, were farming the land in the present, in the everydayness of production processes.[24]

Religious Congregations and New Competing Patrimonies

When Catholic and Orthodox religious congregations took up residence in the places traditionally devoted to the commemoration of Mary's "Visitation" to Elizabeth, renewed competition for landholdings ensued, leaving the stewards of the Waqf Abu Madyan unable to resort to using the same tools they used to settle their recurring conflicts with the tenant farmers. The same holds true for patrimonial claims over the Western Wall that were coming to light by 1840: the increasing power of Western interests in the Holy Land left the Waqf Abu Madyan open to fresh legal challenges, notably after the imperial rescript (Hatt-i Humayun) of 1856, which recognized the principle of property rights for foreigners, and even more so after the enactment of the 1867 Property Code regarding landholdings by foreigners, which set out the conditions for applying this principle.[25]

To shed some light on relations between the stewards of the Waqf Abu Madyan and the religious congregations, let us take a brief side trip to the archives of the Franciscan Custodia Terrae Sanctae in Jerusalem, which had a church built in Ein Karem in 1674: the Church of Saint John the Baptist in Montana, whose stewardship was entrusted to a community of Spanish origin. In the Custodia's financial archives is found a batch of documents containing receipts from rents paid to the "Magravinos" for the occupation of the "Terreni di San Giovani in Montana" during the period dating 1762–99 (figure 14).[26] Another batch bears the title "Affitto que se paga todos los años a los Magravinos de S. Juan," and contains receipts for three continuous sequences: 1675–99, 1740–57, and 1801–18.[27] More interesting still, we note that this charge is collected not only for the actual occupation of the land, but also for the use (*usanza* in the Spanish text) of an easement (*istitrak* in the Arabic text) on another waqf plot. The total annual rent, depending on the years, ranges between sixteen and twenty-two piasters (a piaster corresponding to one one-hundredth of an Ottoman pound). Certain receipts indicate that it was paid "al Capo dei Granadini," which reads literally "to the Chief of the Grenadians," the inhabitants of Grenada; for these Franciscans of Spanish origin, the Jerusalem Maghrebis were either "Magravinos" (transcription of "Maghrebis") or "Grana-

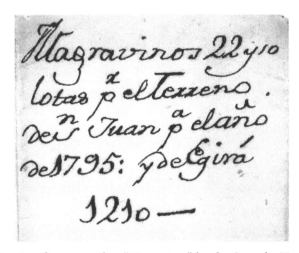

FIGURE 14. Receipts for rent paid to "Magravinos" by the Custodia Terrae Sanctae in Jerusalem, 1795. Source: © Archives of the Franciscan Custody of Jerusalem, Ein Karem: San Giovanni Battista in Montana.

dini," an echo of the Muslim presence in Andalusia, particularly in Grenada.[28] Let us note finally that the receipts are written in Arabic before being roughly translated on the back of the document, and that it is the Franciscan tenants who add to the rental fee two piasters "*al escrivanos*," to remunerate the public scribe assigned to draft the receipt. Even though we do spot a few chronological inconsistencies in these bundles of receipts that have been handed down to us, these documents prove that the "Granadini" of the Waqf Abu Madyan regularly collected rents owed to them by the Franciscans of Ein Karem. This is yet another convergent indicator demonstrating that the Ottoman era was one of legal and financial consolidation of the Waqf Abu Madyan.

The period of Egyptian occupation of Palestine (1831–40), followed by the establishment of the first European consular offices in Jerusalem by 1839, gradually shifted the balance of power between local Muslim institutions and new Western entitlements, as shown by the historian Musa Sroor, who points to a trend of "privatization" of certain waqf assets in the Late Ottoman period.[29] One document included in the file compiled by the French Consulate in 1949 is worth closer scrutiny, for it demonstrates that the Waqf Abu Madyan was immediately challenged by this new historical context: it is a translation, a handwritten draft typed later as the final version, of a "Letter by Muhammad Serif, secretary of Ibrahim Pasha al-Masri, written to Achmed Agha Dousdar, Governor of Jerusalem," on 19 November 1840 (24 Ramadan 1256).[30] The letter, drafted in Cairo, refers to "a Khedival *irade* [decree] issued by His Highness" regarding the Waqf Abu Madyan's rights to the pavement adjacent to the Western Wall or Al-Buraq: ". . . It has been made known after deliberation by the Khedival Council of Jerusalem that the location which the Jews wish to pave is contiguous with the wall of the Mosque of Omar, where 'Al-Buraq' was tied. This location is included in the Abu Madyan bequest. There is no precedent indicating that the Jews restored this place."[31]

With this letter, we leave the relatively well-delineated Ein Karem landholdings dossier to surreptitiously come upon the issue of property rights with respect to the Western Wall and its contiguous pavement, a subject we shall return to later;[32] but the interest of this document lies chiefly with its date and its presence in the documentary folder compiled by the French consular official in 1949. What it shows is that even at the end of the Egyptian occupation, a period considered favorable to foreign interests overall,[33] the administrators of the Waqf Abu Madyan were capable of asserting their rights against the attempts at encroachment and appropriation to which they were subjected. The remainder of the document seals the legal position of the waqf on this decisive issue of access rights to the Wall: "We legally attest that it is impermissible to provide them assistance to pave this place. The Jews must be warned not to raise their voices when praying or speaking. They need to be given authorization to come venerate this place in accordance with their ancient custom."[34] In 1840, speaking from Cairo just before full sovereignty over Palestine was about to revert to Ottoman administration, the khedive of Egypt, Ibrahim Pasha, reasserted the legal validity of the endowment created at the time of Saladin. We grasp the value of this document in the eyes of the French Consulate as it prepares to take charge of legally safeguarding the Maghrebis of Jerusalem a century or so later.

Among the items compiled in 1949, a final batch of documents dating from the 1860s helps us picture the new challenge created by the steady arrival of Christian congregations to Ein Karem. On 6 July 1864 (1 Safar 1281), the Jerusalem tribunal ruled on the case brought by "Muhammad Effendi Abdelkassem Moghrabi, steward of the waqf," who demanded from "Michail Effendi Rahil" a sizable annual rent increase subsequent to the construction of several buildings on two parcels of land belonging to the waqf.[35] Even though the document does not state as much, we infer that it refers to the first edifices built by the congregation of Our Lady of Zion, established in Jerusalem since 1856, which had two tracts of land rented in 1862 by a front man, a Christian and Ottoman citizen, who was moreover "the current paymaster of the Jerusalem Treasury."[36] These first constructions—still standing today, with an engraved stone commemorating the inauguration date (1 July 1864)—must have been particularly imposing, if we are to believe the description produced by the court clerk of the time:

Mr Michail Effendi commenced construction and built on the first plot of land a house with seven rooms and a divan, two latrines and two kitchens, one at ground level and one upstairs [...] and erected a second floor above that one [...]. In front of the building's entry, he has built a stable [...] and next to the stable, he had a cistern excavated, and had it all roughcast and whitewashed, and the terraces paved [...]. He then commenced construction

on the second plot; he had a grand salon built, and two rooms atop one another, and had a cistern excavated on the southwest side of the house. He had
pavement laid and had iron and woodwork done, and ordered the very best
roughcasting and whitewashing."[37]

The construction costs for the two buildings were assessed by the tribunal
at eighty thousand piasters in all, which compelled the waqf steward to demand
a reassessment of the total amount of annual rent, levied at the time at thirty
piasters, a ludicrous sum in fact, given the upgrade brought about by the two
new buildings. The lower court dismissed the waqf steward's claim, but just
over two years later, his efforts were rewarded. On 23 September 1866, the Jerusalem tribunal officially announced the construction of an "Establishment of
Sisters for the Education of Orphaned and Abandoned Girls" and a transfer of
the lease to the French state, in the presence of "Mr. de Bérard, Consul General
of Jerusalem, accredited by His Majesty Napoleon," by reassessing the rent
up to 108 piasters annually.[38] This documentary record is emblematic of the
unprecedented financial influence wielded by the new religious congregations
settled in Jerusalem starting in the mid-nineteenth century, but also of the
attempts by the Waqf Abu Madyan stewards to come to terms with this new
acquisitiveness.[39]

The Accounts Ledger: Financial History, Effective History

In all, the documentary record compiled in 1949 by the French Consulate
provides the unambiguous legal basis of the Waqf Abu Madyan. It also sheds
light on the process of accretions and mergers that came to strengthen the endowment over time by broadening its base of landholdings and built properties.
And finally, it helps demonstrate that whenever attempts at appropriation came
before the Jerusalem tribunal, the court always ruled in favor of the endowment. Even so, the compiled documents pertain only to the legal validity of
the Waqf Abu Madyan and to the challenges it had to face, and say nothing of
the tangible actions implemented by the administrators to fulfill the objectives
set by the donors. To ascertain that the Waqf Abu Madyan was not merely
an empty shell, capable of defending its *rights* without necessarily fulfilling
its *duties*, we need to step back momentarily from the judicial archives and

look more closely at how the waqf was run—and in particular, at the archived accounts ledgers, which kept track of all activity and expenditures undertaken by the administrators. Today, the archives of the Palestinian Ministry for Religious Affairs at Abu-Dis are available to researchers, and this is where a financial history of the Waqf Abu Madyan might be outlined, at least from the second half of the nineteenth century onward.[40]

To get to the Abu-Dis archives from Jerusalem these days, one has to make a long detour and circumvent the separation wall that isolates the Palestinian territories from the Jerusalem agglomeration. Although the building is located less than a kilometer from the old city, as the crow flies—and until 2005 one could bike there in a few minutes, passing by the Mount of Olives, Ras al-Amud, and Wadi Qadum—today it involves a sixteen-kilometer drive via Sheikh Jarah, Mount Scopus, the az-Za'ayyem checkpoint, Ma'al Adumim, Jahalin, and al-Eizariya before getting to the archives of the Palestinian Ministry for Religious Affairs, located right in front of the separation wall, on the eastern side. During an on-site investigation in January 2017, I was able to access fourteen balance sheets covering the sixty-year period from 1855 to 1913, an entirely satisfactory sampling of 25 percent, fairly evenly distributed over the period.[41] The endowment's annual accounts are generally presented on a double-page spread, handwritten in black ink with an occasional addition in red at the bottom to order that the accounts be transferred to the waqfs' administration for validation by a certified public accountant.[42] At the bottom of the document the name of the steward appears consistently, where he dates and signs the balance sheet after summarizing the key elements (total annual income, total annual expenditures, annual balance, and eventual carryover or deficit.)

Until the 1870s the accounts are presented horizontally: a list of revenue sources, then on the opposite page a list of expenditure items (figure 15). Each input or outlay item is described in a few lines, with the corresponding amount written beneath a little horizontal line; then at the bottom, a horizontal line spans the entire width of the page displaying the total amount, generally written slantwise. There are no subtotals calculated for the *categories* of income and expenditures, which for that matter do not appear consistently in statement order.[43] Starting in the late 1870s, the accounts are presented in vertical columns, still over two facing pages, with subtotals calculated for each of the categories of revenue (housing rentals, shops, land use, gardens, etc.) or expenditures (bread and meal purchases, construction work, wages, various taxes, etc.), which facilitate analysis.[44] By 1900 we note the introduction of pre-printed ledgers with headers, columns and subcolumns, single or double lines to differentiate at a glance between subtotals of one-time income or outlay items; but we do still see some loose-leaf balance sheets after 1902.[45] After 1900, even when the accounts appear on loose-leaf pages, the lines are more consistently hand-drawn by the accounts drafter. In all cases, for all the ledgers I was able to consult for the years 1855 to 1913, they were all *retrospectively* written annual balance sheets, free of any erasures, produced in one go in the same hand at the end of the fiscal year—and not accounts books updated on a daily basis.

The procedures for accounts validation are described at the bottom of each balance sheet, with dates for when the ledgers were transferred from one department to another. Once checked and signed by the steward, the accounts were jointly reviewed by the court clerk and the head accountant of the waqfs administration; the document was then forwarded to the executive board before returning to the head accountant for final approval. For the year 1288 (March 1871–March 1872), the accounts were approved and signed by the steward on 30 September 1872, sent to the executive board on 2 October, and definitively approved on 13 October 1872.[46] For the year 1325 (February 1907–February 1908), the process took a bit longer since the steward's signature occurred on 7 September 1908, transmission to the executive board on 21 September, and final approval on 3 October. It is conceivable that the Young Turk revolution, extensively celebrated in Jerusalem in August and September 1908, may well have disrupted the otherwise regular administrative shuttling.[47]

Increased Budget and Rising Agricultural Revenues

Before getting into the details of revenue and expenditure items, we can note a substantial increase of the endowment's overall budget, from twenty thousand piasters in the mid-1850s to around eighty thousand piasters in the 1910s—in other words, a fourfold increase in sixty years. This rise is consistent and uninterrupted, with a first threshold at about thirty thousand piasters around 1870, then a second one of about sixty thousand during the 1890s, and finally a

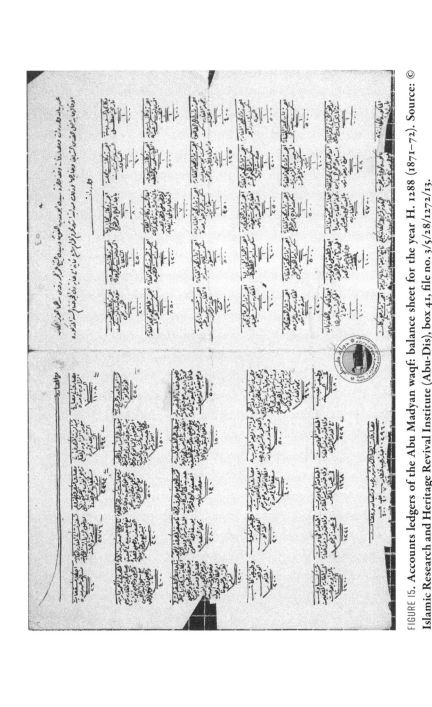

FIGURE 15. Accounts ledgers of the Abu Madyan waqf: balance sheet for the year H. 1288 (1871–72). Source: © Islamic Research and Heritage Revival Institute (Abu-Dis), box 41, file no. 3/5/28/1272/13.

budget of around eighty thousand on the eve of World War I. Hardly an institution in decline in the Late Ottoman era, the Waqf Abu Madyan was showing
a steady strengthening of its scope of action, whether in legal terms, as seen
earlier, or in its finances. This rising trend also provides an informative vantage
point for witnessing the demographic expansion of Jerusalem in the Late Ottoman period, with the city growing from about fifteen thousand inhabitants in
1850 to some seventy thousand on the eve of World War I—a fivefold increase
for the period.[48] Of the fourteen balance sheets I was able to view, six are in
the black while eight are in the red, with a trend toward more deficit years at
the end of the period, related to increased expenditures on improvement work.
Among the revenue sources, there are certain landholdings belatedly added to
the endowment's properties: for instance, the rents from a bread oven and a
grist mill in the Maghrebi Quarter, a residence in Bab Hutta and another in
the Armenian Quarter, a stable in Bab Hutta, a vegetable garden in Silwan, an
olive grove in Lydda, and several shops in Gaza. The long history of successive
accretions to the Abu Madyan endowment is succinctly summarized here in
a few lines on some balance sheets, several centuries after the perpetuity vow
was issued by the donor.

The revenues from the village of Ein Karem were generally collected
through lease, following a public auction procedure (*muzayadah*) comparable
to a call for bids (*munaqasa*), as was customary in the municipality at the time.
Among the tithe collectors who would secure the market year after year are
found the venerable Jerusalem families most involved in this type of activity,
such as the Dajani, Dawudi, and Nashashibi families. The tithe on revenues
from Ein Karem's farmlands was generally levied twice annually, in winter and
summer, with a far more substantial amount levied, of course, on summer revenues. Due to underlying conflicts that prevailed among Ein Karem's farmers,
this item was not consistently available in all the budgets I was able to review,
particularly in the earlier part of the period, though I did come across "larger"
entries where it is specified that they cover in part an adjustment for arrears,
as was the case in 1860.

Thanks to a summary document that lists all the revenues yielded by Ein
Karem over the period 1894–1911, we can calculate that the tithes collected in
winter amount on average to 7,000 piasters, with a minimum at 4,736 piasters
(in 1900) and a maximum at 10,326 (in 1910), and that the total amount of

summer tithes comes out to an average of 21,000 piasters, with a minimum of 19,500 (in 1900) and a maximum of 24,000 (in 1894).[49] In total, the annual average (summer and winter) revenues issuing from Ein Karem's land amount to 28,000 piasters, a little over one-third of the endowment's overall budget for those years. Another batch of documents provides the names of the tithe collectors at Ein Karem for five fiscal years over the period 1876–1903, with the total amount of tithes collected for each year.[50] The average amounts to 27,000 piasters, which indicates relative stability of this property revenue. One final document can help us evaluate the relative importance of Ein Karem's revenues in the endowment's overall budget: in the budget ascertained for the two years 1275–76 (August 1858–July 1860), the tithe collected from Ein Karem farmers amounted to 38,128 piasters, or about 19,000 piasters per year, which translates to nearly two-thirds of the endowment's overall budget for those years.[51] The agricultural income yielded by Ein Karem was thus quite stable and trending very slightly upward over the period as a whole. Logically, it weighed more heavily in the endowment's overall budget earlier in the documented period (about two-thirds of the budget in the 1850s) than in the later period (a little over one-third of the budget by the 1910s).

Recurrent Expenditures and Increased Rental Investments

By analyzing the expenditure items, we gain a much closer approximation of the actual initiatives undertaken by the endowment, and conclude that the demands issued at the time of the bequest were still being scrupulously respected several centuries later. In the context of a markedly expanding budget, we should first note that the allowance paid to the stewards remained modest, and increased very little during the period overall. The *mutewalli* (steward) earned 200 piasters annually in 1855–56 (1272), still 200 piasters in 1907–8 (1325) and 300 piasters in 1912–13 (1331). His two associates, the *kâtib* (registrar) and the *nakib* (secretary), were paid 200 and 180 piasters respectively until 1909, after which the registrar's earnings fell to 180. In all, the three endowment administrators' allowances represented 580 piasters in 1855–56 (3 percent of the budget) and 660 piasters in 1912–13 (less than 1 percent of the budget). Clearly, we can conclude that no undue profit can be attributed to the administrators, who during that period discharged their duties practically pro bono.

If we focus on recurring costs, we find that the four specific instructions set forth in the founding act were consistently implemented. The purchase and distribution of bread for the poor during the three months of Rajab, Chaabane, and Ramadan cost 5,613 piasters in 1855–56, 8,250 piasters in 1878–79, 21,055 piasters in 1898–99, and 25,357 piasters in 1912–13, a fivefold increase over the period. The distribution of two daily meals during the Ramadan celebrations (*Eid al-Fitr*), the day of sacrifice (*Bayram*), and the birthday of the Prophet (*Mawlid*) incurred costs of 919 piasters in 1855–56, 4,323 piasters in 1875–76, 7,020 piasters in 1898–99, and 9,435 piasters in 1910, a tenfold increase over the period. The steep increase in these two expenditure items shows that the endowment was responding tangibly to the most urgent needs of Jerusalem's Maghrebi pilgrims, who were arriving in ever greater numbers. A further demand of the founding charter, to provide warm clothing in the winter, incurred 1,600 piasters in 1871–72, 5,036 piasters in 1901–2, and 9,210 piasters in 1910–11, a sixfold increase over the period.

Add to this, starting in fiscal year 1898–99, a specific expenditure for the purchase of coal during the winter months, for an annual sum varying between 800 and 1,600 piasters, depending on weather conditions. Finally, in the fourth cost provided by the charter, the budget indicates that burial expenses including a shroud were regularly covered at a cost of 470 piasters in 1859–60, 1,343 piasters in 1876–77, and 2,132 piasters in 1910–11, a fivefold increase over the period. In all, given the recurrent expenses and their upward trend, we can conclude that the requirements specified in the founding charter were rigorously respected. Within this logic of support for the Maghrebi pilgrims, one last recurrent expense should be mentioned: the coverage of travel expenses for insolvent pilgrims who wished to return home (3,742 piasters in 1855–56, 10,143 piasters in 1898–99, and 6,931 piasters in 1912–13). Clearly, the Waqf Abu Madyan was fully accomplishing its mission in the Late Ottoman period.

Beyond these recurrent actions, serial analysis of budgets dating from 1855 to 1913 attests to the endowment's expanded scope of operation starting in the 1890s. Upon closer inspection we note that numerous new expenditure items appear in fiscal year 1898–99: the purchase of coal during the winter, as mentioned earlier, but also specific financial assistance for the Maghrebi Quarter's widows, orphans, and the blind (1,720 piasters in 1898–99, 6,816 piasters in 1912–13); the annual replacement of the wicker mats that cover the floor of the zawiya (395 piasters in 1898–99, 321 piasters in 1912–13); and, lastly, the payment of an employee in charge of cleaning, watering, and resupplying candles in the zawiya (375 piasters in 1898–99, 324 piasters in 1912–13). All these additional expenses, however modest, attest to an endowment active and invested in the life of the quarter. Other expenses bear witness to the day-to-day existence of Jerusalem's Maghrebi community: the purchase of oil for lamps in the zawiya (201 piasters in 1855–56, 900 piasters in 1898–99, 1,225 piasters in 1912–13); an allowance for the reciter (*hafiz*) in charge of chanting the prayers at the Dome of the Rock during the months of Rajab, Chaabane, and Ramadan (500 piasters in 1871–72); and the purchase of maintenance utensils for the zawiya (broom, watering can, bucket, rope, basket: 318 piasters in 1910–11). Out of this litany of facts and figures there emerges a picture of the daily existence of those living in the Maghrebi Quarter during the Late Ottoman era, one that testifies to the essential role played by the Waqf Abu Madyan in this modest neighborhood life. These statistics also allow us to better document a few aspects of the economic and social history of Jerusalem at that time. We note, for instance, that salaries did not increase, but that the endowment's operating costs rose steadily, due to price hikes in certain basic commodities (e.g., lamp oil), but especially due to increases in the number of pilgrims, including those arriving from the Maghreb, during this period of modernized transport.[52]

Before closing the accounts ledgers, let us attend to the very end of the documented period, the years 1908–13, for the disruption of the local sociopolitical context in connection with the 1908 Young Turk revolution and the subsequent 1912–13 buildup to war did have tangible repercussions on the endowment's governance. In 1910–11 (1328), undoubtedly swept up in the excitement and optimism of the Young Turk revolution, the endowment officials embarked upon grand renovation and restoration projects involving rooming houses (thirty-three dwellings renovated that year, for a total cost of 12,488 piasters), but also the endowment's "public" buildings (mosque, cenotaph, zawiya, and the quarter's outer wall, for a total cost of 10,135 piasters). That year, over 22,500 piasters were thus invested for improvements to the rental housing stock and the endowment's hospitality buildings, a significant portion of the overall expenses (91,538 piasters), producing a record operating deficit of 14,381 piasters. The endowment's mutewalli, al-Hajj Muhammad, had drawn up the decision in a brief report addressed to the Jerusalem Governorship on 29 January 1908, in which he deplored the fact that out of the fifty dwellings rented out by the endowment, only eleven were cost-effective, and moreover, that the list of Jerusalem Maghrebis requesting housing was growing, with fifteen families who had applied but were still waiting.[53] The improvement work begun a few months later was part of this ambitious renewal project aimed at enhancing the volume and profitability of the endowment's rental stock.

But the timing of this investment program proved inopportune, due to economic downturn and rising political tensions that were rocking the region by 1912.[54] This reversal is clearly visible if we compare the 1908–9 accounts ledger to that of 1912–13. We note that in the earnings column of the budget for the year 1326 (February 1908–January 1909), more and more housing units located outside the Maghrebi Quarter were rented to non-Muslim residents, Armenians (*al-Armani*), Greeks (*al-Rumi*), Latins (*al-Franji*), and especially Jews (*al-Yahudi*). This did not breach the founding charter, however, since these were rooming houses accreted belatedly to the endowment portfolio for the express purpose of increasing its rental income. It also shows that a certain diversity still prevailed in the different quarters of Jerusalem's old city, despite what was long held to be true.[55] The rising number of Jewish tenants is particularly noteworthy between 1900 and 1910 (figure 16), with an especially large proportion of Ashkenazi tenants (*al-Siknaji*), recorded in the registry under somewhat surprising phonetic transcriptions: "Zeineb al-Siknaji," and "Mordohayi al-Siknaji," among other Jewish tenants such as Ayyash al-Yahudiyya, al-Yahud al-Kandrici, Barukh al-Yahudi, Sasun al-Yahudi, Yakub al-Yahudi al-Maghribi (the only tenant identified as both Jewish *and* Maghrebi, along with Mordohayi al-Maghribi). In the budget for the year 1331 (November 1912–November 1913), it appears that the Jewish tenants had left their lodgings, since it is noted in the income column that the endowment would "need to recover owed rent from tenants Zeineb al-Siknaji, Yakub al-Maghreibi, Barukh al-Yahudi, Mordohayi al-Siknaji, and Mordohayi al-Maghribi."

The massive departure of Jerusalem's Jewish communities and a sharp drop in the diversity of the city's different neighborhoods effectively started in 1912, with the Young Turk government's nationalist Pan-Turkist turn, the economic slump, the coalescing of an openly anti-Zionist discourse and threats of war and conscription.[56] It is interesting to note that these departures were

FIGURE 16. The Western Wall, circa 1910. Source: © Matson Photograph collection, Library of Congress.

immediately perceptible in the accounts ledgers of the Waqf Abu Madyan. The upheaval caused by the political crisis and its socioeconomic consequences becomes readily apparent if we focus one last time on the financial record of the year 1912–13. Only ten shops were being leased (instead of fifteen in 1901–2); the rental housing was empty, or showed increasing signs of unpaid rents; and in total, if we exclude the arrears payments from Ein Karem, the net revenues earned that year amounted to only 24,624 piasters, for 70,744 piasters in expenses. The budget of the Waqf Abu Madyan proves an insightful gauge of the region's deepening crisis; and a new expenditure item, however modest, tells of a historic turning point taking place before our eyes. For the first time, 1,206 piasters were paid out that year by way of a new "war tax" (*harb vergisi*) levied on the Ein Karem property income.

Maghrebis in the Empire: Enlightening Insights
from the Istanbul Archives

The juxtaposition of different sets of documents allows for a change of scale and an expansion of viewpoints. After scrutinizing the accounts ledgers compiled in Abu-Dis, let us now move to the archives of Istanbul and Ankara to gauge how important the imperial administrative setting was to the endowment's evolution during the Ottoman period.[57] After glimpsing the day-to-day operations at the local level, let us turn to regulation procedures at the center, for the future of the Maghrebi Quarter, from its endowment to its eventual destruction, was always closely linked to the benevolence or ill will of the successive sovereigns who reigned over the Holy City.[58] In this particular case, the Ottoman sultan-caliph, protector of pilgrimages and custodian of the holy cities of Islam, had good reasons to look upon the fate of Maghrebi pilgrims in Jerusalem with kindly attention.[59]

Consulting the collection is a tricky business, however, since the Ottoman archives relating to religious endowments were reshuffled at every step along the Tanzimat's administrative reorganization starting in 1839, and then were divided up between Ankara and Istanbul after 1936 by the new Turkish Republic. Further complicating an inquiry is the sheer variety of forms these documents could take—from the *ewrak*, a document isolated in different administrative series, to the *defter*, a bound registry bearing a succinct description, to the *gömlek*, a liner or delivery sleeve collating several items pertaining to a same case—all of which often makes it hard to see the whole picture and find the conclusive ruling in a case. And lastly, we should note that the central Ottoman archives contain a number of documents I had come across previously—in original version, translation, summary, or copy—in other collections, notably Abu-Dis and the French consular archives. This is particularly clear for the additions of family waqfs to the Waqf Abu Madyan in the seventeenth and eighteenth centuries.[60] That being said, if we focus on the archives produced specifically by the central administration, the cache of documents identified does demonstrate that the Ottoman imperial structure was fully invested in overseeing and supporting the Waqf Abu Madyan, especially when it came to appointments to the position of steward (mutewalli) and responses to petitions regularly issued by the quarter's residents.

The appointment of the endowment's stewards illustrates a general trend in the history of Ottoman administration: while the office was still passed down by default to a male heir until the early nineteenth century, the new Tanzimat framework recentralized it through its "Bureau of Professions" (*Cihât Kalemi*) starting in the 1840s.[61] Thus, on 25 March 1802, following the death of Ahmed Halif Ibn-i Mehmed Demmûri, the man referred to as El-Hajj Bilal al-Moghrabi asked to be appointed as the endowment's mutewalli, a request that was granted once it had been ascertained that his predecessor had died without a male descendant.[62] On 11 November 1860, on the other hand, Sheikh Mehmed Arif Effendi al-Moghrabi was appointed without any mention made of a legacy appointment to his eventual descendant, and that would remain the case for all appointment decrees enacted henceforth.[63] The serial analysis of appointment and stipend registries also shows that by the 1860s, all religious endowments present in the Maghrebi Quarter were consolidated under one directorship, fully in line with the administrative rationalization endeavor underway during those years.[64] Finally, these decrees inform us that by the mid-seventeenth century, oversight of the markets had been virtually monopolized by the Maghrebis of Jerusalem; and that in the early eighteenth century, the steward of the Waqf Abu Madyan was automatically appointed as "head of the town criers" (*Sheikh Dellal* or *Dellal Başi*, according to the texts). This indicates how well integrated the Maghrebi figures had become within the Jerusalem citizenry, since we know that the policing of markets and the function of town criers played a key role in how news circulated within Ottoman urban spaces.[65]

The inclusion of the Waqf Abu Madyan into Jerusalem's network of religious endowments was confirmed by the allocation of a ration of soup and bread for the employees of the Maghrebi zawiya, drawn from provisions at the Khasseki Sultan soup kitchen, which is regularly mentioned in the ledgers of the famous imperial foundation.[66] This same impression of special attention paid to the Jerusalem Maghrebis by the power center is again illustrated by imperial almsgiving devoted specifically to them, every year, at the start of the pilgrimage season.[67] In the ledgers that document the dispatch of these imperial alms, it is stipulated that they had to be issued in Jerusalem "to the imam, the muezzin, the ulemas, and the poor people of the Maghrebi Quarter."[68] Other documents testify to the high profile of Jerusalem's Maghrebi Quarter within the central Ottoman administration. In 1783, for instance, the historic links between the Waqf Abu Madyan and the "Salah ad-Din waqfs" (*Vakf-i el-Melik en-Nâsirî Selâhaddin*)[69] are highlighted: in 1871, the Mosque of the Maghrebis overlooking the Haram al-Sharif was renovated at the sultan's expense, with a plan to embellish the door with the sultan's seal (*tughra*) and an inscription in Arabic, and the inauguration was scheduled to coincide with the sovereign's birthday, "in the presence of the Quarter's notables."[70] The specifics of this double ornamentation and inauguration exemplify the particular prestige enjoyed by Jerusalem's Maghrebi waqfs, but also the imperial power's wish to incorporate the quarter into its ideological sphere while still respecting its own unique features.

Beyond this attention from the imperial power, as evidenced by the consistent presence of documents in the Ottoman archives that deal with the Maghrebi Quarter, certain "documentary bulges" suggest the emergence of a one-time problem or a particularly complex conflict. This is what happened between 1900 and 1904, when the appointment of a new mutewalli stirred up the Maghrebi community of Jerusalem and set in motion all the workings of the Ottoman administration. This case is remarkably well documented in the State Council archives (*Şura-yi Devlet*), the empire's loftiest administrative jurisdiction, by a dossier containing some thirty documents totaling over fifty pages.[71]

The case began on 11 November 1900 when, following the death of al-Hajj 'Arabî ibn Halif bin Kasim al-Konstantini al-Moghrabi, a successor was appointed as first mutewalli (*mütevelli-i evvel*) in the person of al-Hajj Bashir Effendi al-Moghrabi, of Moroccan origin, with, as deputy mutewalli (*mütevelli-i sânî*), Seyyid Ahmed Arif al-Tunsi—who was of Tunisian origin, as his name suggests. This dual governance, conceived as a way to curb the risk of malfeasance or misappropriation, rapidly devolved into conflict; and the deputy mutewalli resigned, to be immediately replaced by al-Hajj Salih bin Asab al-Zevâdî al-Moghrabi al-Cezâyirî, who was of Algerian origin, also as the name indicates. On 18 August 1902, Hajj Bashir addressed the Imperial Council (*Divan-i Hümâyûn*) to denounce the collusion of special interests between his deputy of Algerian origin and the "French government," and got the deputy removed. On 13 January 1903 the State Council took up the case and called for the intervention of the Ministry of Waqfs (*Evkâf Nezâreti*), which stated in its first report, written on 16 March, that "the Moroccan Bashir Effendi,

principal mutewalli, and the Algerian Salih Effendi, deputy mutewalli," were
unable to collaborate effectively, and that consequently "the keeper of the
Tomb of the Prophet David" (*Hazret-i Davud türbedarinin*) was appointed
the interim mutewalli of the Waqf Abu Madyan. On 14 April, the "Tunisian
and Algerian emigrants" of Jerusalem (*tunus ve cezâyir muhacirleri*) drew up
a collective petition bearing nineteen seals, to denounce the sidelining of the
interim mutewalli by the deputy premier of the Jerusalem tribunal (*kadi nâibi*).
On 2 June a new petition, this time bearing twenty-nine seals and twenty-
three signatures, denounced the collusion between Hajj Bashir and the local
courts, accusing Hajj Bashir of illicitly selling certain of the endowment's real
estate assets to the benefit notably of the Khalidi family; it demanded that the
judicial proceedings be moved to Damascus or Beirut. On 5 July, the deposed
mutewalli, Hajj Salih, denounced in turn the collusion between Hajj Bashir
and the Jerusalem tribunal.

On 5 August the case was taken over by the president of the State Council
in Istanbul (*Şura-yi Devlet Reisi*), which called for a rapid inquest at the Ministry of Waqfs. On 3 September it was the Ein Karem notables' turn to petition
the courts, denouncing Hajj Bechir's mismanagement, claiming that he had
neglected to undertake in a timely manner some much-needed renovation
work on the village mosque. The same day, an impressive petition drawn up by
the "emigrants originating from Tunisia, Algeria and Fez," bearing eighty-two
seals (figure 17), called for the immediate removal of "the illiterate" Hajj Bashir
and the appointment of Hajj Salih, "friend of the poor and the dervishes" (*fa-
kirleri ve dervişleri sever*). Between September and December 1903, three-way
correspondence was exchanged between the "Bureau of Professions" (*Cihât
Kalemi*), the Ministry of Waqfs, and the State Council, resulting in the Waqf
Abu Madyan accounts being frozen by Jerusalem's chief waqf accountant and
management of the endowment temporarily entrusted to the city's governor.
This guardianship allowed for a settling of the dispute, which was steadily
moving toward resolution. On 21 January 1904, the president of the State
Council, after consulting with the minister of imperial waqfs, ruled that Hajj
Bashir be removed. On 5 April 1904 the ruling was upheld on final appeal by
an irrevocable fatwa by Sheikh al-Islam Mehmet Cemâleddin, who, as hierarchical superior of the provincial courts, ordered that the Jerusalem tribunal be
divested and that the case be moved to the Damascus tribunal.

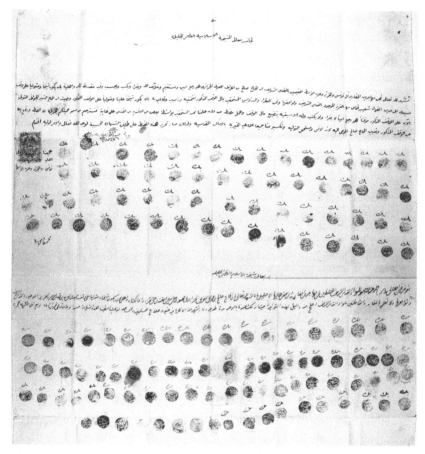

FIGURE 17. **Petition by the inhabitants of Ein Karem (top) and by the inhabitants of the Maghrebi Quarter (bottom) regarding the management of the mutewalli Hajj Bashir, September 1903. Source: © BOA, ŞD.2296.40.**

This murky episode offers valuable insights. First, it demonstrates the Ottoman administration's deep involvement at the highest levels in the governance of the Waqf Abu Madyan. More broadly, it reiterates how central the Holy City was to the concerns of the imperial authorities, and that it was not a forsaken city "on the fringes of the empire." It also illustrates what a decisively important role individual or collective petitions could play in the Ottoman system of government;[72] and lastly, it indicates that the Maghrebi community of Jerusalem was not one and indivisible, but was traversed with fault lines that could split open whenever internal conflicts arose.

Two final documents drawn from the central Ottoman archives are worth highlighting, for they illustrate the specifically political interest granted to the Jerusalem Maghrebis by the Ottoman authorities, but also the consequences of the geopolitical upheavals that rocked the years 1908 to 1914. On 25 January 1908, the governor of Jerusalem, Ali Ekrem Bey, drafted and sent to Istanbul a long three-page report, archived today in the series of correspondence sent to the cabinet of the grand wazir (Bab-I Ali Evrak Odassi), expressing concern over the protection that the Jerusalem and Jaffa Maghrebis might be enjoying from foreign consulates, the French Consulate in particular.[73] Ali Ekrem Bey, one of the most famous Ottoman governors of Jerusalem despite his relatively brief tenure (December 1906 to July 1908), was polyglot, Francophone, and Francophile, a seasoned observer of the major geopolitical issues at stake in the Holy City. Thus he was fully aware of the privileges of extraterritoriality that the Jerusalem Maghrebis could use to their benefit, and he intuited—a half century ahead of time—what France stood to gain as the reigning colonial power in North Africa. On 5 June 1913, while early conscription campaigns were underway in the Ottoman Empire, the governor of Jerusalem, Mahir Pasha, in a statement to the Ministry of the Interior (*Dahîliye Nezâreti*), refuted the rumors spread by the French Consulate claiming that the Jerusalem Maghrebis could be drafted into the army. This was a further indicator of how important the Maghrebi Quarter was to the Ottoman authorities, at both the central and the local levels (figure 18).[74]

Maghrebis in the City: The Oblique Light of the Municipal Archives

After the lofty view from Istanbul's imperial archives, let us complete our survey of the Maghrebi Quarter's archival visibility in the Late Ottoman era with a brief incursion into Jerusalem's municipal archives. Unknown and ostensibly lost until the late 1990s, they have for the last fifteen years undergone a collective effort of identification, transcription, translation, digitization, and indexing.[75] The current state of the archives thus far identified makes available seventeen registers of the minutes of Jerusalem's municipal council deliberations, covering with very few omissions the period 1892–1917, which represents some 1,200 pages of handwritten text, divided into about 3,400 paragraphs. This amounts to an equivalent number of individual rulings by the municipal

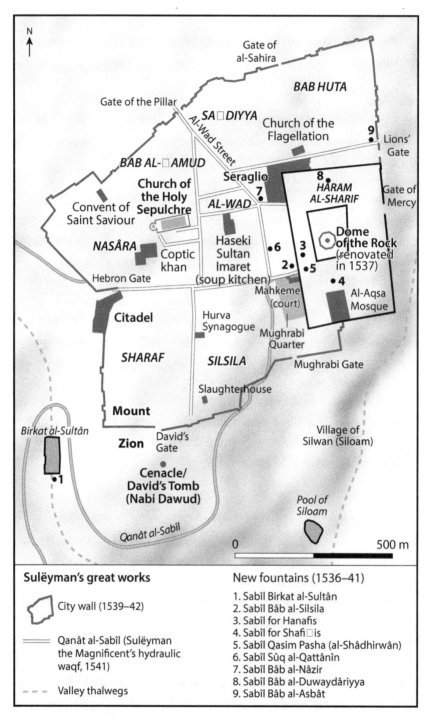

N

Gate of
al-Sahira

BAB HUTA

Gate of the Pillar

SA☐DIYYA

Al-Wad Street

Church of the
Flagellation

9
Lions'
Gate

BAB AL-☐AMUD

Seraglio

8
*HARAM
AL-SHARIF*

Gate of
Mercy

7

Church of
the Holy
Sepulchre

AL-WAD

Convent of
Saint Saviour

Dome
of the Rock
(renovated
in 1537)

NASÂRA

Coptic
khan

Haseki
Sultan
Imaret
(soup kitchen)

•6

3
•
2•
•5

Hebron Gate

•4

Mahkeme
(court)

Al-Aqsa
Mosque

Citadel

Hurva
Synagogue

Mughrabi
Quarter

SHARAF

SILSILA

Mughrabi Gate

Slaughterhouse

Mount

Birkat al-Sultân

Zion

David's
Gate

Village of
Silwan (Siloam)

•1

Cenacle/
David's Tomb
(Nabi Dawud)

Pool of
Siloam

Qanât al-Sabîl

0

500 m

Sulëyman's great works

City wall (1539–42)

Qanât al-Sabîl (Sulëyman
the Magnificent's hydraulic
waqf, 1541)

Valley thalwegs

New fountains (1536–41)

1. Sabîl Birkat al-Sultân
2. Sabîl Bâb al-Silsila
3. Sabîl for Hanafis
4. Sabîl for Shafi☐is
5. Sabîl Qasim Pasha (al-Shâdhirwân)
6. Sabîl Sûq al-Qattânîn
7. Sabîl Bâb al-Nâzir
8. Sabîl Bâb al-Duwaydâriyya
9. Sabîl Bâb al-Asbât

FIGURE 18. Jerusalem during the Ottoman era, 1516–1917. Source: © Dario Ingiusto.

council, slightly under half of which are written in Arabic, with the remainder in *osmänle*.[76] Thanks to the new full-text research tools of this data base, we can locate entries that pertain to the Jerusalem Maghrebis, thus making it possible to measure how integrated the quarter was within the urban community.[77]

One thing is clear: not only was the Maghrebi Quarter not isolated from the rest of the city, but on the contrary, it appears to have been at the very heart of municipal politics and the sociability networks woven around this new urban institution.[78] In the very workings of the Waqf Abu Madyan, the municipality appears as a decisive support structure, especially when it came to conveying the calls for bids on the substantial purchases of bread, clothing, and coal that took place regularly. For instance, on 7 September 1904, the municipal council convened a meeting with the local bakers who had offered a wholesale price for bread purchases that the endowment would be making in the course of a year. "After some necessary coaxing," the price submitted by Hasan Bin-Muhammad was lowered by 0.05 piasters to settle at 2.2 piasters for a *rotol* of bread (around four hundred grams).[79] The endowment's active involvement in housing orphans made it a partner in the municipality's social endeavors. For instance, on 13 April 1897 the city entrusted Khalil al-Maghribi with the custody of an orphan, and provided a thirty-piaster monthly allowance for his daily needs, as well as a one-time allotment of a *majeedi* (i.e., twenty piasters) to purchase clothes, monies to be drawn from the municipal budget set aside for helping the neediest.[80] On 27 December 1904, an orphan girl "found abandoned on the Haram al-Sharif" was taken in by the municipality and entrusted to Hajj Abd al-Daïm al-Maghribi, "who promises to raise her and care for her," in exchange for which the municipality allotted him thirty piasters monthly "for her food and daily care."[81] The officers of the Waqf Abu Madyan, a charitable institution that specialized in accommodating the lonely and destitute, were thus mobilized by the municipality to provide relief to Jerusalem's orphans, including those who were not of Maghrebi origin.

A further gauge of the Maghrebi Quarter's integration was the number of municipal employees of Maghrebi ancestry mentioned in hiring and salary decisions, particularly for the posts of tax collector, overseer, comptroller, and watchman, all jobs that assumed trust on the part of the institution. For instance, we find Hajj Ahmad al-Maghribi in charge of overseeing the collection of toll fees at the entrance to Jerusalem on the road from Jaffa on 13 June 1899,

and in charge of collecting municipal taxes in the Bab al-Wad quarter in 1915.[82]
On 16 March 1899 it was Hajj Qasim al-Maghribi who was tasked with overseeing the "Sultan's Pool," located outside the city walls and farther down from
the Jaffa Gate, to ensure that water from that basin, "intended for municipal
sprinkling," was not used "for horses and camels to drink" (figure 19).[83] On 29
June 1899, in order to reduce dust on the streets and roads located between the
Jaffa Gate, the Fast Hotel (at the northwest corner of the city walls), and the
Damascus Gate, nine street sweepers were hired to work "under the supervision
of the Maghrebi who is already in charge of overseeing the Sultan's Pool."[84] On
23 April 1902 the municipality was complaining about the stench of urine and
garbage in the streets located around the Kanqah Salahiyya—a Sufi convent
founded by Salah ad-Din, just to the north of the Holy Sepulchre—and it was
Hajj Muhammad Ali al-Maghribi who was put in charge of remedying the situation, in exchange for a monthly salary of five *majeedi* (one hundred piasters).[85]

In the same vein, on 30 July 1901, in response to a complaint "by residents
and merchants in the Quarter," the municipality decided to clamp down on the
animal waste and urine around the livestock market, and put Hajj Qasim al-
Maghribi in charge of monitoring and fining the offending livestock owners.[86]
Residents of the Maghrebi Quarter would show up at other municipal proceedings, and what emerges from this documentary evidence is an impression that
they occupied a special place in the urban monitoring and supervision system
that the municipality was gradually implementing from the 1880s onward.
This pervasive impression is confirmed by the unusual wording of a decision

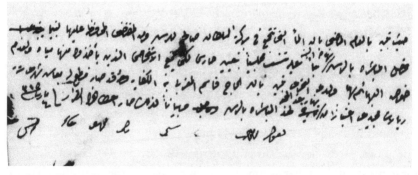

FIGURE 19. **Hiring of Hajj Qasim al-Maghribi as municipal employee in charge of overseeing the sultan's pool.** Source: © HAJM, RJMCO, vol. 3, p. 21a, item 154, 4 Mârt
1315 [16 March 1899].

taken on 12 July 1904, when the Municipal Council noted that "a sizable pile of severed olive branches" had been illegally discarded near the train station "by inhabitants of Dayr Aban."[87] Pending the identification of the perpetrators, the municipality sought to prevent gleaners from helping themselves to the pile, and decided to hire "a watchman recruited among the residents of the Maghrebi Quarter."

All indications are that all these appointments of Maghrebis were hardly random, and that the community enjoyed a particular prerogative for jobs involving surveillance and security, a prerogative that undoubtedly dates back to the eminent position they had occupied as policers of the markets since at least the seventeenth century.[88] On this point, the testimony of Chateaubriand lends further support to the items present in the municipal archives: when he visited Jerusalem in 1806, he roamed the "quarter of the Maugrabins [...] descendants of the Moors driven out of Spain by Ferdinand and Isabelle," and he highlights how tightly woven the inhabitants were into the civic community: "These exiles were received into the Holy City with great mercy: a mosque was built for them; still today, they receive bread, fruit and a little money. The proud heirs of the Abencerrajes, the elegant architects of the Alhambra, have become gatekeepers in Jerusalem, sought after for their intelligence, and couriers, valued for their adroitness."[89] Porters and mail carriers were valued for their intelligence and agility. The Maghrebis occupied Jerusalem's positions of confidence, and this reinforced their connections with different communities in the city. The childhood memories of the historian Nazmi al-Jubeh also corroborates this dual characteristic of the Maghrebi Quarter inhabitants, as both highly integrated into civic life and at the same time singled out for a certain number of distinctive traits:

> A large part of my daily life took place in the Maghrebi Quarter, for our house was located at Wadi Hilweh, 100 meters outside the walls to the south of the city. And my school Al-Omariya was located in the north of the city. So every morning I walked across the Haram passing through the Maghrebi Gate. On the way back home, I would stop at my father's grocery, at the Gate of the Chain, to shop for the family. And then I walked back through the Maghrebi Quarter, down Abu Madyan Street. At that time, I had a lot of friends in the neighborhood, we would play soccer, I got to know the smells of Maghrebi

cooking. Many of the inhabitants were my father's customers since his gro-
cery was nearby. The quarter was a place I could explore. We would often see
a guardian who would open the Maghrebi Gate when a foreigner wanted to
visit the Al-Aqsa Mosque. We noted that the inhabitants wore traditional
Maghrebi dress and that they were more likely to wear a "fez" than the taller
Jerusalem tarboosh. Also, the Maghrebi dialect was much more complicated
and faster than our local Jerusalem dialect. All of that used to spark my
curiosity.[90]

The Jerusalem Maghrebis thus were fully included in the civic community
(*civitas*), but we can also say that their quarter was tightly integrated into the
overall urban morphology (*urbs*). This is observable in the daily decisions regarding all built space, which came under municipal responsibility with the law
of 1877.[91] On 1 August 1901 it came to the municipal council's attention that,
even though it had been declared unsafe, a dangerously unstable wall in the
Maghrebi Quarter had in fact gone unrepaired, resulting in the intervention
of a municipal engineer at a cost of 1,731 piasters, which the homeowner was
required to pay.[92] On 4 March 1907 a demolition procedure "for imminent
danger" was initiated against another wall in the Maghrebi Quarter deemed
unsafe, "pursuant to the terms of Article 48 of the building code," and a
tripartite committee comprised of the municipal engineer, the district chief
(*mukhtar*) and an officer of the municipal police was mandated to coordinate the demolition and then arrange to be reimbursed for all costs incurred,
"minus the sale cost of the rubble."[93] Several documents from the judicial
archives testify, moreover, to monitoring operations carried out on a regular
basis in the gardens and orchards of the quarter, particularly in the orchard
located to the far north of the Western Wall, below the al-Tanqiziya madrassa,
which housed the city tribunal. In city planning terms, it is clear then that the
Maghrebi Quarter was governed by the same rules as the rest of the city; it was
not a reclusive entity surviving on the fringes of an urban system, much less a
"zone of lawlessness."

This is also in evidence starting in the 1880s, when the municipality
launched large public works campaigns, especially to modernize the potable
water supply. On 29 January 1902, while the city was undertaking a massive

renovation of the pipeline network instigated by the municipal engineer George Franghia Bey,[94] sewage pollution was detected in its main line (*Qanat al-sabil*), where it passed beneath the Maghrebi Quarter. Upon inspection, it was found that "17 houses belonging to the Waqf Abu Madyan, as well as three other houses," were connected to the wastewater drain responsible for the contamination.[95] The "Sheikh of the Maghrebis Hajj Bashir Effendi"—yet to be removed at that time—made it known that he could not cover the repair costs (1,570 piasters) without a prior agreement of the waqfs' accounts division. Given the urgency of the situation, the Municipal Council decided to undertake the work at its own expense, and then get reimbursed at a later date. Some two weeks later, on 17 February 1902, it was established that the job of cleaning and insulating the sewer pipe has been effectively executed "for a cost of 1,400 piasters," and that the balance of 170 piasters would be used to complete the project with a few other "partial repairs."[96]

Finally, it should be noted that if the Maghrebi Quarter was fully integrated into the municipal governance of the Holy City, it was about more than dealing with sanitation and zoning issues. The quarter also benefited from modernization efforts and urban enhancement projects undertaken by the municipality. The archive shows, for instance, that the quarter was included in a program of regular street sweeping and cleaning starting in the 1900s; and especially that on 6 June 1900, an inspection tour devoted to night lighting concluded that three street lamps were missing in the Maghrebi Quarter, "at al-Buraq Gate," another "at Dâr' Abdu," and a third "in the cul-de-sac of the Sheikh Eid Mosque."[97] Bidding was opened for the installation of these three new street lamps, financed by a new budgetary line devoted to municipal expenditure on lighting.

———

There is nothing quite like a deep documentary dive into archival collections that bear witness to the urban history of a city embedded in several scales of sovereignty. Only this painstaking data collection makes it possible to concretely gauge the relative visibility, and therefore the degree of integration, of a neighborhood within this or that administrative structure. The Maghrebi Quarter, in this case, far from appearing as an isolated neighborhood relegated to the fringes of the Holy City, emerges at the heart of Jerusalem's urban community, fully embedded in the workings of the Istanbul administration in the Late Ottoman era. It stands to reason that this robust integration, nurtured by centuries-old ties woven between the Maghrib and Jerusalem since the era of Saladin, would be jeopardized with the destabilization and final collapse of the imperial Ottoman structure on the eve of World War I.

2

IN THE TURMOIL OF WAR AND THE MANDATE

A COVETED AND UNDERMINED QUARTER (1912-36)

In the dossier compiled in 1949 by an official of the French Consulate in Jerusalem, we find a thirteen-page summary note, typed and unsigned, titled simply "The Waqf Abu Madyan," in which the history of the religious endowment is broadly summarized, from its origins to the creation of the State of Israel. There can be little doubt that for the drafter of this note, the period of war (1914–17), military occupation (1917–22) and then the British Mandate (1923–48), represented a time of extreme fragility for the Waqf Abu Madyan. This historic turning point, which radically contrasts the Ottoman period (1516–1917) with the British period (1917–48), is accurately summarized in this excerpt:

> The Waqf Abu Madyan was validated after the Ottoman conquest by the provincial authorities and the sovereign authorities of Istanbul, jurisdiction of the Empire not subject to appeal. Indeed, the Waqf Abu Madyan is cited in numerous imperial firmans [. . .]. The Turkish authorities respected the waqf as a charitable endowment and protected it [. . .]. Soon after the British Mandate over Palestine was made official, and once the general department of cadastral surveying was created, numerous tenants of the Abu Madyan landholdings in Ein Karem were able to obtain property deeds

drawn up in their name, arguing that they had effectively occupied these plots for many years, despite previous rulings. The failure of mutewallis to intervene favored the establishment of these land deeds. A great many Jews were able to acquire newly registered plots of land and began to settle a colony on the former waqf lands.[1]

Much is said in this note, which further confirms the Waqf Abu Madyan as a pertinent illustration of the overall history of Palestine, but also helps us understand why this religious endowment was so profoundly affected by the new historical context that began with General Allenby's entrance into Jerusalem in December 1917.[2] Two supportive and protective structures for the Waqf Abu Madyan effectively disappeared or were considerably undermined after 1917. One was the imperial Ottoman structure, which provided an advantageous political and judicial framework for the endowment's interests, first, because Islamic law undergirded the pyramid of Ottoman administrative authority; second, because the sultan-caliph, responsible for the safety of all pilgrimages, had the particular duty of safeguarding the Maghrebi pilgrims to Jerusalem; and finally, because this supranational Islamic empire derived part of its legitimacy from its capacity to keep alive and thriving these same long-standing transnational solidarities that had formed around the holy sites. What the note does not state, however, is that at a different scale, another administrative structure protective of Maghrebi interests in their quarter was considerably eroded by the arrival of the British occupants: the municipality of Jerusalem, already weakened during the war, whose purview would be steadily curtailed over the following two decades. Jerusalem's mayor, Musa Qazem al-Husayni, was abruptly removed from office after the Nabi Mussa riots of April 1920, and the municipality was further destabilized by the 1927 elections. It could no longer manage to overcome the growing rift between Arab and Jewish councilmen after the municipal elections of 1934, which served only to accelerate its institutional and political collapse.[3]

In place of these two institutional protectors, in the wake of World War I, the Waqf Abu Madyan now had to deal with new institutions that were less positively disposed toward it, and which posed new, increasingly explicit threats. The new British authorities, first of all, had every reason to oppose the Maghrebi Quarter officials: they looked favorably on the Zionist project, and mistrusted a Maghrebi community that might serve as a conduit for French interests in Palestine. In concrete terms, they were attempting to limit the autonomy of Muslim endowments by placing them under the auspices of the Supreme Muslim Council. Finally, they encouraged the trend of remapping and privatizing the land, which paved the way for the incremental usurping of the Waqf Abu Madyan's landholdings.[4] In short, the fundamentals of British policy in Palestine seemed unfavorable to the interests of Jerusalem Maghrebis.

Furthermore, the new political and institutional leverage wielded by the Zionist movement after 1917 represented an even more serious threat, pinpointed by the drafter of the note, who speaks of "a great many Jews [. . .] acquiring newly registered plots of land," and of a "colony" gradually taking root "on the waqf lands."[5] The British Mandate represented an indisputable historic opportunity for the actors within the Zionist movement, who realized with the Balfour Declaration in November 1917 that this new imperial tutelage would be more favorable toward their interests than the Ottoman authority had been.[6] In this regard, the rich lands of Ein Karem were not the only target of the Zionist project, but the Maghrebi Quarter itself was equally threatened in its location directly across from the Western Wall, which would become the focus of world attention during the bloody riots of August 1929. The village of Ein Karem and the Maghrebi Quarter of Jerusalem, the two founding pillars of the Waqf Abu Madyan, would become two targets of choice for the various actors of the Zionist movement.

The rivalry between France and Great Britain, the rise of nationalisms, community polarization, the weakening of Muslim religious endowments, the surging power of the Zionist movement—the structuring factors of the new political state of affairs in Palestine during the interwar period contributed to the gradual fracturing of the institutional, judicial, and financial base of the Waqf Abu Madyan. The British Mandate period thus appears as the first stage in the endowment's long disintegration process. This new context compels us to look toward other information sources best able to document the strategies of these new actors, and to detect the new decision-making centers that were emerging with the 1911–12 "march to war." The first of these was the Central Zionist Archives, created in 1919 in Berlin, transferred as a matter of urgency to Jerusalem in 1933, and located today in a modern building inaugurated in

1987, where the archives of all the Zionist organizations produced since the late nineteenth century have been retrieved and housed under one roof.[7]

Next were the different sets of documents produced by the British authorities, which are rather poorly described and difficult to access since they are archived in several places: partly in the vast series of the British National Archives in London, partly within today's Israel State Archives (for the documentation that was left behind in 1948), and partly within various conservation institutions in Israel (the Jerusalem Municipal Archives, notably) or in Great Britain (the Middle East Center Archives at Oxford, for example). With respect to the Maghrebi Quarter, we will be particularly interested in the proposals of urban developers who, like Patrick Geddes in 1919, openly advocated for its elimination, for the sake of a new "plaza-focused" urban plan. Finally, to document the 1929–31 crisis over the Western Wall, a new documentary stratum emerged in the long history of the Maghrebi Quarter: the archives of international organizations, especially the League of Nations, which was addressing with increased regularity the thorny issue of Jerusalem's holy places, one of the most contentious of which was the Western Wall / Kotel ha-Maaravi / Al-Buraq.

Zionist Projects and Projections around the Western Wall

The Central Zionist Archives stores the memory of the Zionist movement as both ideal quest and territorial conquest—in other words, both as a body of discourses and theoretical writings and as the more scattered traces of initiatives undertaken by various actors within the Zionist project to bring this common design into concrete existence, as outlined at the founding Basel Convention in August 1897.[8] Created in Germany in 1919 (based in Berlin from 1911 to 1920, in Cologne from 1905 to 1911, and in Vienna from 1807 to 1905) and then moved to Jerusalem in 1933, the Zionist archives were designed to centralize all documents produced by the institutions and actors of the Zionist project. This accounts for the foundational distinction between its two large pools of documents: "groups and organizations" on the one hand, and "people and personal papers" on the other.[9]

Not surprisingly, the boundaries between these two blocs are porous, since part of the correspondence exchanged between organizations may well have been preserved in the private homes of certain of their officers and, conversely, semiprivate correspondence may have ended up in the offices of their respective organizations, especially between 1912 and 1918, when war in the Middle East and in Europe threw institutions into disarray, forcing certain actors into a sometime hasty exile. As is often the case, to piece together the decision-making process, various documentary series need to be cross-referenced. This was particularly true after the move to Jerusalem in 1933, when the Central Zionist Archives were implementing an intensive policy of retroactive compilation among Zionist institutions and actors to recover batches of archival material that predated World War I. Thanks to this effort, it is today possible to reconstruct some of the strategies put in place during the months leading up to the war to buy out the Maghrebi Quarter.

On 2 February 1913, from his home in Jerusalem, on letterhead stationery of the "Works of the Jewish Colonization Association of Jerusalem"—the organization directed by Edmond de Rothschild, a regular collaborator of his—Albert Antébi (1873–1919) wrote to the governing board of the Anglo-Palestine Company, a bank based in Jaffa (figure 20). The original letter was naturally filed among the correspondence received from the Bank Leumi le-Israel, which took over the assets and archives of the Anglo-Palestine Company in 1950 after the creation of the Israeli state:[10] "Gentlemen, I received your letter of 28 January relating to Kotel Maaravi. I presented to Mr. Dizengoff the background and current state of the issue. I have no idea whether Mr. Yellin is handling this, but I do know that several 'Vaadim' [notables] are involved in this business [. . .]. I do not understand the contract that you want to establish, I do not believe there is one. The point is to begin the process and see where it leads."[11] To read the follow-up exchange, absent from the Anglo-Palestine Company correspondence files, I had to delve into dossiers kept in the personal archives of David Levontin (1856–1940), the director of the Anglo-Palestine Company in Jaffa. On 16 February, Antébi complained that too much action was being taken in this regard: "It is a thorny issue that requires certain circumstances to ensure a solution. It is unfortunate that certain steps have been taken officially and are slowing down the process. We did indeed issue a request to rent houses, and all we managed to get in return was a decision from the Administrative Board blocking our request."[12] On 11 May, Antébi announced that he would no longer involve himself in the matter: "I had taken steps and was mustering a significant base, but one of your own has been working at it concurrently by offering astronomical figures. Why then continue to operate in a vacuum to do harm? I therefore prefer to discontinue and leave the way open to these gentlemen."[13]

The enshrinement of the Western Wall (Kotel ha-Maaravi) by Jerusalem's Jewish communities starting in the sixteenth century, and then its gradual assimilation into the Zionist political perspective from the late nineteenth century onward, represent two complex historical processes that have been the subject of countless studies, and which will not be the main focus of my

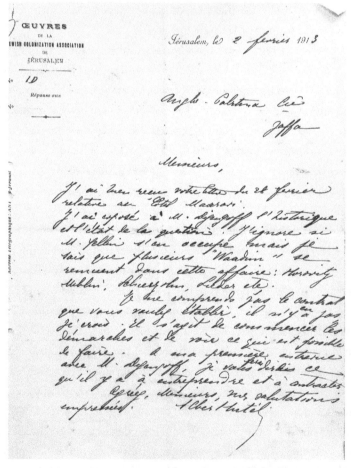

FIGURE 20. Letter from Albert Antébi to the governing board of the Anglo-Palestine Company, 2 February 1913. Source: © Central Zionist Archives, L.51/14.

inquiry.[14] Nonetheless, once it was no longer only about defending the right to pray in front the Western Wall, but also the explicit aim of buying out and destroying the Maghrebi Quarter for the purpose of creating a vast plaza, the history of the Western Wall then reconnected directly with that of the Maghrebi Quarter, and the two chronologies would unceasingly intermingle until the final act on 10 June 1967.[15] This shift took place gradually, according to a timeline that started in the 1870s, with individual initiatives and little oversight, building toward the phase in which large Zionist institutions took the matter in hand in the 1910s.[16]

Starting in 1912, the plan to buy out the Maghrebi Quarter emerged in several documents scattered among various series within the Central Zionist Archives, as if the geopolitical tensions were opening up opportunities and encouraging initiatives on all fronts. Close analysis of various archival holdings reveals that all the large organizations and major actors of the Zionist movement were effectively engaged in this project. Antébi himself mentions Meir Dizengoff (1861–1936), the future mayor of Tel Aviv who was already heading a little urban community near Jaffa. He also names David Yellin (1864–1941), a municipal councilman in Jerusalem and a major intellectual and eminent member of Jerusalem's Sephardic community. Finally, he refers more broadly to the "Vaadim," a sarcastic jab penned by the Syrian Antébi to designate the members of the representative committees (*Vaad*) of Palestine's more recent Jewish communities, those originating from Central Europe.[17] By probing the personal archives of these major figures of the new and the old Yishuv, we can observe that these initiatives were well synchronized and that information was widely circulated. For instance, in the archives of David Yellin on file at the Central Zionist Archives, there are copies of certain letters from David Levontin on the subject. On 13 November 1912, Levontin wrote to Eliezer Friedmann, who, writing from Kiev, had offered to partially finance the acquisition of the Maghrebi Quarter:

> I really do hope that this holy site will be bought from the non-Jews who took ownership of the land of Israel and who have defiled the ruins of the Temple. This matter has already been taken up on numerous occasions and each time there have been impediments and problems along the way [...]. We need to be aware that even now, this matter will not be easily accomplished and that

it will require patience, moderation and sustained work. Furthermore, it is
not possible to assess ahead of time how much it will cost, but we should be
figuring at least 200,000 francs if we are to reach our goal.[18]

On 4 January 1913, Levontin wrote again to Friedmann to lay out the legal
challenges of the project in further detail:

> At this location, there are some houses that belong to different persons and to
> the waqf. Because of waqf regulations, we will first have to obtain the authori-
> zation of the central government in Constantinople, and then negotiate with
> the homeowners and the waqf officials [...]. At any rate, we will not be able
> to conclude this purchase at one go; rather, it will take gradual negotiations
> with the owners and with the waqf. We will also need to incur some covert
> expenditures.[19]

Despite the challenges, the project was arousing enthusiasm among many Zionist sympathizers in the diaspora. For instance, in Levontin's correspondence
files we find this surprising missive written from Kiev by Moshe Halperin,
dated 20 May 1913: "I hereby pledge to pay up to 150,000 francs by notarial
deed in order to acquire in my name the tract of land adjacent to the Western
Wall in Jerusalem, which will remain in my possession in perpetuity."[20] Here is
clear evidence of the "astronomical figures" referred to by Antébi. In response,
on 5 June, Levontin attempted to dampen Halperin's fervor by providing a few
important particulars:

> . . . We are not on the verge of purchasing the Western Wall itself, this his-
> toric vestige cannot be bought by any fortune on earth; consequently, we are
> pouring all our effort into purchasing the buildings located in front of the
> Western Wall, so that the immediate vicinity of the Wall belongs to us, and
> thus the Wall itself, in a way [...]. Owing to the current political situation,
> and because of the piousness of the Muslim Maghrebis living in those houses,
> it behooves us to act wisely.[21]

These lines demonstrate that the decision makers in the Zionist movement
are fully aware of the Maghrebi Quarter's distinctiveness, and of the genuine
"piousness" of its inhabitants, a further challenge to the project's success. At
the same time, a committee was set up in Jerusalem whose purpose was not to

purchase but to rent certain houses in the Maghrebi Quarter, as a pragmatic first step.[22] Unsurprisingly, David Yellin and Joseph Meyuhas (1868–1942) were members, Arabic-speakers, natives of Jerusalem, and representatives of the "old Yishuv" of the Holy City, undoubtedly more keenly aware of local realities than were certain Zionists in the diaspora. In the archives of Joseph Meyuhas held at the Central Zionist Archives, we find the minutes of one of this committee's meetings (22 March 1912), which makes sense, since we read that Meyuhas is appointed as "session secretary." The lively discussions that ensue revolve around two main issues. First, should the committee budget be spent on renting or purchasing houses in the Maghrebi Quarter? And, if it is for renting, for how long should they rent the property before moving on to the purchasing stage? Next, should they act in secret, or should they fund-raise by placing an advertisement in European newspapers? Yellin advises caution: "Mr. Yellin reiterates that it will take great patience to implement the plans to purchase these historic sites, that it will not happen in a year or even three; he added that we should emulate the way the Christians deal in such matters, their endless patience and ability to seize the right opportunities."[23] As if to confirm these intuitions, there are no further documents to be found regarding this committee in the archives of Meyuhas.

In the Midst of War, Bargaining with Jamal Pasha

Between the autumn of 1915 and the summer of 1916, the military alliance between Germany and the Ottoman Empire gave the story a new twist, with direct negotiations started between the directorate of the World Zionist Organization and Ahmad Jamal Pasha (1872–1922).[24] Jamal Pasha was one of a three-member triumvirate that ruled de facto the Ottoman Empire as of January 1913, and was also the civilian and military governor with plenary power over Syria, Lebanon, and Palestine starting in 1915.[25] The Maghrebi Quarter of Jerusalem was thus becoming the object of intense bargaining carried out—in German—at the highest levels of the Ottoman state and the Zionist directorate in Berlin. For this reason, we find traces of these negotiations in the Central Zionist Archives in Berlin (1911–20) in the archive's Z.3 series, which takes up thirty-one linear meters on the shelves.[26] The correspondence file, totaling some forty pages, provides insight into how the collapse of the Ottoman Empire and the breakdown of its ideological and religious structures could make the demolition of Jerusalem's Maghrebi Quarter a viable option. The title written on the dossier cover is "Vorschlag Djemal Pacha's betr Verkauf des Platzes vor der Klagemauer au die Jüden" (Proposal by Jamal Pasha to sell the plaza in front of the Wailing Wall to the Jews). The dossier opens with a letter that Arthur Ruppin (1876–1943), director of the Palestine bureau of the World Zionist Organization, addresses on 17 November 1915 to his superiors in Berlin, in which he convincingly lays out how this operation might go forward:

> His Exc. Jamal Pasha appears interested in a dignifying upgrade to the open space in front of the Wailing Wall [*Klagemauer*], which today is a rather dreary place. As things stand today, there are some thirty Muslim houses occupied by Moroccans [. . .]. His Exc. Jamal Pasha has explained to Mr. Antébi that it would be possible to dismantle these 30 Moroccan houses and that, out of the entirety of the new space—which could be as long as the Temple Wall [*Tempelmauer*] (around 50 meters) and from 30 to 40 meters deep—10 to 12 meters directly in front of the Wall could be reserved exclusively for Jewish prayer, and the rest of the plaza could be turned into a public park. How this might be established legally over the long term has yet to be elucidated. Perhaps with a decree from the Sultan authorizing the registration of the entire perimeter as a Jewish Waqf [*Vakuf der Jüden*] placed under the authority of the Chief Rabbi of Constantinople. According to His Exc.'s estimate, the whole undertaking, to compensate the homeowners and develop the space into a plaza and park, would cost around 20,000 Turkish pounds, 2,000 would be paid now, and the remainder after the war. The demolition of the houses would begin immediately after the first payment of 2,000 Turkish pounds.[27]

This letter represents a radical departure from the documents I was able to consult on the same subject for the prewar years: the precision and credibility of the scenario proposed by Jamal Pasha is striking. This can be attributed to the high level of the discussions between the Ottoman leaders and the directorate of the World Zionist Organization, as mediated by Albert Antébi in Jerusalem and Arthur Ruppin in Jaffa. As a matter of law (with the creation of a waqf subject to the authority of the chief rabbi of Istanbul), and likewise of urban planning (with the installation of a public park on two-thirds of the new plaza), Jamal Pasha demonstrated a certain creativity which made his proposal all the more credible. This would explain why Arthur Ruppin, ordinarily somewhat skeptical on this subject, chose to get involved and encourage Berlin to follow:

> . . . I suggest that you write to Mr. Morgenthau [American ambassador to Istanbul] and present the matter to him [. . .]. Right now, this project cannot be achieved without help from America. Even though we're currently facing a lot of financial needs, I suggest we give this offer our *most serious* consideration. Jamal Pasha's interest in this subject, backed by his unlimited powers [*unbegrenzten dienstbefugnisse*], means that many things are possible today that will not be once the war is over. This clearance project has been hanging over our heads for years, but thus far hadn't seemed achievable. But now it could truly happen.[28]

We can gauge from these few lines how the entry into war had opened up unimaginable opportunities, for it is indeed the military context that explains Jamal Pasha's omnipotence in the Middle East, the disenfranchisement of Sultan Mehmed V, and the replacement of an imperial ideology by a Turkish nationalist deviation that was leading the Ottoman army toward the premeditated genocide of the empire's Armenian populations.[29] The context of war, whether in 1915 or 1967, brought with it a suspension of the rule of law, opening the way to projects unrealizable a few years earlier, as Ruppin so rightly stated.

The entire first semester of 1916 was taken up by these negotiations. On 31 December 1915, Victor Jacobson (1869–1935), representative of the Zionist Organization in Istanbul, wrote to Berlin to indicate that he "fully shares Ruppin's opinion as to the importance of taking firm ownership of this matter," and that from his standpoint, the plaza property "would be better secured if it were in the hands of the J.N.F. [Jewish National Fund, or KKL] or another similar structure" and that he "advises against entrusting this foundation to the Municipality of Jerusalem."[30] In any case, we ascertain that the project was entering a very tangible phase, since Jacobson adds that he is also "staunchly opposed to putting up a fence that would separate the park from the prayer space, for under no circumstances do we want to enclose our pious Jews in a kind of monkey cage [*affenkäfig*] to be gaped at by curious tourists." The same day, Jacobson wrote to Louis Brandeis—a wealthy Boston lawyer and reliable channel between the Zionist organization and President Woodrow Wilson, and one who would be appointed a few months later to the Supreme Court of the United States—to present the project to him and solicit a financial contribution:

> Jamal Pasha has a credible plan [...]. In Jerusalem, everyone strongly supports the plan, Dr. Ruppin staunchly recommends it, Mr. Antébi has also heartily embraced it and he has already contacted the Hakham Bashi [chief rabbi] in Constantinople. Mr. Lichteim has presented the plan to Mr. Morgenthau who is also interested, and who will be contacting his friends in America about it [...]. Further, we feel it is essential that a man of Jamal Pasha's stature should also be highly enthusiastic [...]. All we ask is that you *do not make this project public under any circumstances.* For the moment, all we need to do is raise 2,000 Turkish pounds."[31]

On 9 March 1916, Jacobson wrote again to Richard Lichteim to let him know that Menahem Ussishkin (1863–1941), then in Odessa, declared he was ready to promptly send the two thousand Turkish pounds required to get the project off the ground,[32] and to emphasize that the project's success "would provide an immense moral and political boost, above and beyond the importance of the purchase itself," because "the organization is constantly frustrated by endless internal problems." We get an idea how much the clearance of the Western Wall had become an emblematic objective for the Zionist movement, capable of mobilizing Jews in the diaspora beyond the movement's differing tendencies.

The project negotiated between Jamal Pasha and the Zionist organization would not be implemented right away. This was partly due to the mistrust of Richard Lichteim; partly because Albert Antébi was often away from Jerusalem starting in the summer of 1916; partly because Jamal Pasha was also away from the Holy City during the spring of 1916 (notably, to brutally suppress the Syrian nationalists in Damascus); partly because the local political context was exacerbating intercommunitarian tensions; and finally in part because, once the initial enthusiasm had subsided, partisans of a "down to earth" Zionism, focused on material issues and wary of possible religious deviations within the movement, were taking the floor to express their opposition to the project. For instance, on 28 April 1916, responding to a financial solicitation from Berlin, the governing board of the Jewish National Fund meeting in The Hague openly debated whether it was appropriate to get involved in this matter.

The minutes to this decisive meeting are available in the archives of the

Jewish National Fund (Keren Kayemet LeIsrael, or KKL), housed in the Zionist archives. The agronomist Jacob Oettinger declared that he "fears the purchase of holy places will engage substantial resources from the Fund," while the primary vocation of the organization was to "pursue a policy of farmland acquisition," and that "other organizations could raise funds for the purchase of historic sites."[33] The economist Nehemia De Lieme, president of the Dutch Zionist Organization and future president of the National Jewish Fund, was even more trenchant: "Mr. De Lieme is opposed to mobilizing JNF structures as well as to the use of JNF funds for the purchase of holy places." On 13 June 1916, Salomon Kaplansky and Nathan Gross, both members of the JNF governing board, wrote to the Action Committee of the World Zionist Organization in Berlin to apprise it that certain members of the JNF board of directors wanted to "withdraw from the project," while others were believed to be prepared to mobilize the organization without draining its other rollover budgets, which amounted to the JNF refusing to assume the financial burden of the project.[34]

On 17 July 1916, Jacob Thon (1882–1950), one of the leaders of the Ashkenazi community of Jerusalem,[35] confirmed that the negotiations had reached a stalemate: "Nothing can be done concerning the Wailing Wall. Antébi has once again changed his mind and does not want to negotiate with J.P. [Jamal Pasha] on the subject. What's more, he has left Jerusalem again [. . .], no one knows where he is or when he will be returning."[36] In a note attached to the letter, we read that "six months have elapsed" since the negotiations opened, but that "Antébi has grown quite aloof on the subject and no longer wants to deal with J.P. for the moment. He explains that J.P. has carried out numerous executions against Arabs, which has them very upset, and which makes it difficult for him to favor Jews at this time."[37] The public hanging of 21 nationalist militants in Damascus and Beirut on 6 May 1918 did represent a major trauma, and it is easily understandable that Jamal Pasha would not wish to make matters worse by having several hundred pious Maghrebis expelled from Jerusalem.[38] On 23 July 1916, in the last piece of correspondence from the dossier held by the Central Zionist Archives, Jacob Thon lays out the basic data of the issue, and his assessment heralds the conditions of the future disappearance of the Maghrebi Quarter, fifty years before the fact:

In any event, the reparations that will have to be paid to the homeowners [*hausbesitzer*] for the destruction of their houses will be a worthwhile investment for us. These houses have always been the greatest obstacle to the proper rearrangement of the space in front of the Wall. In normal times, no one could so easily clear them away. But if the demolition were decided at the highest level, without overly fussy procedures, then it would be easy to handle this clean-up [*aufwaschen*] in a single operation.[39]

Town Planning: Patrick Geddes or Planned "Decongestion"

The British military victory and General Allenby's entry into Jerusalem on 11 December 1917 radically tipped the balance of opposing forces with regard to the Maghrebi Quarter. This geopolitical shift also modified the geography of archival production. The central reference authority was located no longer in Istanbul, but in London. Germany fell into the camp of the defeated, and the executive Zionist headquarters left Berlin and moved to the British capital, as close as possible to the new imperial authority.[40] Furthermore, the British arrived in Palestine empowered by a long colonial experience, which they would soon be mobilizing to leave their mark on the town planning of the Holy City. In 1918, William H. McLean—whose previous town planning work has taken him to Khartoum and Alexandria—was mandated to draft a development plan intended for the War Office.[41] This first town planning scheme, even though it would later be criticized and rendered obsolete in certain aspects, did theorize the basic ideological framework of the mandate years: the old city was to be decongested and preserved "in its medieval aspect," and would be surrounded by green space—a "clear belt," to quote McLean—made up of parks and promenades.[42] These basic principles were taken up by the Pro-Jerusalem Society, which was forming during the same period under the leadership of C. R. Ashbee: "Our aim is rather to discover and preserve all that remains of the past and to undo so far as we can the evil that has been done."[43] This commitment to an explicitly backward-looking restoration of the Holy City "in its ancientness" also involves an obsession with freeing up "view points" in front of the oldest monuments, which in the long run would serve to undermine the Maghrebi Quarter.[44]

A year after this first master plan, Patrick Geddes—who was teaching sociology at the University of Bombay while at the same time preparing a first architectural project for the future Hebrew University of Jerusalem—was commissioned to draw up a more detailed development scheme. Significantly, we find today an original copy of this report in the series Z.4 of the Central Zionist Archives, composed of documents brought back from the World Zionist Organization headquarters, opened in London in 1917. The Geddes report, completed in November 1919, was received at the organization headquarters on 4 January 1920, as indicated by the stamp on the cover.[45] In his report, Geddes broadly endorses the conceptual framework laid out by McLean, emphasizing that tourists and pilgrims were to be considered henceforth as the primary users of the Holy City: "Most visitors come to *see* Jerusalem; and these desire to feel as deeply as possible what Jerusalem has meant to the world, or at least to their own faith."[46] This focus on the religious and touristic experience of the city had him imagining a new "place de la gare" (in French in the text), a specialized plaza designed to better welcome visitors, but especially to give total priority to "the magnificence of the general view," the parks and green spaces, which he sums up in an emblematic formula: "Park as view point for planning."[47] Regarding the old city, Geddes advocated a double strategy, calling for "decongestion" of residential spaces and "restoration of religious edifices," which placed the Maghrebi Quarter in an awkward position:

> The village of the Moghrabi Arabs should also be attended. Some of those who require to remain in the city may be rehoused along the vacant areas immediately west or south of their present homes; while it also need not be impossible by and by, when archaeological enquiries are fully satisfied, to house a small group of them outside the walls, upon some portion of the southward slope.[48]

The expulsion of part of the Maghrebi Quarter residents was thus anticipated in the near term by Patrick Geddes, who explicitly spells out the rehousing alternatives, including an *extra muros* site on the slopes of Silwan. As we read the rest of the report, we see how his proposal for the Maghrebi Quarter fit into a specific framework: "This decongestion will also afford opportunity for the various religious communities to acquire and develop such moderate

extensions as may be necessary to them." Lastly, one paragraph is devoted specifically to the Western Wall, in which Geddes shows more caution, at least
where the physical design is concerned:

> The long discussed and long delayed improvement of this area admits of a very
> simple treatment. If the unfinished houses above referred to could be obtained
> and improved, or a few others built to the north of these, they may perhaps be
> exchanged for the very few Moghrabi houses which are alone necessary for the
> improvement of the Wailing Wall, leaving the rest of the village undisturbed.
> [...] With the removal of a single row of houses and with the acquirement
> of the small garden at the north end, the length of the Wailing Wall will be
> about doubled, and the space in front of it sufficiently increased, while a row
> of cypress trees can be planted along the west side and whole enclosed by wall
> and gates."[49]

Reading Patrick Geddes, we are struck by the troubling analogy with the
Jamal Pasha project, which three years earlier had sought to replace part of the
Maghrebi Quarter with a prayer space and a public park. Beyond institutional
positionings and political strategies, then, it was also a new urban ideology, a new
urban decongestion plan with green spaces and plazas, which would threaten the
Maghrebi Quarter in the long run. This ideology, already entrenched in Western
cities during that same era, was gaining both visibility and especially legitimacy
in Jerusalem with the arrival of British town planners in the wake of Allenby's
army.[50] To this new urban planning consensus was added the special case of the
Western Wall, pressure from tourism and religious devotion, and especially the
political will to offer a sanctuary reserved for the Jewish communities of Jerusalem, as evidenced by the mention of "a wall and gates" intended to close off the
new prayer space and, in the strict sense, turn it into a sanctuary.

The Patrick Geddes project would meet the same fate as so many other
urban schemes, both before and after, abandoned for their incompatibility with
the political context in Palestine, which began to gradually worsen around the
spring of 1920. The directorate of the Zionist movement, by then split between
London and Jerusalem, pursued its endeavor to acquire the Maghrebi Quarter either covertly, as was the case between 1918 and 1920 at the prompting
of Chaim Weizmann (who headed the Palestine delegation of the Zionist
organization and was attempting to manipulate Amin al-Husseini toward

this purpose),[51] or more and more overtly, as was the case starting in 1925. In the Zionist Archives, a document produced by the Jewish National Council (Vaad Leumi) points to the Zionist executive of Palestine deliberately opting to politicize the issue beginning in autumn 1925 by leveraging the resources of the Keren ha-Yesod, the movement's main investment fund:

> What took place at the Western Wall over the last Yom Kippur [. . .] has led the Jewish National Council to raise the issue of the Western Wall and its ownership within a broader context. At the general assembly meeting of the Jewish National Council on 30 September 1925, it was agreed that we should present the following claim before the High Commissioner for Palestine: *Since the Western Wall belongs to the Jews, it should be restored to our possession* [. . .]. There can be little doubt, nevertheless, that vast resources will be necessary and we think that the Keren ha-Yesod should also be taking part in this project.[52]

After the individual initiatives pursued by isolated benefactors in the late nineteenth century, followed by the trend to institutionalize these attempts at purchase in the 1910s, by the mid-1920s the Jewish claim with regard to the Maghrebi Quarter had clearly become more *politicized* with this head-on initiative by the Palestine Zionist executive. This politicization of the issue would not produce any more concrete results than the previous sequences, but it would definitely contribute to rising tensions that would culminate in the Wall riots of August 1929. In this latest sequence, David Yellin, who headed the Vaad Leumi from 1920 to 1929, once again exercised caution, as we see in a message he addressed in March 1927 to Eliezer Friedmann (the same who had already offered his financial support in 1912):

> With regard to the ramshackle houses in front of the Western Wall, I must inform you that they all belong to the waqf of poor Moroccan Muslims, and that everything having to do with Muslim waqfs is dealt with through the Supreme Muslim Council of Palestine, and that it is therefore impossible for any collective or private person to purchase even a part of this place. The benefactor who founded this waqf hundreds of years ago wrote into the founding act that a curse would befall any person who transferred the ownership of any part of these properties.[53]

With his deep knowledge of Islamic culture, Yellin was reminding his interlocutor how protective the waqf status had proven over time, bringing him back to the historical and judicial reality of the Maghrebi Quarter.

11 July 1927: Earthquake in Jerusalem

On Monday 11 July 1927 at 3:04 p.m., a violent earthquake struck Palestine. According to seismologists, it was the most powerful quake to hit Jerusalem and its region during the twentieth century; it measured 6.3 and its epicenter was located in the Jordan Valley, a few miles north of Jericho.[54] The Jordan River, between the Sea of Galilee and the Dead Sea, ceased to flow for some twenty hours. The quake was strongly felt in Amman but also in large cities located along the crest of the Palestine ridge, all along the fault line involved that day: Hebron, Bethlehem, Jerusalem, Ramallah, and Nablus. That evening, an early assessment set the death toll at 192, but today's estimations place the number of dead at more than 350 in Palestine. In Jerusalem in particular, apocalyptic rumors were spread by newspapers, with reports of huge crevasses opened in the ground and clouds of dust rising from the bowels of the earth, notably at the bottom of the Gehenna Valley, and even of a volcano rumored to have awoken at the bottom of the Dead Sea, heralding a great catastrophe.[55]

If all this was greatly exaggerated and revelatory of the eschatological anxieties within monotheistic cultures,[56] it is nonetheless true that material damage in the Holy City was indeed substantial, as is witnessed today by the X- or S-shaped tie-rods and braces that are visible on the facades of many buildings in the city.[57] The Western press immediately relayed the news of the catastrophe. The *Milwaukee Journal* of 12 July spoke of "scenes of terror" and of a "state of siege" atmosphere; it reported that "four children died beneath the rubble of their home on the Mount of Olives and five women lost their lives in Ein Karem, the modern name of the village where it is believed John the Baptist was born."[58] On Mount Scopus, the walls of the Hebrew University inaugurated in 1925 were extensively cracked. On the Mount of Olives, the top of the bell tower of the Augusta Victoria hospital was toppled and the private apartments of the British high commissioner, Lord Plummer, lay in ruins. In the old city, numerous buildings were damaged, the streets were strewn with debris, and the dome of the Holy Sepulchre collapsed.[59] The eastern colonnade of the al-Aqsa Mosque was destroyed, and the houses of the Maghrebi Quarter below also suffered from the quake ([figure 21).

Like all natural catastrophes, the 1927 earthquake can be used as a vantage point for the historical context in which it occurred.[60] In Jerusalem in particular, earthquakes are commonly considered as divine signs, and some are more particularly related to the history of the Maghrebi Quarter. A local Jewish tradition reports, for example, that the quake of 1546 opened a breach in the Western Wall, allowing the Jews of Jerusalem to finally come there and pray.[61] That tradition lent an aura of divine will to the inaugural moment of the Jews bestowing sanctuary status on the Western Wall, a move that effectively took place in the first decades of Ottoman rule while work on the exterior walls of the city was in full swing.[62] Nothing of the sort occurred in 1927, even though the catastrophe did give rise to a wealth of particularly invaluable documents for historians, as so often happens in such cases.[63] In the French consular archives, for instance, the retrospective annual budget of the Waqf Abu Madyan for the year 1927 is exceptionally detailed, for it has to integrate all the expenses incurred that year to repair damaged houses, and

FIGURE 21. The earthquake of 11 July 1927 in Jerusalem. Source: © Matson Photograph collection, Library of Congress.

thereby offers a comprehensive overview of the endowment's circumstances at that time.[64]

In an appendix, the 1927 financial records list all seventy-eight properties belonging to the endowment in Jerusalem: their location, the names of their occupants, an estimate of their market value, the total expenditure needed for their renovation, and finally the amount of rent paid—when there was a payment, which was rare. In fact, out of the seventy-eight dwellings managed by the endowment, only eighteen yielded rent payments that year, for a total of 529 pounds (52,900 piasters). In the Maghrebi Quarter itself there were sixty-six dwellings, only seven of which were leased, for an average rent of only fifteen pounds a year. The other fifty-nine dwellings were "occupied free of charge," which corresponds to the endowment's initial vocation. By contrast, out of the twelve dwellings located outside the Maghrebi Quarter ("Armenian Quarter," "Jewish Quarter," "El Wad," "Bab el-Silsileh," "El Nassara," "Bab Hutta" . . .), eleven were leased, for an average rent of forty pounds annually.[65] This record provides insight into the endowment's real estate history, with a clear distinction between the Waqf Abu Madyan's initial property base, intended to house the poorest Maghrebis free of charge, and the later donations, meant to produce rental income. Lastly, we observe that the two dwellings located in the "Jewish Quarter," rented respectively to "Altar El Siknaji" and to "Tobi El Siknaji" (both of Ashkenazi origin), were those that not only ranked among the highest rents (seventy-five pounds for the first, twenty-eight for the second), but also produced the best value ratio, since these two rents brought in annually 8 percent of the value of the dwelling, while the others mentioned on the list earned barely 5 percent on average.

In the "Earnings" column of the budget for the year 1927, the 529 pounds earned annually thanks to rental housing is complemented by 417 pounds, corresponding to "annual income from the Ein Karem land." As it turns out, ever since the Muslim waqfs of Palestine were placed under the authority of the Supreme Muslim Council in December 1921, the stewards of the Waqf Abu Madyan had no longer been paid directly the amount owed by the Ein Karem tenants, but rather a lump sum drawn from the overall volume of duties and taxes collected by the British fiscal administration. This policy of taxation and flat fee payment obviously served to further distance the waqf stewards from their tenants, and in doing so, it increased the risk of the land being usurped and appropriated. We have confirmation of this new procedure in an exchange between the representative of the district of Jerusalem and attorney Hassan Budeiri, legal counsel for the Waqf Abu Madyan, in February 1929:

> I do hereby inform you that the ACHOURS collected in this village are registered under general earnings of the Government which disburses to the Supreme Muslim Council (formerly the Department of Waqfs), on behalf of the WAQF ABU MADYAN the sum of £P. 417 annually, a flat-amount ACHOUR to be distributed to the mutewallis.[66]

Like all the Muslim waqfs of Palestine, the Waqf Abu Madyan had thus lost its stewardship autonomy in favor of the British fiscal authorities and the Supreme Muslim Council, headed by the grand mufti of Jerusalem, Amin al-Husseini.[67] Financially speaking, this disenfranchisement is ambiguous: though the change to a lump sum did secure the annual amount of rent earned by the endowment, it also prevented it from benefiting from price hikes resulting from the exponential rise in real estate values during the mandate years. Whatever the case, this was a major disruption in the judicial and financial history of the endowment: from the 1920s onward, the Ein Karem revenues were set at 417 pounds per annum—which corresponds roughly to the amounts earned prior to 1914, according to what we were able to evaluate based on the accounts records of the Late Ottoman period.[68] When we add this amount to the 529 pounds in rent collected on the Jerusalem dwellings, the "Earnings" column of the budget for 1927 shows a total of 936 pounds (93,600 piasters). This represents a moderate overall increase from previous budgets of the Ottoman period, since we had found budgets of around 80,000 piasters for the 1910s and subsequent years.[69] We might also emphasize that the Ein Karem revenues made up over 40 percent of the endowment's disposable income, which matches the proportions we found for the Ottoman period—and which helps put into perspective how financially catastrophic the sudden loss of this income after 1948 must have been.

The last page of this archival dossier is a tally sheet with the heading "Expenses incurred by the mutewallis of the Waqfs Abu Madyan of Jerusalem and elsewhere during the year 1927." Analysis of these expenditures shows that, even though the commitments provided by the endowment charter were always met, some represent a smaller share of the budget than was the case in 1914. The subsidies paid out to the poor, widows, and orphans represented, for example, an expense of 5,186 piasters in 1927, nearly equivalent to the prewar payment (6,816 piasters in 1912–13). Expenses linked to lighting and maintenance of the holy endowment ("oil, kerosene, lamps, brooms, etc.") represented 1,316 piasters in 1927, an amount once again equal to the same item for the prewar years. By contrast, the item "Expenditures for the feasts of Ramadan, Bayram and Mawlid," which corresponded to distributions of bread and meals stipulated in the endowment charter, amounted to only 4,504 piasters in 1927, which is markedly less than before the war, since the expense registered over 20,000 piasters for the bread and nearly 10,000 for the feast day meals, for a total of around 30,000 piasters. Importantly, this item then represented over a third of the endowment's budget, compared to barely 5 percent of the 1927 budget.

Conversely, structural costs and operating expenses were accounting for a far greater share: 3,925 piasters for "servants' wages" (compared to a few hundred piasters before the war), but especially 8,300 piasters for the "salaries of the mutewallis" (nearly 10 percent of the total budget), compared to 500 to 600 piasters before the war (less than 1 percent of the budget of that time). This difference can be explained by a professionalization of the positions, but also by a judicialization of procedures, as evidenced by the 2,575 piasters spent in 1927 on "stamps for lawsuits filed in the courts" and the 1,500 piasters for "travel expenses involving the waqfs." Whatever the case, this increase in operating expenses did not bode well for the coming chapters of the endowment's financial history.[70]

The budget for the year 1927, as we have said, was severely destabilized by the 11 July earthquake. The summary table of the endowment's seventy-eight housing units anticipated renovation expenditures of 89 pounds per dwelling on average, and the actual budget implemented in 1927 indicates that three houses must have been eligible for exceptional repair work that year, for a total of 883 pounds, or nearly 300 pounds per dwelling on average: the "house at Daraj El Tabouneh" (350 pounds), the "house at Bab El Silsileh" (235 pounds) and the "house at Harat El Nasara" (298 pounds). In addition to these three houses, the budget mentions "repairs in various locations" for a cost of 108 pounds, which brings the total expenditures for actual repairs to 991 pounds (or 99,179 piasters) for the sole year of 1927, with the total projected amount

budgeted for repairs set at 6,542 pounds (654,000 piasters)—a colossal and un-
attainable sum, if we recall that the endowment's annual revenues amounted to
936 pounds (93,600 piasters) that same year. It is interesting to note that a copy
of this same budget can be found in the registry of correspondence compiled
by the Quai d'Orsay as an attachment to a letter dated 22 May 1928 from the
French consul general in Jerusalem, who wished to draw the attention of Paris
to "the scale of damage caused by the 11 July earthquake," and thereby to argue
for sending "an Algerian support delegation" to Jerusalem.[71] On 2 August,
Algiers replied to Paris that "it is not possible to consider such a delegation, as
the Colony's budget includes no funds for covering the expense."[72]

In an earlier correspondence sent on 14 February 1928, the French consul
had already solicited the administration in Algeria so that funds might be
raised there in support of the residents of the Maghrebi Quarter of Jerusalem,
victims of the quake. Algiers's response to Jerusalem could not have been less
sympathetic: "The mutewalli of the Maghrebi waqfs Mohammed El Mehdi El
Fassi solicits the authorization to send to North Africa a delegation tasked with
raising funds toward the repairing of damage caused to assets of the Palestine
waqfs by the earthquake of 11 July 1927. [...] The current economic situation
of Algeria does not allow us to grant a favorable response to the request of the
Muslim personage in question."[73] The Maghrebi Quarter of Jerusalem was thus
in an especially tight situation in the late 1920s: it was constantly threatened
by Jewish claims to the Western Wall, it had lost control of its property assets
in favor of the Supreme Muslim Council, its Ein Karem tenants were taking
advantage of the new registry to privatize plots of land, it had sustained major
damage from the 1927 quake . . . and the French authorities were displaying
little eagerness to provide any relief. It was against this backdrop that the
"Western Wall Riots" broke out in August 1929 (figure 22).

August 1929: The Maghrebi Quarter in the Heart of the Battleground

The riots of August 1929, sometimes wrongly considered "the year zero of the
Israeli-Arab conflict," were anything but a bolt from the blue.[74] Since 1925, signs
of a worsening situation had been increasing, and once again the Maghrebi
Quarter proved an excellent barometer for measuring the successive stages of

N

Geula

Sheikh Jarrah   Wadi Joz

Bab az-Zahra

Musrara

Nablus Road

Herod's Gate

Zikron Moshe   **RUSSIAN COMPOUND**

Municipal hospital (1891)

Café Belediye (Municipal café)

Damascus Gate

Seraglio (governorate)

Saint Stephen's Gate

Municipal park (1892)

Jaffa Road

New Gate (1889)   **Church of the Holy Sepulchre**

Golden Gate

Mahkeme (court)   **Dome of the Rock**

Mamilla Cemetery and Pool

New Municipality (1896)

Jaffa Gate (1898)

Palace Hotel (1929)

Fountain (1900)

Citadel

Mughrabi Quarter

Al-Aqsa Mosque

Khalidi Library

Mughrabi Gate

King David Hotel (1931)

Mount

YEMIN MOSHE

Sultan's Pool

Zion Gate

Silwan (Siloam)

Ras al-Amud

Qatamon

Zion

Pool of Siloam

Aqueduct

Talbiyeh

Abu Tor

Hebron Road

Railway station (1892)

Baka

0   500 m

Old City wall

Zones principally inhabited by …

Muslim Arabs

Main late nineteenth-century Ottoman administration buildings

Christian Arabs

Jews

FIGURE 22. **Jerusalem in the early 1930s. Source: © Dario Ingiusto.**

this race toward the abyss. After the failed legislative elections of February–March 1923, the Mandate authorities managed in 1927 to organize municipal elections in the large towns of Palestine. But the victory of the moderate Na-shashibi Party (with the tacit support of Zionist organizations) served only to further radicalize their adversaries, structured around the Husseini family and the mufti of Jerusalem, Amin al-Husseini, who opted to wage the conflict on a religious sectarian basis in order to preserve their leadership.[75] On the other side, since 1925, the Jewish National Council (Vaad Leumi) decided officially to make the Western Wall a priority; financial transactions were giving way to increasingly explicit political claims.

In late summer 1927, a tragic event would come to highlight the noxious atmosphere surrounding the Western Wall. On 31 August 1927, the daily newspaper *Davar* (close to the trade union federation *Histadrut*) reported "a loud explosion heard near the Western Wall, yesterday evening around 21:00. [. . .] The explosion occurred in an Arab house located in front of the Wall, which was in large part destroyed, though there were no casualties. The blast was so powerful that the neighborhood inhabitants fled in panic."[76] The next day, the same paper reported that the blast had been heard "as far away as Talpioth," but that the cause of the explosion was still unknown: "Rumor has it that it had to do with a settling of scores among Arab residents, and three Arab suspects have been arrested."[77] On 2 September, *Davar* indicated that the criminal nature of the explosion was proven, but that the three Arab suspects had been exonerated and released. The same article reported that the *Times* saw in this explosion "an attempt to destroy the Western Wall" (highly unlikely, given the site's layout and architecture), while mentioning concurrently that the newspaper *Al-Jami'a al-Arabiya*, the news outlet of the Husseini family, saw in this blast "a Zionist attack initiated by Vaad Leumi."[78] On 3 September the daily *Sawt al-Shaab*, close to the Arab High Committee, denounced even more explicitly "a Zionist attack against the Waqf Abu Madyan, with the aim of expanding the prayer area in front of the Wall."[79] The symmetry of reactions reveals how wide the gap had grown between the different users of this space.

On 5 September, an editorial in *Davar* went one step further in its political interpretation of the event: "We are not trying to sow panic in Zionist public opinion, for we know how easy it is to spread conspiracies [. . .]. Still, yet another tragedy has taken place, an indescribable catastrophe for the Jewish people: an explosion next to the Western Wall, that monument of our national and religious history."[80] Lambasting the "contempt" of the British authorities, the paper drove the point home by taking direct aim at the Waqf Abu Madyan: "Our protest will endure until the expropriation of the current owners of the Western Wall and its vicinity and until it is handed over to the Jews, who are the real owners, since they alone have ties to it."[81] A Zionist attack for some, an anti-Jewish attack for others, the explosion of 30 August 1927 would inevitably feed the anxieties and projections of the various actors, while illustrating the accelerated worsening of the situation. As for responsibility for the attack, at any rate, a recent discovery has settled the matter once and for all. Yosef Hecht, commander of the Haganah between 1922 and 1931, reports in his notebooks that he organized this attack with the intention of intimidating the inhabitants of the quarter, following a series of incidents with Jewish worshippers who had come to pray at the Wall.[82] The operation, which was undoubtedly approved by David Ben-Gurion (general secretary of the Histadrut, which supervised the Haganah), was implemented on the ground by Avraham Tehomi, Haganah commander in Jerusalem and future founder of the terrorist group Irgun.[83] The takeaway here is that in the summer of 1927, for the first time, a house in the Maghrebi Quarter was directly and deliberately targeted by an official Zionist organisation.

This ramping up of sectarian and political concerns thus occurred in tandem with an "upscaling" of the actors involved and, consequently, a geographical extension of available news sources as well. On 14 October 1928 there is mention of "Moroccans living in the dilapidated huts of the Wailing Wall quarter" in a missive that the Vaad Leumi addressed to the Permanent Mandates Commission of the League of Nations in Geneva.[84] A fortnight earlier, on 30 September 1928, the *Echo d'Alger* reported that the "Jewish colony" of Jerusalem "had gone on strike for an hour" to "protest against alleged police brutality" against them during an altercation in front of the Wall.[85] On 8 October 1928, the Supreme Muslim Council decided officially to make the defense of the Buraq al-Sharif an emblematic cause of the national Palestinian struggle.[86] Through no fault of its own, the Maghrebi Quarter was henceforth at the heart of the conflict, and would remain in that perilous position until its destruction in June 1967.

The "Wall Riots" of 23–29 August 1929 claimed more than 250 lives, of whom 133 were Jewish and 116 Arab, according to the official toll.[87] This traumatic event has left a permanent mark on Israeli and Palestinian memory to the present, for although the first clashes took place in the Maghrebi Quarter of Jerusalem starting on 23 August, they soon spread to all of Mandatory Palestine, with deadly episodes most notably in Hebron, Safed, Motsa, Jaffa, Tel Aviv, and Nablus. These clashes have given rise to a plethoric bibliography and to massive archival material, especially from the weeks and months subsequent to the events. In order to avoid the distortions of this "blast effect," and to continue to observe the events from the standpoint of the Maghrebi Quarter, we must at least temporarily keep our distance from the archives produced by the Special Commission of the League of Nations set up after the fact, and place ourselves once again as close as possible to the site. By focusing on the days preceding the outbreak of violence, we can attempt to understand what precisely, in the minds of the local actors, might connect the Waqf Abu Madyan neighborhood to the hostilities surrounding the Wall. Toward this purpose, the series of personal papers housed at the Middle East Center Archives (MECA) of St Antony's College, Oxford, are of great value, for they contain numerous documents produced on a daily basis by officers in charge of peacekeeping in Mandatory Palestine.[88] Sir Harry Luke (1884–1969), deputy to High Commissioner John Chancellor (on leave in England during the month of August), thus wrote a preliminary report on Saturday 17 August 1929:

> On [Thursday] 15 August, during the Fast commemorating the Destruction of the Temple, in addition to the large numbers of Jews who proceeded in the ordinary way to the Wall to worship, some hundreds of young Jews exercised their right of access for purposes not confined to the usual practice of prayer but were associated with the making of a speech and the raising of a flag. At about 1 p.m. on the 16th of August, about 2,000 Moslems left the Haram, where they had been celebrating the Prophet's Birthday, and proceeded to the Wailing Wall through streets lying in the Abu Madian Waqf, which also includes the pavement in front of the wall. A wooden table that was standing on the pavement was overturned by the pressure of the crowd and was broken, and papers containing prayers lying in the crevices of the Wall were taken out and burnt.[89]

Already, from his very first report, written a week *prior* to the onset of deadly clashes, Sir Harry Luke placed the Waqf Abu Madyan at the center of the conflict that pitted Jews against Muslims with regard to use of the Western Wall / al-Buraq. He also points out that the reaction of the Muslim rioters took place on Mawlid, the Prophet Muhammad's birthday, celebrated in particular, as we know, by the inhabitants of the Maghrebi Quarter, since that was one of the days when they were granted a meal free of charge at the religious endowment's expense. Other sources confirm that groups of young nationalists did indeed opt to turn the Wall into an arena of confrontation. A year earlier, on 8 October 1928, in the daily paper *Do'ar Hayom*, Abba Ahimeir, a member of the revisionist Zionist Party of Vladimir Jabotinsky and founder of the splinter group Brit Ha'Birionim, criticized the attempts at financial deals and advocated instead for a balance of power: "There are certain things, my friends, that we are forbidden to buy, even if there are four million Jews in America. We must win the Wall by dint of our own political power."[90] On Sunday 18 August 1929, the day after Sir Harry Luke drafted his report, again in *Do'ar Hayom*, Abraham Isaac Kook, chief Ashkenazi rabbi of Palestine, expressed his "deep gratitude" to the young nationalist demonstrators, and attacked head-on the "cramped courtyard housing" of the adjoining neighborhood, asserting that "nothing stands in the way of expanding the prayer area except for the secular waqf of Maghrebi beggars."[91] By contrasting "the holy rage of the sublime soul of Israel" with a supposedly "secular waqf," the Rav Kook was not only stating an untruth; he was deliberately placing the Maghrebis of Jerusalem in the front lines of the historic clash that was taking shape.

Further confirmation of the key role played by the Maghrebi Quarter in various narratives and explanations of the Wall riots is obtained by a quick lexicometric analysis of the Wailing Wall Commission's famous report sent to the League of Nations in December 1930.[92] In the report's forty-seven pages, the term "Moghrabi" or "Maghrebi" is used twenty-five times and the term "waqf" or "wakf" appears sixty-five times. In its preamble, the commission retraces how the quarter came to be: "In the year 1193 an area in front of the Wailing Wall was constituted Waqf by King Afdal, son of Saladin [. . .]. About 1320, the houses which are now called the Moghrabi Quarter were constituted Waqf by a certain Abu Madian. This Quarter was donated for the benefit of Moroccan pilgrims and derives its name from that."[93] We know that in its conclusions, the commission emphasized both (a) that Muslims had "the sole ownership of, and the sole proprietary right to" the premises (Wall, adjacent alley, and Maghrebi Quarter included), and (b) that the Jews must have "free access" for the purpose of carrying out their "devotions."[94] By distinguishing in this way between eminent ownership and right of use, the commission rendered their decision perfectly emblematic of the contradictions inherent to the British Mandate in Palestine that would inevitably lead to confrontation.

By processing the logbooks of the Quai d'Orsay's correspondence in the 1929–30 period, we can gauge the growing concern of the Maghrebi Quarter's inhabitants, but also the reluctance of the French authorities to be dragged into what they then considered a "propaganda" move. On 12 October 1929, the mutewallis Muhammad El Mehdi and Ahmad Amer wrote to the French consul general of Jerusalem to protest against "the closing of the zawiya on Saturdays and Jewish holidays [. . .] and against the installation of objects on the waqf wall, which had heretofore been forbidden."[95] The appeal to France as the colonial power in the Maghreb is stated explicitly: "The places where rights are being infringed [. . .] belong to Your Government, given that it is your nationals who are in possession of them; it is you over any other that have the right to defend them, and should you fail to do so, your silence would cause us to lose our rights."[96] Two days later, the inhabitants of the Maghrebi Quarter wrote to the British high commissioner to protest against "the installation of a second lux lamp in front of al-Buraq, and against the closure of the Muslim zawiyas," ending their letter with a bombastic phrase that could easily have been formulated by Mirabeau in 1789: "You have trampled on our rights on behalf of others, by tyranny, out of hatred, and at the point of your bayonets."[97] For the first time, faced with a heightened nationalization of the conflict that was threatening them, the Maghrebis of Jerusalem thus described themselves as French "nationals" in an attempt to seek France's protection.

The consul, Jacques d'Aumale, refused to play that card, fearing that he would be used as a political tool:

> The mutewalli of the Waqf Abu Madyan [. . .] has just issued me a protest regarding the installment at the edge of the terrace of said waqf of one of those lamps that serve as streetlights in Jerusalem. This protest, which on its face applies only to the safeguarding of waqf constructions, has in reality a political objective, since the building is not damaged in any way by the installation of a streetlamp that is helpful for foot traffic. It was the Mufti who prompted the Algerian mutewalli to issue the complaint, attempting to get us involved in this Wailing Wall business.[98]

The same arguments marshalled by Consul Neuville in 1949 in favor of French intervention are here inverted in order to refuse any assistance to the Maghrebi community of Jerusalem: where Neuville would pinpoint an *opportunity*, d'Aumale discerned a *trap*, in a context admittedly different in every respect. This refusal went beyond the political issue, since Jacques d'Aumale had asked Paris to prohibit Algeria, Tunisia, and Morocco from organizing "fundraising in favor of Muslim victims of the events in Palestine."[99]

His arguments amounted to aligning the French position with that of the British authorities, "who might find it extraordinary that we consent to the organization in French North Africa of major fundraising efforts in favor of individuals who are ultimately nothing but rioters."[100] Via telegram on 16 October, he once more stood against any French intervention, in even more direct terms: "On the pretense of safeguarding Maghrebi interests, the Arab Committees are seeking to involve us in the Wall issue, which they would like to see moved beyond a mere Palestinian problem to become internationalized. We have no interest in falling for this tactic."[101] The internationalization of the holy places, which was to become the pivot of France's diplomatic strategy in Jerusalem from 1947 onward, was here being overtly ruled out by d'Aumale, who demonstrated a certain lack of foresight in this matter, grasping neither France's moral responsibility with regard to the Jerusalem Maghrebis . . . nor the political advantage France would stand to gain.

In fact, Consul Jacques d'Aumale seems to have been especially driven by the fear that the politicization of the issue would lead to a large-scale Muslim insurrection, a fear echoed by the colonial Algerian press. In the *Progrès de Sidi-Bel-Abbès* of 10 September 1929, the paper headlined "Blood on the Wailing Wall" and underscored the fact that "Muslim turmoil could overtake Syria. Does this not herald the reappearance of Sultan Al-Atrash, our sworn enemy?"[102] The *Echo d'Alger* of 30 August claimed outright that "Sultan al-Atrash is marching on Jerusalem at the head of Druze armed units [. . .] to protect the Mosque of Omar."[103] By foregrounding the man who had led the armed insurrection against France in Syria a few years earlier (1925–27), the colonial press was voicing a muted concern shared throughout the diplomatic corps.[104] Indeed, the figures among the political opposition to French colonization supplied arguments that fed this agenda. For instance, on 21 July 1930, Saïd Abd el-Kader El-Jazairi, "grandson of Emir Abd el-Kader Sultan of Algeria" (author of the *Letter to the French* in 1855), who presented himself as "working for over eighteen years uninterrupted for the independence of his country," sent the French Foreign Ministry a memorandum "concerning our particular rights and those of Muslims in general over the Maghrebi waqf where the Western Wall of the al-Aqsa Mosque and the al-Buraq al-Sharif are located," in which he notably asserted, for instance, that "Algerians are the most devoted to the sacredness of this place which belongs to them directly."[105] Against this backdrop, we can understand that an apprehensive consul, unsure of how best to channel these demands to France's advantage, would advocate for caution.[106] In March 1936, a few weeks before the outbreak of the armed Palestinian uprising, a denunciation further fed the illusion of a possible alliance between the Palestinian insurgents and the Jerusalem Maghrebis. This peculiar document, signed "Mohammed Aklil," is housed in the archives of the French Consulate in Jerusalem:

> Monsieur the Consul General, it is my honor to hereby inform you that a meeting of North Africans was convened in their quarter with the purpose of organizing a charitable fundraiser last Friday. It was to my great astonishment that I saw the event take on a wholly political cast, and heard them criticizing France and its government with regard to its policies abroad and in the colonies. They went so far as to insult any person who might have, or had already had a certain relationship with France or its government.[107]

In the margin of this denunciation letter, the consul wrote in longhand: "Bring this person in and talk to him." This was done on 14 March, and a handwritten note summarizes the interview: "The Mufti had a door opened up between the Sharia court building and the Maghrebi Zawiya. It is through this secret door that he enters the Zawiya where meetings with the Maghrebi chiefs of Jerusalem take place. They talk about, among other things, Syrian issues, a mutual assistance society and Moroccan issues, attacking French policies. Several deserters from the French army have joined the Maghrebi ranks."[108] It is difficult to assess whether these accusations were well founded, and especially whether this door was truly "secret," since the opening of new access points to decongest the neighborhood is frequently referred to in the endowment's archives, notably during the decade of 1920–30, when the issue of access was becoming a source of recurrent conflict in the neighborhood (figure 23). But however true it may have been, this missive—and the way it was processed by the consulate—does point to the new *political* and even *strategic* dimension acquired by the quarter. Itself a mandatory power faced with a consolidated nationalist movement in Syria—which would attain independence a few months later—France did not yet know how to take advantage of the legitimate concerns of Jerusalem's Maghrebi community, which in these troubled times was naturally casting about for any protection it could find.

———

It is in this context, in the early 1930s, that the young Yasser Arafat, four years old at the death of his mother Zahwa Abu Saud, came with his brother Fathi to live with his uncle Salim Khalil Abu Saud in one of the loveliest homes in the Maghrebi Quarter, on an overlook along a slope that led through an eponymous gate all the way to Haram al-Sharif (figures 24 and 25).[109] Between 1933 and 1936—until he was seven—in the highly charged atmosphere that followed the Wall riots and which heralded the armed insurrection of 1936, Arafat attended numerous political gatherings, for the various branches of

FIGURE 23. **Jewish worshippers at the south entrance to the Maghrebi Quarter, early 1930s. Source: © Matson Photograph collection, Library of Congress.**

FIGURE 24. German zeppelin over Jerusalem, 11 April 1931. Source: © Matson Photograph collection, Library of Congress.

FIGURE 25. Aerial photograph of the Maghrebi Quarter, taken from the zeppelin on 11 April 1931. Source: © Archiv der Luftschiffbau Zeppelin GmbH, Friedrichshafen.

the Abu Saud family were tied to the major figures of emergent Palestinian nationalism.[110] In late May 1964, at the founding congress of the Palestinian Liberation Organization (PLO) in Jerusalem, Arafat returned for the last time to that childhood home, and met his grandnephew Azzam Abu Saud, who recalled that day a few decades later.[111]

Although this stay in the Maghrebi Quarter between 1922 and 1936 by the Palestinian national struggle's guiding figure might be considered nothing but an anecdote, the same cannot be said for its "political wake," faithfully culti-vated yet today by three photographs exhibited in the Yasser Arafat Museum in Ramallah, which accompany the reconstitution of his childhood bedroom. Far from anecdotal, Arafat's childhood memory in the midst of the Maghrebi Quarter appears, on the contrary, as a further sign of the neighborhood's transformation into a political object precisely during the 1930s, those pivotal years for the imbricated destinies of Jerusalem and Palestine before the first Arab-Israeli war of 1948 broke out, upsetting regional balances.

3

PROTECTION AND IMPERIAL AMBITION

FRANCE UP AGAINST THE WALL (1948–54)

The way archives are structured is always significant, provided that one takes the time to dwell on the *container* before rushing to look through the *contents*. At the diplomatic archives of Nantes, in the material recovered from the French Consulate, four boxes are labeled "Waqf Abu Madyan" and cover the period 1949–69.[1] They are filed under the category "Political Affairs" (as are, for example, the boxes labeled "Status of Jerusalem," "Palestinian Refugees," and "Suez Canal"), and not under the category "Religious Affairs and Holy Places." The Waqf Abu Madyan is thus considered a political issue, processed and classified as such by the officials of the French Consulate in Jerusalem. It is also interesting to observe that an original call number, 8, is used to identify all documents pertaining to this matter, which was thus singled out at the very time of its development; the four boxes now held in Nantes are but the material translation of this operational filing system organized in situ in Jerusalem starting in 1949.

I would come across this call number 8—with the note "To be filed under 8," for example—on certain other documents that ended up being filed under other categories (notably "Jewish Affairs," "Arab Affairs" or "Status of Jerusalem"). This helped me keep track of what the diplomats in charge of this dossier were having to grapple with. Inside these four boxes we find the classic file-processing structure for complex issues of this type: first the documentary dossiers involving judicial and historical matters; then dossiers of correspondence, organized chronologically with the oldest at the bottom of the stack and the most recent at the top. Because these are repatriated consular archives, we should bear in mind that they allow access to all *incoming* correspondence (attachments included), but that the *outgoing* correspondence appears only as a draft or a copy, without attachments, with some exceptions.

Jerusalem to Algiers, via Damascus: Rumblings of Empire

Let us take up the first bundle of correspondence and flip it over to discover which missive "opens" the "Waqf Abu Madyan" dossier inside the consular offices right after the first Arab-Israeli war of 1948. Significantly, it is an epistolary exchange between Algiers and Jerusalem: Friday 17 June 1949, the governor general of Algeria, Marcel-Edmond Naegelen, writes to the consul general of France in Jerusalem, René Neuville.[2] The subject of the letter is the "Hubus of Sidi Bou Mediene in Jerusalem." A nasty rumor spreading through the streets of Tlemcen has reached the ears of the governor, worrisome enough for him to put pen to paper:

> I hereby bring to your honorable attention that a certain BEN YELLES (or BEN ILLES), born in Tlemcen, currently a professor in Damascus, member of the DERKAOUA HEBRIA brotherhood, has returned to his native town. He has spoken of a waqf long ago founded in Jerusalem by the faithful of Tlemcen, and which goes by the name of "Hubus Buraq" (the name of the Prophet's mare) and also the name "Hubus SIDI BOU MEDIENE," in honor of the famous saint buried in Tlemcen and patron saint of the town."[3]

Algiers seemed to be setting the history of the Waqf Abu Madyan in motion once again, and the immediate impression is one of a political history on a Mediterranean scale. The professor in question was Ahmed Ben Yelles, son of Hajj Mohammed Ben Yelles, a refugee in Damascus since World War I because of his nationalist activism and his opposition to the drafting of Algerians into the French army. The father and son were both members of the Derkaouiya, a Sufi brotherhood founded in the late eighteenth century by Moroccan mystics, particularly well established in Algeria and renowned for its resolute opposition to French colonization. Its members included some of the great figures of Algerian protonationalism, including Emir Abd el-Kader (also a refugee in Damascus until his death there in 1883) and Messali Hadj, a native of Tlemcen and founding figure of the independence movement.[4]

From the Algerian governor general's viewpoint, therefore, it was an ominous wind that was channeling the rumors of the "Hubus Buraq," and he appeared ill-equipped to deal with it. Naegelen was the pure product of the *résistance*-era Section française Internationale ouvrière (SFIO), the French section of the Workers' International. A teacher before the war, he was appointed governor general in February 1948 even though he "he knew nothing of Algeria, and nothing designated him for this task," as indicated by the Maitron biographical dictionary.[5] We sense a certain consternation but also an incomprehension in this short missive from Naegelen to Neuville, when he evokes the "Hubus Buraq (the name of the Prophet's mare)" without understanding that in Jerusalem it is the Western Wall itself that the Muslim faithful call "al-Buraq," according to a tradition dating back to the late Middle Ages and reactivated in the nineteenth century.[6] At any rate, it is not trivial that the rumor linking Jerusalem to Tlemcen passed through Damascus, which was the administrative capital of Jerusalem until 1872, when the Holy City had been an integral part of Bilad al-Sham province.[7] Damascus—intellectual and political capital of the Levant, a hotbed of unrest during the French Mandate years, capital of the newly independent Syria since the pullout of French troops in April 1946—played its logical role in the geopolitical reactivation of the Waqf Abu Madyan in the aftermath of World War II.[8]

In fact, the subsequent correspondence confirms the incendiary nature of the dossier: "The property of this religious endowment, adjacent to the Wailing Wall, is much coveted by the Israelis, according to Ben Yelles, and is liable to be diverted by them from its proper purpose. These rumors have not failed to grab the attention of religious circles in Tlemcen."[9] When he mundanely refers to what is "much coveted by the Israelis," Naegelen seems completely detached from reality: prior to 1948, nearly half of the Waqf Abu Madyan's financial resources have come from its property income in the village of Ein Karem, and this village ended up in the Israeli zone following the 1948 war, which abruptly interrupted all payments.[10] Located a little over a kilometer from the village of Deir Yassin, where some one hundred civilians were massacred in April 1948 by

Irgun irregulars, Ein Karem was totally emptied of its Arab population during the Israeli offensive of 9–18 July 1948.[11]

According to Benny Morris, the Deir Yassin massacre was one of the events that triggered the flight of the Palestinian civilian population, an explanation strengthened by the case of Ein Karem, located only a few hundred meters downhill from Deir Yassin.[12] At any rate, from the vantage of Algiers, only the faintest echo of these faraway battles was registered, since the loss of Ein Karem was described as only one element of what was "much coveted by the Israelis," and since all that worried Governor Naegelen was the possible unrest it could cause to "the religious circles in Tlemcen." In reality, from Jerusalem's standpoint, the situation was far more bleak: since the loss of Ein Karem, the Waqf Abu Madyan had been virtually asphyxiated. Cut off from a large part of its financial resources, it simply could no longer function. Though the seriousness of the situation was underestimated in Algiers, its potential political impact was fully grasped:

> If the situation is indeed as Mr. Ben Yelles has described it, perhaps there might well be cause to get the Minister of Foreign Affairs involved, leading to a possible diplomatic intervention, which would have the advantage of emphasizing to the Muslim world that France is interested in preserving not only the Christian religious establishments of Jerusalem, but also the same kind of institutions founded by French Muslims.[13]

All the ingredients of an imminent "French history" of the Maghrebi Quarter of Jerusalem come together in this passage. The Algerian context had been marked by continuous political unrest since the Sétif massacres in May 1945. The Movement for the Triumph of Democratic Freedoms (MTLD), headed by Messali Hadj, had been founded in 1946, and its armed wing, the Special Organization, was taking shape by 1947. There was thus a specifically Algerian political opportunity to take up the issue to show that France as a power was acting to protect the holy Islamic sites, and that it was carrying out a genuine policy with regard to Muslims, thereby fulfilling an authentic imperial ambition. This Muslim Policy of France, the importance of which has recently been reassessed by Jalila Sbaï, aimed specifically at curbing any ambitions for national independence among the civilian population of the Maghreb and was designed as a deliberate action, expressed at the highest state levels.[14]

René Neuville, the Man of the Hour

While the political context in Algeria partly accounts for the subsequent chain of diplomatic events, the geopolitical context in Jerusalem also contributes. The message from the governor general of Algeria effectively landed on the desk of the French consul general in Jerusalem in the thick of negotiations over the internationalization of the holy places, an issue where France fully intended to remain in the forefront. The United Nations Partition Plan for Palestine was approved by the UN General Assembly on 29 November 1947, and fighting erupted as soon as the British troops pulled out in May 1948. After the failure at the French Consulate of the Truce Commission—whose action was interrupted by the assassination of UN special representative Folke Bernadotte in September 1948—the Israeli army made a series of specific moves intended to consolidate its positions and to modify in its favor the cease-fire lines that stabilized in the spring of 1949. Bilateral talks then opened up with the Arab neighbors: an armistice agreement was signed with Egypt on 24 February 1949, with Lebanon on 23 March, and then with Jordan on 3 April. On 11 May 1949, a few weeks before the epistolary exchange between Algiers and Jerusalem, France voted to admit Israel into the United Nations, nearly a year after its declaration of independence.[15] In June 1949, while Ahmed Ben Yelles was shuttling between Damascus and Tlemcen to denounce Israel's "coveting" tendencies, negotiations were in fact underway between Israel and Syria, and would lead to a definitive cease-fire signed between the two countries on 20 July 1949.[16]

The letter from Algiers might well have gone unheeded like so many other epistolary exchanges between chancelleries, but it happened to be read this time by a diplomat capable of fully grasping its broader implications. In this sense, we can say that France's consul general in Jerusalem, René Neuville, was truly the man of the hour, in the right place at the right time, capable of seizing the political opportunity as it emerged. Born in Gibraltar to a diplomat father, he was only twenty-seven when appointed chancellor of the Jerusalem Consulate in 1926, a position he would hold until 1937. He knew the Holy City perfectly, but he also had extensive knowledge of the Maghreb, since he had been stationed successively in Morocco, Algeria, and Tunisia during World War II, before returning to Jerusalem as consul general on 28 February 1946, an appointment he would hold until his death on 23 June 1952 (figure 26).[17]

FIGURE 26. French Consul General René Neuville (front left, with walking stick) in the no-man's-land between the French Consulate and the Jaffa Gate, 1949. Source: © EBAF.

Neuville's career path seems somehow to have preordained him to reconnect the Maghrebi Quarter with its historic Maghrebi roots. A handwritten comment at the top of the letter received from Algiers indicates that he was not at all taken unawares by the governor general's request: "In return provide me with files on Algerian *wakoufs*." And just a few days later, he drafted a long report on the Waqf Abu Madyan, which he sent to Algiers on 6 July 1949. It presents a rapid recapitulation of the endowment's history, but especially makes clear why it was so important to France's new diplomatic strategy in the Middle East. From the opening lines, Neuville makes the point to his interlocutor that the issue not only concerns the "religious circles in Tlemcen" but that it intersects with some of the most emblematic episodes of the territorial conflict in Palestine. In the strictest sense, Neuville puts the governor general of Algeria in his place:

> The affair is not a new one and the threat at issue was notably what caused the bloody events of 1929. It led the League of Nations at that time to appoint a Special Commission in charge of determining the status of the famed wall.

But what is certain, with the establishment of Israel and the considerable extension of Jewish aspirations [. . .], the affair will undoubtedly return to the agenda and will soon take a very serious turn."[18]

Neuville—diplomat, but also archaeologist, prehistorian, epigraphist—knew that the chronological horizon of this dossier was not confined to the 1929 riots.[19] He reminds his interlocutor that "a bit of history is required to situate the issue," since the first endowment dates back to "the year 720 of the Hegira," by "Sheikh Sayed Abu Madyan ben Khousib ben Sidna Sheikh Saleh." He emphasizes the point that the Wall itself is also venerated by Muslims "owing to the memory left there by the Prophet Muhammad when he tied up his mare Buraq there." This "entanglement of spiritual, political, and material interests" was, according to Neuville, emblematic of the complexity of the situation in Jerusalem, which "the United Nations augurs have yet to entirely realize, it seems."[20] Tasked by the UN Security Council to host in Jerusalem the Truce Commission, headed by mediator Folke Bernadotte, Neuville was able to witness firsthand the international organization's prevarications, and its first historic failure in the resolving of the 1948–49 armed conflict. He was particularly affected by this episode: the General Consulate building was regularly targeted by Jordanian gunfire, and the French Colonel André Sérot, heading the team of UN observers in Jerusalem, was assassinated alongside Folke Bernadotte on 17 September 1948 by the Stern group.[21] In early July 1949, Neuville wanted to make the internationalization of the holy places the main thrust of French policy in the region, as demonstrated by Frédérique Schillo in a study on that particular period: "If one had to picture the Palestine issue from the perspective of French interests, the Holy Places would lie at the very center."[22] In this respect, the letter from the governor of Algiers was well timed to consolidate this position by saving France from appearing to protect only the Christian holy places.

For his interlocutor in Algiers, Neuville broadly outlined the long history of how the Waqf Abu Madyan had come to be: "To its founding by the patron saint of the town of Tlemcen were then added other bequests from the Maghreb, which together eventually constituted what has come to be known as "the Waqf Abu Madyan." The assets were located in Jerusalem and in Ein Karem, Gaza, Ramallah, Lydda, and Nazareth. In spite of the terms set out by the endowment, some of these property rights—notably those in Ein Karem which encompassed the entire village—were reassigned, to Jews among others."[23] Although he may not yet have grasped the minutiae of this real estate story, Neuville still summed up rather well the two asymmetric processes that structured the history of the Waqf Abu Madyan, and which, from this perspective, make it quite typical of a general history of Islamic endowments in Palestine:[24] an *accretion* process which made the Waqf Abu Madyan the backbone of a series of related endowments that gradually aggregated; followed by a process of *reassignment* of property rights, which saw this theoretically inalienable land handed over, either temporarily or definitively, to tenants who in the end behaved like genuine landowners, themselves leasing or subleasing the property in a cascade of holders, until the link between eminent property and use property was finally lost in the labyrinth of subleases passed down through inheritance.[25] In his report, Neuville is explicitly critical of how the French administration in Algeria had long disregarded the endowment. We understand here that he is preparing to revive a strategy that he himself had attempted to elaborate during the Mandate years:

> In 1928, following the notorious earthquake the previous year, and a no less disastrous handling of it, my predecessor of that period had suggested to the Minister of Foreign Affairs that the Algerian Administration take charge of managing these properties […]. Your predecessor made it clear […] that it would be "impossible for him to consider such an assignment, as the [Algerian] Colony had not budgeted any funds to meet this kind of expense.[26]

Neuville's resentment was all the more justified in that he had been chancellor of the French Consulate of Jerusalem in 1928—in other words, top advisor to Consuls General Alphonse Doire (31 December 1925 to 20 October 1928) and Jacques d'Aumale (1928–37).[27] Governor Naegelen's letter thus enabled him to reopen a dossier he had reluctantly closed twenty years earlier, following the twofold rejection he had suffered at the hands of the Algiers administrators and his own hierarchical superiors in Jerusalem.[28] For Neuville at that time, it was less a matter of "obtaining financial support" from Algiers than of using French sovereignty in Algeria to prevent Palestinian religious endowments from falling under the authority of the Supreme Muslim Council created in 1921.[29]

Return of the "Prodigal Sons"

In his letter, Neuville pursued his narrative, referring to the new withdrawal of French positions during World War II: "Later on, in 1940, the English took advantage of our defeat, not to exclude us—which had already been done—from administering the Maghrebi waqf, but to split us off from the North African Muslims established in the old city, notably by enabling their acquisition of Palestinian nationality and by tormenting in countless ways those who intended to stand by us."[30] Here again is testimony to Franco-British competition in the Middle East, and to how the Vichy regime had weakened France's diplomatic network. In 1948, the end of the British Mandate, the partition of Jerusalem and the loss of land in Ein Karem represented for Neuville "a turn of events": "Reduced to joblessness and destitution, the Maghrebis of the old town had no recourse but to turn to us and appeal for our generosity." The return of those he labeled the "prodigal sons" would allow the French Consulate to turn what it called the "waqf clientele" into a decisive component to "exploit the unique place occupied by the Zawiya Abu Madyan in the Holy Places question." This is where Neuville developed the core of his argument, which would provide the framework for French intervention in the years to come: the partition of Jerusalem between the Jordanian zone in the east (including the old city) and the Israeli zone in the west made access to the Western Wall a key issue, and the Maghrebi Quarter an even more strategic zone than previously. The fact is that at the time he was writing this letter, situation was completely deadlocked:

> By December [1947], the Jews could no longer venture into the Wailing Wall neighborhood, located in the heart of the Muslim quarter of the old city. After a heroic resistance, they were even expelled, in late May 1948, from the sector they had occupied within the ramparts for centuries. Henceforward, Islam was the sole master of the whole Haram al-Sharif plaza, of its mosques and its venerable enclosure. Despite various UN Security Council resolutions prescribing that free access to the Holy Places be reestablished, not a single Jew has returned to the wall in eighteen months [. . .]. Delegated by the Truce Commission, I myself negotiated with the opposing parties over access, at least

symbolic, to this religious site. The Israelis proved intransigent, when they countered by not allowing Arabs access to Christian or Muslim Holy Places taken over in the Israeli occupation zone."[31]

All eyewitness reports converge to confirm the scale of destruction, following the evacuation of the Jewish Quarter of the old city in May 1948, particularly the systematic burning of synagogues. Constantine Mavrides, an interpreter at the Greek Consulate, having taken refuge inside the Greek Orthodox Patriarchate, describes in his journal the corpses "left in the open air, in an advanced state of decomposition and which the Arabs must have burned on 28 May after their conquest of the Jewish Quarter." He also points out that "everything remaining was pillaged," though he does take care to note that it was inhabitants of neighboring villages, and not the citizens of Jerusalem, who took part in the looting.[32] At any rate, access to the Wall was henceforth denied to Jews, and it was precisely this deadlocked situation that enabled Neuville to design a French strategy that consisted of acknowledging the failure of bilateral negotiations in order to once again propose the internationalization of Jerusalem—or, at the very least, the Holy Places—thanks to the slice of sovereignty France could claim to exercise over the Western Wall. France, methodically pushed aside by the British authorities during the Mandatory period, discredited during the Vichy period, and humiliated by its Israeli and Jordanian interlocutors at the partition of Jerusalem, would recover a trump card, thanks to the Maghrebi Quarter, in the diplomatic game that was about to open:

> Amidst the relatively far-reaching scope of the current turmoil, what might be the possibilities offered to us by the claims of our North Africa to this site venerated by both Islam and Israel? [...] If the vicissitudes of international politics warrant increased caution with regard to the Holy Sepulchre and to France's centuries-old role in the Holy Places, can we hope to profit from the Abu Madyan situation? It is a matter for government. From my humble perspective, nevertheless, I believe we have every reason to presume that our unique position beside the Wailing Wall may prove quite useful.[33]

From Neuville's standpoint, the decision whether or not to seize this opportunity of "relatively far-reaching scope" could be taken only at the highest level. In a classic understatement, he ended his report by stressing that this tiny piece of France, a minuscule neocolonial speck facing the most sacred holy place of Judaisim, "would be far from irrelevant." To ensure the political impact of his missive, he not only sent it to the governor general of Algiers but had copies sent to Amman, Rabat, Tunis, the French Foreign Ministry, Louis Massignon, and finally Claude Bréart de Boisanger, French representative to the UN Conciliation Commission for Palestine, then headquartered in Lausanne.

As Neuville had hoped, the government immediately took up the issue, and at the highest level. On 30 July, the minister of foreign affairs, Robert Schuman, confirmed "the timeline of French rights to this parcel of ground of the Holy City," acknowledged "that these property rights at this current moment take on a very special value in the search for a solution to the problem of the internationalization of Jerusalem and the Holy Places," and added that he would personally confer "all necessary support to continue to bestow French protection upon the Maghrebi waqf of Jerusalem."[34] Neuville's strategy was thus totally validated, in terms even more explicit than those expressed by the consul, since Schuman spoke of France's "property rights" over a "parcel of ground" in Jerusalem.

On 5 August, Schuman received a telegram addressed to him by the meeting of the "Committee for the Defense of Palestine" in Algiers, chaired by Sheikh El-Okbi, who demanded that he "defend the Algerian Muslim religious endowments in Palestine, notably the Waqf Abu Madyan."[35] No coincidence, of course, in the synchronicity of exchanges on the same theme: the historic situation was coming into sharper focus, strategies were taking shape, the actors were eyeing one another, the French history of the Maghrebi Quarter was beginning. On 10 August, Schuman reiterated his position: France "will continue to defend Algerian rights to the religious endowments of Palestine, in particular the Sidi Bou Mediene [Abu Madyan] waqf, and, more broadly, to seek the protection of Muslim Holy Places within an international framework."[36] Eager to promote an expansion of France's traditional role as protector of Christian holy places by integrating Muslim sacred sites as well, Schuman leaped at Neuville's proposal, which had the twin advantage of addressing the Algerian Muslims' concerns while consolidating France's position at the United Nations.[37]

What was the position of the key stakeholders, the inhabitants of the Maghrebi Quarter of Jerusalem, the ones Neuville calls "the prodigal sons"? Certain pieces of correspondence addressed to the consulate reflect their involvement in the issue starting in autumn 1949. On 26 September, Hajj El Mehdi ben El Mehdi ben Abdesselam wrote, in Arabic, to Neuville on behalf of "North Africans, Moroccans and Algerians as well as Tunisians, French nationals who possess important waqfs in this country, among which the village of Ein Karem itself [. . .] with its lands, its trees and its springs."[38] He asserted that "the ownership of this waqf has been confirmed by various rulings" and then denounced "the Jews who, with the purpose of alienating our rights, have [. . .] taken hold of the properties and their revenues." He emphasized that "Your Government, as the protector of the rights of its nationals," had to intervene because "the village is a waqf property of Muslims under your protection."[39] The use of the term "nationals" strengthens the legal rationale and lines up with the narrative stated by Neuville a few weeks earlier, when he referred somewhat sarcastically to the return of the "prodigal sons."

On 11 November 1949 it was the turn of Hajj Ali Nakib, "Chief of the Zawiya Abou Mediene," to put pen to paper, again in Arabic, to write to the consul: "On behalf of the North African colony of Jerusalem (Moroccans, Tunisians and Algerians), I send you my best wishes on the occasion of Armistice Day, with respectful greetings and fervent hopes for the success of the principles of the Union of all peoples of the French Empire."[40] Less procedural than the previous letter, this one aimed for greater affect and patriotic fervor, arriving on a well-chosen day, since World War I had been an occasion for the populations of the Maghreb to demonstrate their loyalty toward the metropole.[41] In his response to Hajj Ali Nakib, Neuville thanked him "for these kind wishes and for the faithfulness to your respective countries and to France that they convey," thereby echoing all the ambiguity of the vocabulary elaborated within the Union Française, officially adopted with the Constitution in October 1946.[42] On 25 December, Hajj Ali Nakib sent Christmas greetings to Neuville and thanked him for his recent visit, but apologized for having to express himself in English, which is symptomatic of the rift opened up between the inhabitants of the quarter and the French Consulate during the British Mandate years.[43] Included with the letter were a few small gifts ("souvenirs, crockery, artifacts"). In response, Neuville sent a donation of twenty-five Palestinian pounds to the "Charitable Club of the French North African Colony of Jerusalem." Recently created "by a group of young people," the club occupied "a room in a waqf house in the Maghrebi Quarter," its treasurer was

Hajj Ali Nakib himself, and its board included two teachers: Mohammed Dadesi Tijani, "instructor at the Ibrahimiyeh College," and Mohammed el-Mukhtar, "instructor at the Maghrebi School."[44] Many exchanges of this type are to be found in the consulate's correspondence from the year 1950, testifying to a resumption of contact between the two parties.[45]

Beyond these exchanges of courtesies, the consul's answer to the request for "protection" shows that, although the framework of France's strategy with regard to the Maghrebi Quarter was by then well established, the judicial means for implementing it were sorely lacking: "In order that I might usefully act upon your request, I would be grateful if you would: 1) specify in as much detail as possible the nature and current condition of the Ein Karem assets; some of them indeed appear to have already been disposed of; 2) provide me with the ruling on which the Mandatory Authorities based the yearly royalty they paid you with respect to these assets."[46] During the winter of 1949–50, Neuville had to face a stark reality. The step between the political objective and its juridical achievement was huge: the evidentiary record of Maghrebi rights was so slim that the consul was reduced to asking the endowment steward for basic legal support documents. At the top of a letter dated 26 September 1949, an associate of Neuville's wrote in longhand: "Do we have a file? Does Mr. Neuville already have something?" thereby demonstrating the consular officers' relative bewilderment. The key to the issue was in effect the question of temporal precedence, both historically and legally, illustrating in the process a structuring feature of the contemporary history of Jerusalem.[47]

In Louis Massignon's Papers: The "Displaced Persons of Belief"

As evidenced by his ubiquity in the archival material that documents the French history of the Maghrebi Quarter, Louis Massignon (1883–1962) emerges as a key figure in this brief but intense sequence of the quarter's history. A close friend of René Neuville and a brilliant Islamologist, member of the Arabic Language Academy in Cairo, chair of the *aggregation* jury in Arabic, professor at the Collège de France, (chair of Muslim sociology and sociography), a fervent Christian but a fierce defender of "Franco-Muslim friendship," founder of the "Christian Committee for Franco-Islamic Understanding" and of the "Islamic-Christian Pilgrimage of the Seven Sleepers of Ephesus" in Brittany, and a man increasingly critical of the Zionist project, Massignon effectively emerged as the linchpin of this new diplomatic strategy.[48] Until his death in 1962, he tirelessly defended what he called "France's sacred mandate" toward the Maghrebis of Jerusalem, in his view the decisive element of a foreign policy that had to assert itself as not only "Arab" but "Muslim," to show Maghrebis lured by independence that France was tangibly concerned with their interests, including those outside the Maghreb.[49] Thus we find his tiny and progressively illegible handwriting, his increasingly crossed-out typescripts, his calling cards and signed publications disseminated throughout the French consular archives in Jerusalem, the Foreign Ministry archives at the Quai d'Orsay, and those of the Government General of Algiers (figure 27).

Massignon's personal archives, housed for a long time at his home, Rue Monsieur in Paris, were deposited in 2012 in the department of manuscripts at the National Library of France (BNF) and can now be consulted by appointment.[50] Through them, we better understand the intellectual origins of his commitment to the Maghrebis of Jerusalem, but we also grasp more deeply the overall logic of his action. Adjacent to files labeled "Maghrebi Waqfs of Palestine," for instance, there is an abundance of documents regarding the internationalization of the Holy Places or the refugee issue.[51] Newspaper clippings slipped into files also allow us a glimpse into Massignon's mindset. For instance, on 9 November 1949 he annotated an article from *Le Monde* titled "New Course of Action by Algerian Islam in Favor of the Internationalization of Jerusalem."[52] In the same files, there is an offprint of the article "Les Lieux saints: Le drame Palestinien" (The holy places: The Palestine crisis), published by his friend Jean Scelles (secretary of the Christian Committee for Franco-Islamic Understanding)[53] and envelopes full of photographs labeled "Palestine—Destructions 1949–1950," which he collected on-site.

Clearly, Massignon considered the Maghrebi Quarter to be a crucial factor in France's overall diplomatic strategy aimed at defending the internationalization of the Holy Places, based on the 1947 partition plan. This idea is again foregrounded by Jean Scelles in an article with an intentionally provocative title, "Du Mur des Lamentations au Wakf algérien" (From the Wailing Wall to the Algerian Waqf), written in October 1949 and published in the *Revue de la Méditerranée*: "Mr. Massignon has undertaken staunch action both to protect the Holy Places of the three great monotheistic religions and to keep

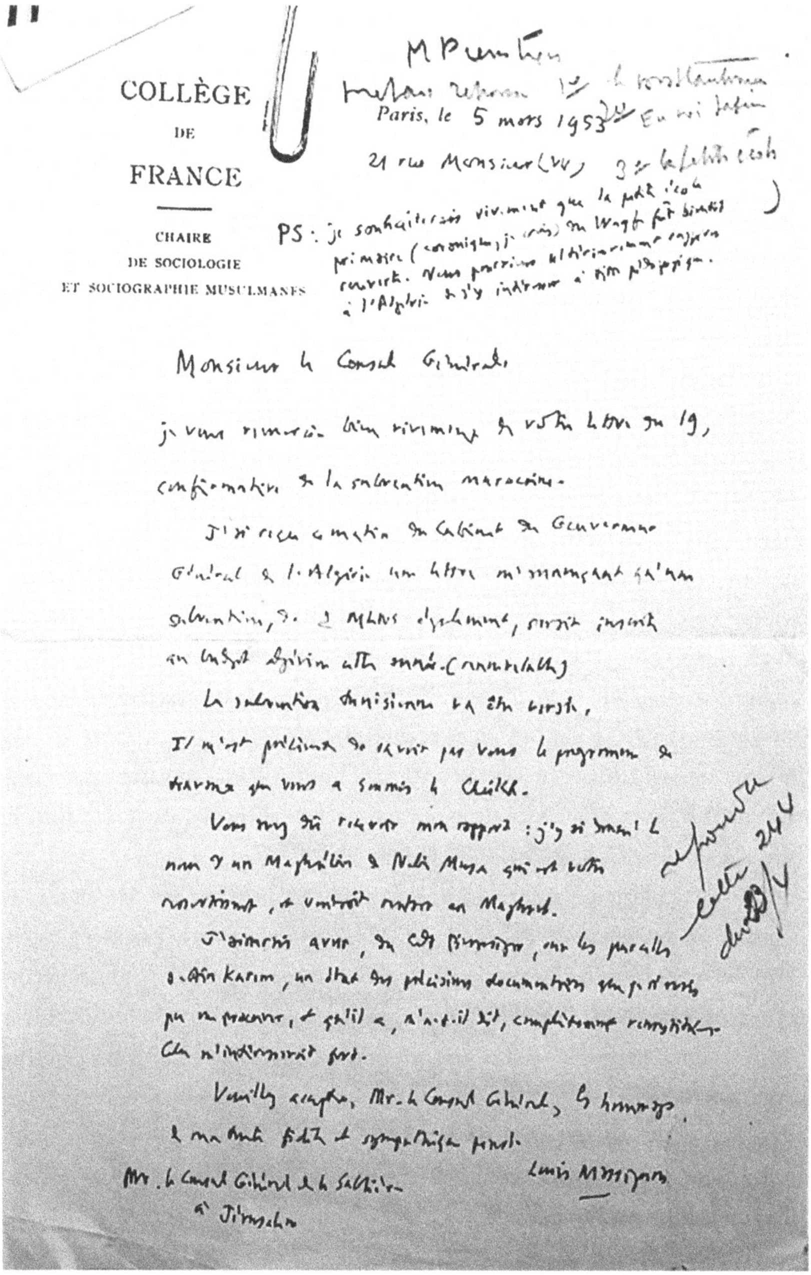
COLLÈGE
DE
FRANCE

CHAIRE
DE SOCIOLOGIE
ET SOCIOGRAPHIE MUSULMANES

Paris, le 5 mars 1953
21 rue Monsieur (VII)

PS : je souhaiterais vivement que la petite école primaire (coranique, je crois) du Waqf fût bientôt rouverte.

Monsieur le Consul Général,

je vous remercie bien vivement de votre lettre du 19, confirmation de la subvention marocaine.

J'ai reçu ce matin du Cabinet du Gouverneur Général de l'Algérie une lettre m'annonçant qu'une subvention, de 2 millions également, serait inscrite au budget algérien cette année (conditionnelle).

La subvention tunisienne va être versée.

Il m'est préliminaire de recevoir par vous le programme de travaux que vous a soumis le Cheikh.

Vous avez dû recevoir mon rapport : j'y ai donné le nom d'un Maghrébin de Nabi Musa qui est votre ressortissant, et voudrait rentrer au Maghreb.

J'aimerais avoir, du côté ..., sur les parcelles d'Ain Karim, un état des précisions documentaires ... et qu'il a, m'a-t-il dit, complètement reconstitué. Cela m'intéresserait fort.

Veuillez accepter, Mr. le Consul Général, les hommages de ma bien fidèle et sympathique pensée.

Louis Massignon

Mr. le Consul Général de la Sablière
à Jérusalem

FIGURE 27. **Letter from Louis Massignon to the French consul general in Jerusalem, Rochereau de La Sablière, 5 March 1953. Source: © CADN, Jerusalem, 294 PO/2, 37/1.**

refugees safe. Thus, in August 1949 [. . .] he was mandated by the Muslim Rescue Section of the Committee for the Defense of Palestine to both provide aid for Muslim refugees and protect those Algerian religious endowments of the Waqf Abu Madyan."[54] The inhabitants of the Maghrebi Quarter, who were at once exiles and stewards of a Muslim holy place, thus found themselves at the intersection of the two great causes defended by Massignon.

In the article he himself devotes to the religious endowment, and which he published in 1952 in the *Revue des études islamiques*, Massignon clearly expresses the connection between protecting the holy places and protecting the refugees: "The waqfs of the Holy Places of Islam, of its four 'Harams,' are the most significant, the ones that allow us to best grasp their essential role: to perpetuate the community in time and space, since they permit the maximal extension of the Hejir, the Hijra of voluntary expatriates."[55] According to Massignon, Islamic law offers pertinent legal support to address the issue of displaced populations, whether they be pilgrims (whom he calls the "displaced persons of belief"), war refugees, or even immigrant workers. To boost his cause, Massignon relies on "the judicial resources of ancient Semitic law, to restore less harsh and more humane international relations based on the notion of *right to asylum*, of *Amân* [safety], *Dhimma* [protection], and *Ikrâm al-Dayf* [hospitality], which safeguards the notion of hospitality for any unarmed guest, without discrimination, with no exceptions to it whatsoever, absolutely like the International Red Cross."[56]

This articulation between Islamic law and asylum law led Massignon to consider an extension of waqfs to non-Muslims (commonly practiced in the Ottoman context), an idea particularly well adapted to the decolonization context: "This extension of the Muslim notion of waqf to foreign establishments in Muslim countries might well be the object of a second expansion, of a genuine, universal internationalization of culturally valuable religious endowments, effectively neutralizing them in times of conflict and gradually exterritorializing in peacetime: universities and scientific research centers, art treasures and museums, hospitals and camps for the wounded, settlements of pilgrims and refugees, of displaced persons."[57] Forged at the very moment UNESCO was elaborating its own response programs,[58] these ideas shed light on the intellectual horizons within which Massignon was acting: the Maghrebi Quarter was a "settlement of pilgrims," its inhabitants "displaced persons of belief," and as such they should benefit from the protection that the international community afforded to all "culturally valuable religious endowments."

The ostensibly disparate elements of this ambitious thought process, combining moral, cultural, and geopolitical issues, are to be found among the files of the archives that Massignon created, and which are available for consultation today at the BNF: his handwritten notes about France as a "Muslim power"; the correspondence he maintained with Hajj Hamou, the court interpreter at the Algiers Court of Appeals who translated for him certain legal materials having to do with the Waqf Abu Madyan; drafts of a map of the Maghrebi Quarter that he surveyed by hand on-site; the distribution of 250 offprint copies of his article from the *REI* (50 copies for the French Embassy in Amman, 50 for the Jerusalem consulate, 50 for El-Okbi in Algiers).[59] All this material testifies to the "clout" of his contributions, which also aspired to move beyond communitarian boundaries. Thus, on 8 November 1950, Jean Scelles informed Neuville and Massignon "of action taken by Algerian Judaism in support of Algerian claims in Palestine" and wondered, more doubtfully, "How will it resonate?"[60] The previous spring, Massignon had asked the famous Algerian reformist ulema Tayeb El-Okbi—known for his stance in favor of the Algerian Jewish community under the Vichy regime—to visit the Maghrebi Quarter of Jerusalem. Once there, he was approached by Mohammed Aklil, the same person who had sent a denunciation letter to the consulate in March 1936, and who, it was learned in passing, had taken "refuge in Jenin."[61] It was not surprising to see Tayeb El-Okbi, in sympathy with the stance of Albert Camus for an autonomous Algeria that would remain in the French fold, take action to defend France's involvement with the Maghrebis of Jerusalem.

From the Western Wall to the Maghrebi Wall: The Political Stakes of an Etymology

From 15 December 1950 to 23 January 1951, Massignon undertook his "12th annual cultural mission" to the Middle East, and visited Egypt and Jordan. One need but read the table of contents of the report he drafted upon his return to sum up his state of mind as he forged his agenda: "a) evolution of the Mediterranean policy of Islamic-Christian rapprochement, between Egypt and Latin powers; b) Franco-Egyptian pedagogical relations and the Academic

Congress of 27 December 1950; c) the future of Franco-Arab culture and the training of those preparing an Arabic *aggregation* degree in France; d) the problem of Arab refugees and the international status of displaced persons; e) the safeguarding of the Algerian waqf Abu Madyan and the supranational character of the Holy Places."[62] Repeating over and over that "France must realize that it is a Muslim power," that "France should be giving pledges not of colonial defeatism but rather of cultural humanism," that it must "train a Muslim elite that is loyal to France," and that "it is nonsensical and mean to forbid pupils from speaking in Arabic during their playground breaks," Massignon first developed the themes he had held dear which corresponded strictly to the scope of his *cultural* mission: defense of the Arabic language in the Maghreb and in France, and promotion of interreligious exchanges with Muslim elites.[63]

That year, however, it was in fact the Maghrebi Quarter of Jerusalem as paradigm of a "supranational holy place" that took up most of Massignon's report, no fewer than five pages out of twelve. Addressing a range of recipients at the Quai d'Orsay, mostly unfamiliar with the issues at stake, Massignon began by recalling that "the Tlemcenian waqf (*thus Algerian, thus French*) of the village of Ein Karem is by far the most important" of the Maghrebi waqfs in Palestine.[64] Further on, he specified that "the mutewalli, in keeping with the endowment's charter, is always a Maghrebi, *and therefore a French national*," acting as if he did not know the differences in status between the categories of inhabitants in Algeria itself.[65]

Massignon next pointed out that due to "British opposition," France had not succeeded in effectively defending the religious endowment during that Mandatory period: "From 1920 to 1928, the Mandatory power allowed the Keren Khayemeth [KKL] to purchase from the waqf's Arab sharecroppers tracts of land they were only farming and did not own, and to settle kibbutzim." The ultimate break occurred at the time of the first Arab-Israeli war: "In 1948, the Israeli army had little trouble expelling the Arab fellahs, as well as the Christian Arabs, from the village (I saw some in Bethlehem, in Amman, in refugee camps, during my previous visits) and settling kibbutzim on all the waqf land [...]. The endowment has lost two-thirds of its revenue at least since 1948." Once he had laid out this diagnosis, Massignon summarized the reasons that should impel France to get involved in this issue:

In the midst of all these claims, France has the duty to defend the Waqf Abu Madyan: first because this gives it an *axial* arbitration position between Israel and Islam (Jordan); since this waqf enjoys not only joint ownership but also access to ground level and the pavement of the famous *Kotel Maaravi* (Hebrew name for the Wailing Wall, where "Maaravi" = Maghrebis, because of the Tlemcen waqf), upon which, subsequent to violent incidents, the royal British decree of 19 May 1931 acknowledged, with Jewish usufruct and easement, the right to ownership of our Tlemcenian waqf.[66]

The geopolitical demonstration outlined by Neuville a few months previously was now rendered more explicit as penned by Massignon: by protecting the Maghrebi Quarter, France would recover an "axial arbitration position"— the term is a powerful one—in current or future negotiations "between Israel and Islam." Largely marginalized up to this point, the French Consulate in Jerusalem could hereby get back into the thick of the diplomatic fray by instrumentalizing what Massignon called "the right to ownership of *our* Tlemcenian waqf" on the most sacred prayer site of Judaism. In passing—and parenthetically—Professor Massignon slipped in his own etymological interpretation of the Hebrew place-name "Kotel Maaravi." In his view, the name should not be translated as "Western Wall," with reference to the tradition of the western wall of the Temple, but rather as the "Westerners' Wall"—or, even more literally, the "Maghrebis' Wall," since the two terms "Maghrebis" and "Westerners" were effectively synonyms, whether in Hebrew or in Arabic.

This etymological power play was not without scientific basis, since the settling of Maghrebi pilgrims in this area effectively dates back to the late twelfth century, while the Jewish enshrinement of the Wall dates only to the sixteenth century.[67] Historical anteriority is thus claimed by the Maghrebis, and could thus solidify the hypothesis of an anterior "Maghrebi" etymology, subsequently covered over by later "Jewish" etymology, as is quite common in the intermingled history of shared holy places.[68] Beyond the scholarly debate, it is Massignon's deployment of the issue that should be highlighted: the Islamologist brings to bear the full weight of his scientific authority to serve a political demonstration, a tactic he would use again in his article published the following year by the *Revue des études islamiques*: "The Kotel ha-Maaravi ('Western,' the Hebrew translation of 'Maghāriba,' Maghrebis)."[69]

After justifying the French intervention plan by citing the geopolitical situation in Jerusalem, Massignon tackles the second component of his
demonstration, which relates to the political situation in Algeria: "We know
that in 1947, the French government, cognizant of its centuries-old duty to
protect the Christian Holy Places, and particularly the endowments founded
there for French Catholic pilgrims, felt that it was bound to *equally* ensure the
safeguarding of endowments founded there for French Muslim pilgrims; and
it made this point to its United Nations delegate, within the framework of the
internationalization that it was seeking."[70] It was thus the political climate
in Algeria as well that motivated Massignon, who also referred to the new
Algerian statute of 1947 according to which Muslim worship henceforth must
receive treatment equal to that of other faiths.

Finally, Massignon recalls that Robert Schuman, during a visit to Paris
by the Grand Mufti of Algiers, made a public commitment to "safeguard the
religious patrimony of Muslims on an equal footing with that of Jews and
Christians."[71] Massignon speaks even more directly when he observes that his
plan has met with "the comprehensive sympathy of the Governor General of
Algiers, concerned by anti-France exploitation by the dissident ulemas under
the leadership of Sheikh Brahimi of the 'double Palestinian question,' the Holy
Places and the Arab refugees." It is thus to counter the rise of independence
movements in Algeria that France must intervene in favor of the Maghrebis of
Jerusalem, because, Massignon concludes, "Algerian Islam would not forgive
our allowing this distinguished religious endowment to be wrested from its
hands without defending the cause of our Muslim citizenry."

To evaluate the endowment's financial resources and needs, Massignon got
in touch with the Supreme Muslim Council, in charge of managing the waqfs
since its creation in 1921. In response, on 7 January 1951, its president Amin
Abdul-Hadi sent him the following assessment:

> Attached is a statement of Maghrebi waqf assets with their 1947 revenues
> listed, and what they amounted to in 1950. These revenues amounted to 1,063
> dinars; they have now fallen to 383 dinars. This decrease is due to damage
> caused to buildings from the 1948 bombings and to the situation of certain
> properties in the Israeli zone. The waqf revenue is all used in the interest of
> the rightful Maghrebi beneficiaries, either for meals when necessary or during

holidays, or to pay paltry stipends to the neediest among them, to the Imam, to the muezzin and to the second mutewalli, Sheikh Mohammed Al-Mouhdi, as well as to cover costs of burying the dead and repairing certain properties.[72]

Cited here once again are the charitable acts required by the founding charter (meals, alms, burials), but this report gives evidence especially of the serious financial crisis triggered by the loss of Ein Karem. Further on, the Supreme Muslim Council precludes its coverage of the endowment's deficit, thereby implicitly acknowledging the legitimacy of France's intervention. The indulgence of the local authorities toward France was confirmed on 24 February 1951 when, "in response to a petition presented (with the backing of the Consulate General) by some fifty members of the North African colony, the Qadi of Jerusalem has just approved the appointment of Hajj Hidoussi Ali Mohammed Saleh, nakib of the Zawiya Abu Madyan (Algerian), as the second mutewalli of the Maghrebi waqfs, replacing the administrative officer of the waqfs."[73] The French intervention seemed on its way to materializing. But the dissolution of the Supreme Muslim Council on 1 May 1951 tempered Neuville's optimism and presaged that a new rivalry would arise with Amman: "King Abdallah's new measure appears to belong to his plan to assimilate Arab Palestine [. . .], with oversight of financial management of the waqfs reverting to Amman and the Sharia Courts returning to the fold of the High Jordanian Judge."[74] The political conditions of France's intervention in favor of the Maghrebis of Jerusalem thus needed to be placed in the broader context of the Hashemite power's defiance of the Palestinian elites, further intensified by the assassination of King Abdallah at the Haram al-Sharif on 20 July 1951.[75] Henceforth, the French consul in Jerusalem knew he would have to contend with a fastidious Jordanian administration wary of any form of meddling that could contest its authority in Jerusalem. It is also against this backdrop that we need to understand the decision to organize a tour of the Maghreb for the endowment's new steward in the spring of 1952.

Colonial Archives and Mobilization of the Union Française

To document how the French colonies in the Maghreb were mobilized in favor of the Waqf Abu Madyan, one has to visit the Archives nationales d'Outre-Mer

(ANOM), France's archives of its history overseas. Created in the aftermath of Algerian decolonization and established in 1966 in Aix-en-Provence, this archive notably preserves the holdings of the Ministry of Algerian Affairs.[76] In the "Political Affairs" series, subsubseries "Muslim Faith," we find the file box (call number 81.F-844) labeled "Waqf Abu Madyan of Jerusalem, financing, Algerian Assembly subsidy, study mission reports, notes, correspondence, real estate litigation," covering the period 1951–63.[77] It contains nineteen folders organized in basically chronological order, with a few overlaps. Amid this material, not surprisingly, we find two (annotated) copies of the article Massignon published in the *Revue des études islamiques*. The Islamologist was very much in the forefront of the action, and it was his mobilization that kicked off this new sequence, which saw Algeria, Morocco, and Tunisia intervene in the attempt to save the Maghrebi Quarter of Jerusalem. Although Tunisia and Morocco, as we shall see, were quick to step away from the issue once their respective countries had declared independence, French Algeria remained at the heart of the proceeding for much longer. Two years after El-Okbi's trip from Algiers to Jerusalem, it was now the turn of the endowment steward to make the same trip in reverse, from Jerusalem to Algiers. On 25 April 1952 the cabinet of the governor general of Algeria wrote to the Quai d'Orsay:

> Mr. Hidoussi Ali Ben Mohammed Salah (nakib of the "zawiya Abou Medi-ene" also called the "Maghrebi Zawiya" of Jerusalem, and mutewalli of this establishment) [...] arrived on our premises on 10 April, bearing a letter from Mr. Neuville, recommending him to the authorities of Algeria, France and Morocco. He described the difficult situation of the Maghrebis in Palestine who number, it seems, around 2,000 [...]. Sheikh El-Okbi, whom he met two years ago on the trip the latter made to Palestine under the auspices of the "Franco-Islamic Committee," is able to host him at the *Cercle du Progrès*, but cannot underwrite him financially, as his own works are barely subsisting. In such conditions, Mr. Hidoussi is soliciting a major subsidy from Algeria and is considering trips to Tunis and Rabat to make the same request.[78]

If this missive hardly bubbles with enthusiasm, it does testify to the enduring material and spiritual ties among the Maghrebi populations residing in Palestine with their countries of origin. On 13 June 1952, the Muslim Faith Commission of the Algerian Assembly did address the issue, and a statement by one of the deputies shows that the French authorities of Algiers actually were under tremendous pressure, despite what they might say: "Mr. Cadi considers the Assembly's action too timid; since we are talking here about Muslim and North African assets located in Israeli territory, we could, if need be, take action in reprisal against Israeli assets of the same kind located in North Africa; Mr. Cadi specifies that he is intervening on behalf of 400,000 Algerian combatants."[79] On 17 June 1952, the Algerian Assembly adopted a resolution revising the text voted six months earlier by the Union Française, adding the explicit demand for immediate financial backing."[80]

The initiative undertaken by the endowment steward thus scored a first victory, even though an article published a few months later by *Le Jeune Musulman*, a news outlet run by the association of Algerian ulemas, showed that the subject was still a sensitive one: "By virtue of what right can the French government, which has yet to restitute the stolen Hubus in Algeria, claim to protect the Abu Madyan Hubus in Jerusalem?"[81] On 20 August, the cabinet of the governor general of Algeria informed the Quai d'Orsay that a defense committee for the Waqf Abu Madyan had been formed in Tlemcen, and Massignon's personal archives reveal that it was "in the office of the sub-prefect of Tlemcen" that the founding meeting of this committee took place on 17 May, which confirms that the mobilization of the so-called "moderate" Muslim elites was indeed part of a political strategy deliberately assumed by the French authorities.[82] On 30 August the Quai d'Orsay asked that Algiers consider making subsidies available following the vote by the Algerian Assembly.[83] As it happened, in order to get aid from Algiers, Massignon purposely organized a kind of sponsorship competition with Morocco and Tunisia, as evidenced by the letter addressed by his friend Jean Scelles to the minister of the interior in early October 1952:

I do hereby ask a contribution by France to the safeguarding of the Maghrebi endowment "Waqf Abu Madyan" in Jerusalem, to conclude the trip made by Sheikh Hidoussi Hajj Ali, steward of this endowment, who traveled to North Africa from March to October and is now in France for this same purpose [. . .]. [In Rabat] His Majesty Sidi Youssef took interest in this charitable foundation, seven centuries old, and disbursed a donation from his personal accounts. Elsewhere, the Hubus service also decided upon an annual grant of two thousand. His Majesty Sidi Lamine did likewise for Tunisia and held private talks with the mutewalli […]. France, a great Muslim power exercising sovereignty over Algeria, must not fall short.[84]

On 22 October, Jean Scelles added, rather shrewdly, still addressing the minister of the interior, that "the French Muslims of Palestine, uninformed as they are of our budgetary rules, would likely fail to understand why we are taking so long to accomplish what their fellow Muslims of Afghanistan and Pakistan have already achieved for their countrymen in Palestine, and whose Hubus have met the same fate as that of our North Africans" (figure 28).[85] In addition to a Maghreb-wide competition, a world-scale competition was being staged, based on an equation that was difficult to challenge: if France wished to keep hold of its colonies, it had to provide tangible proof that it was still "a great Muslim power" and that it could fight on equal footing with other emerging Muslim powers such as Pakistan or Afghanistan. On 21 October an unsigned report, handwritten on Ministry of the Interior stationery, indicated that the message had hit home: "Nothing has been done thus far by Algeria in favor of the Palestine Hubus. Morocco and Tunisia are believed to have given 2 million each, for a total of 4 million […]. It is surely in the national interest that the French citizens of Algeria residing in Palestine be provided assistance."[86] What was leveraged by Scelles and Massignon throughout this sequence, in fact, went beyond mere political and administrative circles, since we find, for instance, in the archives of the Algiers Archdiocese a handwritten letter from Madame Jeanne Scelles-Millie to Archbishop Duval, dated 8 April 1952, with regard to the visit by Sheikh Hidoussi, who had "come from Jerusalem to beg in North Africa."[87] In total, this six-month tour proved a success, as summed up by Jean Scelles in a warm-hearted letter to Hidoussi in the form of an assessment:

> As you leave France and make your way home to Jerusalem after a very long absence […] I can assure you that it was well worth your time […]. By the grace of God, you return guaranteed of contributions from Morocco and Tunisia, whose bequests will amount annually to 4 million. A personal gift of the Sultan from his royal funds has been pledged, and another from President Robert Schuman. I await the reply of the Minister of the Interior as to the Franco-Algerian contribution […]. You thus return to Jerusalem having fulfilled the wish of the late Consul General Mr. Neuville [who died on 23 June 1952]."[88]

Sheikh Hidoussi's tour was finally written up in a long conclusive report drafted by Jeanne Scelles-Millie.[89] As others before her had done, she emphasized the geopolitical stakes of the issue when she highlighted that "the zawiyas of Afghanistan and of Pakistan present in Jerusalem have sent delegates to their respective countries to be aided and replenished, and they succeeded in doing

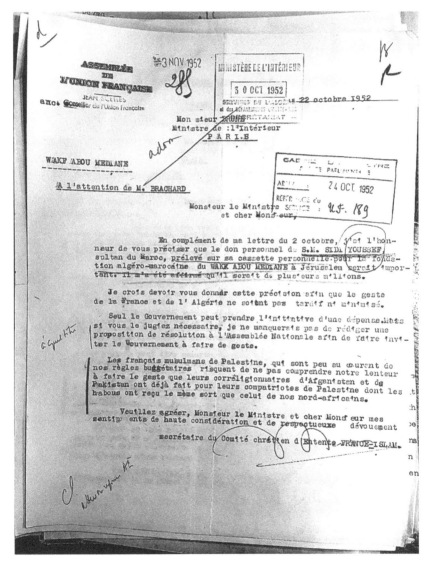

FIGURE 28. Letter from Jean Scelles to the minister of the interior, 22 October 1952. Source: ANOM, 81.F-844.

so." She reported that Hidoussi went to Tlemcen "to pay his respects at the tomb of Saint Abou Mediene," but also went "to the Aurès, to his land of origin at Oued Abdin, in the township of Aris, a village he had left when he headed to the Middle East when he was 20; the Caïd of Oued Abdin Mr. Khalifa Khalif held a grand celebration in his honor; he learned of the deaths of close relatives but also met his nephews and cousins." She emphasized that ties between the Maghrebis of Jerusalem and their regions of origin were still alive and well. The narrative of his visit to Paris shows that the Waqf Abu Madyan was indeed considered an important matter, since Hidoussi was given a presidential welcome at the Elysée Palace on 2 October and was received at the Grand Mosque of Paris the same day. Scelles-Millie, who shared the "moderate progressive" ideas of her husband with regard to France's colonial territories, concluded her report with a broader political perspective: "The political circumstances of this trip were challenging in North Africa, where certain parties had to be humored, but equally challenging is the climate of opinion among Muslims right now in all three countries, two of which (Morocco and Tunisia) are making demands in the midst of turmoil."[90] On 23 August, an article titled "The Abu Madyan Hubus in Danger" was published in the Moroccan newspaper *Es-Saada*, confirming the sensitivity of the issue and focusing on the fact that "Jews are depriving the Hubus of its main revenues."[91]

A School, Bread and Sacks of Cement

After the return of Sheikh Hidoussi to Jerusalem, it was time for his benefactors to make good on the donations they had promised during his tour. For that, the new French Consul Rochereau de La Sablière (1952–55) spared no effort and drafted several alarmist letters throughout the autumn and winter of 1952–53. On 5 November he drafted a long report in which he estimated the number of Maghrebis in the old city of Jerusalem at around 700, with 200 in Jericho, 75 in Hebron, 60 in Bethlehem, 50 in Ramallah, 50 in Gaza, some 15 in Latrun, and 10 or so in Nablus, for a total of about 1,200.[92] He stressed that the zawiya of Jerusalem, "in serious disrepair," its "walls permeated with saltpeter," hosted more than four hundred pilgrims every year, "on their way back from Mecca, or on a stopover on their way there," who "sleep on flagstones covered with mats, old carpets or rags," with "a few utensils allowing them to cook their food." He observed that the quarter's health conditions were "deplorable" even though its inhabitants enjoyed "consultations free of charge with the chief physician at the French Hospital," and that the water supply had been cut because the endowment was "too poor to pay the Municipality the fees it owed," which meant that the residents had to purchase sixteen-liter containers of water sold at "one piaster, or 10 francs." Finally, despite a few jobs as "day workers, night watchmen at garages or worksites," joblessness was endemic, which led to a certain "loosening of morals" within the quarter, though "no cases of prostitution were found among the women."[93]

Concluding that the Maghrebis of Jerusalem "display dignity and base their hope in France's protection," the consul reported on a situation that seemed to have considerably worsened since the Ottoman and Mandatory periods.[94] On 6 January 1953, he indicated that he had gone to the scene and had "visited the main buildings in need of repair"; he once again stressed "the state of disrepair of virtually all the waqf houses," and explained that "if the drop in revenues due to the Israeli occupation of the village of Ein Karem, the waqf's chief source of income, is the main cause of its poor upkeep, we can also blame the mismanagement of Sheikh Hidoussi's predecessors, when the Waqf Abu Madyan was placed under the general waqfs management and the Supreme Muslim Council."[95] This reduced stewardship autonomy during the Mandate period and the loss of Ein Karem in 1948 were indeed the two basic reasons why living conditions worsened in the Maghrebi Quarter.

Within this challenging context, we can well understand that the influx of pledged subsidies would amount to a much-needed shot in the arm. Six million francs (or six thousand Jordanian dinars) were disbursed via the consulate to the endowment in early 1953, on the basis of three subsidies of two million each from Morocco, Tunisia, and Algeria. On 23 April 1953, the French Consulate sent to Paris the first reports drafted by Hidoussi to list details of how the money was being spent:

> In compliance with the wish expressed by His Sharifian Majesty, virtually all of the Moroccan subsidy is being used to help the needy and to distribute bread, according to wafq stipulations, to the Maghrebis of Jerusalem during the three months of Rajab, Chaabane, and Ramadan. This distribution, at the rate of 400 gr. per person per day, will represent the sum of 588 Jordanian

dinars [...]. The Tunisian subsidy, which has just been disbursed to the waqf, will be used to restore a house located in the former Jewish Quarter of the old city which, once renovated, will yield income for the waqf; to repair and furnish the school and the zawiya; and finally, to provide relief for the needy and to serve them a meal on the holidays of Eid el-Fitr, Eid el-Kebir, and the Birthday of the Prophet, as prescribed by Sheikh Abu Madyan."[96]

If it is rather startling to find translated into accounting terms the requirements formulated by the founder from a distance of several centuries, it is equally interesting to remark the nuances that distinguish the donors' requests, with a clear priority granted by the sultan of Morocco to charitable spending (recurrent expenditures), while the Tunisian subsidy is used more for renovation work (notably the school)—in other words, investment expenditures. This requirement had been explicitly transmitted by the resident general in Rabat, who reiterated in November 1952 the need to spend the Moroccan subsidy "on the needy [...] rather than on restoration work on the buildings still in the hands of the waqf."[97] At any rate, this fresh influx of funds allowed for urgent repairs on buildings "for which the municipality of Jerusalem has issued a formal notice to promptly consolidate." A handwritten note slipped into the consular archives, written by Hidoussi, draws up (in dinars) a "statement of expenses for the restoration of the Abu Madyan zawiya and of a house in the Maghrebi Quarter: 50 sacks of cement (42.5 dinars); 42 m³ of gravel (63 dinars); 1.2 of lime for whitewash (42 dinars); 15 m³ of water (1.8 dinars); one foreman at 0.7 dinars per day, 1 foreman at 0.5 dinars per day, 9 laborers at 1.8 dinars per day (43.5 dinars) = 192.8 dinars."[98]

In August 1953 the Algerian subsidy replenished the endowment's coffers, and one year later, in August 1954, Hidoussi drafted a new expenditures report, adding one decisive piece of information: "The needy pilgrims passing through Jerusalem were all supplied free of charge with bread and pocket money during their entire stay here. Travel expenses from Jerusalem to Amman were also covered. I should point out that the number of pilgrims this year was very high (about 600). By way of example, for the period of 12 June to 25 July 1954, 135 pilgrims, of whom 125 Moroccans, showed up at the zawiya."[99] On the flip side, although Hidoussi's tour of the Maghreb did raise unprecedented funds, it also raised the profile of the endowment, leading to an increased number of visitors, and consequently a spike in expenses. At any rate, the figures supplied by Hidoussi (six hundred pilgrims over the course of a year) and the details he gives about the aid provided (bread, cash, travel expenses) show that the foundation created in 1320 was still fulfilling its role in the mid-1950s.

Beyond its material usefulness, the political scope of the activity undertaken was clearly foregrounded by the French Consulate when in early October 1953 it dispatched three messages simultaneously to Tunis, Algiers, and Rabat to inform them that "talks" had just been initiated with "the Government of Tel Aviv" regarding the "plundered" land parcels of Ein Karem, but that, owing to the proceeding's foreseeable time frame, it was asking them to renew their subsidy.[100] To substantiate his request, the consul emphasized that aid granted thus far had produced "certain effects over the last few months at the political level" by strengthening the "loyalty of the North Africans of Jerusalem," even though "the unrest stoked by the local committee of the 'Friends of the Arab Maghreb' [. . .] would make Jerusalem, in the days to come, a hub of public opinion directed against France." In this uneasy political context, while independence movements were steadily gaining ground, the consul asserted that this "tangible token of France's protection" had already proven its "effectiveness."[101]

Louis Massignon, in a report he drafted at the same time following his fourteenth annual cultural mission, also stressed the political impact of these subsidies. Under a hopeful heading ("The first achievements secured for the Algerian Muslim waqf Abu Madyan in Jerusalem"), he first listed the actions already undertaken, before spelling out what he believed were the more long-term objectives of this French restoration of the religious endowment:

> The funds raised will make it possible to repatriate certain Maghrebis now hospitalized at the waqf (notably the Constantine native Darraji, who has worked for 20 years at the Nebi Musa mosque on the road to Jericho: he expressed his desire to do so back on the 25th). Nevertheless, we should refrain from emptying the waqf of guests and stranded pilgrims who are basically its reason for being as a religious hostel at a pilgrimage site. On this subject, I demand forthwith that, as before, we have certain of our Muslim North African pilgrims make their way to Jerusalem and Hebron, the 3rd and 4th most sacred sites of Islam, upon their return from the annual pilgrimage of the first two most sacred sites, Mecca and Medina.[102]

Massignon was therefore justifying the granting of subsidies to revitalize the Muslim pilgrimages in Palestine and to reassert France's role as imperial Muslim power. Anxious not to allow Saudi Arabia—broadly in the British and North American sphere of influence—to monopolize the direction of the pilgrimages, Massignon thus ranked political and cultural influence at the top of his concerns, differing on this point with the wishes expressed by the governor general of Algeria, who had pled on several occasions for a partial repatriation of Jerusalem's Algerians back to Algeria, possibly with the help of the UN Relief and Works Agency for Palestine Refugees in the Near East (UNRWA). This same notion of a strategy of influence, both French *and* Muslim, shows up in a handwritten note that Massignon adds, on Collège de France letterhead, for the attention of the consul: "I would strongly hope that the little primary school (Koranic, I believe) of the waqf will soon be reopened. We could later suggest to Algeria that they get invested pedagogically."

This focus on education issues is a persistent feature with Massignon, who remarked that the inhabitants of the Maghrebi Quarter had lost their command of French—as we can observe upon analysis of the petitions regularly addressed to the consulate, whether to deplore the seriousness of the situation, to support the steward, or conversely, to complain about him, as is the case in this nearly incomprehensible handwritten petition drafted in Arabic, translated into French on 11 August 1953, and signed by twenty-one inhabitants of the quarter (figure 29): "Hajj Ali Nakib it is not good for the people of North African, for example, a sick man he doesn't give nothing and he doesn't help, he stays. And he doesn't visit, because that Hajj Ali now like a Lord [. . .] because he does it benevolently."[103] On 13 August a counter-petition was signed by seventeen inhabitants in support of the steward ("We have never seen anyone care for our interests better than he has"), but this time it was written in Arabic and then translated and typed in French by a scrivener.[104] Massignon's obsession with linguistic issues can also be explained by his concern over the English gaining ground in the Middle East, a process he compared to the rise of Pakistani waqfs in Jerusalem. He went so far as to seek intelligence from the legal counsel of the Waqf Abu Madyan, Hassan al-Budeiri, who replied on 9 May 1953 that "contrary to what you may have been told, that waqf is neither financed nor operated by the Pakistani government; like the Waqf Abu Madyan, it is independent, managed by the Sheikh of the Indians, Munir Ansari."[105] In the world city of Jerusalem, transnational religious endowments were indeed bases—whether proven or imagined—of the new imperial rivalries.

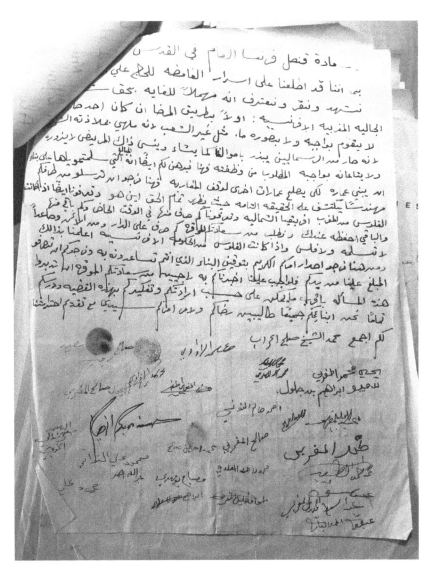

FIGURE 29. **Draft of petition handwritten in Arabic, 11 August 1953. Source: © CADN,** Jerusalem, 294 PO/2, 37/2.

An Airlift between Jerusalem and the Maghreb

In the early 1950s, visits increased between the Middle East's Holy City and the diverse communities of the Muslim West. After the protracted inaugural mission of Sheikh Hidoussi from Jerusalem to the Maghreb and Paris in 1952, several missions in the other direction followed in succession, generally shorter but no less significant. On Saturday 19 September 1953, Tunisian Minister of Justice Sadok Djaziri arrived in Jerusalem "accompanied by his wife, on a flight coming from Cairo [. . .], for an in-depth visit to the Maghrebi Quarter and in particular the zawiya," as indicated by a consular report, which specifies that the Tunisian minister took advantage of this trip to visit "our national Domain of Saint Ann," the next afternoon before leaving the same day for "the Kalandia airport to fly back to Cairo."[106] The visit also took on a political significance with Tunisian public opinion, as shown by the minister's declaration to the Arab Information Agency: "Alluding to the plaza that surrounds the Wailing Wall, and which belongs to the Maghrebi waqf, S.E. said: 'We will authorize the Jews to use it so long as they respect the terms of our waqfiya, but should they violate those terms, our government will take the necessary measures.'"[107] In the same vein, Djaziri made it known via the media that he had granted "a personal donation of 40 dinars" toward the restoration of the Dome of the Rock.

In the report he drafted upon his return, Djaziri highlighted the uniqueness of Tunisia's contribution compared to that of Algeria and Morocco: "If the funds allotted by the other territories have been used to relieve the Maghrebis who have lost their jobs due to events in Palestine, ours, totaling two million, have been channeled in large part toward restoring certain buildings [. . .]. I personally witnessed the repairs at a meeting with Maghrebis in the restored zawiya, where I provided lunch for everyone, at my own expense."[108] Beyond the paternalistic rhetoric, what we perceive here are two Maghrebi states moving toward independence—Tunisia and Morocco—attempting to differentiate their contributions in order to showcase them to their respective constituencies. The minister also takes advantage of his brief stay to profile the Tunisian community of Jerusalem, and this allows for a better glimpse of the quarter's social reality:

The North African colony of Jerusalem includes some one hundred members of Tunisian origin. Among them they make up a dozen or so family groupings, including one household of fourteen persons and two of twelve. The other families have at least two children. In the largest family (ten girls and two boys), the father is jobless. Ten boys in another family are being raised by a widow [. . .]. Most Tunisian families have been settled in Palestine for a generation or more, which explains their commitment to this country despite the turmoil and the economic slump it has experienced. The men get work only on an irregular basis, mostly as day laborers on construction sites. Some have started small, rather unprofitable businesses, such as the head of a large family who sells lime-based products for whitewashing walls [. . .]. A dozen waqf dwellings are occupied by Tunisian families who pay no rent. Four Tunisian bachelors live in the zawiya. Sheikh Hiddousi is having a hard time meeting the colony's educational needs in Arabic and French.[109]

One might well have imagined the Maghrebi Quarter inhabited by a few pious, ailing elders, but what appears here is a lively neighborhood with children and large families, accurately illustrating this Arab world of waning colonial empires within which people circulate and settle for a few years or a few generations, all the while preserving the identity of their country of origin. In the end, the Tunisians of Jerusalem appear torn between two cultures, one transnational and imperial in the process of dissolution, and the other an emerging national Tunisian culture. Concluding his report, Djaziri writes, "These Tunisians are reluctant to accept being repatriated, and to do so they require a formal guarantee that they be resettled in their country of origin," while making the point that "the children of all these Tunisian families were born in this country [Palestine]," which compels them to formulate this median position, according to which "it seems more practical to supply them with temporary assistance where they currently live than to meet their demand for a formal guarantee."[110]

According to the Quai d'Orsay, the political success of Djaziri's visit confirmed the project's relevance and encouraged the Foreign Ministry in late December 1953 to ask Algiers "to entrust a similar mission, on the occasion of the upcoming pilgrimage to the Holy Places of Islam, to a figure who would represent the Governor General of Algeria."[111] As Sheikh El-Okbi was unwell, the role fell to Ahmed Kirèche, an *agrégé* professor of Arabic at the lycée in Blida, heartily recommended by Massignon. On 11 June 1954, the Ministry of the Interior sent the Quai d'Orsay an individual briefing report on "KIRECHE Ahmed Ben Hajj Benellès, called 'Djedou' or BENDJEDOU," born 20 October 1906 in Bou-Saâda [...]. Married to a daughter of the Algerian bourgeoisie [...]. *Agrégé* in Arabic in 1953 [...]. Calm and studious [...]. Political leanings: faithful friend of Sheikh Tayeb EL-OKBI. Shares the latter's views: nonsectarian reformist."[112] This document, for all its mundaneness, testifies to the rising political tensions in Algeria, since Massignon's recommendation could no longer preclude a preliminary inquiry. On 17 June a mission brief was finally drafted "whose objective is to strengthen the interests of the North African *départements* for the Tlemcen waqf Abu Madyan and to establish ties between the Algerian colony of Jerusalem and its territory of origin."[113] On the mission brief held in the archives of the Jerusalem Consulate, the consul added in the margins: "Ties with families. Look for families. Funds for the unallied."[114]

Ahmed Kirèche left Algiers on 6 July, "overland, all the way to Cairo," and from there accomplished a multiweek pilgrimage to Mecca before going to Jerusalem, from 24 to 29 August, on the way home. In addition to his inspection mission, Kirèche was also entrusted with handing over to the endowment steward the sum of 78,000 francs, the result of a fund-raising effort organized in Tlemcen by the "Committee for the Defense of the Sidi Abou Mediene Waqfs in Palestine," recently created at the instigation of the imam of the mosque of Tlemcen.[115] In Massignon's personal archives there is a nominative list of all the donors to that fund-raising campaign, from the fabric merchant and the butcher to the innkeeper—a tangible testimony to this renewal of ties between Jerusalem and the Maghreb.[116] The lengthy mission report that Kirèche drafted upon his return suggests an impression of optimism, at any rate, as if the worst was behind them:

> Our first visit was to the zawiya which forms the core of the Waqf Abu Madyan. We were welcomed by the mutewalli, Sheikh Hidoussi Hajj Ali, whom we had met two years earlier at the Circle of Progress in Algiers. Pleased to receive us, he was joined by some twenty other Maghrebis, whose faces conveyed their joy [...]. Sheikh Al-Mahdi, a venerable seventy-year-old elder, joined the group a short while later [...]. We were served Turkish coffee on

the terrace, after which we visited the mosque of the zawiya; a group of young people bid us to come over to their circle [...] to present to us their athletic and cultural programs. We made a donation of a few dinars toward the purchase of soccer balls [...]. We were able to see firsthand the repair work on several houses, which will guarantee substantial income for the colony or will allow its members to be decently housed. Other repairs are underway. In this regard, Hidoussi Hajj Ali's activities are limitless; he is in the process of tearing down old hovels to rebuild them, ensuring they be clean and habitable.[117]

Beyond the slightly pompous style of the Arabic *agrégé*, this heartfelt testimony shows that the subsidies received the previous year had triggered a genuine *restoration* of the endowment, materially, morally, and legally, as indicated by another excerpt from the report: "Mr. Pierrestiger presented us with lengthy documentation on the waqf's assets and on all the steps taken to compensate the North African refugees."[118] Kirèche then proceeded to the inauguration of the new classroom, where Hidoussi imparted "a few rudimentary notions of French and Arabic, taking turns with another instructor, awaiting someone better qualified." When he then made his way to the "North African Philanthropic Club" hosted by the neighborhood youth, Kirèche was overcome with emotion when they recited "a welcome in verse form," and he expressed how he felt the "solid bonds" that connected them all to him.[119]

Likewise, when Kirèche came upon Nabi Musa on the road to Jericho, the old caretaker, "native of M'sila, a locality only seventy kilometers from where we live," mentioned that "since we know his brother Ma'youf Ahmed in Bou-Saâda, he gave us a letter for him."[120] Kirèche repeatedly emphasized how many letters he was entrusted to deliver to relatives back in Algeria, and at the end of his report he noted that his visit had "nurtured many friendships," to the point that he continued to receive "letters every day from them, asking us for news of everyone after the Orléansville earthquake [10 September 1954]."[121] Even if it is likely that Kirèche sought to project the most positive image possible of the ties established between Jerusalem and Algeria, the concrete examples he reports do tend to demonstrate that the actions engaged in since 1949 were beginning to produce tangible results: the renovated houses in the Maghrebi Quarter, the young people of the neighborhood taking part in a collective project, and the reactivated ties with the Maghreb (figures 30 and 31).

FIGURE 30. View of the Maghrebi Quarter, looking south, mid-1950s. Source: © EBAF.

FIGURE 31. The streets and plots of the Maghrebi Quarter in the early 1950s. Source: Map by F. J. Salmon, updated in 1947.

———

This same impression of optimism emanates from the report drafted a few months earlier by Massignon: "Since my visit in January 1954, restoration work has proceeded apace thanks to the continuation of the three North African subsidies. A shop located across from the Muslim orphanage is being rented to them by the waqf for its exhibit space [...]. Two toilet facilities have been set up in front of the (Buraq) Mosque wall [...]. The mosque is well-kept and the muezzin is on duty."[122] The investment had paid off, to Massignon's great pleasure, for now the argument could be made to renew the subsidies. In hindsight, however, the optimism emerging from these reports seems more like a kind of swan song. The years of an active "French restoration" of the Maghrebi Quarter were coming to an end. In this latter part of 1954, Morocco and Tunisia were definitively embarked upon the path of emancipation, and by leaving the French colonial orbit, they would soon forego their commitments vis-à-vis the Maghrebis of Jerusalem. An armed uprising erupted in Algeria, and France's "Muslim policy" would soon be stifled by an increasingly ferocious logic of repression, leaving less and less room for partisans of an inclusive policy of cultural influence. The age of empires was long past, the nationalization of identities and political priorities was underway, and the Maghrebis of the Holy City would soon be counted among the castaways of this major historical tempest.

4

COLONIAL CONTRADICTIONS AND GEOPOLITICAL UPHEAVAL

THE ORPHANS OF EMPIRE (1955–62)

By late 1954, the history of the Maghrebi Quarter of Jerusalem had once again reached a fork in the road. The propitious momentum that had been building since 1949 was grinding to a halt, undermining the geopolitical equation that had ushered in a brief period of "French restoration" of the Waqf Abu Madyan. The eruption of the Algerian insurrection in autumn 1954, intensifying in the Constantine region in the summer of 1955;[1] the increasing autonomy of the former Moroccan and Tunisian Protectorates and the proclamation of their respective independences in March 1956;[2] the special alliance with Israel by the latter administrations of the Fourth Republic, symbolized by the joint military operation against Egypt at the Suez Canal in late 1956; the deteriorating relations between France and the Arab world, which stood in solidarity with Algeria's nationalist combatants; and the complete break in diplomatic relations with Jordan after the Suez crisis in late 1956 and until 1962, which resulted in the French consul in Jerusalem being denied access to the old city, and therefore to the Maghrebi Quarter[3]—all these factors converged to inexorably counter France's strategy of support for inhabitants of the Maghrebi Quarter. A new phase was opening: that of the waqf's slow decline, marked by both its legal collapse and its gradual financial suffocation. This dismantling of the po-

litical scaffolding constructed in 1949 concluded in 1962, when Algerian independence definitively excluded the Maghrebi Quarter from French diplomacy's
scope of intervention. The loss of this diplomatic protection in turn created
conditions favorable for a possible physical destruction of the quarter—which,
as we know, would take place immediately following the 1967 war.

At this point in the narrative, symptomatically poised between past, present, and future, we need to head down the path of counterfactual history to try
and evaluate how *inexorable* this historical shift really was. Nothing gratuitous
is at play here: only this "what if" scenario can keep us from falling into teleological misinterpretations. It helps us to situate ourselves in the present of the
actors involved in these "uncertain times," and to understand their belief in the
future and their occasionally misplaced obstinacy.[4] Though French support
did officially extend until 1962, this was indeed because the loss of Algeria was
simply not on the radar of French political officials at that time. At any rate, and
including for those who could theoretically project it, the likelihood of Algerian
independence was not the scenario upon which political decisions were being
taken; quite the contrary, they were taken in an attempt to modify the course
of history, against all odds. The inertia of administrative and decision-making
processes, the chronological lags, the sheer blindness of those who believed
to the bitter end in a revamped "community of destiny" between France and
Algeria—all this slowed down the decision-making and postponed deadlines.
Nevertheless, the sequence opened in 1949 was slowly closing again by 1955: the
contradictions inherent to the colonial system had become all too glaring, the
political breakup of the Maghreb was speeding up, and the so-called moderate or
Francophile Algerians were now called "collaborators" and were being targeted
by the insurrection. The inhabitants of the Maghrebi Quarter of Jerusalem,
who had momentarily benefited from the last rays of France's colonial project,
were thus turning into "orphans of empire," battered by the ill winds of history.

Two events might be analyzed as symptomatic of this shift. One is high-
profile and tragic: the 1957 assassination by Algeria's National Liberation Front
(FLN) of Professor Hajj Lunis, who had carried out an inspection mission of
the Jerusalem Maghrebi Quarter in 1955 and again in 1956. In a message addressed to the consul general of France in Jerusalem, André Favereau, in early
July 1957, Louis Massignon speaks of Lunis as "a friend fallen in my stead," a
hard-hitting expression of his utter bewilderment and undoubtedly his sense

of guilt at seeing one of the architects of his committee shot by insurgents as the last sacrificial victim of a lost cause. The funeral eulogy composed by Massignon is commensurate with the trauma he experienced:

> One of our dearest Muslim friends, an Algerian born in Djidelli, Professor Hajj Lunis (Mahfud Ben-Messaud), of Lycée Albertini in Setif, mortally wounded on 4 June in Setif by a mechanic, Belloud Mohammed Taher, died yesterday, leaving a widow and two children [...]. It is he who, at our urging, had accepted the annual mission as inspector of the Tlemcen waqf of Abu Madyan at the al-Aqsa Mosque in Jerusalem, and as defender of France's loyalty to this endowment for the care of indigent pilgrims [...]. It had been insinuated that we involved him, by our union in prayer, in a passive nonviolence resigned to a collective repression of which we have always disapproved, as did he and the mufti of Setif. What Hajj Lunis believed is that there were holy places that give asylum to Muslims and to Christians determined to wrest from the one God, Father of all believers, through prayer, fasting and sacrifice, a serene peace, *Salaam Allah.*[5]

This oration reveals how symptomatic this assassination was of the contradictions inherent to the "Franco-Muslim" project undertaken by Massignon and his entourage, a political and spiritual project for which the Maghrebi Quarter of Jerusalem was supposed to be its symbol. Massignon himself acknowledges that the inspection mission that Hajj Lunis had accepted designated him as an unambiguous "collaborator" in the eyes of the FLN. This intermediary position between Algerian nationalist insurgents and the partisans of a fierce "collective repression" pursued by the French army had become effectively untenable by 1956, when the revolutionary war was producing its first effects. By surgically targeting all those who stood between the insurgents and the French army, the FLN succeeded in creating the conditions of a frontal attack and in encouraging those who backed an ever crueler military repression against civilian populations who, in turn, joined the insurgents more massively with each new act of repression. Some four thousand kilometers away, the Maghrebis of Jerusalem, the offspring of former imperial political structures, now finding themselves at odds with the rise of national struggles, would in the end become the collateral damage in a showdown far beyond their control.

The second event we might consider symptomatic of this historic shift is much less dramatic, but is nonetheless significant. On 25 May 1954, the Tunisian government's Council of Ministers took up the issue of renewing the annual subsidy of two million francs to the Waqf Abu Madyan. According to a report drafted by the resident general in Tunis, "the Minister of Muslim Institutions objected from the start to granting any subsidy to this institution given that funds available in the local budget are already being stretched to assist needy Tunisians."[6] The process of nationalizing collective identity went hand in hand here with a process of renationalizing public spending, at the very time when Tunisia was attempting to gradually emerge from under French authority. A reading of this otherwise dry administrative report reveals what may have been the arguments developed by the minister, keen to spend his budget on helping his nationals rather than resuming responsibility for the colonial power's previous obligations.

In April 1954 the French consul in Jerusalem had already written to Massignon that, although renewal of Algeria's annual subsidy was all but guaranteed, "on the part of the Tunisian and Moroccan Protectorates, the news is rather disappointing."[7] Decolonization was underway, the increasingly inoperative reins of imperial tutelage were being loosened, and the Waqf Abu Madyan was obviously not the priority of the new Tunisian and Moroccan governments eager to assert their autonomy. That being said, in this spring of 1954, when independence had not yet been proclaimed, it was time for compromise; and at the request of France, the Tunisian government did finally consent to free up a final "relief assistance of 500,000 francs for the Waqf Abu Madyan," instead of the two million requested. In January 1955 the French Consulate in Jerusalem did note, however, that "the year 1954 has come to an end without our receiving the promised subsidy," and it called for renewed intervention from the resident general.[8] The picture of postcolonial transition comes into progressively sharpening focus before our eyes, between begrudgingly conceded accommodations, passive resistance, multiple restarts, and constant delays. Colonial *power*, in the real sense, was treading water.

From Jerusalem to Tel Aviv: Israel Imposes Its Conditions

When one approaches a dossier in the archives to comprehend a chronological bend, it is not imperative that every dispatch and piece of correspondence be

read in extenso, at least not immediately. Instead, one should take the time to
spot new actors rising to the surface, first as attachments, then as direct interlocutors. In dossiers archived in Algiers and at the Ministry of Algerian Affairs
pertaining to the Waqf Abu Madyan, the turning point is especially distinct:
where the French Consulate in Jerusalem had earlier been the chief counterpart
of the Algerian governor general, by 1955 the French Embassy in Tel Aviv was
now the indispensable communication vector. First, this was because the scope
of jurisdiction of France's consular office in Jerusalem, set during the Ottoman
era, forbade it from entering into official negotiations with the Israeli government. Second, the severance of diplomatic ties with Jordan in 1956 accentuated
the consulate's isolation, depriving it of the only interlocutor that it could still
call upon to act. Finally, the context of the Algerian war engaged France in a
strategy of preferential alliance with Israel, which took logical advantage of the
situation to gradually impose its conditions in the negotiations regarding the
Waqf Abu Madyan and the dispossession of the Ein Karem lands.

The Israeli governor of the district of Jerusalem, in a stinging response to
the French consul, made his position clear: "The issue of the Ein Karem waqf is
being dealt with directly between the French Embassy and the Foreign Ministry."[9] At the judicial level, the Israeli position is practically unassailable, since the
village of Ein Karem was located a few miles west of the green line, and therefore
inside the internationally recognized Israeli border endorsed by France. In the
archives of the Ministry of Algerian Affairs there is a long report drafted by
the French ambassador to Israel, Pierre-Eugene Gilbert, regarding "provisions
laid out by the Israeli government with regard to the settlement of the Waqf
Abu Madyan issue," dated 9 May 1955. The report shows that, although the
French Consulate was still attempting to sustain the subsidies issuing from the
Maghreb, it was actually Tel Aviv, and thus Israel in the end, that took control
when it came to the crucial matter of compensation for the Ein Karem lands:

> Our dossier was delivered on 5 May 1953 to the Israeli authorities, who had
> the time to assess its seriousness, but also to gauge its weaknesses [...]. By
> asking us "what was the annual fee paid by the Mandatory authorities to the
> endowment's administration at the end of the Mandate period," the Israeli au-
> thorities know that we cannot put forward a figure in excess of 417 Palestinian
> pounds [...]. What's more, the advice of our counsel Szczupak, attorney for

this embassy, [...] is categorical: in the event that we were unable to ensure the furtherance of the trial suspended in 1947, which set the waqf and Ein Karem against some forty seemingly good-faith occupants [...], we would engage in a legal proceeding whose final outcome would be hard to foresee. This is also the conviction of the Department [Quai d'Orsay] itself, which asks nothing more than to obtain, by way of a simple de facto regulation, concrete offers of indemnity.[10]

This missive is fundamental because it sets up the framework—and particularly the limits—of the negotiation with Israel regarding the dispossession of the Ein Karem lands in 1948. According to the ambassador, it was no longer a matter of a "legal resolution," that is, "the legal acknowledgment of the waqf's full rights and a new assessment of its property values," but of confinement to a "de facto regulation" to obtain a simple "indemnity." The Mandate years, which saw numerous tracts of land escape the control of the endowment stewards, involved similar issues, but the Waqf Abu Madyan's weakened legal position was also an archival weakening, as the ambassador indicates: "The Waqf Abu Madyan's archives were managed by its legal counsel Anwar Nuseibeh, who has since become the Jordanian Minister of National Defense and Education, and who lost the archives during the hostilities [...]. Therefore, it does not appear possible to provide the Israeli authorities, within a reasonable time frame, additional information on the various points that they have raised. The admission that we are bound to make about this [...] will most certainly weaken our negotiating position."[11] We recall that as early as 1949, Consul René Neuville was already worried about how weak the documentary case was for establishing the endowment's rights, and had asked the consular officer, Pierrestiger, to reconstitute it as best he could, by digging into the archives of the Jerusalem tribunal most especially,[12] but also by rallying the French ambassador in Ankara, so that he might obtain certain copies of Ottoman documents, as was accomplished during the summer of 1953.[13] Six years later, it becomes clear that this archival gap was due to negligence on the part of the endowment's former legal counsel, who in the interim had become one of the most eminent political figures of the Hashemite kingdom and of the Palestinian notables of East Jerusalem—but we must also entertain the hypothesis that the archives may have been dispersed or destroyed during the 1948 clashes.[14]

At any rate, it was this archival shortfall that led the ambassador to set the negotiation at the *political* rather than the *judicial* level, repeating nearly word for word the proposals stated a few years earlier by Neuville:

> This de facto regulation, these concrete offers of compensation, we stand a chance of obtaining them in a timely manner only if, by coming to an agreement with the [Israeli] Minister of Foreign Affairs to set aside the legalistic discussions, we immediately meet him on the field of political opportunity. Once there, all arguments will be open to discussion, and I shall not refrain from asserting in particular the one to be made of the geographical location of the Maghrebi zawiya in Jerusalem, that property belonging to the Waqf Abu Madyan that commands access to the Wailing Wall. I believe we can say that the extent to which the inhabitants of this quarter remain loyal to France and in compliance with the advice of our Consul General in Jerusalem who administers them will determine whether we can expect to obtain their cooperation for the application and accommodation that we hope, at least, will come to pass one day between Israel and Jordan in view of granting Jewish pilgrims, on certain occasions, access to the Wailing Wall.[15]

The embassy in Tel Aviv chose to refrain from defending the "full rights" of Maghrebis in Jerusalem in an attempt to monetize their "compliance" in the framework of a potential political negotiation between Israel and Jordan regarding access to the Wall; and in doing so it was either demonstrating a certain realism or, on the contrary, taking a huge risk by weakening the French position before the negotiations had even begun. What is certain is that the ambassador chose not to conceal from the Israeli interlocutors any vulnerabilities of French diplomacy in this dossier: "Nor do we have any reason to conceal from our interlocutors that the subsidies are proving ever more difficult to obtain and that the donors have lost interest, such that maintenance of the waqf poses an increasingly troublesome financial problem."[16] By choosing to play entirely "above board" and disclose the dwindling subsidies from the Maghreb, the ambassador positioned the Israeli authorities to take charge of the negotiation. The point was to encourage them to get involved, but it was still a gamble.

Inalienability, Indemnity, Restitution: the Ulemas' Uneasiness

On 29 May 1955, the Official Register of Israel published expropriation deeds for four parcels of land located in Ein Karem, an area of about 520 acres, "for the building of a School of Medicine, a nursing school, a hospital, and university residence halls" (figure 32).[17] We know today that these expropriations were the first stages in the construction of the sprawling Hadassah hospital complex, effectively erected on the land of the village of Ein Karem.[18] In hindsight, we cannot help but be disturbed by the chronology of this expropriation proceeding, which immediately follows the new negotiation strategy stated by

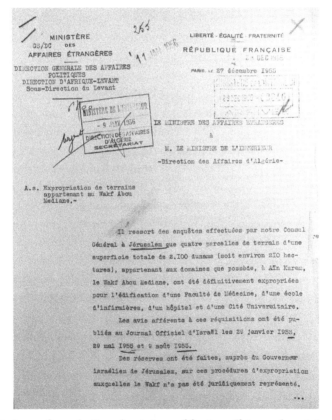

FIGURE 32. **Letter from the French minister of foreign affairs to the minister of the interior regarding expropriation of lands belonging to the Abu Madyan waqf in Ein Karem, 27 December 1955. Source: ANOM, 81.F-844.**

Ambassador Pierre-Eugene Gilbert in early May 1955. Where France chose to keep a low profile, the Israeli authorities were quick to play the power game. Immediately alerted, the Quai d'Orsay could only conclude that the expropriation measures were "legally unassailable in the Israeli courts" since they were enacted "by virtue of the 1943 British law, against which the Supreme Muslim Council, mandated back then to defend Islamic interests, had raised no objection," and that Article 24 of that law "expressly stipulates that the provisions are applicable to assets belonging to the waqfs, irrespective of their nature."[19]

The noose was tightening; in order to try and obtain an expropriation indemnity on behalf of the Waqf Abu Madyan, the Quai d'Orsay needed the consent of the Algerian ulemas, the same ones who had been summoned since 1949 to defend the principle of the inalienability of waqf properties. This inconsistency is clearly expressed in a letter from the Quay d'Orsay's Africa-Levant Bureau to the governor general of Algeria on 20 January 1956:

> Although it may be in the best interest of the waqf to participate in the operations for setting the expropriation indemnity, the very principle of this compensation does nonetheless infringe the rule of inalienability of assets belonging to the waqfiya [...]. Given the violent hostility that prevails between the Arab World and the State of Israel, the Foreign Ministry deems it impossible to issue such directives to the steward of the Waqf Abu Madyan without the consent of the designated moral authorities in North Africa [...]. I would therefore respectfully request that you consult on this matter with those Muslim officials in Algeria in charge of managing hubus assets, and provide me with their advice at the earliest opportunity [...]. I have also asked the Resident General of France in Morocco and our High Commissioner in Tunis to submit this matter to the Moroccan and Tunisian Governments."[20]

On 10 February 1956, the governor general of Algeria submitted a draft declaration to the members of the Tlemcen Support Committee, the qadi and the mufti of Algiers, and a few other ulemas "representative of marabouts and reformist trends": "The undersigned [...], apprised of the expropriation ruling made by the Israeli authorities with respect to four parcels of land (around 520 acres) located at Ein Karem and property of Waqf Abu Madyan, [1] do strenuously protest this measure entirely at odds with the principle of inalienability of waqfs [...], [2] consider nevertheless that this religious endowment must be represented at the proceedings now underway in Jerusalem to assess the total amount of the expropriation indemnity."[21] In its definitive version, the second sentence and the term "nevertheless"—which explicitly indicates a climb-down when faced with Israeli pressure—are replaced in the margins by a more skillful formulation: ". . . [2] *demand* that the religious endowment be fairly compensated and that its interests be defended and represented at the proceedings currently underway."[22] This rhetorical prevarication, formally rather trivial, reveals the fundamental collapse of a colonial system itself compelled to weigh the terms it uses on the scale of indignation, so that the ulemas involved in consultations will not find themselves at odds with public opinion plunged into turmoil.

It was a losing battle, since despite repeated attempts, the governor general of Algeria reported in April 1956 that "Mr. Baba Ameur, Mufti of Algiers, has deferred, preferring for now to remain out of the limelight; Mr. Tchanderli, the Qadi of Algiers, has equivocated, which amounts to a refusal; Sheikh El-Okbi has recused himself, not wishing to accept any transaction on the principle of inalienability of hubus; Mr. Lachachi, president of the Tlemcen committee, has not responded."[23] The unease of the Algerian ulemas was thus conspicuous—and easily understandable, since they were experienced enough to realize that, whatever the rhetorical coating, an "indemnity" amounted to an acknowledgment that rights had been usurped, and that this represented a breach, term for term, of the waqf's basic principles. Qadi Benhoura stated as much in a long argued response that he drafted on 18 March 1956:

> It goes without saying that I shall gladly sign the protest against the violation of the unalienable rights of the Maghrebi colony of Jerusalem by the State of Israel. Allow me, however, to direct your attention to the final paragraph of this declaration to be signed, whose wording could be interpreted as an implicit acknowledgment of the fait accompli. Indeed, asking to be compensated for violation of a right amounts to admitting, via compensation, that this right goes unfulfilled. To dispel any misapprehension, it is my view that the best way to ensure the waqf's inviolability would be to demand not a "fair compensation" but a "restitution of the usufruct" [. . .]. If there is nothing to expect in this regard from the Israeli courts, there might well be something more hopeful at the International Court in The Hague, providing the French government wishes to defend the interests of its nationals."[24]

The Maghrebi Quarter of Jerusalem appears once again as a telltale indicator of the general history of how Israel dealt with the populations residing in Palestine prior to 1948. Confronted with the circularity of Israeli law, Qadi Benhoura could but emphasize the legal trap of indemnity as an acknowledgment of the "fait accompli," and call for the arbitration of international law to counter the Israeli expropriations. But given how urgently the French authorities had been confronted, the suggestion to call upon the court of The Hague could serve no immediate purpose; the preparation of the case file by Israeli attorney Szczupak "already involves translating out of Arabic and Turkish into Hebrew numerous pieces of documentary evidence, deeds, and court rulings," thereby incurring substantial costs, as mentioned in a consular dispatch—a further indication that the process of setting the indemnity amount had already commenced.[25] Here again we find certain recurring elements of Israeli strategy consisting of judicializing the land expropriations while imposing its own conditions for regulating the litigation: defining the jurisprudential framework, controlling the calendar, requiring recourse to an Israeli attorney, and insisting that all supporting documentation be translated into Hebrew.

The escalation of the war in Algeria—the Palestro ambush in spring 1956, the Battle of Algiers in early 1957—only further intensified the unease among the solicited ulemas; and to no surprise, the governor general of Algeria indicated on 15 March 1957 that "in light of the present situation, there were problems getting the Muslim notables to approve the text they had been submitted."[26] The following month, consulted by the Quai d'Orsay on the indemnity proposal put forward by the Israelis, he expressed his readiness to unburden himself of so thorny an issue when, right outside his office windows, the Battle of Algiers was raging:

> You informed me that the Israeli Government was willing to pay, for the Ein Karem lands belonging to the Waqf Abu Madyan of Jerusalem, an annual indemnity of 3,000 Palestinian pounds (some 480,000 francs) retroactively effective from 15 May 1948, the date of the creation of Israel (which, by next 15 May will amount to a total of around 4,320,000 francs) [...]. You ask me to share with you my feelings on the matter [...]. I personally feel that it is now appropriate to accept the offer.[27]

Lending support to the Maghrebi Quarter, a move envisioned in 1949 as a factor of cultural and religious soft power aimed at convincing the Muslim elites of France's solidarity with Maghrebi Islamic institutions, was no longer on the agenda as far as the governor general was concerned, coming as it did in the midst of a decolonization war that was further polarizing the population with each passing day. The letter closes with an even starker reference to this misalignment, questioning the worth of Algeria's subsidy, for explicitly political motives:

> I had suggested, given the feelings of hostility toward France manifested by the Maghrebi colony of Jerusalem, that you continue to include the subsidy in Algeria's upcoming budget, but that you postpone the transfer. The subsidy was indeed included in the 1957–1958 Algerian budget, recently endorsed. But my feelings have not changed about the appropriateness of granting financial aid to a community that speaks of breaking all ties with France and even waging war against us [. . .]. Consequently [. . .], I intend not to grant any subsidy this year to the Waqf Abu Madyan.²⁸

What emerges from this letter is not only the worsening situation in Algeria and the increasingly massive hostility of Middle Eastern public opinion—including the Maghrebi inhabitants of Jerusalem—with regard to the French army's repressive measures, but also the rift between Paris and Algiers, between the Quai d'Orsay's attempts at diplomatic compromise and Algiers's openly repressive strategy. Algiers was no longer meekly obeying the Quai d'Orsay, even when its demands were relayed through the Bureau of Algerian Affairs to the minister of the interior, who exercised direct oversight of the Algerian governor general. We know that this rift between Paris and Algiers would only grow wider over the coming months, leading finally to the Algiers putsch and to the fall of the Fourth Republic. The inhabitants of the Maghrebi Quarter of Jerusalem, dragged unwittingly into this historic upheaval, were also victims of the widening divide between the metropole and its colonies on the path to emancipation.

Conflicts and Generational Divides:
The Maghrebi Quarter under Stress

The rising tension between the French authorities and the younger inhabitants of the Maghrebi Quarter appeared as yet another symptom of the new political situation emerging in 1955. This generational divide expressed a kind of disengagement between those attempting to salvage the machinery of colonial tutelage, or to accommodate it, and those wishing to free themselves by declaring their solidarity with their struggling compatriots. This situation of political overlap, typical of the decolonization process, struck Louis Massignon when he visited the Maghrebi Quarter in January 1956. In a report he drafted after this visit, Consul Laforge pointed out that "during his visit to the 'Maghrebi Club,' created by the colony's younger set, Professor Massignon became aware of the need to provide a few upgrades to the club's facilities, since its principal usefulness is to provide leisure activities to somehow deter these young Maghrebis born in Jerusalem from the influence of Jordanian nationalists who currently seem to be engaging them."[29]

For instance, Massignon suggested purchasing a radio and "a dozen large photographic reproductions of sites and monuments in North Africa" to decorate the club's walls, as if such cosmetic additions could truly change the state of mind of his young interlocutors attracted to the fresh political perspectives of Arab nationalism. A few months earlier, in March 1955, Consul Laforge (22 February 1955–23 December 1957) related one of his visits to "the young people of the waqf," emphasizing that they were "more numerous than their elders and more turbulent," and mentioning that as he was entering the club, "one of them hastily took down a portrait of former Sultan Muhammad V," by then an exile in Madagascar and a rallying figure for Moroccan nationalists.[30] The discrepancy here is glaring between Massignon, who wished to decorate the club with images of cultural heritage devoid of any political significance, and these young people, who were spontaneously drawn to nationalist engagement.

This same impression of a generational disconnect can be read in the report drafted by Hajj Lunis upon his return from an inspection mission in the summer of 1955: "Arriving in Jerusalem, I found the majority of Maghrebis, composed mostly of young natives of Jerusalem, standing against the steward Hajj Hidoussi [. . .]. Certain young French nationals were on the verge of casting their passports into a pile, taking them to the French Consulate, and relinquishing their French nationality."[31] While they were bluntly accusing the steward of malfeasance and breach of trust, Lunis points to a mere "misunderstanding" and urges Consul Laforge to speak to the youth in "a fatherly language"—thereby revealing a typically colonial paternalist posture, singularly at odds with the new political context. Beyond the generation gap, Lunis describes a religious endowment that was struggling, benefiting in some ways from the restoration efforts undertaken over previous years, but also suffering from haphazard management, with increasing costs and structurally insufficient financial resources:

> Here is the situation of the immovable assets belonging to Waqf Abu Madyan located in Jerusalem [. . .]. A) The zawiya, consisting of 25 rooms, 3 of which are very spacious, all occupied by indigent, invalid and unmarried Maghrebis, numbering 40 permanent lodgers. Besides this function, these dwellings receive between 300 and 400 transient Maghrebis during the three-month pilgrimage season. Out of these 40 permanent Maghrebi lodgers, 15 receive individual relief assistance worth 400 francs monthly, and on a daily basis, a large flatbread. The 25 others receive bread only. As for the 300 to 400 seasonal residents, they benefit from one flatbread per day, and the neediest among them receive a modest stipend for their trip to Mecca or the way back home to their country of origin. B) The Maghrebi Quarter, restricted to those who are married; it includes 54 dwellings having 3, 4 or 5 rooms; all these dwellings guarantee free housing to over 700 persons of North African origin. Certain occupants take the liberty of subletting rooms in their home for their own benefit [. . .]. Finally, this Maghrebi Quarter also includes 14 residential homes furnished by the Mutewalli that bring in an annual revenue of 989,000 francs. C) In the old city, the waqf also manages 16 shops, a communal oven and two parcels of land, whose annual income amounts to 188,000 francs [. . .]. The deficit for the current year: 2,050,000 francs."[32]

This exhaustive description draws up a positive assessment of the work undertaken thanks to the subsidies obtained, and it shows that the endowment continued to fulfill its basic obligations, as confirmed by the detailed annual budget published by Lunis in the appendix of his report: "Distribution of clothing and food on the occasion of 4 feast days to the needy at the zawiya = 135,000 francs"; "Miscellaneous expenses (kerosene, lamps, brooms, mats) = 21,000 francs"; "Purchase of shrouds + burial expenses and some medical care (there were 2 deaths this year) = 12,000 francs."[33] But it also points to a deficit of more than two million francs for the current year, despite the subsidies, and precisely because of the major sums invested in restoring the endowment's built properties.

In fact, it would seem that the loss of the Ein Karem revenue stream, coupled with too long a period of underinvestment, had produced a structural shortfall in the annual budget, even while the quarter's underdevelopment was conspicuous in various areas, as indicated by a petition from the "North African Club" which highlights "the extremely dilapidated state" of one locale "deprived of electricity and running water."[34] In the draft budget for the previous year, Hidoussi had already committed seven hundred Jordanian dinars (around seven hundred thousand francs) for "repairs to three houses damaged by the destruction of sewers in the quarter during the winter season."[35] The Maghrebi Quarter, located on the lowest ground of the old city, at the mouth of the central valley (Rue al-Wad), along the path of conduits that for centuries had been evacuating sewage and rainwater, was no doubt especially affected by the city's obsolescent sewage system.[36] This constraint, linked to urban topography, is confirmed by a dossier of documents that can be consulted in the archives of the Abu-Dis waqfs, which give evidence through numerous invoices of work carried out in 1947 both to connect the zawiya to the potable water pipelines and to ensure that the sewer pipes were leakproof.[37]

Hajj Lunis undertook one final inspection mission to Jerusalem in August 1956, and the documents filed as "confidential" that we can now read in the archives of the Bureau of Algerian Affairs show that the context by then had changed irreversibly. On 4 August, when Hajj Lunis was already on the scene, the North African liaison officer wrote to the Quai d'Orsay indicating that "in light of the current situation in Algeria, I would be deeply grateful that you do not make known the mission of Mr. Lunis Mahfud."[38] A further indicator of the deepening divide between the Quai d'Orsay and Algiers, between the diplomatic line and security imperatives, this note also strongly suggests that the strategy put in place in 1949 was being entirely called into question, right when the Suez crisis was on everyone's mind, with Gamal Abdel Nasser's announcement on 26 July that the canal was to be nationalized. Where all effort had been made in the past to widely advertise actions in favor of the Waqf Abu

Madyan, equal effort was now being exerted to deflect the attention of Algerian public opinion, considered as definitively beyond the reach of a peacemaking discourse on "Franco-Muslim solidarity." The intelligence notice devoted to Lunis indicates that he supports "a Franco-Muslim reconciliation" and that he "has collaborated with Mr. Massignon for a study about 'The Cave of the Seven Sleepers.'" The notice concludes on a reassuring note: "*Reputation*: Good. *Influence*: Leads a very reclusive life. *Political attitude*: Nothing unfavorable. Fulfilled this mission conscientiously and dexterously."[39] This man, who would be assassinated a few months later by the FLN, was effectively considered a zealous minion of the colonial system (figure 33).

In his final report, Lunis stresses that "the tragic events that have been unfolding in Algeria for a while now and the solidarity campaign conducted by the Jordanians in favor of the Algerians" have led to "a situation of distrust" against French interests in Jerusalem. He adds that "the announcement of the French Consulate's choice of a Jewish attorney to defend Maghrebi interests in the Israeli courts" provoked "a huge outcry," also relayed by "Jordanian radio and the Arabic-language dailies of Jerusalem."[40] The shifting geopolitical equation was fresh in Lunis's mind, even if he perhaps had not gauged the full extent. The result: "The authorities of the Mahakma [Court] appealed to by the Amman Public Prosecutor and influenced by the violent press campaign against the Consulate" launched a vast investigation into the waqf's finances to monitor "the exact budget of the waqf since 1951."[41] Lunis, given over entirely to his reconciliation mission, did not grasp the obvious political dimension of this legal probe; he attempted to organize an unlikely encounter "at the Israel-Jordan border" (at the Mandelbaum Gate, a few hundred yards north of the old city), between "on one hand, the Qadi of Jerusalem, the Consulate's Muslim attorney in the Arab zone Mr. Budeiri Hassan and myself, and Attorney Szczupack on the other," in an attempt to quell the conflict. This was to no avail, of course, since "the Qadi refused to attend or to meet up with a Jew [. . .], so that the border meeting failed, in the end."[42] This improbable encounter, which inevitably turned into a missed opportunity, was symptomatic of French diplomacy's shrinking scope of action with regard to the Maghrebi Quarter.

The waqf steward Hidoussi, who had been appointed to this position in 1951 at the request of the French Consulate and with Amman's assent, was thus "suspended from duty" and replaced by Muhammad Ibrahim Abdelhaq on

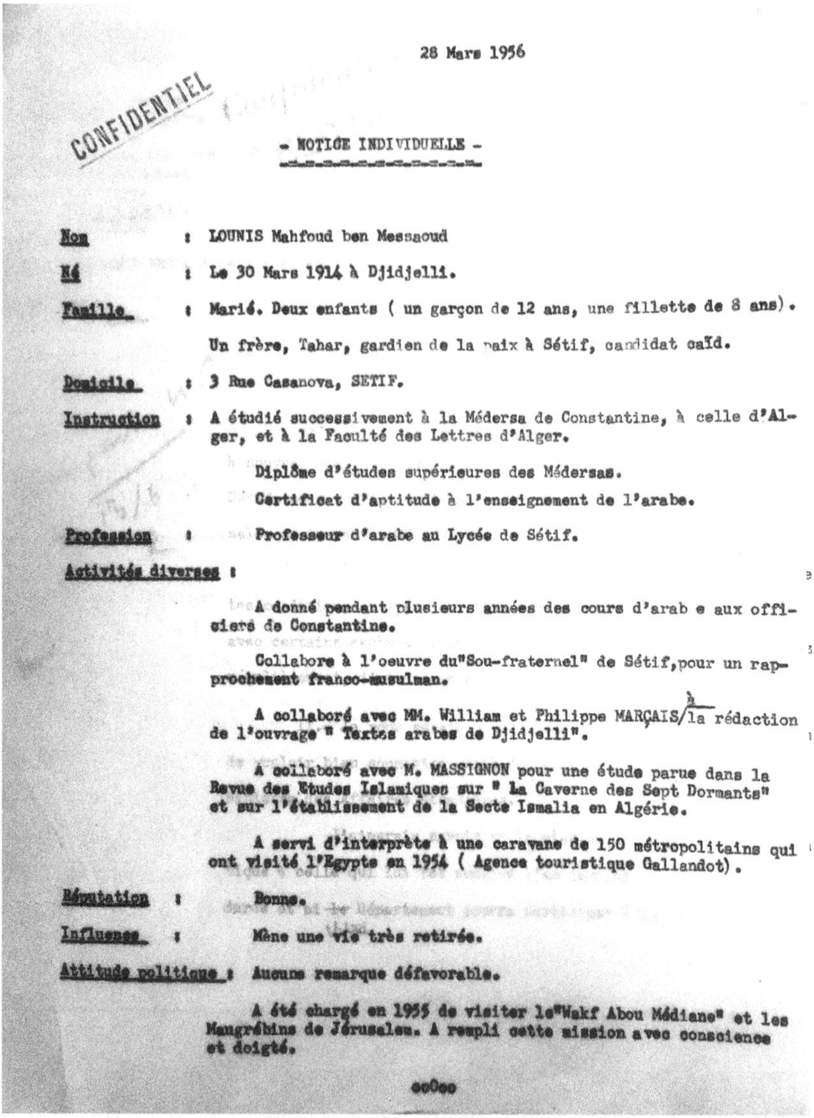

28 Mars 1956

CONFIDENTIEL

— NOTICE INDIVIDUELLE —

Nom : LOUNIS Mahfoud ben Messaoud

Né : Le 30 Mars 1914 à Djidjelli.

Famille : Marié. Deux enfants (un garçon de 12 ans, une fillette de 8 ans).

Un frère, Tahar, gardien de la paix à Sétif, candidat caïd.

Domicile : 3 Rue Casanova, SETIF.

Instruction : A étudié successivement à la Médersa de Constantine, à celle d'Alger, et à la Faculté des Lettres d'Alger.

Diplôme d'études supérieures des Médersas.

Certificat d'aptitude à l'enseignement de l'arabe.

Profession : Professeur d'arabe au Lycée de Sétif.

Activités diverses :

A donné pendant plusieurs années des cours d'arabe aux officiers de Constantine.

Collabore à l'oeuvre du "Sou-fraternel" de Sétif, pour un rapprochement franco-musulman.

A collaboré avec MM. William et Philippe MARÇAIS/la rédaction de l'ouvrage " Textes arabes de Djidjelli".

A collaboré avec M. MASSIGNON pour une étude parue dans la Revue des Etudes Islamiques sur " La Caverne des Sept Dormants" et sur l'établissement de la Secte Ismalia en Algérie.

A servi d'interprète à une caravane de 150 métropolitains qui ont visité l'Egypte en 1954 (Agence touristique Gallandot).

Réputation : Bonne.

Influence : Mène une vie très retirée.

Attitude politique : Aucune remarque défavorable.

A été chargé en 1955 de visiter le "Wakf Abou Médiane" et les Maghrébins de Jérusalem. A rempli cette mission avec conscience et doigté.

ooOoo

FIGURE 33. Individual report concerning Hajj Lunis, 28 March 1956. Source: ANOM, 81.F-844.

25 July 1956. In his report, Hajj Lunis was not overly harsh with regard to Hidoussi, describing him as "a simple man, not very cultured, even-tempered, who indulged in magnanimous alms-giving to needy Maghrebis and in unrecorded payments to persons employed for the construction and renovation of waqf buildings."[43] Hajj Lunis remarked that Hidoussi "never suspected that one day the Qadi would be calling him to account," and ended up offering himself to perform the duties of "administrator-inspector of the North African waqf," in collaboration with the endowment's new local steward.[44] The qadi of Jerusalem acquiesced to this compromise offer, and one reader of the report inside the Bureau of Algerian Affairs in Paris wrote in pencil in the margins: "Excellent move from the political and technical standpoint." But the assassination of Hajj Lunis Mahfud by the FLN on 4 June 1957 sealed the definitive failure of this ultimate attempt at appeasement: the Maghrebi Quarter of Jerusalem was henceforth at the heart of an intense battle between France and Algeria, but also between France and Jordan.[45]

After the Suez Crisis: The FLN at the Gates of the Maghrebi Quarter

By the summer of 1956, the winds of history had decisively shifted. The march toward decolonization and the momentum of Arab nationalisms were placing the Maghrebi Quarter at cross-purposes with the new geopolitical trends that were structuring the Middle East. In Egypt, Gamal Abdel Nasser secured the departure of the last British soldiers on 13 June 1956, got the new constitution adopted on 23 June, and announced the nationalization of the Suez Canal on 26 July 1956 during his famous speech in Alexandria. The government of French Prime Minister Guy Mollet, who was not unaware that FLN headquarters were located in Cairo and that the group was trained by the Egyptian military, opted for a strategic alliance with Israel in an attempt to overthrow Nasser: after an initial secret meeting held in Paris in late July, a second gathering brought together French, Israeli, and British delegates from 21 to 24 October in Sèvres, in the presence of Guy Mollet, David Ben-Gurion, Moshe Dayan, and Shimon Peres. The "Sèvres Protocol" provided for a surprise Israeli attack against Egypt on 29 October, followed by a Franco-British military intervention two days later.[46]

We know that this operation resulted in a partial success militarily and a resounding failure politically. Nasser remained in power, consolidating his role as Arab nationalist leader, and ordered the expulsion of some eighty thousand Jews still living in Egypt, while France wound up isolated within the United Nations and stigmatized in Arab public opinion.[47] Jordan, though it had a military pact with Great Britain, refused to open its airspace to French and British warplanes, and broke off diplomatic relations with Paris, as did all the Arab states with the exception of Lebanon. France therefore no longer had an ambassador in Amman until 1962, which meant that during this same period, its consul general in Jerusalem could no longer enter East Jerusalem, except by dint of long and arduous bargaining. Concretely, French interests in the old city were henceforth to be handled, to the extent possible, by the Belgian Consulate, and this only further accentuated the isolation of the Maghrebi Quarter.

It is within this eroded environment that we must reposition the challenges Hajj Lunis encountered during his final mission in summer 1956, notably the dismissal of the waqf steward by the Jordanian judicial authorities on 25 July 1956. In the archives of the French Consulate of Jerusalem, there is much evidence of this weakening of the French position and the tangible consequences of this new situation for the Maghrebi Quarter. For instance, in an envelope postmarked in Jenin on 14 July 1956, we find the copy of a letter addressed by "Mohammed Omar Aklil El-Jazairi" to the qadi of Jerusalem—the same man who in 1936 had been denouncing the nationalist activities of the mufti of Jerusalem, and proclaiming his loyalty to France,[48] was now being called "the Algerian" and was forthrightly attacking France's support of the Jerusalem Maghrebis:

> To His Excellency the Qadi of Jerusalem. I have been astonished to learn of a news item published in *Falestin* which reports that you have received from the French Consulate the sum of 100 dinars to be handed over to the mutewalli of the Maghrebi waqf, to then be distributed by that mercenary among the needy of that colony. By this act you are collaborating with imperialism and are attempting to erase the ill effects of the barbarous French authorities' criminal conduct in Algeria.[49]

The wording is harsh, and no doubt expresses an elderly man's bitterness in his isolation, exiled as he was in Jenin; but it also reveals that a new discursive repertoire was emerging, and that it was now available to anyone with a grievance about France's support for the Maghrebis of Jerusalem. On 6 September 1956 a more coordinated offensive was aimed at the French Embassy in Amman, still open and running for a few more weeks. Signed and claimed by "The Maghrebi Colony of Jordan," the petition appears to have been drafted by militants close to the FLN, or at any rate, familiar with the anticolonialist rhetoric, and we find certain parallels with the vocabulary used by Aklil a few weeks earlier:

> The massacres perpetrated by France in the Maghreb and its barbarous campaigns against the unarmed Algerian people struggling for their freedom and independence have revealed France's criminal intentions. Thus do we come forward and proclaim to France, the self-described protector of liberty and democracy, that all Maghrebis have rid themselves of the deadly germ that assumes the shape of protection or nationality, and with no regrets we now consider ourselves free from all ties with France and its embassies in Jordan.[50]

Here again, the issue is not so much to gauge how *representative* such diatribes might be, but rather to observe how they *circulate* and duplicate— evidence of the rise of FLN militancy inside its rear bases in the Middle East. On this point, it is worth diving into a series devoted to the organization of pilgrimages from Algeria to Mecca, documents preserved in France's National Overseas Archives. Included are numerous tracts distributed by FLN militants to Algerian pilgrims, calling for the "destruction of France and the victory of Algerians."[51] Certain of these pilgrims would then transit through Jerusalem on their way back home, so we can easily imagine that they too contributed to spreading the nationalist message to the inhabitants of the Maghrebi Quarter. One of these tracts, written in Arabic, was translated by French services: "Noble and generous Muslim: Algeria, Muslim and combative, calls upon you for help in the relentless battle she wages against godlessness and colonialism; grant her your assistance, God will grant you his."[52]

This foregrounding of the "godlessness" of colonial powers is one of the recurring motifs of nationalist advocacy discourse, and we can imagine that it must have been particularly potent among the pious pilgrims in Jerusalem. We find signs of this in a thick dossier preserved at the Archives of Waqf Administration at Abu-Dis, involving a petition drafted by Hajj Aghrabi al-Marakshi against the steward Hidoussi. In this somewhat muddled text, this resident native of Marrakesh ("al-Marakshi") denounces a steward "under the influence of French Algeria" who is "religiously ignorant" and "incapable of applying the principles of Islam."[53] Without ascribing undue importance to these denunciations, which might well be explained by any number of personal motives and resentments, we can nevertheless note the resonance of these themes, their recurrence from one document to another, and especially their increasingly widespread dissemination by the years 1955 and 1956. This trend intensified as the war in Algeria gathered momentum, as is confirmed by this opinion piece published in the Jordanian daily *Ad-Difaa* on 11 September 1958:

> The members of the Maghrebi community reject any aid provided by the French government, in whatever form. They declare that they shall not acknowledge any person who might attempt to disseminate French imperialist propaganda among the members of their community, either by building mission schools, or by distributing funds or gratuities of any nature. They emphasize that they consider France as the enemy of Arabs and Muslims. Finally, they are willing to sacrifice everything they hold dear in order to halt France's imperialism in Algeria, in keeping with FLN guidelines.[54]

In this text, based on a particularly well-structured political demonstration, it is striking to note that all France's modes of support are specifically itemized and denounced, as if the point was to show that these modes were known and that a campaign of intimidation of the Maghrebi Quarter's inhabitants could for that reason prove effective. Again, it is hard to gauge to what extent, and in what proportions, the Maghrebis of Jerusalem genuinely subscribed to this political line, but it would appear in any case that the message was being more openly broadcast. The inhabitants of the quarter were now in an untenable position, trapped between Israeli maneuvering to speed up the plundering of Ein Karem land, and the intimidation campaigns deployed by the FLN's Jordanian branch as France's position grew ever weaker.

We can imagine the sense of divided loyalties that some must have been experiencing, by simply paging through dossiers at the French consular archives, bundles of receipts clumsily signed (sometimes with just an X or a fingerprint) by the most ailing and needy: "Aid to Aït Fergane Taher, Algerian, entitled to a military disability pension. 1 DJ. 5/1/56. AÏT"; "Aid to Hassan Tagal. DJ 0.500. 13 July 1956"; "Received from the Consulate General of France the sum of 500 fulûs in aid, on 25 September 1956. Muhammad Ben Brahim"; "Received from the Consulate General of France the sum of 500 fulûs in aid, on 29 September 1956. Allal Ammar" (figure 34).[55] We also understand—upon discovering, for instance, a petition signed only by the "Committee of the Moroccan Community of Jerusalem," declaring its "loyalty" and "deferential regards" to the French consul—that rifts were deepening between the different nationalities present in the Maghrebi Quarter of Jerusalem. In any event, the French intelligence services were taking very seriously the FLN's activity in Jordan and Jerusalem, as evidenced by a note drafted by the External Documentation and Counter-Espionage Service (SDECE) on 3 November 1958, which describes the Jerusalem Maghrebis as "terrorized by representatives of the FLN."[56] A few weeks earlier, a memorandum inserted into the archives of the French Consulate in Jerusalem referred to "FLN killers" directly threatening the stewards of the Waqf Abu Madyan.[57] Clearly, the history of the Maghrebi Quarter of Jerusalem had tipped into the bloody history of French decolonization.

Qadi Benhoura, the Last Emissary of a Lost Cause

The report drafted by Qadi Benhoura upon returning from his mission in September 1957 was the last in a long series. After him, no one would ever again be mandated by France to inspect the Waqf Abu Madyan and to comfort the inhabitants of the Maghrebi Quarter. Significantly, the final emissary was sent not from Algiers, in fact, but from Paris, undoubtedly to minimize risk, a few months after the assassination of Hajj Lunis. Qadi Benhoura was considered a "moderate Muslim reformer," close to Massignon; he continued to advocate for a "common destiny" between France and Algeria, by participating, for example, in the Paris branch of the "Movement for Community," a Gaullist splinter group aiming to counter the actions of the OAS.[58] As a consequence, this last emissary performed an explicitly political reading of the situation in his report, unlike Lunis Mahfud, who, on the contrary, chose to conceal the contradictions of the French position. From the opening lines relating his arrival in East Jerusalem, Benhoura describes his "anxiety" and "moral solitude," pointing out that the absence of the French consul general represented a "major hindrance"

FIGURE 34. Receipts signed by inhabitants of the Maghrebi Quarter who benefited from "relief" from the French Consulate General, May–September 1956. Source: © CADN, Jerusalem, 294 PO/2, 40/1.

for his mission.[59] All the memoranda and data exchanged with the French Consulate were handled "by way of the Belgian Consul General representing French interests," and Consul Laforge himself had to admit that "he had not been able to enter the old city for the last ten months."

Beyond these tangible impacts, France's isolation was first and foremost political, and Benhoura clearly states in his report that he could feel "hostility and hatred" toward France, to the point where he says he himself was perceived as "presumably bearing who knows what diabolic and debasing colonialism."[60] The words were on everyone's lips, and indicated the shift in Arab public opinion, even though Benhoura was meanwhile asserting that "the majority of the population is hostile to the Jordanian government" and to the "kinglet," that "the Communists are being hunted down everywhere," and that East Jerusalem was sliding into "extreme squalor," as evidenced, for example, by the ban on consuming meat "three consecutive days in a week."[61] Benhoura's meeting with the qadi of Jerusalem, Sheikh Muhammad Salah El-Adjuni, only confirms this first impression: the judge "harbors feelings of fierce hatred against France"; accuses the former steward, Hidoussi, of having been "an avowed agent of French policy in Jordan"; and opposes all contact with attorney Szczupack, since "no self-respecting Muslim could have direct contact with a Jew."[62] Pursuing the conversation on this point, Benhoura understood that this anti-Semitic article of faith was actually a cover for an awkward position vis-à-vis Israel: "It's because he feared that the approval by a member of the Jordanian government of an act intended for the Jewish authorities would amount to a de facto recognition of the State of Israel."[63] The inhabitants of the Maghrebi Quarter, politically backed by France and legally defended by a Jewish Israeli attorney, were effectively in an untenable bind.

In an attempt to recover some leeway and to at least obtain the support of the Maghrebi Quarter's inhabitants, Benhoura chose to appeal to their sense of identity and to what he perceived as their defiant attitude toward both Israel and the Jordanian authorities. When he gathered "all the young men and all the firebrands" into the zawiya, his speech was astonishingly forthright: "The leadership of Jordanian waqfs has no business getting involved in matters that concern you alone [. . .]. United, you can challenge anything in defense of your rights; disunited, you are sure to lose everything, starting with the waqf itself, which they are currently attempting to annex. Never forget that

France is backing you and your legitimate interests. Nor must you forget that the Algerians in particular are French nationals and that here, you are all foreigners."[64] Thanks to this straightforward rhetoric, Benhoura managed to get the assembly to vote on a motion confirming the request for "an annual usufruct indemnity in compensation for the occupation of Ein Karem," and he was gratified that this motion bore "the signatures of all the firebrands of the Maghrebi Quarter, as well as the notables delegated by the elders."[65] In a commentary he wrote for the attention of French diplomatic officers, Benhoura was even more explicit: "It was my outburst against the Jordanian authorities and the traditional diatribe against Israel that won them over." Beyond the tactical maneuver, this passage is revelatory of a real political tension between the inhabitants of Jerusalem and the Jordanian authorities, particularly since the assassination in front of the al-Aqsa Mosque of King Abdallah on 20 July 1951: while the inhabitants of East Jerusalem were primarily anti-Israeli, they were also faced with a Hashemite dynasty that was wary of the destabilizing potential of Palestinian political movements.

The Maghrebi Quarter once again proved an excellent vantage point for the general history of Jerusalem, whose eastern sector had been marginalized, as if trapped between the proactive development of West Jerusalem on the one hand, and Amman's administrative and political capitalization on the other. The situation of the Maghrebis of Jerusalem was special, of course, but according to Benhoura, it only intensified what had been a pervasive trend: "Since I arrived here, I have been devoting my days to preaching union, the sacred union that is, in a way, the only bulwark possible against the Jordanian invader."[66] The choice of the term "invader" might come as a surprise—especially from an advocate of keeping Algeria French—but it provides insight into the complexity of the political situation in East Jerusalem. This complexity, moreover, ran much deeper than it may at first appear, since a share of the Jordanian state apparatus was made up of Palestinian elites . . . and since part of those same elites originated from the Maghreb. This was precisely the case of Sheikh Chenguitti, qadi of qadis serving in Amman, whom Benhoura would meet on final appeal: "I myself am from the Maghreb, he told me, smilingly, and if need be, I will make timely use of that fact. Fear not and return to Algeria in peace."[67] Far from pitting ontologically pure "Jordanians" against "Palestinians" or "Maghrebis," entrenched as they were in their own identity standards, the history of the Waqf Abu Madyan reveals, on the contrary, the extreme fluidity of the region's cultural and identity-linked itinerary, particularly in this period of decolonization.

In an appendix to his report, Benhoura provides an overview of the "Algerian" community of Jerusalem, and his description qualifies a few preconceived notions as to what motivated these populations. This final description is all the more interesting for coming at the very moment when the French archives are about to have their last word:

> The Algerians number around 156 × 3 = 468 in all. They have all kept close ties with their kin living in Algeria. In the social hierarchy, they are at an average level, though sometimes a bit lower, which might explain why they left Algeria in the first place. Apart from a few youths whose interest in the local Francophobic newspapers stirs them up somewhat, most Algerians here are right-minded [. . .]. None of them—more out of interest than of genuine sentiment, in fact—intends to forego his status as French national.[68]

If a large part of the Maghrebi Quarter's inhabitants were in effect former pilgrims who stayed on by chance, piety, or necessity, it would appear that others had also moved there for economic reasons. The lack of financial resources was in any case the common denominator among these families, who were constantly living on the brink of even greater destitution, as exemplified by the financial record of Benhoura's mission, where a donation of eleven Jordanian dinars was "paid to a family of Maghrebis on the verge of eviction by the Jordanian tax authorities."[69] Aware of the myriad challenges the Jerusalem Maghrebis were facing, Benhoura emphasizes in the final pages of his report the need to renew the two-million-franc annual subsidy: "This renewal could coincide with the resumption of diplomatic relations, for there can be no question of disbursing to the mutewalli anything whatsoever that is not channeled through the French Consulate General in Jerusalem."[70] As he was writing these lines in late September 1957, he could not have known that the war in Algeria would be raging with even more intensity, and that diplomatic relations between France and Jordan would not resume until 1962, after the signing of the Evian Accords and Algerian independence. As it happened, Benhoura was the last witness to this miniature French Algeria, increasingly isolated and exposed in the midst of Middle Eastern battlegrounds.

A "Debt of Honor" Increasingly Difficult to Fulfill

The larger history of the Algerian war can be easily read in the archival dossiers devoted to the "minor history" of the Maghrebi Quarter of Jerusalem, whether from direct reporting on events or from the momentary dearth of documents available, as if other more urgent matters were calling those involved in the dossier. This is the case for the year 1958 in the archives of the Bureau of Algerian Affairs, when the Algiers coup d'état, the fall of the Fourth Republic, and the subsequent extension of the conflict to mainland France seemed to put on hold any decision concerning ties to cultivate between Algeria and its nationals residing in Jerusalem. Defense of the Waqf Abu Madyan was seeming increasingly ill-advised and perhaps even incongruous for the colonial administrators responsible for "restoring order" in Algiers. After all, Muhammad Boukharouba, the new commander of the Oran branch of the National Liberation Army (ALN), had chosen as his nom de guerre Houari Boumédiène in 1957, when he took command of the 5th Wilaya, to assert his commitment to Algeria's western territory and the border areas disputed by Morocco. The name of the famous Sufi mystic of Tlemcen, until then a symbol of France's "Muslim policy" in Jerusalem, was henceforth the alias of one of the foremost leaders of the ALN, the armed wing of the FLN—the same man who would preside over the fate of independent Algeria from 1965 to 1978.

A memo dated 26 January 1959, slipped into a folder labeled "Waqf Abu Madyan / Timeline" in the archives of the Bureau of Algerian Affairs, leaves little doubt about the mindset of the French administrators: "It is worth noting how the FLN has managed to hold sway over the Algerian colony of Palestine; the latter even addressed a memorandum in September 1958 to the relevant authorities in which it declared its refusal of any aid or relief from France. The persistence of the Algerian conflict has left a looming uncertainty in the mindset of the Algerians of Palestine, which remains worrisome for the future."[71] In this same folder, a memo from 15 May 1959 recalls the religious endowment's record, and then proceeds to back away from an issue whose political connotation has clearly shifted over the previous ten years: "The stewardship of the Waqf Abu Madyan has been ensured since the outset, under the auspices of the Qadi of Jerusalem, by Maghrebis living in this city, who are called *mutewalli*, or stewards. Algeria thus has no part in the waqf's management. However,

Algeria was appealed to, as was Morocco and Tunisia, to provide relief to its nationals, deprived since 1947 of waqf revenues that had been confiscated by the Israeli authorities. Funds were raised in Algeria, missions were sent to Palestine and in the end, subsidies were repeatedly granted."[72] By explaining that Algeria had "no part in the waqf's stewardship," the drafters of this memo stand in diametric opposition to the arguments developed ten years earlier by their predecessors.

Louis Massignon was growing aware of this shift throughout the year 1957, if we are to credit the documents preserved today in his personal papers at the BNF. On 31 March 1957, in a letter to the French secretary of state for foreign affairs, Pierre de Felice, he stresses the need to "tighten up the somewhat loosened bonds of our 'hold' on the waqf [...], to keep from definitively destroying that 'Franco-Muslim community' proclaimed by the Prime Minister [Robert Schuman], to prevent the demise of my France-Islam Committee."[73] The following October, sounding even more desperate, he reiterates that he has "fought for over ten years for this waqf," toward which France, in his opinion, has a "debt of honor" and a "sacred mandate."[74] In early 1959, while carrying out his annual cultural mission to the Middle East, Massignon made a stop in Jerusalem and drafted a personal memo to the French consul general, André Favereau (1957–60), expressing his alarm at Jordan's resolve to "nationalize" the waqf. In his annual report, he describes in no uncertain terms the Jordanian maneuvers:

> The scheme of the Grand Qadi of Amman, determined as he is to replace us as stewards of the waqf, took place in four steps: 1) make us suspicious of Hidoussi [...]. 2) deprecate Lunis Mahfud as "colluding" with Pan-Arabism, which had bearing on his violent death, on 5 June 1957 in Setif [...]. 3) threaten the new inspector, Qadi Benhoura, in the Jordanian press [...]. 4) replace Hidoussi et al. with the two current stewards [...]. The two new stewards are Moroccan: Mr. Issa Ben Hachem is from Ntifa, while the chief steward Mr. Ben-Ibrahim Abdelhak is from Figuig, [...]. Why did the Qadi appoint two Moroccan stewards? [...] He persuaded the 40 Moroccan heads of families hovering around the waqf to abandon their French passports and to apply for Moroccan passports.[75]

The position of Massignon, well connected at the Quai d'Orsay though not a career foreign service officer, allows him to describe the new situation without diplomatic doublespeak: the Algerians of the Maghrebi Quarter were still suspected of being agents of colonial France, but Morocco was taking advantage of its recent independence to heighten its control over the quarter and its residents.[76] By force of circumstance, the Waqf Abu Madyan was "slipping away from" France, and this new context further hampered the endowment's likelihood of a possible transaction with the Israelis, as Massignon next indicates: "The new chief steward, Mr. Ben-Ibrahim Abdelhaq, had only just been appointed when he denied France the renewal of the Israeli attorney (Szczupack) in his capacity of counsel to the waqf for the notorious lawsuit against the Israeli seizure of land in Ein Karem. Right when the Israeli State was offering to pay the waqf eleven years' worth of impounded revenues (1948–1959) or, at least, a considerable deposit." Massignon had every reason to lose hope. On all sides, obstacles and adversaries were piling up, even as the endowment's defenders were ever fewer in number and were losing their motivation. Massignon himself, exhausted, was unable to steer the course of a history that was eluding him. In any case, after 1959, he disappears definitively from the archives devoted to the Maghrebi Quarter. He died on 31 October 1962, in the evening, a few months after Algerian independence.[77]

An "Insider Affair," "of No Political Interest"

Turning once again to the archives produced by the French administration of Algeria, we understand that the Waqf Abu Madyan affair had grown unwieldy and was by no means a priority, while the situation on the ground was deteriorating relentlessly and independence for Algeria was appearing more likely by the day. In fact, the tone of exchanges between Paris and Algiers on this subject continued to harden, a sign that the moment of truth was arriving. On 18 August 1959, the Quai d'Orsay delivered a long letter to the Algerian governor general to present a historical recap and to urge his interlocutor to face his responsibilities:

> The development of the legal proceeding and the mounting costs it has incurred compel us today to take a position on a certain number of issues: What authority has jurisdiction to decide the course of action to be followed and to ensure the financing of these operations? What are the chances for a favorable

outcome? Does it make sense to pursue our action despite the considerable expenditure it involves for the State? The first evidence of our interest in the Waqf Abu Madyan dates back to only 1949. Prior to the creation of the State of Israel, France had left it up to the Ottomans, then the British, to monitor the Muslim magistrates [...]. As it currently stands, according to somewhat inaccurate statistics, there are thought to be in Jerusalem (Jordanian zone) about 40 Moroccan families, 30 Algerian, and 15 Tunisian. This is why, from 1950 to 1957, Morocco and Tunisia were always consulted about issues involving the waqf, and solicited, with dwindling success, to contribute financially to its upkeep. However, since 1957, Morocco and Tunisia have failed to respond to our messages pertaining to the waqf.[78]

This summary of the situation—mostly accurate, historically speaking—sought to demonstrate that Algiers was henceforth on the front line to finance the ongoing legal proceeding, whose basis was defensible since the Ein Karem domain "is thought to comprise an area of 12,000 to 15,000 hectares," whose "theoretical value is certainly considerable (eight million francs according to the waqf attorney)." The purpose of mentioning the total theoretical property value of Ein Karem was, of course, to highlight the utility of the proceeding, even if everything indicated that the endowment's rights had been eroding for quite some time:

> It is important to acknowledge that already under Ottoman domination, the waqf's situation in Ein Karem had been gradually worsening, that its rights were being contested, and that it had effectively lost possession of part of its lands. Inaccuracies in the land registry, administrative mismanagement, scheming on the part of the tenants who, by passing their leases down from father to son, had come to consider themselves as rightful owners, all were the leading causes of this decline. Subsequently, under British Mandate, numerous occupants had deeds issued to them, which they then sold to Jewish immigrants. During the 1948 war, all the Arab farmers were expelled and replaced by kibbutzim. Finally, since 1953, the Israeli government has undertaken a series of expropriations to install public services in the vicinity of its new capital.[79]

In attorney Szczupack's report, attached to the letter, these "public services" are more precisely described: "School of Medicine of the University of Jerusalem, low-cost housing, a memorial to the victims of Nazism."[80] In fact, a law passed by the Knesset on 19 August 1953 provided for the installation on the eastern slopes of the Ein Karem territory, at the foot of the hill that henceforth bore the name *har Herzl* (Mount Herzl), the Yad Vashem memorial, dedicated to the six million Jews who died during the Shoah. The memorial was inaugurated and opened to the public in its early configuration in 1957. In other words, the rural land holdings of the Waqf Abu Madyan were now adjacent to the Yad Vashem, while its urban properties were facing the Wailing Wall. By a strange historical coincidence, the religious endowment found itself surrounded by two of the most emblematic symbols of Jewish religious memory and national Israeli memory.

The end of the letter puts aside these patrimonial considerations to focus on more pragmatic issues: since the legal costs were increasing relentlessly, the Quai d'Orsay asked whether the Government General of Algeria was in a position to "plan for the annual provision on the order of 8 million" to cover both the waqf's operating costs and all fees incurred by the legal proceedings.[81] The amount was substantial, since it would equal a quadrupling of the annual Algerian subsidy. Attorney Szczupack justified these expenses, pointing out that "part of the archives having remained in the old city of Jerusalem," he had to "seek out the necessary documentation not only in Israel but also in Jordan and in Turkey, since some of the documents dating to the Ottoman Empire are located in the Istanbul archives."[82] Here again, we come upon the decisive issue of reconstituting the historic and judicial dossier, already spelled out ten years earlier by René Neuville. We especially recognize that the equation that had once determined France's intervention had been totally modified: the expenditures required for the judicial proceeding were vanishing at the very moment when the FLN's influence in Palestine had largely dampened Algiers's good will, eroding the credibility of the Quai d'Orsay's request.

The response from Algiers took nearly three months and was finally drafted on 6 November 1959, a sign that the issue was no longer a priority. The content is hardly surprising, but the form is quite withering. Michel-Jean Mafart, a high-ranking official who would complete his career at the Cour des Comptes, the national audit court, was then chief of staff of the government's general delegation in Algeria;[83] the very least we can say is that he distanced himself from any notions of "debt of honor" and "sacred mandate" put forward a few months earlier by Massignon:

> It is true that in the past the Israeli occupation of Ein Karem lands stirred feelings among the religious leaders of the Muslim community [...]. But these same notables felt no duty to acknowledge the validity of a ruling even when it compensated the waqf for the expropriation [...]. At present, the Waqf Abu Madyan affair leaves Muslim opinion indifferent, and thereby presents no political interest in Algeria. Developments in its legal proceedings are being monitored by only a handful of insiders, notably Professor Louis Massignon and Mr. Jean Scelles of the France-Islam Committee, Qadi Benhoura [...]. Moreover, Algerian families represent only a minority of the Abu Madyan endowment's beneficiaries, the greatest number of whom are made up of Moroccans and Tunisians, whose respective governments have lost all interest in the matter [...]. Consequently, I find it would be impossible to have the Algerian budget assume the responsibility of these proceedings that no political interest in Algeria can justify, and whose outcome remains at best uncertain.[84]

The divorce was thus consummated between the Algiers authorities in charge of managing a decolonization process that was looking increasingly irreversible, and the "handful of insiders" from Paris who were still defending the Waqf Abu Madyan as a symbol of "Franco-Muslim" solidarity, a slogan that now seemed obsolete. Not without a dash of irony, Mafart reminded his Parisian interlocutors that the Algerians were preoccupied by other matters now in late 1959, while in his 16 September speech, French President Charles de Gaulle opened the way to self-determination with three possible options: "secession," "Francization," or "association."[85] In addition, Mafart bitingly emphasized the judicial-political deadlock that the "Muslim notables" had entered, as they could not formally accept the Israeli offer of compensation without breaching the principle of the endowment's inalienability, even though the Israeli press stated at the same time that the appeal proceedings were ongoing before the Israeli Supreme Court.[86] Finally, if the new Moroccan and Tunisian governments had lost all interest in the matter (which was not entirely true in the case of Morocco), it was, according to Mafart, undoubtedly because its follow-through only made sense within the framework of imperial solidarity, which was no longer of any relevance. The sequence opened in 1949 closed ten years later.

Endgame: Fear and Trembling

When the time came to act upon the decision to discontinue French protection of the Waqf Abu Madyan, decision-making processes ground to a halt with decision makers wringing their hands, and a certain feverishness seemed to overcome the various administrations in charge of the dossier: there was no longer anyone with a stake in defending the endowment, but each person was still reluctant to assume responsibility for the discontinuation. Symptomatic of this ultimate hesitation was that the responsibility level of the parties involved kept moving higher up, which is logical since the lower and middle echelons within ministries could not take on such an eminently political decision on their own.[87] Furthermore, since the financial stakes were becoming the deciding factor, the Ministry of Finance was emerging as the new arbitrator between Algiers and the Quai d'Orsay.

On 9 February 1961, it is the foreign minister, Maurice Couve de Murville, who in person writes to the minister of finance regarding "an exceptional affair, an extremely complex issue."[88] After summarizing the case history, Couve de Murville explains that "Morocco and Tunisia, having gained independence, have stopped responding to communications," and that "Algeria itself, concerned with other problems, has tended to lose interest in the matter." Couve de Murville nonetheless pursues his reasoning at the political level, emphasizing that discontinuing French support would do "irreparable harm," precisely within the context of ongoing discussions about the future of Algeria, since "we run the risk of being accused of sacrificing the interests of the Muslim communities of the Maghreb." Given the urgency of the situation, he asks the minister of finance to allow that the three hundred thousand francs earmarked "for the restoration of the Holy Sepulchre" be made available immediately, since a "persistent disagreement between Christian communities" has been holding up the project.[89] Here we face a surprising paradox at two levels since, thanks to an expansive definition of the mandate to protect Catholic holy places, the minister of a secular republic was suggesting the transfer of budgetary funds set aside to restore the Holy Sepulchre to the judicial protection of an Islamic endowment.

On 4 May 1961 the Quai d'Orsay was compelled to acknowledge that its strategy had failed, since the minister of finance would accept this budgetary transfer only if the appropriation earmarked for the restoration of the supposed tomb of Christ were canceled, placing French diplomacy in an impossible predicament: this "would oblige us to choose between the restoration of the Holy Sepulchre and the continuing defense of the waqf's interests."[90] The Quai d'Orsay then turned to Algiers, concluding that in the prevailing conditions, there would be "no outcome other than abandoning the legal proceedings." Stressing that "a decision to abandon would be used against us," the Quai d'Orsay made one final attempt to get the Algiers authorities to assume responsibility. On 19 May, the minister for Algerian affairs, Louis Joxe, issued a particularly blunt refusal:

> The proceedings underway are both very costly and very slow due to the complexity of this affair. Its outcome, moreover, is most uncertain: the situation is indeed unfavorable to the Muslim endowment that has lost assets in favor of already long-standing occupants, and is coming up against powerful Israeli interests [. . .]. Although the furtherance of the proceedings initiated might constitute an attempt to offset the influence wielded by the FLN over the Algerian colony in Palestine, it is nevertheless doubtful that it could result in anything positive in that regard.[91]

This last sentence is of course the harshest, since above and beyond the legal and financial arguments, Louis Joxe was questioning the *political* equation on which French intervention had been based thus far. As it happened, this exchange of letters took place a few days after the coup d'état of the generals in Algiers (21–26 April 1961), and we can well understand that the gap was now all but unbridgeable between the situation in Algeria and the Maghrebi community of Jerusalem. During the summer of 1961, Couve de Murville asserted that, "all things considered, I have arrived at the conclusion that it was not possible to abandon the proceedings underway" because "the Israeli authorities would be delighted at our turnabout which for them would seal the withdrawal of our argument with regard to the waqf's rights," which in turn could "have people suspecting us of colluding with Israel."[92] Here we can gauge the salience of the foundational reasoning developed over ten years, between the moral commitment to the Maghrebis of Jerusalem and the political risk of too conspicuous an alignment with Israeli interests. Responding to this final pressure from the Quai d'Orsay, the minister of Algerian affairs deployed all manner of administrative foot-dragging, arguing "tight budgetary constraints," requesting additional information as to the amounts to be provided, and demanding "new appropriations" from the minister of finance.[93]

The resolution of this standoff, which marks the end of France's history in the Maghrebi Quarter of Jerusalem, was punctuated by the political history of the Algerian war. On Monday 12 February in the evening at the Quai d'Orsay, in the office of the chief of staff of the minister of foreign affairs, Couve de Murville, a brief conclave was taking place to enact the "discontinuation of the proceedings," as is evidenced by an unsigned handwritten transcript preserved today in the archives of the Ministry of Algerian Affairs.[94] Four days after the 8 February massacre, on the eve of a demonstration that would bring five hundred thousand people into the streets of Paris to accompany the five dead from the Métro Charonne incident to Père-Lachaise cemetery,[95] a month before the signing of the Evian Accords, French diplomacy bowed to the inevitable and decided to "cut off" the Waqf Abu Madyan. Since neither the Quai d'Orsay nor the Ministry of Algerian Affairs cared to assume responsibility for the decision, the format of the meeting conferred a kind of collegiality. The two ministries actually blamed the Ministry of Finance, which had sent "no representative," and which "refused to allocate any funds whatsoever."

The first paragraph of the transcript summarizes the position of the Ministry of Algerian Affairs, which continued to believe that "the political stakes of this affair are insufficient"; the second paragraph sums up the Quai d'Orsay position, which points to the "difficulties" of this affair as "financial" and "judicial," but especially as "diplomatic," since "the Arab governments consider the waqf assets as inalienable and would never acknowledge the jurisdiction of Israeli courts." The final paragraph states the "decision taken": "Discontinuation of the proceedings; liquidation of fees and costs; request to the Israeli government to take on the affair at the diplomatic level, by deeming the waqf as 'absent' from the proceedings and not as 'defaulting.'" There was obvious dithering going on here between judicial and diplomatic actions, but the fact that the Israeli authorities were being asked to consider the Waqf Abu Madyan as falling under the "Absentee Property Law" (1950), and not as a "defaulting" party in the proceedings underway, did not bode well for the religious endowment, since Israeli jurisprudence on "absentee property" actually allows for the ex post facto legalization of dispossession subsequent to acts of war.

On 19 March 1962, in the aftermath of the Evian Accords, a cease-fire went into effect, putting an end to nearly eight years of war. On 3 July, following the referendum on self-determination, France officially recognized Algeria's independence. In early November, the ambassador of France in Tel Aviv informed the Quai d'Orsay that the Israel authorities had accepted "the postponement of the proceedings until 1 January 1963," so as to allow the new Algerian authorities to take over the proceedings.[96] The Zionist associations that had purchased the Ein Karem properties affected to rise up via the press; this was the case, for example, with the Hachsharat Hayishuv (formerly the Palestine Land Development Company), which asserted that "Israel must not cede anything to the Ben Bella regime, whose leaders are responsible for the shedding of Jewish blood and the loss of Jewish assets" in Algeria.[97] On 4 November, an article appearing in *Haaretz* proved more reassuring and especially more consistent with reality: "In the wake of Algerian independence, France has ceased to take an interest in the affair but has sought to bring it to the attention of the Algerian government, alongside other matters it is called upon to hand over [. . .]. If the waqf were to win in court, it would involve only payment of compensation and not recovery of lands."[98]

All indications were that French diplomacy did attempt to transmit the dossier to the Algerian government. In December, Jean-Marcel Jeanneney, the first French ambassador to Algeria,[99] requested that the Quai d'Orsay provide a brief fact sheet that could then be passed on to the new Algerian authorities (figure 35).[100] This four-page memorandum illustrates the postcolonial relationship opening up between France and Algeria:

> France's intervention in the Waqf Abu Madyan affair had but one purpose, to safeguard North African assets subsumed into the State of Israel. The sole aim of its action was to spare the waqf the harshness of Israeli law on absentee property. It is obvious that this waqf should be considered as principally Algerian if we recall its founding personage, a native of Tlemcen. Since Algerian independence, France no longer has any basis for pursuing its action in favor

of the waqf [...]. It is therefore up to the Algerian Government, should it deem appropriate, to resume the action undertaken earlier to safeguard the waqf patrimony."[101]

In the mail exchanges that followed, we note that the Algerian government did not seem especially motivated to take charge of the dossier. On 4 January 1963, Jeanneney indicates that the Algerian minister of foreign affairs, "having no knowledge of the matter," stalls by requesting additional information on "the proceeding's progress" and on "an estimate of the fees" still to be disbursed in order to reach closure."[102] A new postponement was requested of the Israeli authorities, who set a final deadline of 1 April 1963, thanks to a direct intervention by the French ambassador in Tel Aviv with Golda Meir, minister of for-

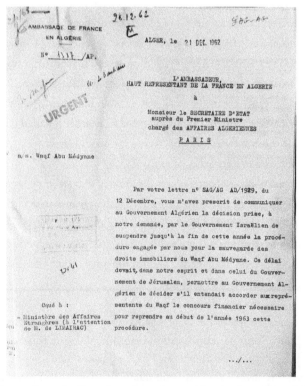

FIGURE 35. Letter from the French ambassador to Algeria, Jean-Marcel Jeanneney, to the secretary of state in charge of Algerian Affairs, 21 December 1962. Source: ANOM, 81.F-844.

eign affairs.[103] In the end, the Algerian government chose not to take over the proceedings that were underway, and it was France that would finally settle the 234,000 Israeli pounds in back fees owed to attorney Szczupack in the spring of 1969—in other words, nearly two years *after* the demolition of the Maghrebi Quarter—as attested in a dossier preserved in the French consular archives, titled "Szczupack—recovery of fees from the French government 1962–1969."[104] In the consular archives, this dossier is the last document bundle devoted to the Maghrebi Quarter of Jerusalem, which, once outside the consulate's scope of jurisdiction, disappeared definitively from its archives.

———

On the Algerian government side, we can posit several theories to explain the decision to discontinue the proceedings. First of all, Algiers was consumed by the countless domestic contingencies it was facing. Furthermore, the dim prospects conveyed by the Quai d'Orsay left little hope for a satisfying outcome; politically, an official involvement by Algeria in the compensation proceedings would have raised the issue of de facto recognition of the State of Israel and the dispossession of land. Finally, from the standpoint of a regime that foregrounded its socialist and revolutionary credentials, a few hundred pious pilgrims lost in Jerusalem would no doubt rank low as a priority. Still, the Maghrebis of Jerusalem found themselves totally isolated as of the first of April 1963; already deprived of a major share of their financial revenue since 1948, they were now bereft of all judicial and diplomatic recourse. Worse still, this isolation took place under the gaze of the Israeli authorities, and at the highest level: Golda Meir, by granting this final grace period, was sending the message that the Maghrebi Quarter of Jerusalem was henceforth living on borrowed time.

5

EXPEL AND DEMOLISH

HISTORY OF A POLITICAL DECISION (JUNE 1967)

The Maghrebi Quarter of Jerusalem was demolished on the night of Saturday to Sunday 11–12 June 1967, a few hours after the imposition of the cease-fire that brought the Six-Day War to an end. On Wednesday 14 June, the date of the Jewish holiday of Shavuot that year, tens of thousands of Israelis marched in procession to the Western Wall. Some took photos to immortalize the historic moment;[1] in the background, behind the smiles and beaming faces, one can see dump trucks removing the rubble, bulldozers filling and leveling the ground, heaps of stone and debris pushed to either side. In a few days, several centuries of urban history would be razed, flattened, erased (figure 36). As often happens in such cases, the history of this sudden obliteration left behind little written evidence. At first sight, the demolition of the Maghrebi Quarter would effectively qualify as "spoils of war" with no written order, hastily decided in the heat of combat, to take advantage of a sudden historic opportunity unlikely ever to recur. Thus, while the centuries-old life of this intensely administered neighborhood had produced a large quantity of archival material, its death appeared at first glance to be shrouded in silence. Unlike the French period of its history, which is perfectly documented, the moment of the quarter's physical *destruction* seemed to also coincide with its documentary *disappearance*, as if the quarter and its inhabitants had become literally "invisible" in the eyes of a historian. Hence a triple paradox, since the destruction of the Maghrebi Quarter is the most famous event of its history, the one that marked its demise, while being by far the least well documented.

The history of this demolition is essentially an Israeli history. With no ingenuousness or false hopes, therefore, I had to look toward sources other than those I had marshaled thus far. It makes sense that these sources are rare, patchy, and incomplete, as are those that could shed "glancing" light on the event. Foreign consulates, for instance, had no access to the prior decision-making processes or to the practical terms of the neighborhood's demolition; consular reports drafted at the time are instructive, for they show that the demolition took place out of sight and that, as a result, its "archival echo" is extremely tenuous, the event having largely "evaded" any possible written documentation.[2] It is worth recalling here what is self-evident: the punishment of cities or "urbanicide"—to quote a term forged by historians of ancient and medieval cities—is widely practiced in the wake of a conquest or siege, and is the very hallmark of victory and transfer of sovereignty; and while it has always contributed to redesigning urban landscapes, it is nevertheless considerably

FIGURE 36. **Wreckage of the Maghrebi Quarter, Wednesday 14 June 1967. Source: ©** **Gilles Caron.**

underdocumented in comparison to development projects conceived and discussed during peacetime.[3]

Even so, to forge the narrative of this destruction, I was reduced to collecting piecemeal evidence and hard-to-date photographs, but also the testimonies
reported in the Israeli press at the time, relating events on a daily basis in a
spectacular fashion, strictly speaking, without necessarily understanding their
political underpinnings. To fill this gap in understanding and reconstruct
the nested decision-making processes that led to the demolition, we shall be
drawing on *technical* documents produced by the Israeli municipality of Jerusalem in the days preceding and following the demolition, focusing particular
attention on the timeline and the scope of meetings, but also on how information circulated, how instructions were transmitted to this or that department.
Being able to meet with Meron Benvenisti, the Israeli historian and essayist
who at the time was a young deputy mayor in charge of East Jerusalem, proved
critical for this study; his personal archives, recently bequeathed to the Ben-
Zvi Institute, and his administrative archives, preserved by the municipality,
demonstrate—for the first time with supporting material—that the disappearance of the Maghrebi Quarter did indeed result from a scheduled and
planned operation, and not at all from some spontaneous initiative.[4] Finally,
in the absence of written sources, we shall resort to the oral testimony of the
youngest inhabitants of the neighborhood, who are still alive today, and to the
testimony of an Israeli entrepreneur, Sasson Levy, one of the last survivors of
taking part in the demolition and its logistical preparation.

What is at issue in this rather challenging "history of a disappearance"
gets to the very heart of the historian's craft, for the event was prima facie
elusive. Somewhere in the recesses of the documentation were the actors who
had to be identified in order to establish responsibility. Although compressed
into the urgency of combat, the successive *stages* still had to be sorted out to
distinguish how each sequential technical operation linked up to provide
the desired result, to open up a plaza as fast as possible with the least outcry:
justifying the decision, expelling the inhabitants, demolishing the buildings,
evacuating the rubble, and finally compensating the former residents. Shrouded
in a mystical memory intermingling religious redemption and nationalist revenge, the *history* still needs to be traced: a ground-level history, purposefully
urban and citizen-focused, persistently anchored in the daily life of those who

experienced it on both sides of the front line. The issue is therefore heuristic and methodological, but also ethical, for the ultimate purpose here is nothing short of relating the *death* of this corner of the city to the history of its life, to weave back together the tenuous threads that connect the short time of its disappearance to the far longer time of its existence, to recall that no matter what object or subject the historian is addressing, its death is part of its life—indeed, very often the culminating point of its meaning. In the tangible case of the Maghrebi Quarter of Jerusalem, the purpose is to demonstrate that beyond overt appearances, its destruction is anything but an accident of history, an unforeseeable, incidental *disruption*; rather, it fits into the *continuity* and even perhaps the logical sequence of previous years and decades.

1962–67: A Neighborhood on Borrowed Time

Even before the actual moment of demolition, we confront a dearth of sources concerning the last years of the Maghrebi Quarter: a few years before being *demolished*, it was being slowly *eclipsed*, relegated to the dead zones of available documentation, or at least of accessible material. Whether we turn to the Jordanian municipal archives, to those dealing with the administration of the waqfs at Abu-Dis, or to the French diplomatic archives, we are struck by this gradual erasure, no doubt symptomatic of the political marginalization process that affected the Waqf Abu Madyan after 1962. Despite this gradual vanishing from view, we can still discern a few documents that deal with the Maghrebi Quarter's final decade.

In the Abu-Dis archives of waqf administration, we find a list of the endowment's properties drawn up in 1959 that provides a final snapshot of the neighborhood a few years before its disappearance.[5] What makes this list worthy of interest is that it supplies a quite precise description of the buildings, their exact locations and respective amenities, and this allows for a better understanding—in anticipation—of the tangible, material dimension of the neighborhood's demolition. A third of the buildings listed, for example, are described as comprising two levels (a ground floor and an upper floor); two-thirds of the buildings have only a ground floor, sometimes topped by a terrace. In the bills and invoices for work carried out during this same period, refurbishing the watertightness of the rooftop terraces or cupolas is in fact often mentioned, as well as applying new coats of whitewash. In the Maghrebi Quarter, the list mentions three vegetable gardens, a few trees scattered around in various court-yards (notably fig, olive, and almond trees), and a vast field planted with prickly pear to the south of the neighborhood (al-Katunya). The list also mentions a public bread oven and a few pantries. And finally, we observe that more than half of the houses are equipped with underground cisterns for drinking water.[6] The ubiquity of underground cisterns typical of traditional domestic architec-ture in Jerusalem would represent both a constraint and an opportunity at the moment of the neighborhood's demolition,[7] as is told to us by Sasson Levy: the cavities precluded the use of overly heavy bulldozers, which more than once crashed through the vaults of cisterns excavated just beneath the surface, but they could also be filled up with some of the debris, thereby accelerating the removal of rubble.

In the archives of the Islamic Tribunal of Jerusalem, a ruling on 27 June 1961 also contains an exhaustive list of properties belonging to the Waqf Abu Madyan, drawn up in the context of a conflict between its stewards and the Jordanian administration. Although it converges broadly with the list pro-duced two years earlier by the Waqf administration, it does a more precise job of locating the houses with respect to their immediate vicinity, in the manner of an official registry: "a house bounded to the east by the Buraq al-Sharif," "a house bounded to the north by the waqf al-Khalidi," "a house bounded to the north and east by an alley and to the west by the zawiya al-Afdaliyya," "a public oven and a warehouse bounded to the north and south by an orchard," "a house bounded to the north by the waqf of Imam al-Husseini...."[8] These descriptions of the neighborhood match photographs of the period, showing a densely built urban fabric, fairly well maintained: low elevation, a few courtyards mostly surrounded by low walls over which rise a few trees, the neighborhood itself being surrounded by several orchards, especially to the south.[9]

We would like to get beyond this exterior panorama of the neighborhood prior to its demise, but analysis of filmed footage from official trips made in the early 1960s provides little compelling evidence. The neighborhood remains unseen—outside the frame, in a sense. This was the case during Pope Paul VI's trip to Jerusalem in January 1964. For the first pope in history to visit the Holy City, it was out of the question that he would include the Western Wall among his site visits, unlike his successors who have commonly made the stop.[10] More surprisingly, however, this was also the case for the extensive tour undertaken by the king of Morocco, Mohammed V, to the Middle East and notably to Jerusalem, from 7 January to 6 February 1960. In the long film directed by Bernard Rouget documenting this trip, we can see shots of Mohammed V visiting the Dead Sea, Nabi Musa, Hebron, the Haram al-Sharif in Jerusalem, and the Holy Sepulchre, but no shots taken inside the Maghrebi Quarter.[11] At minute thirty-five in the film, a tracking shot taken from a moving vehicle shows the official motorcade driving through the old city from the Zion Gate, moving in the direction of the Maghrebi Quarter. When it takes the wide bend that leads to the neighborhood, the convoy slows down, surrounded by hundreds of bystanders waving red Moroccan flags, but we see nothing of the neighborhood itself; we know from the royal archives in Rabat, however, that the king made a sizable donation on that occasion, which allowed for the renovation of a certain number of buildings.[12]

To better capture the Maghrebi Quarter's last years of existence and to reframe it in the broader context of Jordanian urbanism in 1960s Jerusalem, I was able to consult the private archives of the chief engineer for the Jordanian municipality of Jerusalem, Yussuf Budeiri, preserved by his son Adel Budeiri in a little family library adjacent to the Haram al-Sharif.[13] One photograph in the collection notably features a construction site of a rather large building located between the Maghrebi Quarter and the gate of the same name; on the back of the photo, handwritten, we read "Madrassa Bab al-Magharibah," and pictured in the shot is Yussuf Budeiri in the company of a few laborers, a policeman, and Adel Sharaf, the brother-in-law of the mayor of East Jerusalem, Ruhi al-Khatib (figure 37). The photograph is not dated but, based on how his father looks, Adel Budeiri situates it in the early 1960s, thus allowing us to conclude that the famous school so yearned for by Louis Massignon was at last breaking ground thanks to funding from UNRWA, according to Adel Budeiri.[14] In other photographs we glimpse a crane set up on the Temple Mount, as part of the renovation of the Dome of the Rock, the first phase of which was completed and celebrated to much fanfare by the young King Hussein on 6 August 1964 (figure 38).[15]

Kimberly Katz, author of one of the rare studies of Jordanian urbanism in Jerusalem, shows that the years 1959–67 correspond to a genuine push by the Hashemite monarchy to reclaim the Holy City.[16] To overshadow the trauma

FIGURE 37. Group including Yussuf Budeiri and Adel Sharaf in front of the building site of the "Madrassa Bab al-Magharibah" in the early 1960s. Source: © EBAF.

FIGURE 38. Maghrebi Quarter, Dar Abu Saud, and the restoration site of the Dome of the Rock, January 1964. Source: © EBAF.

created by the assassination of his father Abdallah in Jerusalem in July 1951, King Hussein decided in 1959 to proclaim the city the "second capital" of his kingdom,[17] and to showcase the Holy Places within a vast program promoting Jordan as "Holy Land," involving the development of various tourism projects and the renovation of heritage sites—in particular, the Holy Sepulchre and the Dome of the Rock—but also the hosting of prestigious personalities, such as Pope Paul VI in January 1964 or Morocco's King Mohammed V in January 1960.[18] In the same vein, and to assert his authority over the Holy City, Hussein convened in Jerusalem the founding assembly of the Palestinian Liberation Organization (PLO) on 28 May 1964, in the presence of 350 delegates—including the Algerian foreign minister, Abd al-Aziz Bouteflika.[19] It was on this occasion that Yasser Arafat visited his childhood home on the outskirts of the Maghrebi Quarter, if we are to believe the testimony of his nephew, Azzam Abu Saud.[20] In 1965 a new series of postage stamps was available in Jordan showing the profile of King Hussein overlooking the recently renovated religious sites of Jerusalem; the stamps must also be understood in the context of a drive to develop the tourist industry worldwide in the early 1960s.[21] That same year, a number of street signs were replaced or installed on the most emblematic sites of the old city, notably the one reading "Al-Buraq," affixed to the Western Wall / Al-Buraq.[22]

The years leading up to the Six-Day War were thus marked by a determination to reassert the Hashemite dynasty's sovereignty over East Jerusalem, and this resolve translated notably into intensive renovation programs in neighborhoods located immediately adjacent to the Haram al-Sharif, or Temple Mount. In the archives of the municipal engineer Yussuf Budeiri we find a copy of the town plan proposed by the American agency Brown Engineers International in 1963 at the request of Henry Kendall, who was in charge of coordinating the town planning scheme within the Jordanian municipality of Jerusalem between 1963 and 1966—thereby resuming a position he had held during the British Mandate.[23] Upon close scrutiny of his proposals,[24] we realize that several recommendations involved the Maghrebi Quarter or its vicinity: in front of Robinson's Arch (located on the Western Wall), for instance, there were plans for "archaeological sites as garden areas" and a "sitting area with trees and fountains,"[25] as well as "creation of automobile parking areas"[26] both inside and outside the Maghrebi Gate. In a zone encompassing both the Maghrebi

Quarter and the Jewish Quarter, there were plans for a "rehabilitation" of "deteriorating areas," which would presuppose a preliminary "rehousing program" for the residents involved.[27]

In the archives of the Jordanian municipality of Jerusalem, I came across a few traces of these development projects. For instance, the municipal council meeting on 3 July 1963 dealt with the parking lot project planned for the Maghrebi Gate area, with a negotiation engaged between the municipality and the "Maghrebi waqf, owner of the property," concerning the lease amount in particular.[28] On 24 July 1963, the municipal council welcomed the completion of a new school located at Maghrebi Gate—the same worksite photographed a few months before by Yussuf Budeiri—and stressed the need to build a wall around the new structure. A year later, on 8 July 1964, the municipal council ordered the demolition of "wooden shacks" located near the Maghrebi Gate, no doubt in anticipation of the parking lot project. On 5 May 1965, however, it was the municipality that opposed the Jordanian governor regarding the eviction of people living in these shacks, because there was no guarantee they would be rehoused. In the end, it was decided that the shacks would not be demolished until the issue of financing a rehousing scheme was settled. A few years earlier, on 7 June 1956, the Jordanian municipal archives indicate that a small police station was built near the Maghrebi Gate; the municipality covered the utility costs but collected rent from the governorate. These few elements attest to the reality of these redevelopment projects in the vicinity of the Maghrebi Quarter, but also testify to the latitude the Jordanian municipality meant to deploy when issued orders by the Jordanian government.

These stepped-up Jordanian town planning schemes resonate with convergent testimony regarding the 1966 expulsion of a few dozen residents living illegally in the former Jewish Quarter,[29] but also with a dispatch from the French consul on 29 December 1966 that mentions a project aiming to turn part of the former Jewish Quarter in the old city into a "park" and to "allow free access to the Wailing Wall."[30] Vague as this latter formulation might seem, we understand that the southeast corner of the old city, comprising both the Jewish Quarter and the Maghrebi Quarter, was to undergo a broad-based rehabilitation project by urban developers of the time. Already in February 1963, the French consul notes that "seventeen representatives of North American travel agencies have arrived in Jerusalem, old city [. . .] in order to study the

conditions in which tourism might be developed." He adds that "the Municipality of Jerusalem, old city, has taken steps to devise a town planning scheme
that would involve the architect Henry Kendall," and specifies that the project
provides notably for "turning the Jewish Quarter into a public garden," and
that "the Wailing Wall would be kept intact, this vestige of the second temple
being considered a holy site."[31] In December 1964 the consul further explained
that this "urban design plan" would be carried out under the aegis of the East
Jerusalem Development Corporation, and notably that it anticipated "the
demolition of numerous more or less damaged buildings."[32]

In the *Jerusalem Star* of 28 December 1966, an article details "Mayor Khatib's grand plan for Jerusalem in 1967," emphasizing that "this new year heralds
a large number of important state-sponsored public projects [. . .], which the
government gladly announces to visitors to the Holy City in this period of
religious feast days," before going on to mention the upgrading of the Kalandia
airport, the renovation of the al-Aqsa Mosque, and continued restoration work
on the Holy Sepulchre, but also various upgrades of the water supply networks
and electrical grid.[33] Beyond the irony one cannot help but feel when reading
these documents in light of later events, we clearly perceive that the Jordanian
authorities, at both the governmental and the municipal levels starting in the
early 1960s, had committed to a broad scheme of modernization of the Holy
City, with the stated aim of improving tourist attractions.

One final bit of testimony is able to show that the perimeter of the
Maghrebi Quarter was particularly targeted by these tourism development
projects. Fouad Moughrabi, who today teaches at the University of Tennessee,
recalls participating in an archaeological dig in the summer of 1966 under the
direction of William Stinespring, in the vicinity of Wilson's Arch, immediately
bordering the Maghrebi Quarter, in the northern part of the Western Wall.[34]
Moughrabi had a very special connection to this dig, since his father, of Algerian origin, had grown up in the Maghrebi Quarter of Jerusalem in the 1930s.
In February 1966, Stinespring published an article in the American journal
Biblical Archaeologist about an excavation project in the sector, intended to
eventually create a "tourist attraction."[35] The following year, in February 1967,
he reported on an excavation campaign in which Moughrabi took part, stressing that further digging would require an opening up of the excavation area,
and ending with a question: "But can such an opening be made, with many

people living overhead? And can we do any excavating underground without bringing down on our heads large stones or even whole buildings now resting on these ancient structures? We hope to answer some of these questions in the summer of 1968."[36] The answers would come sooner than expected, as the buildings of the Maghrebi Quarter would be effectively demolished, and the "tourist attraction" would indeed be created, but in conditions and proportions that Stinespring could hardly have imagined.

Faint Signals, Warning Signs

The role of the historian sometimes consists of simply making subtle continuities visible, where epic narratives will see only earth-shattering disruptions. In this respect, the Six-Day War is a classic example: just as the destruction of the Maghrebi Quarter in the night of 10–11 June came as no surprise, the outbreak of war on Monday 5 June was not some unexpected event, catching actors and observers off guard.[37] Likewise, the conquest of East Jerusalem on Wednesday 7 June was not the "divine surprise" that certain Israeli editorialists suggest, as if the operation had not been long anticipated, awaiting a historic opportunity.[38] A rapid analysis of the French consular archives shows, for example, that signs of heightened tension over the Jerusalem issue had been growing more frequent over the preceding months: faint signals that issued a warning. On 10 August 1965, the French consul reported that "on this 9 Av, national day of mourning (commemorating the destruction of the Temple), the Hebrew press raised the issue of the pilgrimage to the Wailing Wall to which Israelis had no access since 1948," adding that "as an alternative, numerous pilgrims and Jewish tourists went up to Mount Zion to pray at King David's Tomb, to read the Lamentations and to gaze out over the old city," and mentioning in passing that the *prohibition* of access to the Wall most certainly contributed to consolidating its *sacredness* in the years 1948–67.[39] The following summer, on 30 June 1966, the French consul reported an intense press campaign orchestrated by the Israeli rabbinical authorities calling for "the right for Jews to access the Wailing Wall," theoretically provided for by the armistice agreements signed in Rhodes in 1949. On 6 October, the French consul describes "the zeal of the director general of the Ministry of Religious Affairs, Dr. Cahana," observing that "a sizable crowd" had assembled on Mount Zion to "rekindle" the tradition of religious pilgrimages to Jerusalem.[40]

These faint signals did not involve religious demands alone. They also pointed to urban planning issues revived in the run-up to the new town planning scheme launched in 1966 by Aviya Hashimshoni, Zion Hasimshoni, and Yoseph Schwied under the aegis of the Israeli municipality, which explicitly demanded that the planners work on the assumption of a "reunification" of Jerusalem.[41] Although a draft of this development scheme was not completed until 1968, we can observe that its main recommendations—notably with regard to incorporating services and infrastructures, but also preserving patrimony and developing tourism—had been determined *prior to* the conquest of East Jerusalem, which strongly suggests that "reunification" was the Israeli authorities' vision for the future.[42] Once again, analysis of the French consular archives supports this conjecture. On 10 November 1966, the French consul sent to Jerusalem's mayor, Teddy Kollek, some "documentation on measures taken in France to preserve and beautify cities"—in particular, a brochure titled "Protection of Historic and Aesthetic Patrimony, Safeguarded Sectors and Conservation Operations (law of 4 August 1962)" and another entitled "Restoration of Paris, Doctrine and General Information."[43] A few days later, Kollek thanked him, indicating that "at a time when our attention is focused on our city's urban development scheme, the French example will represent a source of inspiration."[44] Another dispatch signed by Kollek a few years later implies that "the French example" was indeed contemplated: "The publication you kindly forwarded to me about 'Historic Buildings and Urban Reclamation' is all the more pertinent for us in that Jerusalem itself is an assemblage of historic buildings that we are striving to reclaim without defacing."[45] Irony of history: France, which until 1962 had protected the Maghrebi Quarter by virtue of its imperial obligations, was now flaunting its expertise in the area of "urban reclamation" to the Israeli municipal authorities.

In the weeks leading up to the launch of military operations, the region was increasingly on the alert. On 16 May 1967, Nasser called for the departure of UN intervention forces deployed along the Suez Canal; on 22 May he banned Israeli ships from accessing the Straits of Tiran, setting up a de facto naval blockade of the port of Eilat which the Israelis considered a casus belli.

In the ensuing days, the UN Security Council stepped up efforts to avoid an armed conflict that seemed inevitable.[46] These geopolitical maneuvers had direct repercussions on the city of Jerusalem: on Wednesday 31 May 1967, Kollek informed all consulates that a "special commission" had been created within the municipal council to resolve "the problems that could arise during this time of emergency."[47] At the bottom of the memo, in longhand, a French consular officer wrote, "motor bus—about 100 persons," implying that civilian evacuation operations were being planned. Four days earlier, on 27 May, the European consuls had demanded that "the character of the Holy City of Jerusalem" be protected, and that "in the event of a conflict opposing Israel and the Arab countries, the hostilities not be widespread and that Jerusalem be considered as an open city."[48]

On Friday June 2, in a memo to the Quai d'Orsay, the French consul indicated that "the measures taken here in anticipation of armed combat, the prevailing nervousness, the feverish excitation in the Jordanian sector preclude any notion that Jerusalem could possibly remain shielded from military operations. Fighting there might well prove more impassioned than at any point along the border."[49] As it happened, from the very onset of the war, the battle of Jerusalem was engaged, violent, and meteoric. At dawn on Monday 5 June, Israeli warplanes launched their "preemptive attack" and wiped out the entire Egyptian Air Force on the ground before deploying a massive land offensive in the Sinai; by late morning, the Jordanian army had sprung into action in Jerusalem and take the UN general headquarters located south of the city, a position retaken hours later by the Israelis. On the night of 5–6 June, the fighting moved northward into the neighborhoods of Mea Shearim, Sheikh Jarrah, and Wadi Joz; on Tuesday 6 June, the Israeli army definitively got the upper hand, completely surrounding the old city by taking positions on Mount Scopus and Mount of Olives. On Wednesday 7 June, in the morning after an intense artillery barrage, Israeli paratroopers commanded by Colonel Mordechai Gour entered the old city through Lion's Gate and immediately took over the Temple Mount before arriving at the Western Wall around 10 a.m. and deploying throughout all quarters of the city.[50] The conquest of Jerusalem had taken scarcely two days.

Photographing a Disappearance: Gilles Caron as Scout

The French photographer Gilles Caron was one of the first to enter the old city of Jerusalem, on Wednesday 7 June at midday, through Lion's Gate, in the wake of the first Israeli paratroopers. Arriving a few minutes later at the foot of the Western Wall, he was also one of the first to have photographed the Maghrebi Quarter, not knowing that it would be demolished a few days later. Caron, then twenty-seven, had never before photographed war, even though he'd personally experienced war as a soldier in Algeria between 1959 and 1962 after being drafted into the military—a service he completed in prison for insubordination.[51] In 1965–66 he worked for several agencies, covering world politics, the performing arts, and cinema. He photographed de Gaulle, Mitterrand, Sartre, Gainsbourg, Brigitte Bardot, Romy Schneider, Johnny Hallyday, and many other celebrities of the era.[52] In December 1966 he moved to the Gamma agency, and when he accompanied the entertainer Sylvie Vartan's tour in Israel in late May 1967, he sensed that an imminent conflict was brewing.

Caron returned to Jerusalem on Tuesday 6 June to cover the war that had broken out the previous day. Out of the 450 shots he took on Wednesday 7 June (thirteen rolls of Kodak stock, thirty-six shots each), a dozen or so were published in *Paris Match* and became the most iconic images of the Israeli conquest—in particular, the shots of Moshe Dayan posing ecstatically in front of the Western Wall next to Yitzhak Rabin. In the shoot of a documentary by Mariana Otero about Caron's career[53]—from his first war assignment in Jerusalem until his death in Cambodia in April 1970, with Vietnam, May 68 in Paris,[54] the famine in Biafra, and the civil strife in Northern Ireland in between—we are able to see all the shots he took that day, following him step by step throughout those momentous hours that witnessed a major shift in the history of Jerusalem in general, and of the Maghrebi Quarter in particular. To relive the palpable reality of this shift, Caron will be our scout.[55]

Loaded onto a bus Wednesday morning by the press service of the Israeli army, Caron slips away late that morning and drives to the northeast corner of the old city, passing through the Sheikh Jarrah and Wadi-Joz neighborhoods. Behind the Rockefeller Museum, he photographs the corpse of a Palestinian civilian still wearing his white keffieh, with the Augusta Victoria Hospital in the background and a low wall showing traces of blood—a wall easily identifi-

able today from the way the casing stones are arranged (figure 39). After taking
three images of the corpse, one of which has remained particularly memorable,
he heads into the old city on foot, beyond the northeast corner of the ramparts,
down a steep slope leading to the Gethsemane intersection. There, he photographs several Israeli tanks on the side of the road, and then takes off in the
direction of Lion's Gate, through which he passes after skirting the smoking
carcass of a bus, evidence of the intense fighting hours earlier. Once inside the
old city, he takes the first left turn, into the Haram al-Sharif plaza, where he
photographs a group of paratroopers sitting in the shade between the Dome of
the Rock and the Dome of the Chain. The shadows cast help situate the scene
in the early afternoon (figure 40).[56] Caron reloads his camera and heads toward
the Maghrebi Gate, soon finding himself on a rooftop terrace overlooking the
Maghrebi Quarter and the Western Wall, branching off the alleyway sloping
downward, the Zuqaq Bab al-Magharibah.

He takes two shots of the Maghrebi Quarter, oriented southeast by
northwest, in which we glimpse a tree-filled courtyard in the foreground, a
succession of rooftop terraces in the middle distance, and the Church of the

FIGURE 39. Corpse of a Palestinian fighter photographed near the Rockefeller
Museum, with the Augusta Victoria Hospital in the background, 7 June 1967.
Source: © Gilles Caron.

FIGURE 40. Israeli soldiers on the Haram al-Sharif plaza between the Dome of the Rock and the Dome of the Chain, 7 June 1967. Source: © Gilles Caron.

Redeemer and the Holy Sepulchre in the background (figure 41).[57] He descends a metal staircase that then connects him to the Western Wall, he takes a few shots of soldiers praying in front of the Wall, and then he comes face-to-face with the Rabbi Shlomo Goren, chaplain of the Israeli army, who celebrates the event hoisted onto the shoulders of a soldier. Caron captures this joyful scene for posterity, then cuts back across the Haram al-Sharif in the opposite direction and enters the Via Dolorosa, passing in front of the Church of Saint Anne. But he notices right then, as it enters through Lion's Gate, a convoy of jeeps transporting Minister of Defense Moshe Dayan, Chief of Staff Yitzhak Rabin, and General Uzi Narkisss, in charge of operations in Jerusalem.[58]

Caron rushes to follow them, gets ahead of them on the Haram al-Sharif plaza, and turns to take a few group shots, but realizes that he needs to stay ahead of the convoy if he is to get the real scoop shot in front of the Western Wall. The pictures he gets in the next few minutes are indeed historic and aesthetically accomplished: low-angle shots with the Wall rising up to the left, Moshe Dayan and Yitzhak Rabin in full frame, Dayan beaming, Rabin simply smiling (figure 42). Before leaving the scene, Dayan stops in front of a little bush emerging from a courtyard of the Maghrebi Quarter; he picks a bouquet

FIGURE 41. Rooftops of the Maghrebi Quarter, shot from southeast to northwest, with the bell tower of the Church of the Redeemer in the background, 7 June 1967. Source: © Gilles Caron.

FIGURE 42. Yitzhak Rabin (left) and Moshe Dayan (center) in front of the Western Wall, 7 June 1967. Source: © Gilles Caron.

of jasmine flowers. His portrait, with helmet on head, patch over one eye, and bouquet in his hand, will circle the globe.

Caron knows he's got a scoop, but he continues reporting from different neighborhoods of the city, notably the vicinity of Jaffa Gate, where he takes a few stunning shots of the no-man's-land and of the former building of the Ottoman municipality of Jerusalem, which will be razed in the days that follow.[59] In late afternoon he returns to the Maghrebi Gate, where he photographs several groups of civilians gathered together, their hands above their heads. He decides to follow a group of Israeli soldiers heading up toward Zion Gate. On the steep embankment overlooking Al-Faraj Street, he moves ahead of a group of soldiers and takes two low-angle shots against the background of the Western Wall and the Dome of the Rock; and in the middle distance just behind the soldiers, the Maghrebi Quarter is perfectly outlined (figure 43).[60] Caron then follows the group of soldiers in front of a house in the former Jewish Quarter with a family of Palestinian residents.

Then, he walks back down to the outskirts of the Maghrebi Quarter, where he again photographs several groups of civilians, hands raised or on their heads, this time with their suitcases, cookware, and bundles carried by the women

FIGURE 43. **View overlooking the Maghrebi Quarter, shot from the southwest toward the northeast, 7 June 1967. Source: © Gilles Caron.**

and children.[61] In some pictures the men are displaying white handkerchiefs, holding them in their hands or waving them on sticks. These shots are all the more troubling when we know that Caron was mobilized in Algeria a few years earlier, and that in 1967 the Israeli soldiers are wearing French army surplus sold after the 1962 cease-fire, notably the paratrooper uniforms and bush hats (figure 44).[62] Caron follows these groups of evicted inhabitants, snapping shots of them on the road that overlooks Silwan and Kidron Valley. The shadows on the ground indicate that it is now getting toward evening, and Caron has to get his photos to Gamma without further delay. He heads back by way of Wadi Joz and Sheikh Jarrah, crosses back over the border at Mandelbaum Gate, and leaves Jerusalem for Tel Aviv.[63]

From Thursday 8 June to Sunday 11 June, Caron goes on assignment to the Sinai Desert, the Suez Canal, and the Golan Heights. Upon his return to Jerusalem on 12 June, accompanying the famous singer Enrico Macias, who has come to pray at the Western Wall to celebrate the conquest of the city, he discovers that the Maghrebi Quarter has literally *disappeared*.[64] He takes several shots of Enrico Macias at the Wall, surrounded by a throng of admirers, and that evening he photographs the singer in concert in front of Israeli

FIGURE 44. **Inhabitants evicted by the Israeli army, 7 June 1967. Source:** © Gilles Caron.

soldiers (figures 45 and 46). But two days later, he returns to the new plaza on his own to photograph it again, from every angle. A serial analysis of the pictures Caron shot that day testifies to his stunned disbelief: the neighborhood he had walked through four days earlier no longer existed, and he was left to take dozens of shots of piles of unphotogenic rubble while wandering around the flattened neighborhood as if trying to understand what must have taken place in his absence, to somehow fill a blank space, answer a question, perhaps relieve a frustration (figures 47 and 48). It was as if he were seeking in any case to appease an "inner conflict"—to quote the term used by Michel Poivert in speaking of the "useless" photos Caron took in such abundance at his reporting sites—to weave back together what Poivert calls the "parallel narrative" of what Caron did not see and could not bear witness to.[65]

This "parallel narrative" comprises here a multitude of innocuous details, seemingly insignificant, but on which the photographer lingers persistently, even though he knows that none of the photos will ever be published. Amid the rubble and bits of shattered furniture, the large almond tree that grew in the courtyard along Imam Malik Street is still standing, and groups of bystanders seek its shade to shelter from the sun. Dozens of Israeli flags have been hoisted onto pylons, and a few metal barriers are set up to channel the crowd wandering about aimlessly amid the wreckage.[66] And everywhere on the ground, traces of dwellings he saw with his own eyes a few days before: scraps of woodwork, steel beams, twisted piping, electrical wiring, bits of cloth, the odd piece of bed linen, fragments of smashed dishes . . .

This same impression of a gaping space, suddenly unfathomable, is left by most photographs dating from that time. In one, taken by Marylin Silverstone for Magnum, a little girl in a white dress and an old woman in a headscarf search through the rubble and collect what they recover into a square metal can. The little girl gazes directly at the photographer, facing the wide-angle lens Silverstone has chosen in a bid to encompass the outsized perimeter of the new plaza.[67] In the November–December 1967 issue of the magazine *Arab World*, we see several comparable pictures with explicit captions: "A young Arab girl searches through the remnants of clothing where her house once stood, while Israelis gather at the Wailing Wall in the background."[68] In another picture we see two veiled women on the new plaza, surrounded by Israeli civilians and soldiers, and the caption reads: "Two elderly Arab women are told by Israeli

FIGURE 45. Enrico Macias (center, in pale shirt) in front of the Western Wall, 12 June 1967. Source: © Gilles Caron.

FIGURE 46. Enrico Macias performing for Israeli soldiers, 12 June 1967. Source: © Gilles Caron.

FIGURE 47. Wreckage of the Maghrebi Quarter (northwest angle), 14 June 1967. Source: © Gilles Caron.

FIGURE 48. Wreckage of the Maghrebi Quarter (south and east), 14 June 1967. Source: © Gilles Caron.

soldiers they may not cross the Moroccan quarter."[69] Each time, the same dizzying impression of a spatial and temporal abyss that has opened up right in the
middle of the city, such that we have a hard time believing that this is indeed
the timeline of events. How was it possible that some 130 houses were evacuated
and razed in such a short time? The photographs help ask the question, but
they leave us without answers. To attempt to understand, to give voice to these
images, we need to turn to other clues, often sparse and piecemeal.

The Media Narrative: Prophecy Fulfilled

The *Jerusalem Post* dated Monday 12 June is categorical. In an article headlined
"The Western Wall Area Cleared," the paper informs its readers that "there is
now a large open square before the Wall, which rises in its splendor before the
visitor the moment he turns right from the path leading in from the Dung
Gate."[70] The article goes on to explain that "because of demolition work, access
to the Wall was denied yesterday," adding that "yesterday afternoon, a bulldozer
was overturning the last of the houses," and describing in detail the zone as it
appeared on Sunday 11 June: "beds and bedding, other items of furniture and
kitchen utensils, presumably abandoned by those who had fled the area during
the fighting for the city."

   This argument, of a spontaneous departure by the inhabitants of the
Maghrebi Quarter, is stated unequivocally here—even though in the same
article, seemingly unaware of the discrepancy, the journalist emphasizes the
project's timeline, as if the event of the previous day were but the fulfillment of
an ancient prophecy: "The Baron Edmond de Rothschild came down together
with Mayor Teddy Kollek to see the work being carried out. This recalled to
local historians the fact that the Baron's grandfather, the first Baron Edmond
de Rothschild, had in 1887 offered to purchase the area from the Moroccan
Wakf (the religious trust who owned it) in order to clear it, but the project had
fallen through, despite the approval of the Turkish governor Raouf Pasha."[71]
We can infer here, by way of this anecdote about the visit of Baron de Rothschild, the key to the very structure of the event: its tricky double time frame,
falsely paradoxical, yet in fact absolutely logical. It is precisely because this
destruction was hoped for, and was such a long time in planning, that it could
be decided—or rather *confirmed*—so quickly, and then executed in a matter of

hours. The demolition of the Maghrebi Quarter *precipitated*, in the chemistry sense of the term, several decades of history, and this is what allows the event to be placed in the *longue durée*.

Another explanation situates the event in a shorter period while still feeding its prophetic dimension. At the end of the article, the *Post* points out that "a spokesman for the Military Government, Mr. Eliezer Zhurabin,[72] told the *Jerusalem Post* that the narrow passage along the Wall would constitute a serious hazard if more than a few hundred persons ever crowded there." The public safety argument is not raised fortuitously, since the paper next explains that the urgent nature of the operation was dictated by the Jewish liturgical calendar: "The public access route [to the Wall] is now being prepared, and is hoped to be ready in time for Shavuot (one of three traditional pilgrimage holidays) beginning tomorrow night."[73] Effectively, all testimony confirms that starting on Tuesday 13 June in the evening and for the whole day of 14 June, tens of thousands of Israelis arrived in procession before the Western Wall. In this regard, the sound archives of the former ORTF, the national radio and television agency, now preserved at the INA, the national audiovisual institute, represent a priceless resource, since they add an audio dimension to the silent images captured by the photographers. On Wednesday 14 June, at 1 p.m., the radio station France Inter broadcast a three-minute news spot recorded in Jerusalem earlier that day, devoted to the celebrations of Shavuot, or what the French called "Jewish Pentecost," in the Holy City:

> It was three in the morning when the first Israelis gathered at the foot of Mount Zion; at five o'clock the first of them entered the old city, the Holy City, the city that had been off limits for them since the nineteenth century [*sic*]. The prophecy was to be fulfilled, and it was being fulfilled, we were living a historic moment in this land of history. The first to enter were the Hassidim, those strictly religious Jews who acknowledge only unconditional obedience to the Law handed down to the Jewish people on Mount Sinai by Moses. The feast of the Pentecost today in fact celebrates the delivery of this law of the Torah to the Chosen People [. . .]. And at this moment, we are at the entrance to the old city of Jerusalem, *on a vast plaza cleared by the Israelis in forty-eight hours*, we are before the Wailing Wall. The Wailing Wall is the last remaining vestige of the Temple of Soloman destroyed nineteen centuries ago by Titus [. . .]. People have come from Tel Aviv, Haifa, Be'er Sheva, from

kibbutzim and towns, it is two in the afternoon here, and already 150,000 or
200,000 persons perhaps have already passed; by this evening that number
will have doubled. In front of the Wall, people are praying [. . .]. Since 1948,
as we know, the Israelis were unable to come pray before the Wailing Wall,
which somehow symbolizes today their freedom and independence regained.[74]

Beyond the numerous historical approximations, the message transmitted
to France Inter listeners on Wednesday 14 June was precisely this: what was
newsworthy about the event was not the evacuation and destruction of some
130 houses in the heart of the Holy City, but the "freedom and independence
regained" for the Israelis, who could once more come pray before the Wailing
Wall. The journalist sums up in one short phrase the "vast plaza cleared by the
Israelis in forty-eight hours," but does not describe what existed there before,
and mentions nothing of the Maghrebi Quarter or its inhabitants. This holds
true in all the broadcasts aired as of 7 June.[75] This omission should not be
interpreted as a sign of some conspiracy intended to gloss over the demolition
of the Maghrebi Quarter, but rather as a symptom of the silence surrounding
the episode, which is precisely its incapacity to qualify as an "event," to be part
of a narrative. The disappearance of the Maghrebi Quarter did not, in effect,
feed into any narrative, any memory, any story—it came across as nothing more
than an awkward detail, inconvenient and anecdotal, literally *insignificant*,
as compared to that which the France Inter reporter called "prophecy" being
fulfilled before his eyes, and which brought out a procession of "150,000 or
200,000" Israelis to commemorate "the delivery of this law of the Torah to the
Chosen People."[76] Here we have another explanation as to why the destruction
of the Maghrebi Quarter could have been carried out so unimpeded: even
before the demolition, it had already been relegated to a dead end in the collective memory, those former transnational imperial structures removed from
view and banished from the conversation now that the triumphant nation-
states were in ascendency.[77]

A look at the left-leaning Israeli press provides a final confirmation of this
premise. *Haaretz* published a a harsh opinion piece on 21 June 1967 under the
provocative headline "The Barbarians Are Coming,"[78] but we find not the
slightest reference to the Maghrebi Quarter. It was not the destruction of this
medieval quarter nor the eviction of its inhabitants that caused outrage, but

the fact that the bulldozers could have damaged the Western Wall, which now appeared "smaller" and "less majestic." On 23 June, the daily paper *Davar* (close to the trade union confederation Histadrut) reiterated this same aesthetic assessment, quoting the testimony of an elderly Yemeni Jew who compared the new plaza to a "stadium" and regretted that the Western Wall now looked "tiny."[79] On 19 July 1967, *Davar* pointed out that "the houses of the Maghrebi Quarter were not so old," thus minimizing the scope of the patrimonial destruction.[80] In the months to come, *Davar* featured several articles focused on the aesthetic issues raised by the new plaza.[81] On 21 July 1967, *Haaretz* criticized the architectural projects that risked turning what had once been a place of private prayer into a huge, noisy "religious discotheque."[82] The Maghrebi Quarter had not only been *destroyed* during the night of 10 to 11 June 1967; it was literally *erased* from all narration. In an attempt nevertheless to reestablish the narrative of this disappearance, I would first need to gather and assess the testimony of those who had experienced it firsthand.

The Fabric of Memory: Neighbors, Inhabitants, and the Wrecking Crew

Haifa Khalidi was nineteen in June 1967. She was born in 1948, Street of the Chain, in the historic home of the Khalidi family, on the outer perimeter overlooking the Maghrebi Quarter immediately to the north. She is still living there today with her sister, and she insists that this is the house in which she will die. She witnessed the demolition of the neighborhood from her bedroom window, and her memories of that day are still quite vivid:

> On Saturday evening, before nightfall, Israeli soldiers entered the Maghrebi Quarter houses and ordered the inhabitants to evacuate the premises in two hours. Loudspeakers were also used to make the same announcement in Arabic. Bulldozers started knocking down the houses, one by one, even before all the inhabitants had managed to leave. You could hear shouting, the crash of collapsing walls; there were floodlights to light the way for the bulldozers, and clouds of dust were rising up everywhere. I thought our house was going to collapse as well, but finally the bulldozers stopped at the foot of our wall, in front of the bathroom window, right there.[83]

She also recalls the conquest of the city the previous Wednesday:

> At that time we had a wooden door that opened using a rope. The soldiers
> ordered us to open the door, saying that they would not harm any innocents.
> My father came down the stairs to open the door, and at that point one of the
> soldiers tossed a grenade inside, which exploded on the third step of the stair-
> case, right here. Fortunately, my father had time to move back, and he wasn't
> hurt. The soldiers took all men fit for combat and led them to a mosque where
> they were questioned. Lucky for them, my father and uncle were beyond fight-
> ing age, and were allowed to come back home. We were worried sick, because
> we had heard about what happened back in 1948.[84]

Haifa's narrative resonates with the photographs of Gilles Caron; while
the people of the Maghrebi Quarter were evicted from their homes, pure and
simple, all able-bodied men living in East Jerusalem were stopped and checked,
and all inhabitants were urged to leave the city, as evidenced by the narrative of
Ibrahim Dakkak, then a young engineer living in East Jerusalem:

> When the weather report for Jerusalem was broadcast by Radio Israel and no
> longer Radio Amman [. . .], we knew that Jerusalem must have fallen into
> the hands of the Israeli forces. What could we do? Was history going to repeat
> itself? Was it going to be 1948 all over again? [. . .] Vehicles equipped with
> loudspeakers were driving through the streets calling for those who wished to
> leave the city via the Allenby Bridge over the Jordan to head over to a bus that
> was made available for this purpose. A call fraught with implications. Inviting
> and urging at the same time. The ride over the bridge was free of charge, with
> no preconditions for anyone. Some people rushed to get on the bus while
> others stood to the side, entrusting those who were leaving with messages to
> be conveyed to their families abroad.[85]

This kind of testimony gives an idea of how tense the situation was at the time
of the Maghrebi Quarter demolition, and allows for a glimpse into what the
inhabitants were feeling as they were receiving evacuation orders.

Moussa-Issa Ben-Abdallah Ahmed al-Moghrabi, known as Abu Mahdi,
was thirteen in June 1967. He was born in the Maghrebi Quarter in 1954. His
grandparents were natives of Fez, Morocco, and settled in Jerusalem in 1907 on

their way home from a pilgrimage to Mecca.[86] His father was a blacksmith and locksmith. Moussa-Issa (Moses-Jesus in Arabic) has a few childhood memories, notably of soccer games on the Haram al-Sharif and the distribution of food baskets for pilgrims lodging in the neighborhood during the month of Ramadan. Today he lives in the old city of Jerusalem, in the zawiya of the Maghrebis where a dozen or so families sought refuge after the Six-Day War. He vividly recalls the day of Saturday 10 June 1967:

> We lived in a large house on this side of the neighborhood [northern], some twenty meters from the Wall, over there where you see a public fountain today. I remember that my aunts had been telling us for three days not to go out in the street. When the Israeli soldiers entered the neighborhood, we were all gathered in the house; we were looking out the window, we could hear the sound of doors being broken down, the shouts of soldiers, then we heard the loudspeakers ordering us to leave immediately, and not to bring anything with us. We left on foot; some headed toward the Maghrebi Gate and were then taken to the Shuafat camp, or to Silwan for those who had family there. My family and a few other families opted to take refuge in the zawiya of the Maghrebis, located on an adjacent rise. We went up to the roof to watch the bulldozers; I was holding my father's hand, he was weeping.

At this point in our interview, Abu Mahdi got up and went to get a photograph of himself as a baby in the arms of his father, who is leaning against a tree in their courtyard; on the back of the photo a date is written in blue ballpoint: 1957, ten years before the destruction of the quarter. Abu Mahdi was three years old.[87]

Abu Mahdi's story resonates with those of other inhabitants of the quarter, who all recount the same rapid chain of events, the brutality of their eviction, the distraught families fleeing wherever they could. Ghaleb Ben-Daoud al-Labban, known as Abu Rami, was also thirteen in June 1967. He was born in the Maghrebi Quarter in 1954 and lives today in the Shuafat refugee camp, between Jerusalem and Ramallah. His family is of Tunisian origin; he and his children have kept in touch to this day with their Tunisian cousins. He describes the same eviction scenes, their discovery of the demolished neighborhood a few days later, the streets and alleyways where they used to play now nowhere to be found, with only a few trees left standing as reference points for reconstructing a mental map amid the rubble. When I met up with him in March 2017, his memories were hazy, and he apologized. But he was keen to participate in this inquiry, and he drove me over to meet his friend Mohammed Abed Jalil al-Maloudi, known as Abu Munir, who was twenty-eight in June 1967, and who lives today between Anata (a Palestinian locality neighboring Shuafat) and the old city of Jerusalem, in the zawiya of the Maghrebis, where he has kept a small room.[88] Born in 1939 of Algerian parents in the Maghrebi Quarter, Abu Munir recalls that his father had installed a radio set in the Young Maghrebis Club, and that his grandfather cooked the *shorba* fed to the poor of the neighborhood during the month of Ramadan. When I ask him to recount the evening of 19 June 1967, Abu Munir mentions the al-Atrash family, the al-Tawatis, the al-Tayebs, the al-Zawawis; and he is especially keen to recall the name of Hajjah Rasmiyyah Ali Tabakhi, an elderly widow who was found dead beneath the rubble of her house—an incident repeated in all the testimonials of the neighborhood's former residents. Abu Munir also recalls how, years later, he met Meron Benvenisti, former deputy mayor to Teddy Kollek, during the shooting of a documentary short, and he remembers the anger he felt that day.[89]

Mahmud al-Masluhi, known as Abu Marwan, was thirty-three in June 1967. He was born in 1933 in the Maghrebi Quarter, and helped run the neighborhood sports association; he was also its star boxer, winning a tournament in Amman when he was seventeen.[90] His father, born in Marrakesh, moved to the Maghrebi Quarter in the late 1920s and taught in the neighborhood Koranic school. Abu Marwan lives today in Beit-Hanina, north of Jerusalem. He is a fixture in the community, as the local mukhtar since 2002, when he replaced his late predecessor Muhammad Ibrahim Abdelhaq, who had held the position since 1956. Abu Marwan recalls visits by the French consul in the 1950s, when he was in his twenties, and in particular the free medications distributed by the White Fathers in the French-owned Sainte-Anne domain, which Abu Marwan still calls by its Islamic name, Madrassa Salahiya. Abu Marwan's spouse, Nawal Kassem Daraji, was born in 1950 of a family originally from Constantine in Algeria. When asked to pool their memories of the Six-Day War, they recall the confinement, entire days shut inside their houses listening to the radio, and then the arrival of the Israeli soldiers, the sudden eviction, the loudspeakers, young men being separated from their families. Abu Marwan vividly recalls his family's evacuation: "We went outside because we heard the Israeli soldiers shouting orders to evacuate the houses. There was my elderly mother, whom we evacuated first. Then we came back for my sisters and the rest of the family." But, like all the testimony we were able to gather from former inhabitants, Abu Marwan's memories are interrupted right before the demolition, which by definition none of the inhabitants was able to witness.[91]

Sasson Levy was thirty-six in June 1967. He was born in West Jerusalem in 1931; his parents were both born in Iraq and emigrated from there to Palestine in 1921. The last of four brothers, Sasson was his brother Ovadia's associate in a construction business. Today he lives in West Jerusalem near Mount Herzl, and is one of the two surviving participants in the demolition of the Maghrebi Quarter, which he describes calmly, in mostly professional technical terms. He recalls that his older brother Ovadia phoned him on 9 June in the evening, during the Shabbat meal, to ask him to get some machinery and manpower together for the next evening:

> Ovadia called me late on Friday; we weren't religious in our family, so we had no issues with using the telephone. All day Saturday we took advantage of Shabbat to make the rounds of various work sites to pick up the equipment, trucks, bulldozers, backhoes, and drills. We're the ones who supplied the machinery, but the army supplied the gas, the refueling, the floodlights, and the generators, because we worked all night and into the next day. We also had passes from the army to be able to drive around with the equipment. We met at the appointed place on Saturday at the end of Shabbat, just before nightfall. By then, the army had already started evicting some of the residents; the others left when we started tearing down the first houses, the ones on the edge of the neighborhood as you entered the Maghrebi Gate.[92]

When I ask him to recount the actual demolition operation, Sasson focuses on the logistical problems resulting from the neighborhood's extreme density:

> The houses weren't very high, two floors maximum, but the streets were terribly narrow, so that at first we couldn't get the bulldozers in; we first had to open up an access route and level the ground to then be able to work with the heavy equipment brought in by Zalman Broshi, a major Jerusalem contractor. To save time, we drilled through the vaults of the underground cisterns, then

filled them with as much rubble as possible. We evacuated the rest of the rubble through the Maghrebi Gate with dump trucks that we would then offload out behind the Mount of Olives, at the side of the road to Jericho. We worked much faster than usual; it wasn't a normal demolition site. The walls were falling onto the machinery, and the heavier bulldozers got stuck in the underground cisterns. I remember being afraid that one of my workers would get hurt, but we knew we had to get the job done as fast as possible. An elderly woman was found dead in her house; she hadn't heard the evacuation order.[93]

Sasson Levy describes the scene as he experienced it back then, as a thirty-six-year-old construction entrepreneur: first of all, as a particularly tricky demolition. At no moment in the interview does he focus on the religious significance of the operation, but he does repeat several times that the destruction was "necessary" to allow anyone who wanted to come pray at the Western Wall.

When asked to describe the houses he tore down, Sasson does not speak of hovels or slums, but rather of "clean and well-maintained" houses: "We could tell that the people had been living here for a long time; the houses were old but the roofs, terraces, and courtyards were in good condition, the paint and plaster were recent. There were many staircases, of all sizes, for getting up to the roof terrace. The windows also came in many sizes; nothing was symmetrical." Some of his memories help one to better understand the brutality of the evacuation: "We could see that the inhabitants hadn't had time to collect their things. I can still remember posters and mirrors hung on the walls, petrol lamps, a vase with flowers, gas stoves, pots with food in them, mattresses, bedding, suitcases with linens and clothing, large cans of olive oil, in the kitchens or in the cellars. . . ."[94]

During the interview, Sasson Levy shows us an album with a red cover, printed in a two-hundred-copy limited edition in 1983 by an association called "The Kotel Order" (Misdar ha-Kotel), founded, according to the tradition reported in the album itself, on "Sunday 11 June 1967 at three o'clock in the morning, the 3rd day of the month of Sivan."[95] In a montage made in 1968 by the Israeli artist Lea Majaro Mintz, showing the members of the association gathered before the Western Wall, Sasson Levy points to his brother Ovadia, the first on the right, and his own younger self, whom we recognize in the back row (figure 49).[96] Under the montage is a reproduction of a manuscript document signed by the commander of the engineering unit, Eitan Ben Moshe, and addressed to Baruch Barkai, the secretary of the association of building contractors of West Jerusalem.[97] Its wording reveals a deliberate intent to stage a spontaneous, benevolent act on the part of the contractors association, who seem to have acted on their own initiative, with only the "blessing" of an army officer: "By the authority invested in me as officer of military engineering, I approve the *benevolent* action of your organization that made it possible to achieve an exploit at Kotel. Blessed be the organization that knows how to build but also to destroy the impurity around the Kotel. Captain Ben-Moshe to the secretary of the organization of builders gathered at Kotel, Mr. Barkai. Kotel Plaza, midnight, 11 June 1967."

Beyond the fabrication of a glorious legend, this memorial album is enlightening in that it features a valorization of the operation's prophetic dimension, particularly with extensive excerpts from a text written during the British Mandate era by Itamar Ben-Avi, the son of Eliezer Ben-Yehudah, with regard to the creation of a vast plaza in front of the Western Wall.[98] During our interview, Sasson Levy also shows us a photograph of a ceremony organized in 1987 at the Knesset, at which the members of the association received the "Defenders of the Kotel" award.[99]

Sasson Levy's testimony is precious, for it brings the demolition process to life, logistically and materially. Still, as he tells it, he was simply following orders, and complying with the agenda of his older brother and associate. Furthermore, the whole idea of this memorial album, to which Sasson Levy refers insistently, and which was published some fifteen years *after* the events, would suggest that it also functioned as a smoke screen intended to conceal the true history of the demolition. I got confirmation of this impression from the testimony of Ben Moshe, who commanded the engineering unit in charge of supervising the evacuation and destruction of the quarter—testimony published in the (right-leaning) journal *Yorshalim*:

> Prior to demolishing the quarter, an army regiment passed in front of the Arab houses to order the inhabitants to leave their houses in fifteen minutes. After demolishing the quarter, amid the rubble, they found the corpses of some inhabitants who had refused to leave their houses. There were three bodies and I transported them myself to the Bikur Holim hospital in the western sector of the city. There were other bodies, however, and they were buried [. . .]. Under

מסדר הכתל

FIGURE 49. Photomontage in tribute to the "Kotel Order." Source: © Lea Majaro Mintz, 1968.

the Wall plaza, there are vestiges of nine different historical periods, layered one atop the other, so when you dig, you come upon empty spaces [. . .]. We dumped the rubble from the houses there, along with the Arab corpses.[100]

The openly provocative nature of this testimony warrants caution, since Ben Moshe is the only one to speak of "three corpses" transported to Bikur Holim hospital, and especially since no witness mentions the "other bodies" he says were buried on-site along with the rubble of the houses. That being said, we cannot rule out his account entirely, especially given how precise and detailed the rest of his narrative is:

> It all started once the fighting had ended. The mayor of Jerusalem, Teddy Kollek, sketched out on a scrap of paper the zone to be demolished. But the bulldozer drivers defied the order and demolished additional houses. Around 135 Palestinian families lost their houses. Teddy and his colleagues had planned for a limited demolition that would not affect the holy places. But there was a mosque in the zone called al-Buraq, built on the site where the Prophet Muhammad's horse ascended into heavens. And so I said, "If the horse ascended into heaven, why not the mosque, too?" So I completely flattened it, leaving not a single vestige [. . .]. A high official told me that if there was a lot of international reaction, they would say that you did it on your own initiative, and that you'd get a five-year prison sentence, then you'd be granted amnesty the day after.[101]

What does this "zone to be demolished" refer to? Could I possibly recover this "scrap of paper" on which Teddy Kollek supposedly made his sketch? Were historical buildings destroyed in violation of the original orders? To get beyond the unraveled and sometimes dubious fabric of individual memories, to break through the smoke screen of the "Kotel Order" and understand the actual decision-making process that led to the destruction of the Maghrebi Quarter, I had to press on and bring my inquiry to completion by turning to the scant written documents that record the event. For that, I needed to go back to the technical archives of the municipality that preserve the memory of the operation's logistical issues, but also its chain of command.

The Archival Record: A Joint Action of
the Municipality and the Army

Meron Benvenisti was in charge of coordinating municipal policy in East Jerusalem between June 1967 and January 1972. Born in 1934, a historian specializing in the medieval period, with a focus on the Crusades, he was only thirty-three when he was appointed to this position by Kollek, who had spotted this dynamic militant during his victorious 1965 electoral campaign, when Benvenisti was working in tourist development in the prime minister's cabinet.[102] In office for four and a half years, Benvenisti was involved in all decisions concerning the old city; he attended all the key meetings, and his training as a historian most probably predisposed him to preserve as much documentation as possible from this crucial period. After leaving the job at the municipality, he wrote several historical works, some of which were translated into English and French, and carry weight in the field.[103] In the first of them, published in Hebrew in 1973 and translated into English in 1976, he makes brief mention of the destruction of the Maghrebi Quarter, but without dwelling on the political responsibilities for the operation, explaining simply that "whoever initiated this plan," it was "confirmed by the Minister of Defence," Moshe Dayan, and "the city mayor, Teddy Kollek, who volunteered for the task and was in charge of executing it"—concluding that if criticism concerning "the abrupt evacuation of the quarter's inhabitants without any promise for alternative housing" seemed "justified" to him, the operation was in any case "inevitable."[104] In June 2016, at the age of eighty-two, Benvenisti made the decision to deposit his papers with the Ben-Zvi Institute, where they are now accessible to researchers.[105]

In a grey laminated box labeled "Waqf Memorials, Western Wall, Sites, Confidential Papers," there is a pink subfolder labeled "Jordanian Municipality 5–28/06/1967," which contains a certain number of handwritten memos drafted in the early days of the Israeli conquest of the city, at the time when Benvenisti had just started his job and was endeavoring to coordinate his action with the staff at the Jordanian municipality before it was dissolved by military decree on 29 June.[106] A note drafted during a meeting with the health services of the Jordanian municipality indicates that 250 corpses were buried in Jerusalem "the first day" (Wednesday 7 June), and 180 corpses "the second day" (Thursday 8 June), which amounts to a total of 430 bodies. On the next page, no longer in blue ink but black, a new total indicates "430 + 214 = 644," which seems to suggest that the total number of bodies buried in Jerusalem as a result of the fighting in the Six-Day War amounted to 644.[107] In the same note, Ahmad al-Khatib, in charge of sanitation issues in the Jordanian municipality, informs Benvenisti that "30 tons of refuse (apart from the rubble) were evacuated from the old city between 12 and 27 June."[108]

In the same file, another note handwritten by Benvenisti sums up the key points of a meeting held on 24 June with the Jordanian municipality. The fifth point of the meeting is devoted to "deceased persons," among whom is "Abdel Salam al-Moghrabi, municipal gardener," about whom it is mentioned that his house was "destroyed" a few days after the conquest of the city.[109] The file also contains a report of a meeting held in closed-door session on Sunday 27 August 1967 between Kollek and Ernesto Thalmann, special representative of the United Nations.[110] At the fourth point on the agenda, titled "Destruction of Dwellings," after mentioning the demolition of buildings "threatening collapse" around Jaffa Gate, Kollek refers to "the destruction of the buildings outside the Western Wall" and acknowledges that "these were not buildings that were dangerous. This was a bit of a slum area, but was not dangerous." Kollek, known for his outspokenness, chose to reveal a partial truth (the buildings were not dangerous) to more shrewdly embed a falsehood (this neighborhood was a slum). At any rate, we can gauge the full historical value of these internal documents produced by the municipality.

Records of these municipal operations are also found in the historical archives preserved in the underground levels of the current Jerusalem municipality buildings. Even if the records account mainly for the logistical aspects of the destruction, the precise wording of a clearing operation can sometimes reveal valuable insights. In a file labeled "Repairs and restoration work in the reunified city of Jerusalem. 25/05/1967–31/10/1967," we find, for instance, a summary report of a meeting of the municipality's department of public works dated 26 July 1967, which lists the rubble removal operations since the conquest. The fourteenth item on this list reads: "Clearing and leveling of the Western Wall plaza subsequent to the demolition of the houses by order of military command, removal and crushing of rubble = 20,000 I.L. [Israeli pounds]."[111] While Israeli historiography has for a long time claimed that the operation was a spontaneous initiative by a handful of overzealous contractors, we find here an archival record—incidental, but nonetheless significant—of an operation planned and commanded by the army.

In his recent book on the Six-Day War, Tom Segev points out that the purpose of foregrounding the role of the contractors was effectively to mask the operation's political responsibilities: "On Saturday evening, when the Sabbath was over, fifteen veteran Jerusalem contractors arrived at the Western Wall with their bulldozers [. . .]. Given the legal and international sensitivity involved, the operation was carried out swiftly, under the cover of night, and with sufficient obfuscation to claim that neither the military nor the municipality had demolished the houses, but rather the contractors association, a private organization."[112] In foregrounding the "Kotel detail," the scope was effectively to cloud the issue of the real decision-making process that led to the destruction.

Further sifting through this same dossier produced by the department of public works, I identified another document that confirmed the same premise—that the demolition operation was a coproduction of the army and the municipality—but which especially allowed me to better track the timeline of events (figure 50). The document in question is a typed report, annotated in longhand, of a meeting held on Friday 9 June 1967 in the afternoon—a few hours *before* Sasson Levy was contacted by phone—"between the Mayor of Jerusalem Mr. T. Kollek and General Uzi Narkiss."[113] More specifically, it is a record of decisions aimed at formalizing a series of operations, as the introductory paragraph explicitly states:

> During a meeting between the Mayor of Jerusalem Mr. T. Kollek and General Uzi Narkiss—in the presence of members of the municipality's Emergency Commission for matters of public works and civil defense, of the chief municipal engineer and his adjuncts, of the official in charge of water supply and sewage disposal, and of the municipal treasurer, with regard to the municipality—and in the presence of military engineering officers, of central command officers and of the director of military operations and his assistants, with regard to the army—and subsequent to a site visit carried out at the completion of the meeting in the border post area heading toward the Jaffa Gate and on the road that links Mount Zion to Kotel—it was decided as follows: [. . .][114]

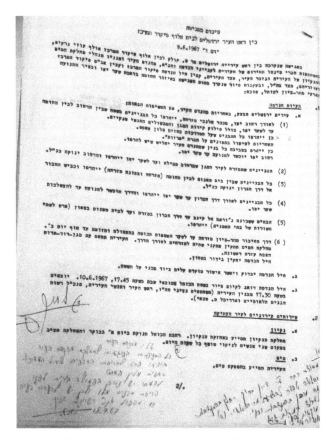

FIGURE 50. Minutes of the meeting on 9 June 1967, headed by Jerusalem Mayor Teddy Kollek and by General Uzi Narkiss. Source: © HAJM, box 1210, file 2/22/6.

It was a bipartite meeting, then, between the army and the municipality, a decision-making assembly organized at the highest level, since it was jointly presided over by Mayor Kollek and General Narkiss, each surrounded by their adjuncts. Narkiss, who had taken part in the Battle of Jerusalem in 1948 and was forever scarred by the Israeli military defeat, was now in charge, nineteen years later, of all military operations in the center region and in Jerusalem,[115] backed notably by Eitan Ben Moshe, who commanded the Engineering Unit, and who therefore was present at the meeting on Friday 9 June. The record of decisions pinpoints the buildings that were to be demolished. Under item A are listed the demolitions to be performed outside the walls of the old city by "the Jerusalem municipality under the supervision of the municipal engineer,"

notably "all the buildings located on Jaffa Street all the way to Jaffa Gate, including the border wall and the antitank obstacles [. . .]; the buildings located
to the east of Mamilla Street all the way to Jaffa Gate [. . .]; the buildings
located on the road to Hebron all the way to Jaffa Gate." Item B specifies that
military engineering units would be on the scene to make sure the right material was being used on the ground by the municipality for the demolitions
mentioned in item A.

Item C is devoted entirely to the "Kotel plaza": "The military engineering
unit will be responsible for organizing a site visit to the Kotel zone tomorrow
Saturday evening at 17:45, on 10/06/1967. They will gather at the municipality
at 17:30 (taking part in the visit: the engineering officers; the mayor, assisted by
municipal staff; the head of the National Park Authority assisted by architect
Mr. Tanai)."[116] The myth of a demolition spontaneously conducted by West
Jerusalem contractors definitively falls apart. During the Friday 9 June meeting
presided over by Kollek and Narkiss, one particular agenda item was devoted
to the demolition of the Maghrebi Quarter, and it was specifically noted that
this operation—unlike the demolitions performed in the vicinity of Jaffa Gate
listed in item A—would not take place under the sole responsibility of the
municipality, but would be placed under the triple responsibility of the army,
the municipality, and the National Park Authority.

The next item, regarding issues of sanitation and hygiene, confirms that the
decision was indeed ratified at this meeting: "The Water Works will take part
in cleanup operations. The Kotel plaza will be cleaned Sunday morning and the
Water Works will assign two employees on-site starting Monday morning to
ensure continuous cleaning throughout the day."[117] Let us recall that on Friday
9 June in the afternoon, at the moment when this report was being drafted, the
Maghrebi Quarter was still intact, and that what was being designated as the
"Kotel plaza" did not yet exist. But everything was already planned, both to
coordinate the demolition logistically (the site visit planned for the following
day at 5:45 p.m.) and to ensure the subsequent cleanup of the site, and its water
spraying by a two-person crew to contain the dust.

The Demolition Plan: Architects and Archaeologists at the Helm

The site visit did take place the following late afternoon, Saturday 10 June, at the very moment when the evictions were starting and Sasson Levy and his crew were working out the last equipment details. This was not a decision-making visit, but an operational one to look at procedures and at the perimeter of the demolition, which had been decided upon the day before. For this reason, the only document that remains as evidence is a roughly drawn and captioned map of the demolition (the very one referred to by Ben Moshe), a digital copy of which is preserved at the Israeli National Archives in a file kept by the National Park Authority devoted to patrimony in Jerusalem (figure 51).[118] The map's key captioning is in Hebrew but, probably to avoid any risk of confusion, the four street names of the neighborhood—which don't exist in Hebrew, and which determine the outer limits of the zone to be demolished—are written in Latin characters, all capitals: AQABAT ABU MADYAN; AL IMAM MALIK RD; AL BURAQ; AL AFDALIEH.

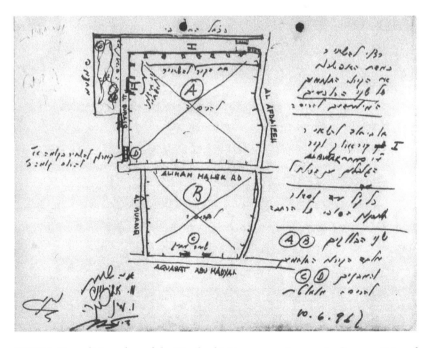

FIGURE 51. **Demolition plan of the Maghrebi Quarter, 10 June 1967. Source:** © Israel State Archives, GL-3847/4.

The five signatures at the bottom left of the document testify to the high level of responsibility of the figures brought on board.[119] The first signature belongs to the architect Arieh Sharon,[120] already world-renowned at the time: winner of the Israel Prize in 1962, board member of the International Union of Architects since 1963, president of the National Council of Israeli National Parks since 1964, president of the Israeli Association of Engineers and Architects since 1965, and honorary member of the Berlin Academy of Arts since 1965; he would be directing a restoration project for the old city of Jerusalem in 1968.[121] The second signature is that of Michael Avi Yohah, historian and professor of archaeology at Hebrew University in Jerusalem, academic secretary of the Israeli Department of Antiquities, and inspector of antiquities for the Jerusalem region.[122]

The third signature belongs to the architect Yohanan Minsker, the author in 1966 of a list of five hundred historical sites to preserve in Jerusalem within the city's master plan in preparation; he was also among those who inspired the renovation of the Roman Cardo in old Jerusalem in the 1970s, and he would defend a dissertation in 1973, "Methodology for Restoring the Jewish Quarter of the Old City of Jerusalem."[123] The fourth signature is that of the architect Dan Tanai, whose name had come up during the meeting the previous day, and who would later be in charge of restoring the four Sephardic synagogues in the old Jewish Quarter, inaugurated in 1973.[124] The fifth and last signature, less legible and off-center to the left, is that of the archaeologist Yaacov Yannai, who headed the National Parks Authority and had published in 1964 a vast overview of historical monuments in Israel, prefaced by the famous archaeologist and former chief of staff Ygael Yadin.[125]

The five signatures at the bottom of the demolition map were intended to render the destruction validated by five established figures whose academic bona fides were indisputable, whether in archaeology or architecture. Paradoxically, all five were, or would soon be, involved in the upcoming historic preservation projects over the next few years. This was paradoxical only on the surface, since the plan makes clear that the Maghrebi Quarter, even if it was founded at the end of the twelfth century, is considered by all five signatories not as a patrimonial element in itself, but as an obstacle to the necessary upgrading of the Western Wall, the only architectural patrimony worthy of conservation within these boundaries. It is also significant that not a single representative of the army or municipality is among the signatories, even though we know—from the previous evening's report—that they were present at this visit, which they themselves had organized. The point, then, was to cover up the *political* responsibilities by showcasing the scientific experts.

If a detailed analysis of the demolition map reveals a certain reluctance on the part of the five experts, the comparison between the initial map and the perimeter that was actually destroyed shows that their misgivings were not acted upon, as Ben Moshe pointed out: in the end, the destruction proved far more extensive than planned. The map legend indicates, in fact, that the exterior walls of two blocks of houses were to be kept intact "to the extent possible [. . .] awaiting the final configuration of the plaza"—notably, the wall running alongside the Al-Buraq alley, the suspended vault located at the corner of the Al-Buraq alley and Imam Malik Street, and finally what is described on the map as an "ancient gate" located in Abu Madyan Lane. This ancient gate is none other than the scalloped arch from the Ayyubid period that marked the entrance to the Madrassa Afdaliyya, fragments of which were uncovered during digs carried out from 2005 to 2009.[126] More precisely, the map indicates that only two blocks of houses were to be torn down: the first, labeled A on the map, faces the Western Wall and is circumscribed by Afdaliyya Street, Imam Malik Street, and Tariq al-Buraq Street. The second, labeled B on the map, is located to the immediate west of the first block and is bounded by Afdaliyya Street, Aqabat Abu Madyan, Tariq al-Buraq, and Imam Malik Street.

Close scrutiny of the photographs taken on-site a few days later reveals that the initial perimeter was greatly exceeded to the south, west, and north, until it finally encompassed the whole quarter—reaching all the way, for example, to the outer wall of the Khalidi home, even though that building was located some fifteen meters beyond the boundaries set by the map. Overall, if we compare the area scheduled to be demolished according to the map and the surface area effectively destroyed by the bulldozers of Sasson Levy and his crew, we come up with a 60 percent discrepancy. We can clearly state, therefore, that the demolition map was *not* followed; its limits were massively exceeded, and not only at the margins.

In greater detail, the five experts asked expressly that the suspended vault and the Ayyubid gate be "preserved," along with the wall that circumscribed the prayer space in front of the Western Wall; yet all these features were immediately destroyed. This massive discrepancy between the demolition map and the area effectively destroyed implies that the five experts summoned to the site visit had been manipulated. In any case, it would appear that their expertise was conspicuously overruled, thus confirming that their scientific opinion had been taken on advisement only, and that the destruction of the Maghrebi Quarter was indeed the result of a political decision taken at the highest state level. Although this premise by now seems rather obvious in terms of historical plausibility, I have still had to make the documentary case to prove it.

Demolition Permit: A Political Decision

In fact, the staging of an operation initiated by West Jerusalem contractors simply strains credulity once subjected to the most basic historical scrutiny: how to imagine that an entire neighborhood of the old city of Jerusalem, located across from the Western Wall, could be evacuated and destroyed in one night, hours after the cease-fire was established, without a prior decision by the highest political authorities? How would these contractors have been able to maneuver the earth-moving equipment, and how would the architects and archaeologists have been willing to commit their signatures if they had not received guarantees that they were acting under cover of a political decision? Two brief notes recently published by Israeli researchers unequivocally debunk the fable of a private initiative. Eli Shiller and Aharon Yaffe write in 2007 that "it was decided that a private entity would be put in charge of the demolition so that it would not be interpreted as a military action,"[127] and Shmuel Bahat writes in 2017 that the army oversaw the demolition site but did not want to be "publicly implicated" in the operation.[128]

Even so, if these researchers highlight a determination to conceal *military* involvement, neither posits a *political* decision. Importantly, no study has thus far been able to produce a document that would attest to such involvement. Yet, at the very core of the historian's métier—and of its legitimacy— documentation remains the defining requirement: though not all past reality has left documentary traces, it is nonetheless true that definitive validation of a historical premise is only as good as its documentary proof, whether direct or implicit, or at least the quality and exhaustiveness of its documentary inquiry.

As for the army's responsibility, the case is settled. Predictably, research into the Israeli military archives has yet to yield any compelling results,[129] but the document identified in the municipal archives is more than enough to demonstrate the army's direct involvement—and that at the highest level, since it was General Uzi Narikss himself who planned the terms and procedures of the demolition during the meeting he cochaired with Teddy Kollek on Friday 9 June in the afternoon.[130] As for the municipality's role, the same document also amply attests to the full responsibility of Kollek, which he will assume ten years later in his memoirs.[131] But can we seriously imagine that Kollek and Narkisss could have made that decision of their own volition, without the backing of some political initiative from the powers that be—that is, from the government?

The journalist Uzi Benziman, who covered the Six-Day War for the daily *Haaretz*, collected his memories in a book published in 1973, where he refers to David Ben-Gurion's visit to the Western Wall on Thursday 8 June, accompanied notably by Kollek, Shimon Peres (Ben-Gurion's young protégé, the secretary-general of his party, Rafi), Air Force Chief of Staff Ezer Weizmann, and Yaacov Yannai, head of the National Park Authority. According to Benziman's account, picked up by numerous other authors, the man Israelis used to call "the Old Lion"—he had not been prime minister since 1963—is said to have flown into a temper when he noticed a public toilet next to the Wall, and reportedly asked Yannai to have it demolished immediately, after which Yannai supposedly engaged Kollek on the subject, adding that it was time, in his mind, to "clean up the whole area."[132] In the same vein, Ben-Gurion is also said to have ordered that the street sign affixed to the Wall bearing the mention of "Al-Buraq" be immediately destroyed; this gave rise to a famous photograph taken by Micha Bar-Am.[133] The narrative is all the more credible in that it converges with the next day's meeting (Friday 9 June), and with the site visit the day after (Saturday 10 June), both in the presence of Kollek and Yannai.

Benziman's testimony thus tends to steer the inquiry toward a verbal register, expressed in rather vague terms by the "Old Lion," Ben-Gurion, who had the requisite moral authority, though not the administrative authority, strictly speaking, since he was only a member of the Knesset. This narrative also resonates with other unwritten orders said to have been issued by the same Ben-Gurion, as prime minister this time, during the 1948 war, when one word—or even a single gesture—is said to have triggered the evacuation and

demolition of the greatest possible number of Palestinian villages.[134] Still, however credible the story might seem, it does still rely on nothing but the good
faith of Benziman himself. The Ben-Gurion archives, preserved alongside his
remains at Sde Boker in the Negev, have kept no trace of the order he is said
to have articulated on his visit, whether in his personal diary entry for 8 June
or in letters written the following hours or days.[135] Moreover, we should note
that even if we accept Benziman's story as valid, he reports only the order to
get rid of the *toilets* adjacent to the Western Wall (the very ones built in 1954
to improve public sanitation), with no mention of the *quarter* itself. Finally,
he places the ultimate responsibility for the decision on Ben-Gurion alone,
which relieves other governmental bodies of all accountability. At this stage
of the inquiry, I could piece together a plausible scenario, partially accurate no
doubt; but the missing link that would confirm the government's involvement
remained elusive.

Just as I was able to identify a key document by processing the technical
files at the municipal archives, I applied the same strategy for the governmental
archives by favoring the *fringes* of the state apparatus rather than its *center*. In
fact, we shall most likely never recover a ministerial council account that would
state in black and white and a priori the decision to destroy the Maghrebi
Quarter. In the current state of available documentation, the only account of
the cabinet meeting held on Sunday 11 June refers a posteriori to the Maghrebi
Quarter issue: after Prime Minister Levi Eshkol raises the question of the need
for a law formalizing the evacuation and destruction of the quarter, Minister
of Industry Zeev Sheref counters that a law would be pointless, since the operation "has already taken place." Minister of the Interior Haim Moshe Shapira
goes even further, indicating that the operation can be justified more simply
"by pointing to the hazard posed by the demolished buildings." The inquiry
most probably ends here, with regard to the core government apparatus: it most
probably did not address the issue officially *prior to* the effective realization of
the fait accompli.[136]

However, it is highly plausible that this decision, if it was indeed validated
in advance at the governmental level, must have left traces in the archives of
the Foreign Ministry, which then had the daunting task of getting the international community to accept the process of "reunification" of the Holy City, so
as to render it irreversible. A search of the archives of the Middle East Division

of the Israeli Foreign Ministry for the period 8 to 10 June yielded a document
that establishes definitively the *prior* implication of governmental bodies in the
decision to destroy the Maghrebi Quarter. It is a typewritten "classified memo,"
dated 9 June 1967, written and signed by Yael Vered and addressed to Yosef
Tekoah, deputy director general of the Foreign Ministry, titled "Jerusalem"
(figure 52).[137] Vered was at that time a reputable diplomat, a graduate of Hebrew
University in psychology and Islamic studies; previously assigned to the North
African Division,[138] she would become director of the Middle Eastern Division
in 1969, then Israel's ambassador to UNESCO in 1979.[139] The memo, written
on Friday 9 June, most likely early in the day, enumerates the decisions necessary to make the conquest of Jerusalem irreversible.

> Our resolve to keep possession of Jerusalem requires the following actions: [1]—
> At the meeting next Sunday, the government must decide that the Jewish city
> and the Arab city henceforward form but one city. This decision must not be
> made public for the moment. [2]—Decision no. 1 presupposes that life will go
> back to normal in the formerly Jordanian part of the city. For that, the follow-
> ing actions must be immediately decided and gradually made public over the
> course of next week: [a] The offices of the military governor of the West Bank
> will not be located in the formerly Jordanian part of the city. [b] The munici-
> pality of Jerusalem will be responsible for all municipal services for the entire
> old city: cleaning, sanitation, drinking water, etc. [c] All the buildings recently
> added in the Wall zone will be demolished, so that the Wall will recover its
> original appearance. This will apply to all Arab buildings built since the mid-
> 20th century by the Arabs around the Wall with the goal of reducing the space
> around the holiest site of world Judaism. The National Park Authority will be
> immediately responsible for this operation and for the rehabilitation, mainte-
> nance, and surveillance of the monuments inside and outside the old city."[140]

This is clearly an internal Foreign Ministry document, dated Friday 9 June,
which makes the demolition of the Maghrebi Quarter one of the necessary conditions for consolidating the conquest of East Jerusalem. It is worth noting that
most of the items listed in the document would be implemented—in particular,
the decision to reunify the city under a single municipal entity, but also, more
broadly, the strategy of rapidly replacing the military occupation regime with
"ordinary" civilian management, unlike in the rest of the West Bank.

FIGURE 52. Note from Yael Vered to Minister of Foreign Affairs Yosef Tekoah, 9 June 1967. Source: © Israel State Archives, HZ-4089-14.

Equally worth mention, this memo's purpose is to list the *actions* to be implemented, but also to embed a *communication* strategy for each, both in terms of timing—calendar deadlines or postponements, as was the case for the dissolution of the Jordanian municipality—and in terms of vocabulary or "talking points," as we would say today. This twin objective illustrates diplomacy's double function, both to decide which actions to carry out, and to establish the right strategy to make them acceptable to foreign powers and international organizations. This was particularly true when it came to the decision to demolish the Maghrebi Quarter, a decision worded as a succession of talking points aimed at presenting the quarter as a group of buildings constructed since 1948 with the purpose of preventing access to the Western Wall. This is why the decision was presented not as a transformation of the site, but as a return to its "original appearance." This is also why responsibility for the operation was handed over to the National Park Authority: clearing the plaza had to be framed as protection of a heritage site. Finally, it is why the demolition had to be carried out "immediately," before international observers or journalists had the chance to realize how ancient the neighborhood was.

The strategic, adjudicative dimension of the memo is further confirmed by a final element that brought my inquiry to a close: in the margins of the document, next to the paragraph concerning the Maghrebi Quarter, the memo's addressee, Yosef Tekoah, added a handwritten commentary: "Must quote plausible technical reasons (e.g. facilitate access or buildings unsafe) to avoid impression of vindictiveness or inhumanity. Decent alternative accomodation for anyone displaced."[141] There is no other marginal annotation on the document, which confirms that the demolition of the Maghrebi Quarter was indeed seen as paramount at the time. The note in the margin is crucial for two reasons. First, it proves that the demolition of the Maghrebi Quarter was indeed an explicit political decision endorsed at the governmental level. On Friday 9 June, more than twenty-four hours before the start of operations, the decision to demolish the Maghrebi Quarter was explicitly approved by Tekoah, number two at the Foreign Ministry.

Second, this internal memo exposes the dissimulation strategy devised deliberately by the government with regard to the destruction of the Maghrebi Quarter. Tekoah, who would be appointed Israeli ambassador to the United Nations in 1968, emphasizes in his commentary that this operation is liable to give an "impression of vindictiveness or inhumanity," which could be avoided if "plausible technical reasons" were put forward to advocate for demolition, notably "unsafe" buildings, while emphasizing that all "displaced" persons would be offered "decent alternative accomodation." It is striking to observe how closely this communication strategy was adhered to, since we can read in the report submitted to the UN secretary-general by his representative Ernesto Thalmann on 12 September 1967: "The Israeli authorities stated that the buildings in a slum area outside the Temple Wall had been destroyed; the inhabitants had been provided with alternative housing."[142]

———

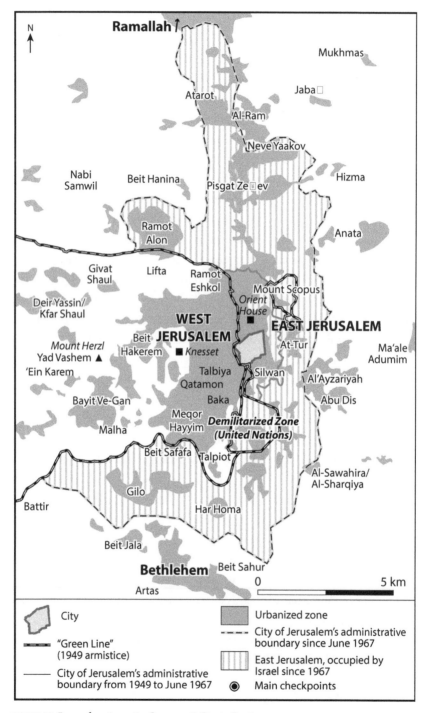

N

Ramallah

Mukhmas

Atarot

Jaba

Al-Ram

Neve Yaakov

Nabi
Samwil

Beit Hanina

Pisgat Ze□ev

Hizma

Ramot
Alon

Anata

Givat
Shaul

Lifta

Ramot
Eshkol

Mount Scopus

Deir Yassin/
Kfar Shaul

*Orient
House*

EAST JERUSALEM

WEST
JERUSALEM

Mount Herzl
Yad Vashem ▲

Beit
Hakerem

Knesset

At-Tur

Ma'ale
Adumim

'Ein Karem

Talbiya

Silwan

Al'Ayzariyah

Qatamon

Bayit Ve-Gan

Baka

Abu Dis

Malha

Meqor
Hayyim

*Demilitarized Zone
(United Nations)*

Beit Safafa

Talpiot

Al-Sawahira/
Al-Sharqiya

Battir

Gilo

Har Homa

Beit Jala

Bethlehem

Beit Sahur

0   5 km

Artas

City	Urbanized zone
"Green Line" (1949 armistice)	- - - City of Jerusalem's administrative boundary since June 1967
—— City of Jerusalem's administrative boundary from 1949 to June 1967	East Jerusalem, occupied by Israel since 1967
	◉ Main checkpoints

FIGURE 53. **Jerusalem in 1967. Source: © Dario Ingiusto.**

By cross-referencing news releases, individual testimony, municipal records, and government archives, I was finally able to establish the decision-making process that led to the demolition of the Maghrebi Quarter of Jerusalem. On Thursday 8 June, during Ben-Gurion's site visit, Yacov Yannai and Teddy Kollek raised the need to "clear out" the zone, with no further details, and undoubtedly after a remark made by Ben-Gurion himself. On Friday 9 June, the deputy director general of the Foreign Ministry considered the demolition of the quarter a necessary condition if the conquest of East Jerusalem was to be irreversible; he explicitly endorsed the decision and set the conditions for its diplomatic acceptability by embedding key talking points into its messaging to the rest of the world. On Friday 9 June in the late afternoon, a bipartite meeting between Kollek and Uzi Narkiss set the terms of the operation, placed under the triple responsibility of the army, the municipality, and the National Park Authority, and planned a site visit for the following day. A few hours later, on Friday evening, Sasson Levy was contacted by phone, along with some twenty other contractors, to take part in the operation; all day Saturday, he and his crew assembled the necessary gear. On Saturday at 5:45 p.m., the site visit took place in which Arieh Sharon, Michael Avi Yonah, Yohanan Minsker, Dan Tanai, and Yaacov Tannai all signed off on the demolition plan, thereby imparting scientific legitimacy; the army immediately began evacuating the inhabitants, and the contractors set about tearing down the buildings, with logistical backing from the army: safe-conduct passes, gasoline, refueling, lighting, generators. The greater part of the quarter was destroyed overnight. On Sunday 11 June at midday, the *Jerusalem Post* reporter noted that "a bulldozer is knocking down the last houses"; at this same moment, the government was pondering the need for a law to ratify the destruction of the quarter, a contingency that seems to have been ruled out. In no way the accidental result of a spontaneous initiative by a few overly zealous contractors, the destruction of the Maghrebi Quarter was on the contrary the logical outcome of an operation decided and coordinated at the highest state level, with the backing of the army, the municipality, scientific authorities, and archaeological and heritage institutions. Fifty years on, this is what history as a discipline can state with certainty, based upon supporting documents.

The actors in these historical events, for their part, were always fully aware of the inside story. On 26 September 1967, long after the dust had settled at the demolition site, Meron Benvenisti wrote to Kollek about the "inhabitants evacuated from the Western Wall area," to deplore how few resources were available to the municipality to provide relief "to the hundreds of people who were evicted right after the war *by the army and the State*."[143] Nicolas Boileau's famous phrase is worth quoting here to comment on this brief but enlightening passage: "Whatever we conceive well we express clearly, and words flow with ease." There is no circumlocution, no communication strategy in this internal memo, which has the advantage of stating bluntly what each of the interlocutors knew full well. The same day, Kollek wrote to Prime Minister Levi Eshkol to convey this same grievance in even more pointed terms, specifying that it was not up to "the city of Jerusalem" but to the "government of Israel" to accommodate the former "inhabitants of the Maghrebi Quarter, which bordered the Western Wall," recalling that "most of the families were evacuated with only a few hours warning and hence lost all of their effects," and pointing out that "in most cases, the evicted families have not been provided with alternative rehousing."[144]

There it is, in black and white: the state's responsibility, the conditions of the evacuation, the wretched plight of the former inhabitants of the neighborhood, the failure to rehouse most of them. In longhand, on the Kollek memo, Prime Minister Eshkol or a member of his cabinet wrote: "300,000 IL. Security issue. Property rights. Ministry of Housing supplies budget." The government's full responsibility is thus acknowledged by Eshkol himself, who draws the logical conclusions by consenting to assume the compensation of the former inhabitants of the quarter. The archives of the Israeli Ministry of Finance attest to the follow-through on that decision: on 27 February 1968, the Budget Department confirmed with the cabinet of the prime minister that, "pursuant to the request for a budget of 300,000 IL from the Ministry of Housing," the amount was made available "the same day" to finance compensation for "persons evacuated from the Kotel zone."[145] To conclude this investigation, we must search for these reparations dossiers, which could shed an ultimate light on the community of Jerusalem Maghrebis, in the manner of a postmortem inventory.

6

AFTER THE CATASTROPHE

COLLECTING THE EVIDENCE,
DOCUMENTING THE DISAPPEARANCE

In the Royal Archives of Rabat, in the received correspondence files, there is a copy of a long letter dated 18 March 1977, signed by "Ruhi al-Khatib, mayor of Occupied Jerusalem," and addressed to the ambassador of Morocco in Amman, with regard to the "plight" of the former inhabitants of the Jerusalem Maghrebi Quarter,[1] and to "the historical and political importance of the Moroccan presence in Jerusalem." Ten years after the quarter had been demolished and its inhabitants dispersed, the former mayor of the Jordanian part of the Holy City (expelled from Jerusalem to Amman by the Israeli authorities in March 1968) was imploring "fraternal Morocco" and its king, "Commander of the Faithful" and "Protector of the Holy Places," to "pursue the mission of the finest sons of Morocco, Algeria, Tunisia, and Libya," and to continue to act to protect the community however possible, as he wrote at the end of his message, in order to "mitigate the catastrophe."[2] To "mitigate the catastrophe" was an apt phrase, for it is precisely the reason behind all the documents produced in the weeks, months, and years following the disappearance of the Maghrebi Quarter.[3]

At the Royal Archives of Rabat I came upon another letter, dated 28 January 1975, signed "Muhammad Ibrahim Abdelhaq and Issa Hasham al-Moghrabi, mutewalli of the Waqf Abu Madyan," addressed to Princess Lalla

Malika, sister of King Hassan II and president of the Moroccan Red Crescent, begging that she "instruct the embassy of His Majesty in Amman" to provide financial relief to the former inhabitants of the quarter, to help the youngest in their schooling, to support the sick, and to speed up the process of obtaining or extending passports. The Moroccans of Jerusalem, they write, "both inhabitants and defenders of the Holy Places," are guardians of a "deep history that testifies to the greatness of Morocco, the generosity of Moroccans, and the patrimony built on Eastern land."[4] The Maghrebi Quarter was destroyed on the night of 10–11 June 1967, but the community of its former inhabitants still existed, since it represented and expressed itself as such, several years later. Not everything had disappeared, in other words. The story was still being written.

What did remain, then, of the former Maghrebi Quarter after the catastrophe? Patrick Boucheron, in *Faire profession d'historien*, reworks the distinction made by Walter Benjamin between *trace* and *aura*. He quotes first a fragment of *The Book of Passages*, in which Benjamin outlines a definition of the two notions: "The trace is appearance of a nearness, however far removed the thing that left it behind may be. The aura is appearance of a distance, however close the thing that calls it forth. In trace, we gain possession of the thing; with the aura, it takes possession of us."[5] Out of caution as much as ethical choice, the discipline of the historian recommends that one keep the aura at a distance and hew as closely as possible to traces, to be more a hunter than a gatherer, more a rag picker than a *flâneur*, to quote the terms used by Boucheron in his commentary on Benjamin: "Where the *flâneur* is in thrall to things, the rag picker looks where he places each footstep, eyes never skyward, and collects rags, which is to say, everything that constitutes a trace [. . .]. What is my point here? A wake-up call that makes the *flâneur* too frivolous and flippant, and renders necessary the time of the rag pickers, those with a more humble and first-hand rapport with the archives."[6]

That being said, trace and aura are often lumped into one document, and this is what Boucheron believes makes for the whole "critical dignity" of historical work, which consists precisely of "dispelling the halo surrounding things to take account of the real, with doggedness and assiduous attention."[7] Thus, the letters written in Jerusalem in 1975 and Amman in 1977 and sent to Rabat involve both trace and aura: they conserve the *trace* of a reasoned complaint that would result in the transfer of hard cash, but their authors also benefited from the *aura* of the Maghrebi Quarter, its former renown and its bygone prestige, in their attempt to ingratiate themselves with the Moroccan sovereign.

The postmortem history of the Maghrebi Quarter, the one that continued beyond 11 June 1967—in a delocalized, dispersed, diffracted manner—involves both trace and aura, the imprint and the halo, the vestige and the echo: documents and discourses, procedures and narratives, remnants of buildings and snippets of legend. This *postmortem* history is the very subject of this final chapter, though its aim is not to tell the story of an erasure, a disappearance, or even an unfolding tale of nostalgia, a sleep-inducing lullaby murmured before switching off the light; if the history of the Maghrebi Quarter is to be told "to the bitter end," which must necessarily include the *aftermath* of its destruction, it is because, on the contrary, this after-the-fact phase offers some invaluable rearview mirroring of life in the neighborhood *before* its disappearance. We can break this view into three broad subgroups that will structure this final chapter.

First, I will attempt to gauge the diplomatic resonance that followed the crashing din of the destruction. The deafening silence offers an essential interpretive key for understanding the diplomatic blind spot in which the Maghrebi Quarter found itself in the final years of its existence, even if Morocco emerges as a relative exception in this respect, since Morocco opted for a strictly humanitarian approach to the issue, thanks to the transnational network of the Red Crescent and the Red Cross.

Secondly, I will document the reparation procedures put in place by the Israeli authorities for the express purpose of containing the outcry that might have been triggered by complaints of the quarter's former inhabitants. The dossiers pertaining to reparations, not unlike insurance claims filed after some natural disaster, offer a snapshot of the quarter—its built space, but also its sociology—right before its disappearance.

And thirdly, I will linger on the lengthy procedures that preceded the destruction of the neighborhood's very last block of houses, Dar Abu Saud, in 1968–69. Like a butte in an otherwise eroded landscape, Dar Abu Saud preserved the last traces of the Maghrebi Quarter for a few months longer, like a silent but reproachful memorial. Because this particular act of demolition did not take place on the sly or in a single midnight raid, but rather in the light of day and over several months, its narrative has the unique potential to *retrace* the reasoning behind the destruction of the major part of the neighborhood. The trace and the aura of the Maghrebi Quarter, captured even long after its death, speak volumes about the history of its life.

The Diplomatic Echo: The Maghrebi Quarter in the Blind Spot

A systematic search through the archives produced by the French Consulate in Jerusalem in the days and weeks that followed the Six-Day War yields evidence that officials there considered the destruction of the Maghrebi Quarter as a piece of anecdotal news, referred to belatedly and almost incidentally. The first mention of the events is not made until more than twelve days after the fact, in the course of a dispatch on 23 June devoted to "the situation in the West Bank and Jerusalem after fifteen days of occupation." After ample focus on the "return to normal conditions" thanks to "the exemplary conduct of the Israeli soldiers," the consul Christian Fouache d'Halloy reports on the fifth page of the dispatch that "the destruction of the Maghrebi Quarter to create a large plaza measuring about a hectare in front of the Wailing Wall, and the ordering of the Arab Muslim population to evacuate the old Jewish Quarter within 24 hours, affected nearly 250 families, several of whom are now homeless."[8]

After this brief observation, the consul moves on to another topic and fails to propose any kind of reaction to his ministry. The Maghrebi Quarter, over which France had still been exercising guardianship a mere five years earlier, had clearly been excluded from the scope of French diplomatic intervention since Algerian independence. In the long eight-page consular dispatch titled "A Three-Day War" and drafted on Monday 12 June, the very day after the demolition, there is no mention, not a single word, about the event, even indirectly.[9] Nor is there any reference in the dispatch written on Wednesday 14 June, which starts with a rather startling general commentary: "The situation remains alarming in the old city where the hostility of the Palestinian Muslim population toward the occupier is delaying the point where more or less normal life can resume."[10]

The deafening silence of the French diplomatic archives helps us understand how this neighborhood could have been so easily destroyed. The European consulates, including the one that in principle should have been the largest stakeholder, looked away. We cannot speak here of an information gap, since it is the consular officials' job to read the Israeli press, particularly the *Jerusalem Post*, which appears in English. So they most certainly read the article of 12 June headlined "Western Wall Area Cleared," which described "a bulldozer knocking down the last houses."[11] But they failed to transmit the information to Paris either in their 12 June dispatch or in that of 14 June, and mentioned the episode only incidentally in their 23 June dispatch. The archives are significant as much for what they contain as for what they do not: namely, if the destruction of the Maghrebi Quarter was glossed over by the French Consulate, it is because it was considered not an *event* that needed to be reported to Paris for an eventual reaction, but rather a predictable *anecdote* to be placed against the backdrop of a broader process underway.

This long process was rightly perceived as dynamic, for a few months later a different project was troubling the French consul On 7 August 1968, he reported on the commemoration of 9 Av (the anniversary of the destruction of the Temple), described as 150,000 persons assembled "on the plaza erected in front of the Wailing Wall," highlighting the fact that "young people from the religious kibbutzim movement" were chanting "a special prayer calling for a speedier reconstruction of the Temple in the reunified Jerusalem."[12] On 11 July, the French ambassador to Israel had already alerted Paris to the Chief Rabbinate's reference to a "service at the restored Temple," before indicating that such a prospect had been firmly rejected by the political authorities.[13] This emerging tension over the future of the Haram al-Sharif is undoubtedly one of the reasons for the dearth of reactions to the destruction of the Maghrebi Quarter; numerous witnesses report that Moshe Dayan had the Israeli flag flying over the Dome of the Rock removed at his very first visit on Wednesday 7 June 1967, and we know that he would later decide, against the advice of military rabbi Shlomo Goren, to confirm the authority of the Jordanian waqf over the entire plaza, forbidding any form of Jewish worship from taking place.[14] With the fate of the Haram al-Sharif seemingly in the balance, we can imagine the relief of European diplomats, prompting them to exercise discretion when it came to the Maghrebi Quarter, located just below.

The French consular archives assure us, at any rate, that there was no reason for outrage. On 25 August 1967, the consul reported on the visit of UN representative Ernesto Thalmann, making the point that the Palestinians of Jerusalem were still expressing hope for a "return to Jordan of the territories occupied since 5 June," mentioning in passing that in order to achieve this, "concessions could actually be made to Israel, the main one involving the surrender of all sovereignty over the Wailing Wall and all the necessary clearance."[15] Within days of the Arab summit in Khartoum (29 August), and in the midst of negotiations over the future of Resolution 242 of the UN Security Council (22 November), all indications were that the destruction of the Maghrebi Quarter had been written off, including by France, which considered the demolition operations as mere "necessary clearance."

Toward the end of my perusal of the French consular archives from the weeks following the Six-Day War, I came across a folder labeled "Relief organized under the auspices of the municipality," and I caught myself believing that the fate of the former inhabitants of the Maghrebi Quarter might finally be raised, at least from the humanitarian perspective. But this was not to be. The dossier contained only one letter, dated 21 June 1967 from the French consul to Mayor Kollek, "to contribute to the relief fund for all those who suffered during the fighting in the city of Jerusalem during the period of last 5 to 7 June."[16] On 26 June, Kollek expressed "his sincere thanks" to the French consul for "the donation of 200 Israeli pounds that [he] generously gave to the city."[17] For the French Consulate, the destruction of the Maghrebi Quarter was decidedly a nonevent.

The four-volume set of *Documents on Jerusalem* published in 2007 by the PASSIA Foundation provided me with a rapid overview of diplomatic reactions to the destruction of the Maghrebi Quarter.[18] If they were swift and virulent coming from Jerusalem's Palestinian notables, they were more circumscribed on the part of Arab governments, including the Maghreb states. On 24 July 1967, in an open letter addressed to Israeli Military Governor Shlomo Lahat, former Jordanian Governor Anwar al-Khatib enumerated seven "illegal actions" committed by the Israeli army since the conquest of the city. The letter described, in third position, "the destruction of two Muslim mosques in the Maghrebi Quarter of Jerusalem as well as the destruction of the whole neighborhood, which is entirely the property of a Muslim charitable endowment."[19] In the memorandum he issued to the UN on 26 August 1967, the former mayor of East Jerusalem, Ruhi al-Khatib, also raised the issue of the destruction of the Maghrebi Quarter, but in far more detailed terms, reporting the demolition of "135 houses" and the eviction of "poor and pious people," who had "no more than three hours" to leave the premises, and about whom "one can easily imagine the consternation."[20]

We know that the UN Security Council was concurrently taking up the issue of Jerusalem with the vote of a first resolution (242) on 22 November 1967, calling for "withdrawal of Israeli armed forces from territories occupied in the recent conflict," and then, six months later, a second resolution (252), voted on 21 May 1968, denouncing more specifically the "expropriation of land and properties thereon which tend to change the legal status of Jerusalem [...]."[21] Meanwhile, in late December 1967, the Kuwaiti delegation—made up in part of Palestinian exiles—dispatched to the Security Council a documentary dossier titled "The Wailing Wall: Magharaba Quarter Completely Demolished," reprinting certain photographs already released in the magazine *Arab World*.[22] On 6 November 1968, the Jordanian ambassador to the United Nations addressed a letter to the secretary-general to denounce Israel's faits accomplis.[23]

On 20 November 1968, again at the initiative of the Jordanian government, the UNESCO General Assembly voted its own resolution calling on Israel to "scrupulously preserve all the sites, buildings, and other cultural properties, especially in the old city of Jerusalem" and to "desist from any archaeological excavations, transfer of such properties, and changing of the features of their cultural and historical character."[24] On this occasion, Israeli diplomats endeavored to react specifically to the issue of the Maghrebi Quarter when they contemplated using the town plan drafted in 1919 by Patrick Geddes, but in the end they decided against doing so;[25] a telegram addressed on 18 November 1968 by the Foreign Ministry to the Israeli delegation to the United Nations stresses that "the British government had intended to destroy the entire Maghrebi Quarter, based upon the Patrick Geddes report, which can be found in the archives of the Rockefeller Museum."[26]

On 8 December, an employee of the Rockefeller Museum handwrote a note (on letterhead stationery of the "Palestine Archaeological Museum, Jerusalem, Hashemite Kingdom of Jordan") to warn that the Geddes report's suggestions "were not approved" by the British government, and that its use might therefore prove counterproductive. The next day, the legal counsel to the Foreign Ministry definitively ruled out the possibility of using the British urban planner's report as justification, emphasizing that "the changes suggested by Geddes were far less drastic than what we have done."[27] In this sequence, it is striking to observe how each party attempts to argue about how old the quarter was, or, on the contrary, how old the demolition project was—a sign that the race for *anteriority* was taking hold as a general rule governing how the patrimonial controversy in Jerusalem was to be structured.[28] As of 1968, at any rate, UNESCO became one of the principal arenas in which a patrimonial memory of the Maghrebi Quarter was developed and has thrived to this day.[29]

This same race for precedence was also taking place in Algeria, as seen in the few rare reactions triggered by the event. If Andrew Bellisari, during his current research on transfers of sovereignty in postcolonial Algeria, has been able to assert that the Algerian government made no explicit statement on the subject,[30] I have nevertheless been able to pinpoint a repercussion in the media over the days immediately following the demolition of the neighborhood, even if the repercussion appears oddly out of step with the event itself: on the cover of the Sunday 18 June 1967 issue of *Algérie Actualité*, there is an old photograph of the Western Wall with the headline "From the Algerian Waqf to the Wailing Wall" (figure 54). Inside, an unsigned full-page article addresses how ancient are the ties that unite Algeria and the Maghrebi Quarter of Jerusalem:

> Irrespective of the sentimental ties that might unite us with the brotherly people of Palestine, with their struggle for freedom that is the same for all Arab peoples confronting imperialism, the following reminder is for informational purposes addressed to those among our readers who have no idea that Algeria possesses, with all the supporting legal documents, somewhere between 10 and 15 thousand hectares of land in occupied Palestine, in Jerusalem and its vicinity [...]. The deed of religious bequest drawn up by Abu Madyan in the year 720 [Hegira] states that "the bequest was endowed especially to Maghrebis residing in Jerusalem and those to come, without discrimination of distinction or profession, men or women, old or young, virtuous or otherwise." The bequest provided not only housing but also distribution of bread and even clothing to needy Maghrebis passing through Jerusalem or residing there.[31]

Surprisingly, but no doubt symptomatically, the rest of the article mentions nothing of the demolition of the Maghrebi Quarter, though it had taken place only days earlier. It prefers to reference a rough approximation of past judiciary procedures, wrapping the narrative in a vague anti-imperialist diatribe with strong conspiratorial overtones:

After the creation of Israel, the waqf lands, by some "remote-controlled" coincidence, ended up on the Jewish side and the administrators on the Jordanian side [. . .]. This is where France prevailed upon the plunderers who then consented unconditionally to pay out annual royalty fees of 3,000 Israeli pounds to the endowment, while taking the liberty to distribute more than two hundred property deeds pertaining to waqf lands. The situation had reached this point by 1961. Taking legal action, the endowment's legal counsel will have to sue for each property deed. The first suit, filed in 1961, was not heard in court until two years later. At this rate, the last one will not be brought to trial for another four hundred years. The forces of evil are ubiquitous. Imperialism, its instrument of execution, taking as its pommel horse a completely fabricated Zionist community, will stop at nothing, whether it be humanitarian concerns or, even less, considerations of a spiritual order, to reach its goal: to gain a foothold in Arab land, a test platform from which they plan to stifle the Arab homeland.[32]

FIGURE 54. Front cover of the magazine *Algérie Actualité*, no. 87, Sunday 18 June 1967.

These rantings, totally disconnected from reality, were undoubtedly meant to conceal the deep malaise felt in Algeria over these events. As we saw earlier, the Algerian government did not follow through on the information shared by French Ambassador Jean-Marcel Jeanneney in early 1963, and thereby relinquished their commitment to ensure the legal protection of the Jerusalem Maghrebis, who were left to their own devices. In the *Jerusalem Post* of 20 June 1967, a brief dispatch under the deliberately eye-catching headline "Algeria Claims the Wailing Wall" refers to the article published two days earlier in Algiers.[33] But the content of the article seeks to be reassuring for the Israeli readership, and confirms that the Algerian reaction will not go beyond virulent but ineffectual media posturing.[34]

From the Red Crescent to the Red Cross: Jerusalem, Rabat, Geneva

Like the aftermath of an explosion, the demolition of the Maghrebi Quarter brought about both the *dispersal* of its inhabitants and the *scattering* of evidence of its history. Still, to track down all the archives that document its *post-mortem* existence, I sometimes needed to take the less likely paths: for instance, those that link up the Red Cross branch office in Israel, the Moroccan Red Crescent in Rabat, and the headquarters of this humanitarian organization in Geneva. Since the former inhabitants of the Maghrebi Quarter were now refugees, this final chapter of their story left a few traces within nongovernmental organizations that handle people with this status.[35] The search began at the Office of the Royal Archives of Rabat, where certain documents testify to an ongoing commitment in favor of the former inhabitants of the Maghrebi Quarter, compared to what I was able to observe—or rather, what is not available for observation—in Algeria or in Tunisia. Nothing is surprising about this, since the king of Morocco, descendant of the Prophet and "Commander of the Faithful," has special responsibilities with respect to the third-holiest city in Islam.

Despite the absence of an accessible catalog, and despite the particular status of the Royal Archives in Rabat (which are more akin to dynastic archives than to public archives), I was able to identify a certain number of documents that attest to the palace's commitment: a brief "report relating to the Waqf Abu Madyan," which makes mention of an Algerian community devoted to the "Sidi Abu Madyan" in Fez, written in April 1930 by palace intendants, most probably within the framework of the League of Nations commission of inquiry on ownership of the Wailing Wall;[36] a note that mentions the visit to Rabat of the mutewalli Muhammad Abdelhaq in 1966, with no further details;[37] the letter from former mayor Ruhi al-Khatib dated 18 March 1977, previously mentioned, in which he stresses the need to continue supporting the Moroccan presence in Jerusalem to sustain the Malikite and Sufi religious traditions; and finally, the letter previously mentioned, signed by "Muhammad Ibrahim Abdelhaq and Issa Hachem al-Moghrabim mutewalli of the Waqf Abu Madyan," on 28 January 1975, which in this case did not go unheeded.

Addressed to Princess Lalla Malika, sister of King Hassan II and president of the Moroccan Red Crescent, the letter is a reminder, first of all, that the Sharifian dynasty had always been involved in supporting the Maghrebi community of Jerusalem, particularly after 1948, initially "through the French Consulate General," then "through the Moroccan Embassy in Amman" after its opening in 1959. The letter then cites "the stepped-up pressure" endured by the Moroccan community of Jerusalem after the "Ramadan War" (or "Yom Kippur War") in 1973, during which Morocco openly backed Egypt and Syria, and which resulted in the eviction of three more Moroccan families from the old city on 24 November 1974.[38] At the end of the letter, the two officials of the Waqf Abu Madyan asserted that the former inhabitants of the quarter "accept no compensation for the property destroyed or confiscated," and implored Lalla Malika to help a community that was more than ever "in a critical situation."[39] Two days later, Lalla Malika, in her capacity as "president of the Moroccan Red Crescent," wrote (in French) to Eric Martin, president of the International Committee of the Red Cross (ICRC) in Geneva:

> Since the occupation of the city of Jerusalem in 1967, Israel has been consistently undertaking repressive operations and mass deportations of Arab inhabitants. In fact, one hundred and thirty-five houses belonging to two hundred Moroccan families have been destroyed. These Moroccan families had been living in a neighborhood set aside for Moroccans for more than five centuries [...]. This Moroccan Quarter was in large part demolished by Israel. This is how the last Moroccan families were driven out on 24 November 1974 [...]. We urge you to graciously keep us informed of the emergency actions that you

will be planning to take within the scope of the Red Cross and in compliance
with the Geneva Conventions, notably the 4th convention relating to the
protection of civilians in wartime."[40]

Two important elements in this letter: first, no mention is made of Algeria
or Tunisia, as if, in the absence of specific initiatives by these two countries,
and given the king's special role as "Commander of the Faithful," Morocco
had somehow monopolized the representation of the neighborhood's former
inhabitants, a position which would indeed impact the historical toponymy,
the quarter being most often referred to as the "Moroccan Quarter" in publications subsequently devoted to it.[41] The other decisive element of this letter has
to do with the choice made by the Moroccan authorities to move away from a
political action, in favor of a strictly *humanitarian* approach. Accordingly, the
rest of my inquiry is geared toward the archives of the Red Cross in Geneva,
which offer the advantage of being perfectly cataloged and accessible.[42]

The appeal to Lalla Malika effectively triggered a social inquiry expedited
by the Red Cross, mandated to a "delegation in Israel and in the occupied
territories."[43] On 5 June 1975, the ICRC office in Tel Aviv sent Geneva a first
summary note in the form of a historical overview, emphasizing that, given
how swiftly the demolition had proceeded, "the ICRC had not carried out an
in-depth inquiry back then," and that as a consequence, the only information
available was supplied "by the local mukhtar Mr. Muhammad Abdelhaq, based
on the report by Aref el-Aref." This first note does provide invaluable data on
the fate of the former inhabitants after their eviction:

> In the aftermath of the Six-Day War, on 10 June 1967, at 22:00, the Israeli
> authorities ordered 350 families of the quarter to evacuate their homes within
> the next half-hour. They then set about tearing down the houses. The families
> did not have time to remove their personal effects [. . .]. A 65-year-old woman,
> Hajjah Rasmiyyah, wife of Hajj Ali Abu Akel Al Tabahi Al Moghrabi, who
> refused to leave her house, died beneath the rubble. The evacuated families
> were not rehoused by the Israeli authorities: 200 among them settled in Jeru-
> salem and the vicinity; 125 in Amman; 25 left for Morocco. Reparations: 102
> of the families who stayed in Jerusalem are said to have received in 1968 a total
> of 94,000 Israeli pounds by way of compensation (or an average of 920 Israeli
> pounds per family).[44]

The note confirms the speed of eviction, and specifies that the inhabitants "were not rehoused" (contrary to earlier assertions by the Israeli authorities); but it also indicates (contrary to statements by Ruhi al-Khatib) that some one hundred families collected "compensation," and that although more than half of the families remained in Jerusalem or its vicinity, a third left for Amman and twenty-five went back to Morocco. The note states that the information derives in part from "the report by Aref el-Aref"; and thanks to this clue, I found in the ICRC archives a thick file titled "List of Demolished Houses Drawn Up by Mr. Aref el-Aref," forwarded to Geneva by the Tel Aviv delegation on 1 July 1969.[45] Oddly, the letter attached to the report presents Aref el-Aref as "an Arab historian from Ramallah," failing to mention that he had been mayor of East Jerusalem from 1949 to 1951, and director of the Rockefeller Archaeological Museum beginning in 1963.[46]

This list, based on data established "by the local mukhtars and waqf officials and by the director of the Muslim waqf on 15 June 1967," was originally drafted in Arabic and translated by "Leila," secretary of the Red Cross delegation in Jerusalem. As the attached letter attests, "For the houses demolished in front of the Wailing Wall, we have a wealth of impressive details."[47] In fact, the list mentions for each destroyed dwelling the name of the head of household, the number of rooms, sanitation facilities (toilets, wells), and an estimated value of the property in Jordanian dinars (figure 55). The list thus describes 135 dwellings, accounting for a total of 282 rooms (two rooms per dwelling, on average) for an estimated overall value of 195,250 Jordanian dinars (1,450 dinars on average per dwelling, with a minimum of 500 dinars and a maximum of 5,000 dinars).

Going down this list, despite a few transcription variations, I unsurprisingly found the names of the witnesses I was able to interview fifty years later, as well as other family names I encountered while working through the archives devoted to the history of the Maghrebi Quarter: al-Lubban, al-Daragi, al-Moghrabi, al-Alami, al-Atrash, al-Marakshi, al-Tunsi, al-Fasi, al-Tabakhi, al-Tawati, al-Tayeb, al-Zawawi. . . . I also came across the local mukhtar Muhammad Abdel Haq, who lived in a four-room dwelling with its own cistern, assessed at 2,500 dinars; but also his deputy, Issa Hashem al-Moghrabi, who lived in a three-room dwelling with cistern, assessed at 2,000 dinars, and the mother of the latter, who lived in a single room, no cistern, assessed at 800

- 5 -

ANNEXE No. 1   Waqf Al MAGHARBA / JERUSALEM

Les propriétés qui ont été détruites dans le quartier Al MAGHARBA à
Jérusalem et une évaluation du prix de la propriété.

No.	Habitant	Description	Nb de Pièces	Prix en JD
1.	Mohyi Eddin Al Shami	mais., toil.,mur	3	1500
2.	Magasin pour construction Waqf	2 pièces, mur, puits	2	1500
3.	Haj Kassem Al Daragi	mais.,s.d.b., mur	2	1200
4.	Haj Kassem Al Daragi	mais.,s.d.b., mur	2	1200
5.	Abdallah Kassem Al Daragi	mais.,s.d.b., mur, puits	4	2400
6.	Hassan Al Jandawi	mais.,s.d.b., mur	2	1200
7.	Zakaria Al Zawawi	mais.,s.d.b., mur, puits	3	1800
8.	Mahmoud Al Jarabi	" " " " " "	3	2000
9.	Ahmad Hamideh	mais.,s.d.b., mur	2	1200
10.	Fouad Hamideh	" " " " " "	2	1200
11.	Yahya Al Zawawi	mais.,s.d.b.,mur, puits	2	1500
12.	Maison Al Zawawi	" " " " " "	1	750
13.	Ali Mohammad Al Zawawi	mais.,s.d.b.,mur	1	500
14.	Omar Al Jarabi	" " " " "	1	600
15.	Mohammad Abdel Jalil Moghrabi	" " " ", puits	2	1200
TOTAL:			32	19750
16.	Abdel Jalil Ayed Al Moghrabi	mais.,s.d.b.,mur, puits	2	1200
17.	Ramadan Mussa Kassem	gde pièce,s.d.b., mur, hall	1	1200
18.	Abdel Mon'im Mussa Kassem	mais.,s.d.b.,mur, puits	2	1500
19.	Abdel Rahman Mussa Kassem	gde pièce,s.d.b., mur, hall	1	750
20.	Vve de Abdel Kader Issa	mais.,s.d.b., mur	2	1200
21.	Ahmad Ata Allah	" " " " "	2	1200
TOTAL:			50	26800

...../6

FIGURE 55. List of the 135 houses destroyed in the Maghrebi Quarter, drawn up by
Aref el-Aref in June 1967 and sent to the Red Cross in July 1969: page 1 of 6. Source:
© Archives ICRC Geneva, B-AG-202-139-073.

dinars. The list also mentions eight shops, two mosques (the "Wall of Tears"
mosque, located in the southeast corner of the neighborhood, assessed at 5,000
dinars, and the "Sheikh Abed" mosque, located in the western part of the
quarter on the Aqabat Abu Madyan, assessed at 4,000 dinars), and a two-room
dwelling allocated to the "ambassador of Morocco," whose value was assessed
at 2,000 dinars.

This list, invaluable for its description of the Maghrebi Quarter on the eve
of its demolition, is a prime example of belated valorization of a previously
neglected archival document. Prepared as early as 15 June 1967 by the neighborhood mukhtars, it was first obtained by Aref el-Aref, who forwarded it to
the Tel Aviv delegation in 1969, which then sent to Geneva a version translated

into French that would not be finally leveraged until 1975 to respond to the plea by Lalla Malika, who in turn was responding to the solicitation by the two mukhtars—the very ones who had taken care to produce the list eight years earlier. The story comes full circle, perfectly illustrating the value of an a posteriori archive, and how decisively important it is to properly file and label such an archive to allow for its future use.

In keeping with the terms of Lalla Malika's initial plea, the Red Cross's social survey focused on only the inhabitants of "Moroccan origin," as indicated by a new list sent to Geneva on 3 July 1975.[48] This list accounts for sixty-eight families of Moroccan origin located in Palestine, and updates their new addresses. Out of the sixty-eight families identified, half (thirty-five) still lived within the city walls of Jerusalem (Moroccan Hospice, al-Wad Street, Bab el-Silsileh, Suq al-Hosor), and one-fourth (seventeen) lived in East Jerusalem neighborhoods outside the walls (Wadi Joz, Beit Hanina, Ras al-Amud, Silwan). Eight families had settled in other Palestinian towns (three in Bethlehem, two in Jericho, two in Nablus, and one in Hebron), and only three identified families had ended up in refugee camps: two in Kalandia camp, near Ramallah, and one in al Fawwar camp, near Hebron. This list also shows that families tended to cluster wherever possible in the same location: the Maslouhi family in Beit Hanina, for example (it was in fact at Beit Hanina that I met Mahmud Al-Maslouhi, known as Abu Marwan, in spring 2017), the Tawati family in Wadi Joz, or the Shankiti family in Ras al-Amud. This list, however, implies a double bias. First of all, it compiles only families of Moroccan origin, to the exclusion of Tunisians and Algerians. Next, by definition, it accounts for only those families that could be located, thus overrepresenting the families remaining in Jerusalem and the immediate vicinity as compared to more isolated ones, scattered around more distant localities.

On 22 September 1975, the ICRC delegation in Tel Aviv submitted its final report to Geneva. Of the sixty-eight families identified, about half could not be contacted. "A social inquiry was thus conducted with 33 families," and the result showed that a certain number of them "were in real need of assistance," as shown in the summary table that lists the families subsisting "thanks to charity" or others (exactly nine) who received support from UNRWA. In conclusion, the report recommended "aid amounting to 21,500 L.I., plus the construction of six houses for around 60,000 L.I. as immediate relief to families, and around 480,000 L.I. as permanent annual aid."[49] On 5 December, Philip Grand d'Hauteville, general ICRC delegate for North Africa, wrote to Lalla Malika informing her that certain families were indeed living "in abject poverty," and that they would therefore "be needing greater assistance than what is currently being granted by Israeli Social Welfare, among others."[50] He warned, however, that "financial relief cannot be distributed without the unpredictable agreement of the Israeli authorities" and that any targeted aid could violate the principles of "non-discrimination." The former inhabitants of the Maghrebi Quarter, already deprived of the support of the endowment, which had housed them until 1967, were now caught up in the legal inconsistencies of the refugee relief system.[51]

Before leaving the Red Cross archives in Geneva, I was able to consult a few other dossiers relating to the Six-Day War that better explain why the demolition of the Maghrebi Quarter did not raise a greater outcry at the time. First, thanks to a waiver, I was able to access the telegrams sent to the Geneva headquarters via a direct telex system, Intercroixrouge, which confirm that the Red Cross teams pre-positioned in Amman and Tel Aviv were blindsided by the swiftness of the operation, and that they had not been able to inspect firsthand the demolition of the quarter.[52] On Saturday 10 June at 5:15 p.m.—the very moment when the architects were drawing up the demolition plan and the evictions were starting—a first telex was sent by the Red Crescent in Algiers to express concern in rather broad terms "about scope situation crimes and massacres committed" and "about exodus civilian populations," and to appeal for an urgent shipment of "increased aid in blood, medications and food." The following day, Sunday 11 June, at noon—by which time most of the neighborhood had been demolished—the Jordanian Red Crescent in turn sent a telex "regarding fate Arab inhabitants Jerusalem."

On Monday 12 June at 11:50 p.m.—by which time the entire quarter had been destroyed—the Tunisian Red Crescent sent a telex indicating that it had been informed by the Amman office "that Israeli forces had driven from their homes some inhabitants of Jerusalem," without specific mention of the Maghrebi Quarter. Finally, on Tuesday 13 June at 3:25 p.m., the Moroccan Red Crescent, "further to information press and radio," denounced the "infringement Geneva Convention" and "raise[d] vigorous protest," with no further details.

On Wednesday 14 June, while tens of thousands of Israelis were heading in procession toward the new Wall plaza, the ICRC headquarters in Geneva was responding to the different alerts received: "Regarding fate Arab inhabitants of Jerusalem stop inform you that have forwarded to our delegation Tel Aviv stop in view assistance that civilian population might require."[53] This real race against the clock between the flow of information and the course of operations on the ground, precisely documented by the sequence of telexes, proves that the intuition of the Israeli political and military officials was on target: the Maghrebi Quarter had to be demolished in the hours immediately following the 10 June ceasefire, in a manner hidden from view, to avoid, for example, an intervention by the Red Cross.

A second element emerges from the Red Cross archives: the fate of a few hundred inhabitants of the Maghrebi Quarter was very quickly submerged by the desperate situation of tens of thousands of refugees fleeing into Jordan.[54] For instance, on 9 July 1967, the ICRC delegation in Jerusalem noted that "65 trucks full of refugees" had crossed the Allenby Bridge into Jordan on the single day of 4 July, and especially that "starting on 6 July, the Israeli government will no longer allow those who cross into Jordan to return."[55] The same report also indicated that the Israeli military was having civilians sign a "no-return declaration." On 1 August, the Jordanian Red Crescent indicated that between five hundred and a thousand civilians were crossing the bridge every day into Jordan, which had already accommodated 260,000 refugees who had fled the West Bank since the start of hostilities. One can easily imagine, strictly from the humanitarian perspective, that the fate of the Maghrebi Quarter's inhabitants was diluted in the endless flow that was raising countless logistical problems. In fall 1967 with the approach of winter, the ICRC headquarters informed the Jerusalem delegation of the imminent shipment of ten thousand sweaters, scarves, and "black stockings for women and girls"; one thousand baby blankets; twelve metric tons of powdered milk, twenty-five thousand blankets, eight thousand mattresses, and five hundred cooking stoves.[56]

Furthermore, as it assumed its monitoring role to document the "expropriations and demolitions of houses" prohibited by article 53 of the Fourth Geneva Convention,[57] the Red Cross was facing other extremely serious events, such as the total destruction of three villages neighboring Latrun (Yalo, Beit Nuba, and Imwas) and the ruthless explusion of their seven thousand inhabitants during the night of 6–7 June 1967.[58] A summary assessment drafted in late 1974 indicated, for instance, that 19,152 houses had been demolished by the Israeli army since 10 June 1967, including 460 in Jerusalem, 10,897 in the Gaza Strip, 1,830 in the Latrun region, 3,112 in Samaria (Nablus, Tulkarm, Qalqilya), around 2,000 in the Golan Heights, 605 in Hebron, and 153 in Bethlehem. In total, the report estimated that at a rate of seven inhabitants per house on average, the destruction of these 19,152 houses affected 134,000 inhabitants.[59] Reading this report, we can only conclude that the 135 houses of the Maghrebi Quarter could hardly have been the Red Cross's focus of concern.

From Reparations Cases to Disclaimer Letters

The Red Cross archives in Geneva leave one question unanswered: Were the inhabitants of the Maghrebi Quarter compensated? If so, how many of them received compensation, according to what procedure, for what purpose, and for which damages? In the letter addressed in 1975 to Lalla Malika by the two officials of the community, the point is stressed that the former inhabitants "accept no compensation for the property destroyed or confiscated"; but conversely, in the first note drafted by the ICRC six months later, it is indicated that "102 of the families [. . .] are said to have received in 1968 a total of 94,000 Israeli pounds by way of compensation (an average of 920 Israeli pounds per family)." To resolve this glaring contradiction, I had to leave Rabat, leave Geneva, return to Jerusalem, stray from the *aura*, and get closer to the *traces*, as close to the event as possible, to persistently hunt down the elusive paper trail that such a compensation operation may well have left. Once again, it was the "rag picker" skill that was needed here, to rummage through the hundreds of archival files produced by Meron Benvenisti at the municipality, with the same strategy as deployed for the demolition archives: with less focus on the political series, and more on the boxes most likely to contain traces of the administrative processing of the operation, particularly its financial records.

   In box no. 5994 of the Israeli municipal archives, a thick grey binder, indexed 5994/4, bears a white label on which is handwritten in red pencil, in Hebrew: "Maghrebi Quarter—Jewish Quarter—~~Kotel~~." The word "Kotel" is crossed out.[60] On the same label of this typical lever-arch binder, which is in rather poor condition, we read two preprinted dates to be completed: "From 196_ to 196_." This indicates that these binders were purchased and used by the municipality during the 1960s, and proves therefore that the file was assembled at the time of the compensation procedure, and not retroactively. In the same box, next to binder 5994/4, are found three other binders; the first is labeled "Old City," the second "East Jerusalem Development Company," and the third "Company for the Development and Reconstruction of the Jewish Quarter," the latter with two preprinted root dates: "From 197_ to 197_" (figure 56). I could infer, then, by this proximity of files, that the aftermath of the Maghrebi Quarter demolition was handled by the same municipal services as was the rehabilitation of the old city and the former Jewish Quarter.[61]

Inside binder no. 5994/4 are preserved some three hundred pages of documents related to procedures for compensating the former inhabitants of the Maghrebi Quarter and the Jewish Quarter of the old city, the two phases of the operation being separated by a blue divider bearing the handwritten notice "Maghrebi Quarter." Most of the documents are letters received or copies of letters sent, written mostly in Hebrew, though sometimes also in Arabic along

FIGURE 56. The four folders of box no. 5994 in the Israeli municipal archives. Source: © HAJM, 5994/1–4.

with a cursory handwritten translation; and the envelope is often stapled to the letter, to attest to the postmark or receipt date. Letters received sometimes come with hand-drawn, multicolored floor plans of a house. There are also lists of names, handwritten or typed, almost all crossed out, with different dates written into the margins, the lists getting longer as the dates get later, the longest dated February 1969 and including ninety-two names.[62]

There are also summary charts, folded over several times, mostly crossed off for the oldest, a clean copy for the more recent. Almost everywhere, whatever the available medium, there are additions, scribbled in, scratched out several times, and redone. Most of the letters are abundantly annotated in various colors and scripts, in the margins, at the top or bottom of a page ("approved for payment," "paid," "to be filed," "to be summoned," "pending," "denied"), which would indicate that these are documents that passed through several hands and several departments. The documents are arranged in roughly chronological order, with most dating from September 1967 to February 1969; but the lever-arch binder also allows for a grouping of several successive documents relating to the same family or to the same compensation application, with, on occasion, an entire batch all stapled, pinned, or paper-clipped together.

This material analysis already provides a wealth of information: the thick, worn-out binder—stained, dog-eared, much handled, and heavily annotated—is all about *trace*, nothing about *aura*. We are here in the heart of the municipal administrative machine, the office of Meron Benvenisti, deep in the workings of the compensation procedure that he steered eagerly, even hastily, as evidenced by the resumptions and regular updates he asks of his assistant Fares Ayub, as also evidenced by certain applications clearly submitted after the deadline. For instance, on 4 September 1968, "Myassar Abdallah El-Jareedi," residing at the Convent of the Sisters of Zion (41 Via Dolorosa), writes—in Arabic—to the municipality to request that she be reimbursed "for the loss of my residence and its furniture," attempting to justify her request: "The residence was demolished on 12 June 1967 together with other houses situated at the Maghrebi Quarter [...]. All the residents and the mukhtars of the quarter witness to the truth of my statement and claim" (figure 57).[63]

Getting no reply from the municipality, she writes on 21 October 1968 to the Ministry of Defense, adding this time that she is a widow with a child to raise, and that she is of Tunisian origin.[64] On 12 November 1968, Fares Ayub

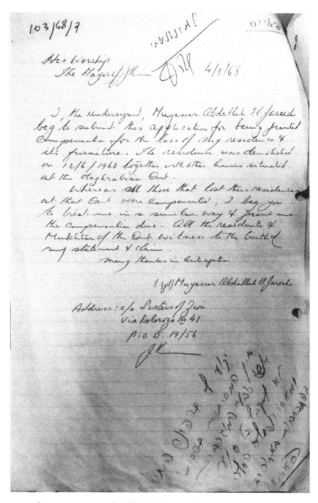

FIGURE 57. Letter from Myassar Abdallah El-Jareedi to the municipality regarding her compensation claim, 4 September 1968. Source: © HAJM, 5994/4.

answers her, in Hebrew and Arabic, that "all the applications for compensation were supposed to have been submitted before 30 January 1968," that "the deadline was extended a final time to 31 March 1968," and that this information has been broadcast over the radio and has appeared in the press.[65] The procedure is thus extended over barely nine months, from July 1967 through March 1968. On 4 May 1969, Myassar Abdallah El-Jareedi writes directly to "Mr. Ted Coleg" to inform him that she has yet to receive any compensation, and that she is therefore renewing her request. On 20 May 1969—this is the last letter stapled into this stack—a subordinate replies that "the municipality has definitively ceased processing the compensation applications of the former inhabitants of the Maghrebi Quarter."[66] According to the list sent to the Red Cross by Aref al-Aref in July 1969, the "Widow of Abdallah El-Jareedi" lived right until the Six-Day War in a one-room dwelling in the Maghrebi Quarter, valued at 750 Jordanian dinars (or 7,500 Israeli pounds, at the exchange rate in late 1967).[67]

For the hundred or so families who were able to submit applications in time, which damages precisely were being compensated? The compensation procedure is described at length in a letter from Benvenisti to Prime Minister Eshkol on 15 November 1967.[68] The document shows that the two ostensibly contradictory assertions dispatched in January and June 1975 by the ICRC and by officials of the Maghrebi community are in fact both strictly accurate: according to the procedure described by Benvenisti, the former inhabitants of the Maghrebi Quarter are paid compensation corresponding to "the difference between the rent they had been paying *prior to* their eviction and the rent they are now paying *since* their eviction," but none of them is compensated "for property destroyed or confiscated." In other words, it is not the value of the "destroyed property" (estimated by Aref el-Aref at 195,250 Jordanian dinars, or 1.95 million Israeli pounds) that is reimbursed, but only the damages linked to the eviction from their homes without notice.

Logically, it is therefore not the *owners*—in this case, the Waqf Abu Madyan—who are compensated, but only the *occupants* of the houses, for an amount obviously far below the real estate value of the property destroyed. Moreover, Benvenisti points out that, in order to benefit from this compensation, the former inhabitants have to provide proof of how much rent they were paying earlier, and that if this proof has been "lost" (at the time their houses were demolished, for instance), they must produce affidavits signed by their former landlords. Finally, Benvenisti specifies that each application is checked by the municipality's social assistance office, that the compensation is granted only "provided that the former and current dwellings are of a similar size," and finally that the compensation will be paid to the former inhabitants only upon their signing of "a disclaimer letter."[69] Clearly then, the scope of this compensation effort is aimed not at redressing a wrong but at attenuating the damage suffered, in order to secure the silence of the former inhabitants.

For the administrative follow-up, Benvenisti was assisted by Fares Ayub, whose name appears sometimes as "assistant" to Meron Benvenisti, sometimes as "supervisor of public inquiries in East Jerusalem." Ayub was the one, in any case, who interfaced between the municipality and the former inhabitants of the quarter, as evidenced by the ten stages of the procedure described by Benvenisti in November 1967:

> 1. The application is filled out in duplicate and handed to Fares Ayub in person; 2. Mr. Ayub checks the form in the presence of the applicant, he checks the address of the residence and other details on the application, then countersigns the form; 3. Mr. Ayub assigns a number to each application and copies out certain elements on his general follow-up chart; 4. Every day in the afternoon, the new applications are sent over to Mr. Benvenisti, along with reviews carried out by the social assistance office and the updated follow-up chart; 5. If no review has yet been performed by the social assistance office, Mr. Ayub sends them another copy of the application and demands a reply within three days; 6. The applicant must appear once again within three days if the review has been performed by the social assistance office. If not, he must appear again within a week; 7. Mr. Benvenisti sets the compensation amount in light of the information he has received and he transmits this recommendation to the municipal treasurer as well as to Mr. Ayub, along with a serialized disclaimer letter; 8. Mr. Ayub transmits the recommendation of compensation to the applicant after the latter has signed, in his presence, the disclaimer letter; 9. All the disclaimer letters are kept by Mr. Ayub in a separate binder; 10. The accounting transactions are handled by Mr. Naor and Mr. Totah.[70]

What is striking about this document is the triple objective of speed, efficiency, and discretion that surrounds this administrative protocol. The procedure is handled personally and solely by Benvenisti and his assistant Ayub; it is validated only by the mayor's social assistance office, which checks only the factual accuracy of the declarations; the processing deadlines are extremely tight, most likely to prevent the claimants from talking among themselves and eventually coordinating their reactions. Special attention, finally, is devoted to the "disclaimer letters," which the claimants must sign *prior to* finding out how much they are going to be compensated (most likely to avoid any kind of negotiation), and which Fares Ayub is to carefully file "in a separate binder." These disclaimer letters are, in effect, the whole point of the procedure, which seeks to shut down any possibility of subsequent complaints.

Letters exchanged between the municipality and the political and military authorities confirm the role discretion played. In the letter that Kollek sent to Eshkol on 26 September 1967, the mayor deliberately emphasizes that "this humanitarian problem also has political implications," and that "several international organizations as well as the personal representative of the UN secretary-general have already taken interest in it," which should justify the immediate release of necessary funds for the reparations. On 30 July 1968, in a rather lively exchange with Mr. Katzenelbogen (head of the Defense Ministry's department of compensations and claims), Benvenisti again emphasizes that without a swift financial settlement, it would be impossible to achieve the "political objective" of this procedure, which consists precisely of "settling this matter once and for all."[71] Further on, Benvenisti points out somewhat maliciously that the Ministry of Defense would be well advised to support the procedure engaged by the municipality, "since after all, this eviction was conducted by Tsahal [sic]."

In a further sweet-and-sour exchange of letters with the Ministry of Defense in September 1968 to prove the soundness of his strategy, Benvenisti attached a letter addressed to Kollek and signed by a group of former inhabitants of the Maghrebi Quarter testifying to "their gratitude to the municipal supervisor for East Jerusalem Mr. Benvenisti and his assistant Mr. Fares Ayub, for their help and the tremendous effort they have made over 15 months to lift them out of their dire circumstances," and adding that their objective was to find "real jobs in order to survive, to keep their dignity and honor intact, so as not to become a burden on the municipality's social assistance."[72] Although we do not know the number of signatories to this letter (the signed original was sent to the Ministry of Defense, and only an unsigned copy is available at the municipal archives), the material analysis would appear to indicate that it was solicited by Ayub and Benvenisti themselves, since it is written in Hebrew, typed (no handwritten version or Arabic version has been found), and stapled together with letters exchanged with the Ministry of Defense. The message was crystal clear: to demonstrate that the reparations paid out to the former inhabitants of the Maghrebi Quarter made it possible to nip in the bud any potential outcry that might have tarnished the political and military authorities, all the way to the highest echelons.

The Objects' Lament: A Retrospective Social History of the Maghrebi Quarter

The letter written (or rather signed) by certain former inhabitants of the quarter in September 1968 raises in turn an important issue: prior to expressing their gratitude, the signatories do mention that they received "compensation for the loss of their housing and compensation for the loss of their furniture and household effects," even though a few months earlier, in November 1967, when he gave a detailed description of the procedure to the prime minister, Benvenisti mentioned only the rent differential between the old and new housing as a basis for calculating the compensation, nowhere mentioning furniture or other effects, and even specifying that there had been no compensation planned for housing "facilities."[73] It would appear that the doctrine established at the outset evolved under pressure of a legal action brought by a few former inhabitants, perhaps more well-to-do and better informed than the majority of their former neighbors.

This parallel procedure, focused on the issue of furniture and objects destroyed in the demolition, is backed by an illustrious figure of the Israeli bar, the attorney Gideon Japhet (1928–2013), whose office was located in West Jerusalem (Shamai Street, between Ben Yehuda Street and Hillel Street). Japhet is known for having been the first to defend the inhabitants of East Jerusalem after 1967.[74] On 10 January 1968 he wrote to the Ministry of Defense to convey the complaint of three former inhabitants of the Maghrebi Quarter (Hajj Jamil Salahi, Issa Musa Abu Shaker, and Musa Sadat Abu Gosh) "whose homes and shops were destroyed after the Six-Day War," and who lost all their furniture and household effects as a result. Japhet indicated at the end of his letter that he would be awaiting "a response regarding compensation for the aforementioned clients prior to initiating legal proceedings" (figure 58).[75]

On 21 July 1968, Benvenisti received a copy of the letter, which provides us with a description of the interior of three houses and shops in the Maghrebi

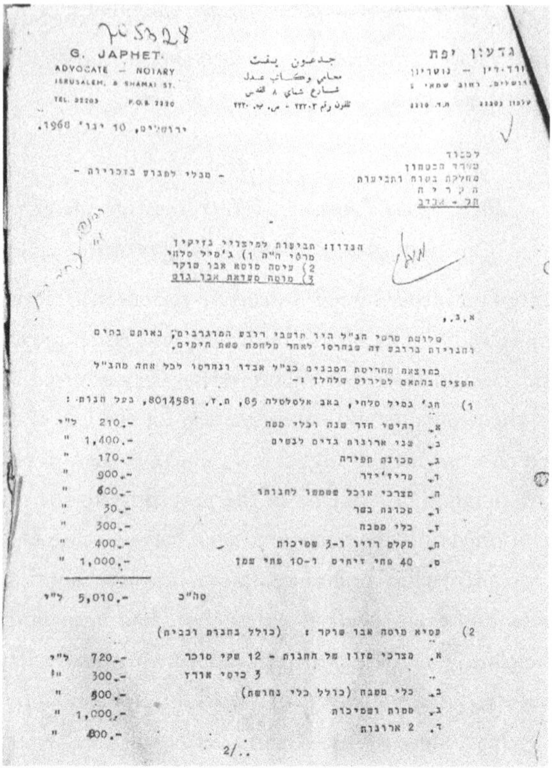

FIGURE 58. Letter from attorney Gideon Japhet to the minister of defense regarding compensation of movable assets, 10 January 1968. Source: © HAJM, 5994/4.

Quarter just before the demolition, as well as the declared value of each object in Israeli pounds. The list drawn up by Hajj Jamil Salahi is the most concise: "Bedding and linens (210 IP); two wardrobes with women's clothing (1,400 IP); sewing machine (170 IP); refrigerator (900 IP); groceries in the store (600 IP); meat grinder (30 IP); kitchen utensils (300 IP); a radio and three tablecloths (400 IP); 40 cans of olives and 10 canisters of oil (1,000 IP). TOTAL = 5,010 IP."[76] This list is the stark expression of the eviction in all its abruptness: almost nothing could be rescued, neither bed linens nor a sewing machine, much less a refrigerator. Even the oil canisters and canned olives had to be left on their kitchen shelves in the frantic rush of departure, as the loudspeakers ordered people to leave their homes immediately, as babies wailed, and as the elderly had to be helped along. This raw document converges with the photographs of Gilles Caron: most of the inhabitants have their hands in the air, and literally could not carry anything with them. They fled, leaving everything behind, even "women's clothing"—bringing with them only their most important administrative documents, slipped into a coat pocket or jacket.

These lists of objects also document the quarter's relative social diversity. This is quite clear if we compare Hajj Jamil Salahi's list with the next two, particularly that of Issa Musa Abu Shaker: "Foodstuffs stocked in the store: twelve sacks of sugar (720 IP) and three pouches of rice (300 IP); kitchen utensils, including copper items (500 IP); beds and covers (1,000 IP); two wardrobes (800 IP); radio (320 IP); propane tank (400 IP); carpet (500 IP); clothing for the whole family (1,500 IP); table (100 IP); fan (50 IP); five wool blankets (150 IP); Singer sewing machine (450 IP); washing machine (700 IP); bedding (150 IP); kitchen cupboard (100 IP); chairs and sofas (550 IP); jewelry (800 IP). TOTAL = 9,090 IP."[77] The kitchen utensils are copper and not brass; the sewing machine is a Singer; the home is outfitted with a washing machine and a fan, the living room is furnished with both chairs and sofas; and in total, the sum declared for all the furniture and objects destroyed (9,090 IP) amounts to nearly twice what Hajj Jamil Salahi claimed (5,010 IP).

If we take our social micro-analysis a step further, and cross-reference these lists of objects with the one Aref el-Aref sent in 1969, which had to do with housing, we observe that the two documents converge. Aref el-Aref's list found in the ICRC archives indicates that Hajj Jamil Salahi lived in a two-room dwelling (one room and a kitchen) whose value was assessed at 1,200 Jordanian dinars, and that Issa Musa Abu Shaker lived in a three-room house (including a "hall") valued at 2,400 Jordanian dinars, twice the value of Salahi's. The two documents correlate perfectly, then, when it comes to estimated value, but also with regard to dwelling size and furniture, Hajj Jamil Salahi lived in a two-room, most likely a room and a kitchen, and declares no living room furniture, while Issa Musa Abu Shaker's house included a "hall," and he declared the loss of several armchairs and a fan. This convergence between the two documents—which are produced neither at the same time nor by the same writers, nor for the same purpose—makes the case for their accuracy or, at the very least, their good faith.

The third and final list attached to the letter from Attorney Japhet, that of Musa Sadat Abu Gosh, is quite similar to the one drawn up by Issa Musa Abu Shaker: "A four-door wardrobe with clothing (2,000 IP); bedding (500 IP);

covers and linens (1,500 IP); carpets (1,000 IP); tapestries and clock (600 IP); sewing machine and radio (800 IP); living room furniture, buffet, armchairs, etc. (1,500 IP); kitchen utensils, including a propane tank and a refrigerator (2,000 IP); small table and chairs (200 IP); gas oven (100 IP). TOTAL = 10,200 IP."[78] Noteworthy are the wall tapestries, a clock, living room furniture, and a buffet, but also a gas oven. Here again, this is a resident who was certainly more affluent than the average, which makes sense, as these are former inhabitants who were availing themselves of the legal services of an Israeli attorney. And his name confirms it: Abu Gosh is the name of a prominent Palestinian family dating back to the Middle Ages, settled in its village of the same name and in the surrounding area.

In early February 1968, a fourth former inhabitant of the quarter took legal action to obtain reparations for his destroyed furniture and effects. Faraj Abdul Halis, for his part, sought the services of the attorney Amnon Zelikha, whose office was located in Tel Aviv and who lodged his client's complaint on 4 February 1968 with the Israeli Office of Public Domains.[79] Two sets of parallel proceedings took place, handled by two different attorneys who chose to apply to two distinct Israeli administrations, even if in both cases the complaints were channeled to the Jerusalem municipality in the end. It is worth noting that both attorneys turned spontaneously to either the army or the Office of Public Domains, an additional indicator that to observers at that time, it was perfectly obvious that the military and political authorities were directly responsible for the destruction of the quarter. Faraj Abdul Halis, writes Amnon Zelikha, "was a resident of the Maghrebi Quarter in the old city of Jerusalem near the Western Wall and he used part of his house as a souvenir shop for tourists."[80] The list of furniture and effects he claimed he left behind testifies to a relatively high living standard:

> Formica wardrobe with mirror (300 IP); six armchairs (300 IP); pedal sewing machine (230 IP); two beechwood bed frames (120 IP); electric washing machine (700 IP); Butagaz brand stove (400 IP); radio (250 IP); carpet (120 IP); 4 mattresses, 16 pillows, and 4 down comforters (200 IP); a large radiator (100 IP); summer and winter clothing for the whole family, including a leather winter jacket and a woolen suit (1,000 IP); various kitchen utensils, including a copper pot, dinnerware, glasses, silverware (600 IP); pantry containing rice,

sugar, oil, flour, tea, coffee (800 IP); merchandise for gift and souvenir shop in front of the Western Wall, including camera film, engravings, wooden crosses, small silver spoons, earrings, and miscellaneous souvenirs (4,000 IP); baby crib (30 IP); Formica chairs and table with little stools (350 IP). TOTAL = 9,500 IP.

Here again, several clues point to a living standard higher than that of the average inhabitant of the quarter: the wardrobes and chairs are Formica (not in raw wood), the bed frames are made of beechwood, the washing machine is electric, the house features a "large radiator," the living room is furnished with six armchairs, and the clothing is widely assorted and of good quality, in leather or wool. These indicators are corroborated by the description of the house sent to the ICRC in 1969: Faraj Abdul Halis was living in a four-room house with a "store" and a "hall" (living room), with an estimated value of 2,400 Jordanian dinars.[81] As a souvenir vendor for visitors to the Western Wall, this merchant also lost the entire inventory stocked in his store, including rolls of film, wooden crosses (which confirm that most visitors to the Western Wall during the Jordanian period were Christians), earrings, and more. Once again, we are struck by how powerfully this simple list of furniture and objects evokes a world; how it makes immediately visible, in its most granular detail, a social reality now vanished; and how it inevitably calls to mind postmortem inventories used by historians to document the material facts of popular culture, particularly in the modern era.[82]

But in this specific case, we are moved even more by this staggering paradox: it is the disappearance of the quarter that triggered its *emergence* before the eyes of the historian; it is its abrupt destruction that enabled its *documentation*. This is a paradox in appearance only, since history ceaselessly feeds on documents produced by the very disappearance of what they bear witness to, whether in the form of written traces or material vestiges: houses of Pompeii frozen in volcanic magma, wreckage trapped in mud after a flood, cargo of sunken vessels after a shipwreck, an insurance claim written up after a fire, an inventory of seized property listed by the bailiff after foreclosure, a declaration of theft filed in the police archives, an inventory recorded by a notary public after the death of an occupant of a dwelling. Oftentimes, disaster, death, and the disappearance of people and property produce *at the same time* their documentation, or rather their transformation into document—in other words, their paradoxical conservation, no longer for use by the living but for the sole benefit of historians and their readers.

In any case, everything indicates that these four parallel proceedings are indeed what modified the doctrine regarding compensation for furniture and household effects; between May and September 1968, a dispute arose between the municipality, which argued for the addition of this second form of reparations, and the Ministry of Housing and Ministry of Defense, which refused. On 1 March, Benvenisti wrote to Kollek to suggest that, out of the three hundred thousand pounds allocated by the Ministry of Housing, they might set aside a balance of about one hundred thousand pounds for the purpose of granting eight hundred to a thousand pounds to each family of the Maghrebi Quarter "for loss of their furniture and effects."[83] On 11 May, the director of the District of Jerusalem, S. Peleg, informed Benvenisti that there was still "no confirmation of the possibility of using the remainder of the 300,000 pounds to compensate the furniture and effects of the residents of the Maghrebi Quarter and the Jewish Quarter."[84] At the same time, attorney Japhet was reiterating his reparations claim at the Ministry of Defense, indicating that "these houses were destroyed by soldiers of the Israeli army [. . .] within the first days of the liberation of the old city."[85]

Benvenisti won the tradeoff by making a distinction between the families of the Maghrebi Quarter, evicted in a few hours, and those of the former Jewish quarter, whose eviction took place over several days or weeks. The first took literally nothing with them, while the second had time to move out the furniture and effects they wished to take away. In a letter to the Ministry of Defense, Benvenisti gets right to the point: "Since it's about a family who lived in the Jewish Quarter, and not in the Maghrebi Quarter, we refuse to compensate them for their furniture and effects."[86] By inference, this distinction provides an additional confirmation of how quickly the Maghrebi Quarter evictions were effectuated, by the Israeli authorities' own admission.

On 27 June 1968, Benvenisti informed the Ministry of Housing that the "inter-ministerial committee for Jerusalem Affairs" had decided to grant 80,000 pounds for this additional reparations operation, "reserved exclusively for the former residents of the Maghrebi Quarter."[87] A summary chart, drafted in November 1968, details the amounts granted to each of the 92 families compensated for "furniture and effects," for a total that effectively amounted to 80,150 pounds, for an average of 850 pounds per family, a maximum of 1,300 pounds (for Hassan Ali Al-Jandawi), and a minimum of 500 pounds.[88] We remark that the four former residents who had triggered the affair with their legal claims (Hajj Jamil Salahi, Issa Musa Abu Shaker, Musa Sadat Abu Gosh, and Faraj Abdul Halis) received 1,000 pounds each, slightly above the average. Nonetheless, the total amount of reparations granted in the end remained considerably lower than the estimate of assets declared, which amounted to 5,010 pounds for Hajj Jamil Salahi and 9,000 or 10,000 for the three others. The compensation thus covered between a tenth and a fifth of the declared value of the furniture and effects destroyed. Here again, this was not about making good the loss, but about attenuating it in order to obtain as many as possible disclaimer letters and to "settle this matter once and for all," to echo Benvenisti's wording.

Compensated and Dismissed: Balance Sheet and Political Impact

The procedure was swift, a sign of its highly political nature. This is clear from how eager Benvenisti was to be done with it, and how quickly cases were opened and shut. By 22 December 1967, six months after the end of the war, Ayub had already drawn up a preliminary review of the ongoing procedure. To date, 311 families had come before him, and 206 had gone ahead and applied for compensation, 119 of whom were former residents of the Jewish Quarter and 87 of the Maghrebi Quarter.[89] Between 10 November and 18 December, no fewer than five meetings took place to set the amount for the first 62 reparations cases. On 9 February 1968, Ayub sent an updated report to Benvenisti; by then, a total of 350 families had come forward, and 252 had gone through the application process, of whom 160 were former residents of the Jewish Quarter and 92 of the Maghrebi Quarter. By that date, 152 compensation cases had been validated and closed, 89 of them for the Jewish Quarter and 63 for the Maghrebi Quarter. To speed up the effective reparations payments, Benvenisti requested a first installment of 100,000 IP to the Ministry of Housing on 25 October 1967,[90] and reiterated his request for an amount of 200,000 IP on 20 February 1968, which brings the total amount granted for the whole procedure (Maghrebi Quarter and Jewish Quarter) to 300,000 Israeli pounds.[91] A first deadline for applications was set for 30 January 1968, then extended until 31 March 1968.[92] With the first anniversary of the quarter's destruction looming, undoubtedly anticipating a possible spike in political tension over the issue, Ayub and Benvenisti accelerated the processing of applications, and an initial list of 74 former residents of the Maghrebi Quarter having received compensation was produced on 26 May 1968.

On 12 February 1969, Ayub handed the *definitive* balance sheet of the operation to Benvenisti (figure 59).[93] With regard to the Maghrebi Quarter, 92 families ended up receiving reparations, for a total amount of 165,624 Israeli pounds, or an average of 1,800 pounds per family. As for the Jewish Quarter, 137 families received reparations, for a total of 103,017 Israeli pounds, or an average of 750 pounds per family. How to explain this discrepancy? First, as we have seen, only families of the former Maghrebi Quarter were compensated for furniture and effects destroyed. There is a document, in fact, that demonstrates the relative share of this specific compensation. In a letter addressed to the Ministry of Housing on 17 March 1969, Benvenisti broke down how the 300,000 pounds allotted by the ministry had been used, incorporating the final corrections sent by Ayub. It indicates that 108 families of the former Maghrebi Quarter had applied for reparations, that 16 were denied, and that 92 had received compensation for a total of 169,824 pounds, "92,674 IP of which for the housing and 77,150 IP for the effects."[94] On average, these 92 families received 1,000 pounds in housing reparations and 840 pounds in damages for furniture and effects destroyed.

But beyond this difference in treatment regarding furniture and effects, a sizable gap still remains. The families of the former Jewish Quarter received, on average, 750 pounds per dwelling, compared to 1,000 pounds for families of the former Maghrebi Quarter. Since the housing compensation was supposed to make up for a differential in rent, it is possible that this gap can be partially explained by the price of the housing, which may have been higher in the former Jewish Quarter; but this is far from certain, and it in no way explains the size of the gap. In fact, it would appear that the Israeli authorities may well have considered, and no doubt rightly so, that the political scope of the Maghrebi Quarter's abrupt destruction was greater than the evacuation, spread out over several weeks, of families living in the former Jewish Quarter. At any rate, careful analysis of the *balance sheet* does indeed reveal a difference in terms of the operation's objective and its *political impact*.

FIGURE 59. **Letter from Fares Ayub to Meron Benvenisti regarding the balance sheet of the compensation process, 12 February 1969. Source: © HAJM, 5994/4.**

The procedure's political sensitivity is confirmed by a further detail, which comes to light only if we scrutinize carefully the summary table of the sixteen compensation applications that were denied in the end. Certain families were not compensated because they simply moved out to the immediate border of the Maghrebi Quarter, notably into the former zawiya of the Maghrebis—where some still live to this day, at the corner of the former Abu Madyan Street (today Kotel Street).[95] The political objective here is clearly stated: the point was to move the former inhabitants out of the Maghrebi Quarter and prevent them from clustering in the vicinity of their former living space, to limit to the utmost any sustained social connection to their former community, and therefore any possibility of political expression. This hypothesis is confirmed by yet another document in which Ayub mentions two former inhabitants "evacuated from the Maghrebi Quarter, who resettled nearby, but who in the end moved into other neighborhoods in order to collect their compensation." Ayub is referring to Latifah Fadel Anwar and Kamel Abdul Halis, who took refuge in the former Maghrebi zawiya and who ended up moving to Silwan, outside the walls of the old city, a move that finally enabled them to be compensated.[96]

In the documents of binder 5994/4, other clues confirm that the procedure was not devoid of political tension. On one of the letters sent by Myassar, widow of Abdallah El-Jareedi, Ayub handwrote in red pencil that she was "one of those who are urging the former residents of the Maghrebi Quarter to refuse compensation."[97] It is indisputable that everyone knew the operation's political objective and that some were refusing to comply—most often women, as it turned out, for the cases of explicit refusal often involved women and widows, like Maria Doloris, widow of Yussuf Musa Zeyda, whose name crops up on several documents with the comment, "Refused to sign the disclaimer letter."[98] In the list of seventeen denied applications in February 1969, one particular case irrefutably confirms the political dimension of the operation: "Muhammad Abdelhaq refused to accept compensation because he is the official in charge of the [Maghrebi] waqf," writes Ayub in the column that records the "motives" for rescinding the applications.[99] In refusing compensation, Muhammad Abdelhaq retained the kind of political latitude that would allow him, for example, to write to Princess Lalla Malika a few years later, in January 1975. In binder 5994/4, there is no specific mention of the community's second mukhtar, Issa Hashem al-Moghrabi; but in consulting different summary tables of compensated families, I noted that his name appears nowhere. He too, in order to continue defending the rights of the former inhabitants of the quarter, refused to sign the disclaimer letter.

By way of conclusion, we can compare the amount ultimately disbursed by the Ministry of Housing with the assessment of the patrimonial property destroyed. In March 1969, Benvenisti indicated that 92,674 Israeli pounds were spent to compensate the former inhabitants of the Maghrebi Quarter for damages linked to the loss of their homes, whose value Aref el-Aref had assessed at 195,250 Jordanian dinars, or 1.95 million Israeli pounds, according to late 1967 exchange rates. The sum total of compensations effectively granted therefore amounted to a little under 5 percent of the value of the property destroyed. To complete this assessment, we can also compare the amount paid out in 1968–69 with the conclusions of the ICRC report in 1975, which recommends that the sum of "480,000 Israeli pounds be allotted as permanent annual aid" for the only families of Moroccan origin, thirty-three in all, who had been located.[100] Concretely, the ICRC was recommending that the Moroccan Red Crescent spend *every year*—and for only thirty-three families—five times what the Israeli government spent on a one-time compensation for nearly one hundred families. Clearly, in light of what is on the whole a fairly limited balance sheet, we can conclude that the political outcome of the compensation operation proved largely positive.

Erasing the Last Remnant: The Destruction of Dar Abu Saud

The Maghrebi Quarter was not entirely destroyed in June 1967. The block of houses known as Dar Abu Saud, located to the south of the new plaza, perched on a butte and flanking the outer wall of the Haram al-Sharif, was not demolished until two years later, almost to the day, on Sunday 15 June 1969 (figure 1 and figure 60). The story of this final destruction offers invaluable hindsight with regard to the events that occurred two years earlier. Indeed, the

FIGURE 60. **Maghrebi Quarter and the Dar Abu Saud. Source: Matson Collection, Library of Congress, https://tile.loc.gov/storage-services/master/pnp/matp c/05800/05898u.tif**

decision-making process that led to the demolition is in several ways analogous to, and in other ways different from, what I was able to reconstruct about the destruction of the Maghrebi Quarter in June 1967. For the analogous aspects, I was struck in particular by the way technical expertise was manipulated, even deflected, to justify the demolition, but also by the ambiguous role of the municipality and the Foreign Ministry, which, after having warned of the operational, political, and diplomatic hazards of such a decision, moved forward and took part in the elaboration of a communication strategy intended to mitigate the effects.

As for differences, the length of the decision-making process in the case of Dar Abu Saud is noteworthy: it was spread over two years under the watchful eyes of journalists and international observers. Equally important, however, is the role of the Department of Antiquities, which attempted, this time resolutely but unsuccessfully, to oppose the decision. Where the demolition of the Maghrebi Quarter, decided as a matter of urgency in June 1967, had practically achieved a consensus inside the Israeli state apparatus, the demolition of Dar Abu Saud showed evidence of a certain fracturing of this consensus, symptomatic of a political upheaval that would become increasingly manifest by the late 1970s, between supporters of a secular Zionism, mindful of maintaining Israel's reputation abroad, and the partisans of a religious Zionism, increasingly aggressive and impervious to reactions within the international community.[101]

These differences between the two sequences also had implications when it came to sources. While the demolitions carried out in June 1967 are broadly documented in the *municipal* archives, the June 1969 operation is better documented at the *national* archives, with dossiers of cross-referenced correspondence involving the Ministry of Religious Affairs, the Foreign Ministry, the Inter-Ministerial Committee for the Preservation of the Holy Places, the Department of Antiquities, and the Jerusalem municipality. Even though current rules of communication at today's Israeli National Archives limit us to accessing only digitized versions, we can still manage to piece back together the order of different documents.[102] Last point: whereas in June 1967 the greater part of the documentation comes from the period *subsequent* to the destruction, here it is, rather, the documentation that *precedes* the destruction, including matters having to do with compensation, heatedly negotiated *prior* to the demolition.

The possibility of a southward extension of the Wall plaza was being hotly

debated by the summer of 1967. On 8 August 1967, the *Jerusalem Post* informed
its readers of a "project at the Ministry of Religious Affairs to clear away an
additional 82 meters of the Wall," which would facilitate the separation of the
sanctuary between men and women and help settle the brewing conflict over
who should be in charge of the perimeter: religious or archaeological authorities.[103] On 31 August 1967, the keys to Maghrebi Gate—precisely where Dar
Saud is located—were confiscated by the Israeli army, a sign that pressure on
the site was mounting.[104] In the municipal archives, the first documents pointing to this project give evidence of the municipality's explicit hostility to the
idea. This animus is expressed first at the patrimonial level. On 14 September
1967, an unsigned memo addressed to the municipal engineer points out that
the sacredness of the Western Wall "is associated with a defined, limited and
specific segment, which has been kept as holy over numerous generations, and
not the totality of the wall erected in its day by King Herod," and that "the
demolition of these houses would nullify what remains of this definite and limited zone," making this sacred vestige "nothing more than an ancient wall."[105]
This memo echoes certain critiques already formulated in June 1967 when the
opening up of the plaza had, for certain observers, tainted the sacredness of
the holy place since, in fact, what defines a sanctuary—wherever it is located
and whatever religious tradition it represents—is that it be somehow bounded,
physically or symbolically, and that it be separated or at least distinguished
from the worldly realm.[106]

In Benvenisti's archives, there are copies of letters that evince the rising
tension overtaking the protagonists in this debate. On 17 July 1968, Minister
of Foreign Affairs Abba Eban writes to Minister of Religious Affairs Zerach
Warhaftig, calling for an emergency meeting of the Inter-Ministerial Committee for the Preservation of the Holy Places, emphasizing that the UNESCO
representative in Jerusalem, Raymond Lemaire, is openly concerned about
this project.[107] On 31 July 1968, the director general of the Foreign Ministry,
Shlomo Hillel, writes to Benvenisti to reassert his ministry's opposition to the
project, citing the director of the Department of Antiquities, Avraham Biran,
for whom "there is no way for Dar Abu Saud to be destroyed, for it's a protected
historic site by virtue of the 'Convention for the Protection of Cultural Property in the Event of Armed Conflict' of 1954."[108] On 23 August, Benvenisti
replies to Hillel that he also "remains opposed to the demolition of Dar Abu

Saud, not only for the archaeological value of its buildings but also because this demolition could block access to the Maghrebi Gate."[109] Benvenisti ends his letter stressing that the partisans of the project will not throw in the towel: "You and I will have to stay vigilant once the matter returns to the agenda, whether formally or after some fait accompli on the ground."[110]

As the project started taking shape, the municipality's hostility was increasingly expressed in strategic terms. In binder 5994/4, devoted to reparations for the evicted families, a note signed by Yehoshua Baruchi and dated 6 February 1969 stresses the multiple impediments to be removed before this demolition could be envisioned:

> In the Abu Saud houses, there are three families that have not yet been evicted: (a) the owner of a souvenir and drinks shop, also owner of a three-room apartment. This man is asking for 350,000 IP, a disproportionate amount compared to the sums granted thus far for expropriated houses and shops. (b) An ailing man who lives in a 2.5-room apartment. (c) A widow of the Abu Saud family who lives in a 6-room apartment. The ailing man says he is prepared to leave if the widow leaves. However, this woman, in exchange for her apartment, is asking for housing of the same size and standard in Shuafat or the vicinity. [. . .] We mustn't give these families the impression that by insisting long enough they will succeed. This impression would not only overburden the budget but it would also prolong the time frame necessary for the complete evacuation of the Jewish Quarter. We therefore propose to put off until later the evacuation of the Abu Saud houses and to move forward with the evacuation of the Jewish Quarter.[111]

This document is crucial because, tactically speaking, it validates in hindsight the method adopted for evacuating the Maghrebi Quarter in June 1967. For himself alone, one of the proprietors still living in one of the Abu Saud houses demanded 350,000 IP, four times the total amount spent in reparations for ninety-two families evicted two years earlier.

On 11 March 1969, Benvenisti once again took a stand to attempt to counteract the project of the minister of religious affairs, or, more precisely, to relieve the municipality of all responsibility. In a particularly harsh letter addressed to Rabbi Dov Perl (director of the Department of Holy Places at the Ministry of Religious Affairs), Benvenisti accused him of deliberately provoking a weakening of the building and seeking to exploit the municipality:

> You would like the municipality to issue a notice about the fissured building, hoping to utilize that notice to have the house demolished [. . .]. However, I get the strong impression that your request is aimed solely at getting the municipality to shoulder the responsibility for the demolition, which has been your plan for a while now. But the weakening of Dar Abu Saud does not result from an act of God over which we have no control. As far as I can tell, it is the result of a violation of instructions issued by the Committee for the Security of the Kotel [. . .]. The municipal engineers will not recommend the destruction of the aforementioned building, but rather will recommend its reinforcement, whatever the cost. Moreover, we will not contact the residents nor will we accept to enter into negotiations with them.[112]

This strong counterattack was not enough to halt the process. On 16 March, Rabbi Dov Perl replied scathingly to Benvenisti that his "impertinent letter," as well as the "personal attacks" it contained, would be forwarded to the ministers in charge of the dossier, implying that the decision would be taken at the highest echelons of government, and that a municipal adjunct like Benvenisti would soon have no more say in the matter.[113]

It would require further digging into the documentation's sublayers to understand how the different levels of decision making line up. A case in point: in the archives of the Foreign Ministry, one dossier (serial no. HZ4293-2) made it possible to track how the decisions were developed and ratified, and then how the operations were coordinated depending upon the diplomatic constraints of the moment. In this dossier, the most immediately accessible document is the minutes dated 30 March 1969, typed and stamped "classified," drafted after the meeting of the Inter-Ministerial Committee for the Preservation of the Holy Places, held on that day and chaired by Minister Zerach Warhaftig.[114] Dar Abu Saud was the only item on the agenda. The minutes indicate that "the Mayor of Jerusalem opens the discussion," in which participate: Zerach Warhaftig (minister of religious affairs), Menachem Begin (minister without portfolio), Yisrael Yeshayahu (minister of postal communication), Haim-Moshe Shapira (minister of the interior), Moshe Kol (minister of tourism), Eliyahu Sasson (minister of the police), Mayor Teddy Kollek, archaeologist Benjamin Mazar, architect Yosef Shenberger, Officer Shlomo Gazit (in charge of military intelligence in the occupied territories), and

Zvi Rafiah (representative of the Foreign Ministry).[115] The minutes also mention
five other people who were present at the meeting but did not take part in the discussion: Meron Benvenisti, Rabbi Dov Perl, Attorney General Meir Shamgarand,
and two members of the cabinet of the Ministry of Religious Affairs. The minutes
indicate that Ministers Abba Eban (foreign affairs), Moshe Dayan (defense), and
Yaakov Shimshon Shapira (justice) were absent.

The minutes do not mention the content of the discussions, but report only
the three decisions taken by the end of the meeting: "1. Architect Shenberger
will draft a plan for an alternative access to the Maghrebi Gate; 2. The Mayor
of Jerusalem will issue a demolition order for the unsafe part of Dar Abu Saud.
The Minister of Religious Affairs will coordinate with the Foreign Ministry to
establish a timeline for the demolition of the remaining two thirds; 3. Reparations for the woman residing in this part of Dar Abu Saud will be addressed."[116]
We understand unmistakably that the position Benvenisti put forward was
struck down, but this document gives little insight into how the municipality
finally accepted taking part in the maneuver, since the minutes do not report
the actual content of the debate.

In the archival dossier numbered HZ 4293-2 of the Foreign Ministry, adjacent to the typed minutes, a five-page handwritten note sheds light on how this
strategy was elaborated.[117] Though it is neither signed nor dated, its content is
enough to determine that it was written during the 30 March meeting by one
of the participants, perhaps Zvi Rafiah, representative of Foreign Affairs—
since this handwritten note is conserved today in that ministry's archives. The
note-taking is succinct, almost telegraphic; but it plainly reveals the content
of the discussion:

Digs near Kotel—Dar Abu Saud. / **Kollek**: evacuate the woman's 6 rooms.
Millions. / general planning of the Kotel plaza and structures. / Shenberger
has a plan for building an access to the Maghrebi Gate—promptly? The slope
leads to the entrance to Temple Mount. / Not all the buildings will be evacuated, only 1/3, where the woman lives—not the shop. / **Ministry of Religious
Affairs**: we do not wish to determine who is responsible for the fissure. According to a report by the Security Committee, the backhoes moved forward
more than 5 meters. / **The Mayor**: Baruchi report six weeks ago / Asked the
Foreign Ministry in writing six weeks ago to set a date for the demolition. /

Begin: mayor's decision to demolish. / **Ministry of Religious Affairs**: we suggest to make the demolition order public and to seek a compromise with the woman. / **Minister Begin**: a fissure is useful. The president of this committee must execute this decision. Let's let the Minister of Foreign Affairs come. The fissured 1/3 has to be demolished. This needs to be announced to the Minister of Foreign Affairs. **Moshe Kol**: my hope that the Kotel backhoes would trigger a fissure has finally come true. / [. . .] **Mazar**: digs at Abu Saud carried out in coordination with the Security Committee. Doubts as to the value of Abu Saud. Substructures might have interest (perhaps Mamluk). The rest is later. / **Gazit**: no objection to the demolition / Access to the Maghrebi Gate. Security committee. For caution and responsibility. **Yeshayahu**: demolish everything. A unique opportunity. As the Minister of Foreign Affairs. / **Kollek**: Shenberger should start thinking about construction / 1. Fissure. No political coordination; 2. Maghrebi Gate; 3. Evacuation without outcry. / Prepare a *project* for the Maghrebi Gate. Without formal help from the planning committees / 1. An architect is going to design an operational project / 2. The mayor is going to issue a demolition order after coordinating with Foreign Affairs *today* / 3. Coordinate the demolition with the Minister of Foreign Affairs, with the promise that not everything will be demolished.[118]

The value of archival traces is revealed here in full force. Thanks to these few scribbled words, nevertheless preserved in an archival dossier, the knotty decision-making process is suddenly disentangled, the forces at play express themselves unequivocally, the primacy of politics over technical issues is unabashedly on display. Menachem Begin quips sarcastically that "a fissure is useful," Moshe Kol is delighted that it was caused by the "Kotel backhoes," each asserts that they must take advantage of this "unique opportunity" to destroy the buildings, and all demand at several points that the minister of foreign affairs should consent to participate in the exchanges to manage the "coordination," the timeline, and the staging of the operation. Shlomo Gazit (an ally of Moshe Dayan, in charge of military intelligence in the occupied territories) does not take part in the discussion, but coldly endorses the decision on security grounds ("no objection"). The archaeologist Benjamin Mazar brings his scientific approbation by asserting that there are "doubts" as to the patrimonial value of the building. Finally, the municipality is being openly manipulated: Benvenisti is present at the meeting but doesn't say a word—we can imagine his humiliation—and Kollek in the end has no choice but to prepare his technical department to shoulder the political decision; he must issue the demolition order that conditions the operation's success. The decision-making process that led to the destruction of Dar Abu Saud, spread over a longer period and better documented than that of the rest of the Maghrebi Quarter, is full of valuable insights.

Antiquities, Foreign Affairs, Religious Affairs: A Fissured Israeli Consensus

Abba Eban, minister of foreign affairs, was still attempting to impede the implementation of the decision over the following weeks. Indeed, as the prospect of the Dar Abu Saud demolition drew ever nearer, dissent grew all the more visible between, on the one hand, the Department of Antiquities and the Foreign Ministry, both firmly opposed to the operation, and on the other, the Ministry of Religious Affairs, followed by most government ministers, who were in favor. On 7 May, Shlomo Hillel, deputy director at the Foreign Ministry, addressed a long memo to his minister informing him that Begin had once again demanded "the immediate implementation" of the decision, out of concern that some new delay would run the risk of timing the demolition, with all its diplomatic fallout, to coincide with the run-up to the UN General Assembly the following autumn.[119] Hillel adds that all ministers present at the last meeting of the Committee for the Preservation of the Holy Places on 4 May "protested against the endless delays to implementing this decision," and that "even Minister of Justice Mr. Yaakov Shimshon Shapira weighed in, categorically in favor." Hillel specifies that Dayan now supports the operation, and asserts that he has found an alternative means of accessing the Maghrebi Gate, which topples the final security argument. Disheartened, Hillel concludes his memo indicating that "since we can no longer oppose the operation [...], we would be better off getting the demolition job done at one go rather than confining ourselves to the one-third of the structure where the fissure was detected, putting off the demolition of the other two-thirds for the weeks to come. We have nothing to gain from it, and it would only give rise to a double reaction."

On 19 May, the director of the Department of Antiquities, Avraham Biran, made one last attempt to halt or at least slow down the operation. In a letter addressed to the deputy director of International Relations at the Foreign Ministry, Ms. Lambert, Biran reiteratese all his arguments, one by one:

> The array of buildings called "Dar Abu Saud" should not be demolished. These buildings which are adjacent to the Western Wall and the Maghrebi Gate date back to the Mamluk period. The foundations of the structure are undoubtedly even older. The demolition of certain buildings could damage the ancient stones of the Western Wall and lead to the collapse of certain structures inside the Haram al-Sharif. The protests against us will be not only political and religious but also cultural (violation of the convention for the protection of cultural property). Let us remember that these buildings were already mentioned on the list of ancient sites to be preserved published during the British Mandate on 15/02/1922. Same thing for the building located to the north of the Kotel known by the name of Mahkamah or Tankeziya, built eight centuries ago.[120]

None of these arguments was able to halt the political machine set in motion by the minister of religious affairs, Zerach Warhaftig. In that respect, this operation is symptomatic of an ideological shift that was altering the balance of power in Israel after the Six-Day War: the jubilation of victory turned the messianic rapture of the religious Zionists into a genuine political agenda, to which an increasing number of government officials subscribed.[121] At a smaller scale, the sequence is also representative of the ongoing power struggle for control of the Western Wall and its immediate vicinity between the Ministry of Religious Affairs and the Department of Antiquities, even if the positions were not airtight since, as we have seen, certain archaeologists—like Mazar, during the decisive 30 March meeting—let themselves be swayed into a dubious compromise with the religious faction, with the goal of maintaining their control over part of the perimeter.[122]

Two years almost to the day after the destruction of the Maghrebi Quarter, it was once again up to the Foreign Ministry to devise the communication strategy to mitigate the diplomatic fallout from the destruction of Dar Abu Saud. On 13 June 1969, two days before the backhoes went into action, Shlomo Hillel sent an "urgent" and "classified" bulletin around to all the Israeli embassies indicating that the demolition could trigger "negative international criticism," and that even if there was "nothing to be gained, of course, by raising the issue ourselves," the following talking points should be prepared:

> These buildings are not sacred. What is sacred, however, is the Western Wall, which the buildings partially obscure. These buildings are neglected, in a state of disrepair, and the filth that surrounds them defiles the sanctity of the Kotel. Among other arguments, you can mention the toilets adjacent to these buildings [...] and the sewers channeled all along the Western Wall, which have marred the site and rendered it impure (we already did away with the toilets several months ago). These buildings are not ancient, they were built some 150 years ago. Even though they managed in the past to be classified as cultural sites, this is hardly comparable to the Western Wall, which dates back 2,000 years. Effectively, these buildings are adjacent to the Temple Mount, but every precaution has been taken to avoid damaging the Western Wall which is—as we all know—the exterior wall of the Temple Mount [...]. The buildings at issue are unstable, they jeopardize the lives of the inhabitants and the public in general. This is why last 5 May, the municipal engineer and the mayor issued a demolition order "to protect the inhabitants and the public." The clearing away of these buildings is thus carried out in accordance with a professional assessment and the demolition order was issued on that basis. As we have done in the case of other building demolitions in the old city, we wish to grant full reparations and guarantee fair and just rehousing to persons evacuated. (*For your information only*: a protracted negotiation with one of the women living in these buildings has proved unsuccessful because, for political and nationalist reasons, she has refused to accept our offer of reparations.[123]

The destruction of Dar Abu Saud sheds a harsh light on the demolition, two years earlier, of the 135 houses situated farther below. The communication strategy was the same, but because the operation was longer in preparation and thought through in finer detail, it came across as more self-assured: the demolition would aim to preserve an ancient patrimonial order and protect an ancestral holy place threatened by a recent structure known to be filthy, shabby, devoid of architectural value, and presenting imminent risk to its inhabitants, who naturally would be rehoused and compensated. Almost everything here is false—or at any rate, almost nothing is true—in this list of talking points, which is all the more astonishing in that it was emanating from a diplomat (Shlomo Hillel) who had been positing the diametrical opposite a few weeks earlier in his written exchanges with Benvenisti, particularly with regard to the patrimonial value of the buildings. But once the decision had been made, the arguments were reversed one by one. On Sunday 15 June 1969, the day of the demolition, a telegram was sent to the Israeli ambassador to UNESCO, Moshe Avidor, indicating that Israel "will surely be attacked on this issue at the upcoming meeting of the General Assembly," and that with this prospect in mind, "Dr. Biran is requested to prepare arguments."[124] It is clear that even the officials most firmly opposed to the demolition, like Avraham Biran, were solicited in an effort to mitigate the political impact.

On the same day, a communique from the Ministry of Religious Affairs was sent to the Israeli embassies in London, Washington, New York (UN), Paris, UNESCO, Rome, Geneva, Bern, Stockholm, Helsinki, Ankara, and Teheran. It reprised the arguments already put forward by Foreign Affairs two days earlier, but in even more emphatic terms and openly seeking to implicate all the leading political and administrative bodies involved in the issue: "The Minister of Religious Affairs has today begun the demolition of buildings adjacent to the Western Wall, at the southern end, which were threatening public safety. The demolition was carried out in compliance with a demolition order issued by the Mayor of Jerusalem in accordance with the decision of the municipal engineer which stated that the buildings represented a threat to public safety, following the discovery of a fissure, and to avert the risk of imminent collapse."[125] The sides clearly had shifted since the 30 March meeting, and everyone now appeared to be doing the bidding of Warhaftig, having no other choice but to fall into line, given the potentially explosive nature of the dossier.

The issue did indeed prove explosive, as evidenced in the next day's *Jerusalem Post*, Monday 16 June 1969. Under the headline "'Dangerous' Houses Next to Western Wall Demolished," Anan Safadi emphasizes all the ambiguities and grey areas involved in the destruction of the Abu Saud buildings, "including one in which Fatah leader Yasser Arafat was born."[126] The journalist notes that "Mr. Meron Benvenisti, in charge of East Jerusalem affairs for the city administration, said the municipality 'had nothing to do with it.'" Further on, he even suggests that "another source in the municipality said that Mr. Kollek had endorsed an engineer's report that the buildings were in dangerous condition but had issued no demolition order." In short, the deception was painfully obvious and no one was fooled, including the *Jerusalem Post*. Reading the article, we understand that Benvenisti and other municipal officials decided to deliberately break with the discipline that their higher-ups had attempted to impose. We also infer that the international observers were the main target of this disinformation campaign; Safadi makes the point at the end of his article that "unidentified officers attempted to prevent journalists from witnessing the evacuation of the buildings. Two foreign journalists, John Wallis of the *Daily Telegraph* and William Schmick of the *Baltimore Sun*, were forcibly removed by two men as they were attempting to get closer to the perimeter."

Four days later, undoubtedly upset by the *Jerusalem Post*'s coverage of the event, the spokesman for the Ministry of Religious Affairs was able to publish a rebuttal, in which he reasserted that "Sunday's demolition became urgent after cracks were discovered," and that "the municipal engineer issued an order which was signed by the Mayor, Mr. Teddy Kollek, after it was determined that there was imminent danger of collapse."[127] To conclude, the spokesperson tirelessly reasserted that "the timing was set after consultation with all concerned, including the Foreign Ministry." With no hope of convincing anyone, the communications officer perhaps imagined at least that all parties would be implicated—or compromised—in an obviously dubious affair that had temporarily split the Israeli consensus achieved after the Six-Day War.

————

On 25 June 1969, in the weekly magazine *Zo Haderekh*, published by the Israeli Communist Party, in an article titled "A Blasphemy," Yosef Algazi sets out to methodically dismantle the communication strategy that the Ministry of Religious Affairs has deployed to justify the destruction of the last houses of the Maghrebi Quarter.[128] In doing so, fewer than ten days after the event, he is doing the work of a historian; though the dust has hardly settled on the rubble of Dar Abu Saud, he is collecting traces to dispel the aura, collecting testimony to counteract the echo so powerfully orchestrated by a well-oiled administrative machinery. After foregrounding the crucial role played by Zerach Warhaftig, Algazi emphasizes that the foreign affairs minister, Abba Eban, was resolutely opposed to the demolition project. To fuel his investigation, he questions Waja Abu Saud, who asserts that her house was built eight centuries earlier, that it was sturdy, and that it was the archaeological digs carried out under its foundations that triggered the fissures. She also tells of the dozens of times she was offered compensation, including by a man who called himself a "mukhtar" but whom she did not know, and who refused to disclose his true identity. She finally declares that she received no written order, and was given less than two hours to evacuate her apartment, bringing with her nothing but her medications.

Algazi then speaks to Tawfiq Abu Saud, a cousin of Waja, who recounts rushing over to Teddy Kollek's office on Sunday morning, when the bulldozers are starting to destroy the house. The mayor reportedly tells him that if he were him, "he would have attempted to resist in the same way"—a comment quite typical of Kollek's rhetoric, mixing bluntness and provocation. Tawfiq Abu Saud replies that he is asking only for a delay of a few hours, so that he can help evacuate his cousin's effects. Kollek seems to agree, and asks Benvenisti to have the operation halted. After several attempts to get through by phone, Benvenisti returns to Kollek's office to say that he has been unable to reach anyone; and when Tawfiq returns to the site of his cousin's house, it has already been demolished. Algazi, the reporter, ends his narrative with a direct accusation against the mayor of Jerusalem: "If Teddy thinks that he can trick anybody with his doublespeak, he's seriously mistaken." He concludes the article by declaring that this destruction illustrates yet again Israel's indifference to international law.

Algazi, in June 1969, did not have access to the archival traces that we can compile, analyze, and connect today. His clear-eyed narrative, however, written as events were unfolding, sheds light on the truth: Warhaftig's deliberate manipulation, Kollek's equivocation, Benvenisti's powerlessness, and the stubborn but ultimately shattered resistance of Waja Abu Saud. Fifty years later, Algazi's testimony, drafted in the heat of the moment, comes down to us to rekindle the cold ashes of the archives.

EPILOGUE

THE ARCHIVES IN THE GROUND

APPEARANCE, DISAPPEARANCE

The paradox of archaeological excavation is that it destroys a
large part of what the ground had conserved.

Alain Schnapp et al., "Archives de l'archéologie
européenne," Les nouvelles de l'archéologie (2007), 100.

One of the storage facilities for the Israeli Antiquities Authority (IAA) is
located three kilometers north of the old city of Jerusalem, in the industrial
zone of Har Hotzvim. Inside, arranged along hundreds of meters of shelving,
is the archaeological material collected at digs run by this public institution
within the Ministry of Education, which in 1990 succeeded the Department of
Antiquities and Museums. It is at Har Hotzvim that archaeological discoveries
made in Jerusalem are sorted and preserved during the time required for their
analysis, before being transferred to huge repositories in Bet Shemesh for final
storage.[1] Under the serial mark "A-6876 / Beit Strauss" are gathered objects
collected during the rescue excavation carried out in late 2013 on the northern
edge of the Wall Plaza during expansion work taking place on "Beit Strauss"
(figure 61). The purpose of this excavation, implemented at the conclusion of a
contentious debate between the Israeli Antiquities Authority and the Western
Wall Heritage Foundation, was to preserve a few archaeological vestiges before
installing new public toilet facilities for use by visitors to the Western Wall.[2]

In eight cardboard boxes are preserved objects dating from the Ottoman period and the contemporary era—in particular, household objects buried in the upper stratigraphic layer, found inside one of the Maghrebi Quarter houses evacuated in great haste on the evening of Saturday 10 June 1967. Here there is no text, no one's voice, no testimony, no paper, no archive . . . no discourse. Only objects, utensils, and tools, stubbornly silent but terribly eloquent, which need to be removed from their boxes and described, or rather named, slowly, one by one: a rusty rake, a shovel, an oil lamp, a gas canister, brass platters, a petrol heater, a blue-and-white tin teakettle, a child's shoe, a wooden knife, glass vials, shards of broken dishes, aluminum cutlery, plastic cups, a saucepan lid, a mousetrap (figures 62 and 63) . . . and then, stored on another rack reserved for oversized objects, a Phoenix-brand pedal sewing machine. Elsewhere, in a plastic bag, a large bowl full of shaving soap. Ortel Chalaf, who was Peter Gendelman's assistant for the Beit Strauss excavation, recalls this bowl of shaving soap found in situ, set next to a razor, a bottle of shampoo, and a toothbrush, all inside a little niche carved into one of the walls of the house, in front of a sink. He is happy to show the few objects he was able to collect and save while under time pressure, just before bulldozers destroyed the premises once and for all to install public toilets in the summer of 2013.

The Beit Strauss excavation is not alone in providing archaeological testimony that helps document the material history of the Maghrebi Quarter before its destruction. In the southern part of the plaza—below the Maghrebi Ramp, which collapsed in winter 2004—an excavation campaign was carried out in 2007 and again in 2012–14, financed by the Western Wall Heritage Foundation, overseen scientifically by the Israeli Antiquities Authority and headed by the archaeologists Hervé Barbé, Fanny Vitto, and Roie Greenwald.[3] Here again, even though the recent history of the Maghrebi Quarter was not a major concern of the funders, the upper stratigraphic layers were rigorously excavated and documented before being dismantled. In the preliminary report they released in 2014, those in charge of the excavation describe their discoveries in quite a bit of detail:

> All the foundations of the houses discovered in this area contained material dating to the Late Ottoman period, such as tobacco pipes. These houses are densely built on either side of an alley forming a curve, which ascends to the

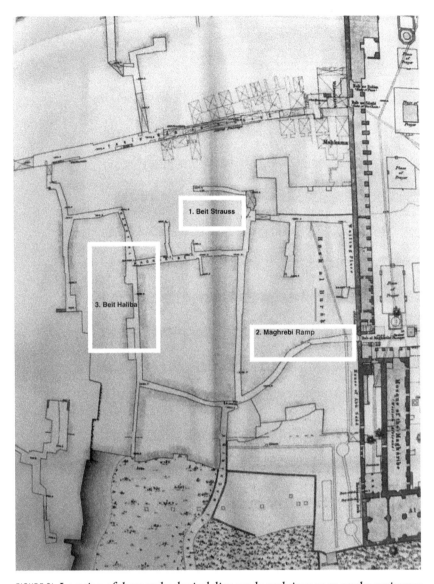

FIGURE 61. Location of three archaelogical digs conducted since 2005 on the perimeter of the former Maghrebi Quarter: 1. Beit Strauss, northern edge (2013); 2. Maghrebi Ramp, southern edge (2007–14); 3. Beit Haliba, western edge (2005–18). Source: © Palestine Exploration Fund (base map).

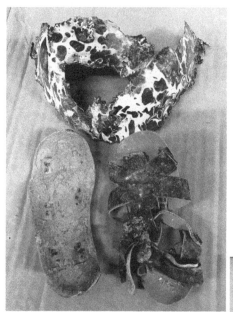

FIGURES 62 AND 63. **Objects recovered at the Beit Strauss dig and preserved at the IAA Har Hotzvim repository.** Source: © Vincent Lemire.

Maghrebi Gate and, from there, to the Haram al-Sharif [. . .]. Originally, most of these houses had plaster flooring. A flagstone pavement often covered the plaster floor and in several cases, a thin layer of concrete had been poured on top of the paved floor. It is possible that at least some of these changes are relatively recent, as shown by a Jordanian coin minted in 1955, which was found under the slab of one of these floors. Barber's clippers and scissors found on the floor of one of the rooms suggest that it was a barber's shop. Several pairs of leather shoes discovered in another room point to a shoemaker's shop. Finally, the discovery of porcelain coffee services, among many other objects, illustrate the hasty departure of the inhabitants in 1967.[4]

Like the Beit Strauss excavations, those carried out along the ramp also provide decisive material clues to the morphology and sociology of the Maghrebi Quarter right before its destruction. Far from being a derelict neighborhood or an assemblage of "slums," as the Israeli administration had asserted in 1967, the quarter was made up of "densely constructed" houses built on solid foundations, whose floors were well maintained and regularly restored right up to the final years preceding its demolition, as evidenced by the discovery, beneath recent flooring, of a 1955 Jordanian coin, minted in the same year as the visit by the Algerian inspector Hajj Lounis.[5]

Beyond these data on the morphological structure of the building stock, the discovery of objects reveals essential clues about the neighborhood's activities prior to demolition: the barbershop and the shoemaker's shop allow us to imagine an altogether mundane neighborhood life until late in the afternoon of Saturday 10 June 1967, when the evacuation order was broadcast over loudspeakers. A visit to the warehouses of Har Hotzvim in December 2019 allowed me to complete firsthand the list of objects described in the preliminary report (figure 64).[6] Under the call number "Maghrebi A-5013" are archived a dozen or so boxes whose contents reveal a few activities of artisans and merchants in this southern part of the quarter: a barber's clippers and scissors, a bottle of hair tonic, several tubes of salves and ointments, a tube of penicillin, meat hooks, knives, tin platters, a few skewers, a ring, pierced scallop shells, religious medals, a necklace, pearls, a blue-and-white amulet against the evil eye, a painted metal matchbox, several assembled or disassembled tobacco pipes, a ceramic coin bank—evidence of a hair salon, a butcher shop, a souvenir shop (perhaps the one described by Faraj Abdul Halis in his February 1968 complaint), whose vestiges are intermingled with those of private dwellings (figures 65 and 66). Fifty years later, the archaeologists who discovered valuable objects (like a porcelain coffee set) or everyday objects that were obviously left behind for lack of time (like the bowl of shaving soap, the razor, and the toothbrush), cannot help but see in them the incontrovertible material evidence of an abrupt eviction. Archaeology, the necessarily fragmented but unquestionably rigorous record of past reality, opens an invaluable window onto the *urbanity* and *civility* of the Maghrebi Quarter of Jerusalem a few hours before its destruction.

Between 2005 and 2009, and again between 2017 and 2019, a third archaeological window was opened on the perimeter of the Maghrebi Quarter—on its western edge this time, next to the former Aqabat Abu Madyan.[7] Headed by Shlomit Weksler-Bdolah and Alexander Onn, the excavation of Beit Haliba was also overseen by the Israeli Antiquities Authority and financed by the

FIGURE 64. **Kitchen utensils photographed at the Maghrebi Ramp dig. Source:** © Fanny Vito.

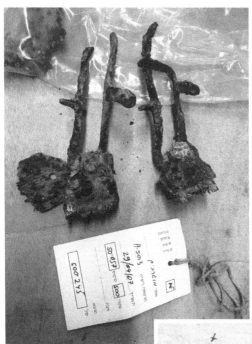

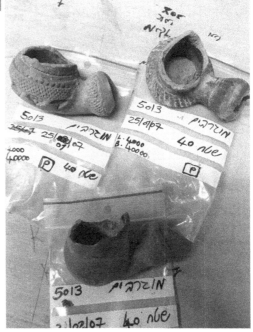

FIGURES 65 AND 66. **Objects recovered at the Maghrebi Ramp dig and preserved at the IAA Har Hotzvim repository: tobacco pipes and rusted hair clippers. Source: © Vincent Lemire.**

Western Wall Heritage Foundation, which built a new welcome center for
visitors and tourists at this location, known as Beit Haliba—a project that
once again triggered considerable controversy in Israel and in Palestine in the
years 2010 to 2015 (figure 67).[8] The excavation, more extensive and deeper than
the two previous ones, enjoyed substantial financial backing, for there were
plans to exhibit *the oldest* stratigraphic layers in the underground rooms of the
future welcome center.[9] Like the two previous digs, Beit Haliba provided its
share of data on the quality of the building stock and the infrastructure of the
Maghrebi Quarter. The preliminary report highlighted, for example, that "at
the end of the nineteenth century or in the twentieth century the street was
paved with small stones," and that just below the new pavement, "a ceramic
drainage pipe was discovered in the middle of the street." At the same time,
one of the houses of the perimeter had been entirely retiled with high-quality
"decorated tiles," several photographs of which are included among the excavation report's illustrations (figure 68).[10]

We can thus compile a certain amount of material evidence that confirms
the clues revealed in textual sources. The Maghrebi Quarter was not a slum;

FIGURE 67. **View of the Beit Haliba dig. Source: © Emek Shaveh.**

FIGURE 68. At the Beit Haliba dig, tile flooring of a house in the Maghrebi Quarter, early twentieth century. Source: © Shlomit Weksler-Bdolah.

it was an integral part of the urban space, its streets were well-maintained, and its infrastructures were regularly updated. We recall that the municipal archives testify to an operation to refurbish the sewer system in February 1902, which would seem to correspond precisely to the drainpipe system discovered by the archaeologists.[11] History is cunning; fifty years after the demolition of the Maghrebi Quarter, it was rescue excavations carried out within the larger program of tourism development by the Western Wall Heritage Foundation that allowed the buried memory of the neighborhood to resurface.

But beyond these spot details about the structure of the built space, two other revelations comprise the specific interest of the Beit Haliba excavation. First, because it went all the way from the surface of today's Wall Plaza down to bedrock eight meters deep, this dig allowed for a highly accurate chronology of the perimeter's urbanization; and on this point once again, the archaeological data correspond perfectly with information gleaned from the textual sources. While the quarter had been uninterruptedly urbanized since biblical times until the end of the Abbasid period (ninth century), the stratigraphy indicates that the sector was neglected or even totally abandoned from the tenth to the twelfth centuries, which includes the Crusades (1099–1187), before being heavily and densely reurbanized starting in the early thirteenth century, with the construction of "large buildings, which continued to be used with slight changes until the twentieth century," as the archaeologists note.[12] This robust reurbanization of the quarter in the early thirteenth century, clearly visible through stratigraphic analysis, thus corresponds precisely with the textual sources that point to the period when the first religious endowments were created to welcome Maghrebi pilgrims, in the late twelfth century, on the initiative of Saladin and his allies.[13]

The second major discovery of this dig is the Madrassa Afdaliyya, founded by the son of Saladin, al-Afdal Ali, in 1193 to encourage the teaching of Maliki law, the dominant school of jurisprudence in the Maghreb.[14] The building, which archaeologists suggest was regularly upgraded and used until the demolition of the quarter in June 1967, notably housed a burial chamber:

> The most important element in this building was a single cist grave, found sealed with stone slabs that were overlain with a built heap of stones, which protruded above surface. The burial cell contained the skeleton of an adult male, oriented east–west in a supine position, whose head was in the west, facing south. The position of the deceased is characteristic of Muslim interments. The skeleton, not accompanied by funerary objects, was transferred for reburial.[15]

We know that, even while they document the past, every archaeological excavation also irretrievably destroys material traces. André Leroi-Gourhan strikingly formulated that radical distinction between textual sources and archaeological sources: "The archives in the ground can be deciphered only once."[16] In this particular case, the paradox of archaeological disclosure is all the more dizzying in that the Beit Haliba dig unintentionally brought to light the Madrassa Afdaliyya, a founding heritage feature in the history of the Maghrebi Quarter, and yet did not conserve the slightest trace of it in the restoration planned for the tourists (figure 69). The archaeological *apparition* of the madrassa, while it did yield *documentation*, was followed immediately by its *disappearance*.

In an interview with *Haaretz* in June 2015, the medieval historian Benjamin Kedar, former president of the scientific advisory board of the Israeli Antiquities Authority (2000–2012) and former vice president of the Academy

FIGURE 69. Festooned arch from the Ayyubid era, above the entrance to the Afdaliyya Madrassa, photographed in the 1930s. Source: © EBAF.

of Sciences (2012–15), characterized the destruction of the Madrassa Afdaliyya as an "archaeological crime": "By the time I found the clue that allowed the place to be identified, it was already destroyed. Had I known about it in time, I would have stopped it. It was done innocently, but somebody needs to understand that if there's a tomb in the heart of the city, it means something."[17] In this case, the tomb very likely contained the body of a certain "Sheikh Ayd," a Sufi ulema buried in one of the rooms of the madrassa in the late seventeenth century.[18]

Beyond the particular case of the Madrassa Afdaliyya, Kedar's outcry points the finger at a more far-ranging blindness among his fellow Israeli archaeologists and historians: the Maghrebi Quarter, destroyed in June 1967 when they were still children or very young adults, had not been integrated into the common core of historical knowledge passed on to them as students.[19] If the Madrassa Afdaliyya could have been so easily demolished, it is because the historical context it illuminated and reified had never been valorized or even taught to Israel's future archaeologists and historians. The demolition of the madrassa is therefore not *accidental*; rather, it is *symptomatic* of how the Maghrebi Quarter was deliberately kept invisible after its demolition in June 1967.

As is often the case, it is the decision makers who best express what they are doing and for what purpose. In the same *Haaretz* article about the demolition of the madrassa, the spokesperson for the Western Wall Heritage Foundation makes no secret of the goals set for the Beit Haliba dig: "Excavations in the area of the Western Wall are intended to reach *the earliest levels possible*. Clearly, this cannot be done without destroying later periods, whatever they may be."[20] The scientific and ethical demands of the archaeological discipline are here unrepentantly brushed aside: since the foundation wishes to valorize exclusively the vestiges of the biblical era, it is out of the question to grant the slightest visibility to other elements of the archaeological heritage.[21] In the face of such constraints, the archaeologists of the Israeli Antiquities Authority are caught in an intractable bind: the vestiges of the Maghrebi Quarter, which they inadvertently bring to light during the rescue excavation, are doomed to disappear, this time definitively.

CONCLUSION

A WALL OF SILENCE

> For a truth to take hold in the memory of a group, it must be represented in the concrete form of an event, a personal figure, or a place.
>
> *Maurice Halbwachs,* Topographie légendaire des Évangiles en Terre sainte: Étude de mémoire collective *(Paris: PUF, 1941).*

Having reached the end of this investigation, let us return to the question raised in the introduction. A harsh question in the form of an enigma, disconcerting, bewildering, a question that bumps up against a wall of silence: Why was this history left so long unspoken? What is behind this long concealment? Why has the history of the Maghrebi Quarter been so late and so rare in the telling? How is it possible that most visitors and pilgrims, when photographing the Western Wall today, are unaware of such a distinctive quarter, *on which they are treading*? How was this silence constructed, and how has it been maintained? How was this absence fabricated, until it finally invaded the entire empty space of the Western Wall Plaza? How has this memory blackout become a gaping hole of history: a place of forgetting, or rather of denial, a nonplace, an off-site, excluded from narratives and expelled from history books, yet located in the very heart of Jerusalem, one of the most monitored and visited places in the world? This question is neither incidental nor ancillary. It is central, paramount, for it questions the very function and ethics of history as discipline, by juxtaposing the mechanisms of *concealment* with the possibilities of *restitution*. It is thus a question that involves *knowledge*, but also *acknowledgment*.

Paradox

Before positing a few responses, let us continue delving into the question, to sound the depths of the paradox. Let us sort out what *should have* and *could have* inspired and sustained a long-running history of Jerusalem's Maghrebi Quarter. Founded by the son of Saladin, intended to host pilgrims coming from the Maghreb, this quarter was anything but a blind spot, anything but a place of banishment. On the contrary, it was a place teeming with life, open onto the Mediterranean, traversed over eight centuries by thousands of travelers. As an Islamic waqf, the quarter in its totality was in fact theoretically protected from any divestiture, spoliation, or destruction. Built in the late twelfth century, it preceded by four centuries the sanctuarization of the Western Wall, which didn't occur until the sixteen century. This *anteriority*, so strategic in the competition of legitimacies that prevail in the holy city, left an enduring toponymic mark on several surrounding urban features—the Maghrebi Gate, the Maghrebi Mosque, the Maghrebi fountain—to which the French Islamologist Louis Massignon even adds "the Maghrebi Wall" (a possible translation of "Kotel ha-Maaravi").

That is not all. The last decades of the Maghrebi Quarter's existence hardly amounted to an inexorable decline. Rather, they were marked by genuine attempts at restoration and refounding. France, the power that claimed to be "protector of the Holy Places" of Jerusalem, invested substantially to reactivate the mission of welcoming Maghrebi pilgrims, to finance reconstruction work, and to strengthen relations with Algeria, Morocco, and Tunisia. After the bloody riots of August 1929, the quarter would regularly make headline news and come under the scrutiny of international observers, who would examine the rights and duties of each of the parties, in landmark reports submitted to the League of Nations. In the 1930s the young Yasser Arafat lived in one of the finest homes of the quarter, to which he returned for a final visit during the founding congress of the PLO in May 1964. Located right in the heart of the city, across from the most famous holy place in Judaism and a few dozen meters from the third most sacred site in Islam, the Maghrebi Quarter could hardly be deemed *marginal*; everything about it was *central*, or even hypercentral, at the crossroads of all the structuring issues of the region, and of all the force fields that have acted upon the history of the Holy City.

Part of the explanation is perhaps to be found nestled in the recesses of this apparent paradox. The Maghrebi Quarter was located in the immediate vicinity of the engine that electrified the religious identities of Jerusalem since its origins: the Temple, the Temple plaza, cradle of monotheisms and tomb of empires. The Temple—founded, according to biblical tradition, around 1000 BCE by Solomon; destroyed by the Babylonian armies in 586 BCE and rebuilt by the Persians, only to be destroyed again by the Roman armies in 70 CE; refounded in the seventh century in homage to the night journey of the Prophet of Islam; and since then become the "mosque plaza" or Haram al-Sharif: "noble sanctuary." We know that on 7 June 1967, the military rabbi Shlomo Goren was toying with the idea of destroying the Dome of the Rock, in view of constructing a third Jewish temple.[1] We also know that Moshe Dayan fended off the idea categorically; and we can imagine that, in those intense hours, the destruction of the Maghrebi Quarter, located right downhill from it, may well have appeared as the "lesser evil," or a "necessary evil," to establish a new status quo, a new sharing of the space—precisely the one that is called into question today. The Muslims have reserved exclusive use of the Haram al-Sharif, and the Jews have carved out a new plaza down below, to assemble tens of thousands of their faithful during major pilgrimages, a compromise called for explicitly by Teddy Kollek in his memoir.[2] This hypothesis undoubtedly contains a measure of truth, and in any event, we can confidently state this: The Maghrebi Quarter was destroyed not *despite* but, quite the reverse, *because* of its topographical situation.

Leads

Nevertheless. This no doubt partly explains the destruction, but not the *silence* of the destruction. To that point, what this inquiry has taught us is that the history of the Maghrebi Quarter is both *local* and *global*, deeply anchored in the holy places of Jerusalem but also continually penetrated by political projects and the most remote geopolitical realignments. Here is where other leads enter in, leads that need adding up to better understand why this history has remained cloaked in silence: why it hasn't been produced, published, and shared. First, as we have seen, it is because by 1967 the inhabitants of the Maghrebi Quarter were effectively "orphans of empire," or rather, empires: orphans of fallen Islamic empires; orphans of an open, imperial Mediterranean; orphans of the last gasp of France's colonial empire. They found themselves on the wrong side of history as nations and nationalisms imposed their agendas, to the detriment of international refugee rights that were being slowly eroded.[3] Victims in the first instance of Israeli expansionism, they were also collateral victims of Algerian nationalists, who failed to take measures after 1962 to protect their nationals, and who remained silent in June 1967 at the moment of the destruction. Disinclined to assume this colonial legacy, the socialist Algerian regime did not mobilize to rescue a few hundred pious pilgrims wandering in the holy land. Too Muslim for revolutionary Algeria, perhaps the inhabitants of the quarter were also too Maghrebi for the new political direction of Palestinian nationalism. Too stateless, in the end, for all the nationalisms that were taking shape all around the Mediterranean, including in Tunisia and Morocco.

This explanation, foregrounding the overall chronological context, does not fully account for the specifically French dimension of this enigma. After having been so intensively involved in the 1950s in defending the Maghrebi Quarter, why did French diplomacy remain so silent at the time of its destruction? Obviously, since 1962, France could no longer ensure the religious foundation any *legal* protection, which ought to have been taken over by Algeria. But it might well have lent its *political* support, if only by denouncing the conditions of the quarter's destruction. France, whose prerogatives in Jerusalem had been acknowledged since the 1536 Capitulations, which enjoyed a permanent seat on the UN Security Council, and which only five years earlier had considered itself the guardian of the Maghrebi Quarter, had the political wherewithal— and undoubtedly the moral duty—to ensure the protection of Maghrebis evicted from their homes in 1967. Instead: nothing. A deafening silence on the part of the consul general of France in Jerusalem, Christian Fouache d'Halloy d'Hocquincourt. Nothing, except this peculiar phrase from a dispatch on 14 June 1967: to express dismay at "the hostility of the Muslim Palestinian population" with regard to the Israeli forces. Realpolitik, of course, is the only word that comes to mind; bogged down in the contradictions of a diplomacy at times pragmatic and at times rhetorical, divested of the North African colonies that justified its "Muslim policy," France opted to abandon the Jerusalem Maghrebis to their fate—the very ones it had attempted to instrumentalize a few years earlier.[4]

Another silence, involuntary in this instance, issuing from international institutions and NGOs, faced with the brutal fait accompli, but also overwhelmed by multiple humanitarian emergencies: we saw that the Red Cross counted some 250,000 new Palestinian refugees and tens of thousands of houses destroyed as a result of the 1967 War, a reality that crowded out the destruction of the Maghrebi Quarter in terms of large-scale humanitarian crises.[5] Indeed, in the months and years following the war, these same institutions would attempt to provide relief to expelled populations, including the Maghrebis of Jerusalem. But, while the Jordanian ambassador to the United Nations regularly included the Maghrebi Quarter in the list of denunciations he would present to the international body in New York, it was especially the local notables who took up the issue and accurately documented it. The former mayor of East Jerusalem, Ruhi al-Khatib (expelled in 1968); his predecessor Aref al-Aref; the former governor, Anwar al-Khatib; the former mukhtar of the quarter, Muhammad Abdelhaq—it is they who, on the basis of their intimate knowledge of the former quarter, would succeed in gaining official acceptance for the figure of 135 destroyed houses and 650 inhabitants evicted, figures that the Red Cross International would pick up in the 1970s, and which today are universally ratified.

Israel, of course, had a stake in the building and consolidation of this wall of silence, a composite edifice that managed to circumscribe the memory of trauma into a closed perimeter. Operational agility, swift execution, and control of messaging and communication—all these ingredients come together to explain the effectiveness of the destruction of the neighborhood on the night of 10–11 June. But there is a further factor, a decisive one, that enabled the *cover-up* of the decision-making process upstream and, consequently, of the political responsibility for the operation. In passing off the destruction as a spontaneous initiative by private entrepreneurs from West Jerusalem, the point was to gloss over the role of the army, the municipality, and the government. This rather unsubtle window-dressing proved sufficient to win acceptance for the fait accompli as "spoils of war": an oft-practiced custom, though in violation of international law "unless required by imperious military necessity," which of course was not the case here.[6] Another decisive element in the Israeli cover-up strategy: the urban renewal argument, whereby for reasons of public health they had to tear down a few "hovels," a set of houses "that were threatening collapse." This argument, make no mistake, was backed by a strong international consensus among major urban planners who, in this same period of the 1960s, on five continents, were destroying anything that stood in the way of the modern, well-aerated city dotted with highly visible monuments and large, unobstructed plazas.[7] Even though I have demonstrated that the Maghrebi Quarter was in no way a collection of "hovels," the argument nevertheless must have made sense to interlocutors who did not have time to come check for themselves.

But none of this would have worked had it not been for a deliberate strategy aimed at securing the discretion of the former inhabitants themselves, locking them behind yet another wall of silence. This issue was crucial, and Meron Benvenisti was the mastermind behind this strategy, which articulated an *individual* compensation, nominal but immediate, in exchange for the notorious "letters of renunciation," whereby the inhabitants were compelled not only to accept their fate but to refrain from lodging any complaint in the future. Isolated, dispersed, deprived of any legal protection or political backing, already impoverished prior to June 1967 and still more vulnerable after their eviction, the inhabitants of the Maghrebi Quarter doubtless had no choice but to accept the meager indemnity they were offered. In this regard, the refusals expressed by two women—Myassar, widow of Abdallah El-Jareedi, and Maria Doloris, widow of Yussuf Musa Zehda—stand out as isolated acts of resistance, all the more striking for that reason.

Analogy

Explanations are multifarious and not mutually exclusive. Quite the reverse, they are cumulative and combine to form an agglomeration of interdependent and convergent causalities. This wall of silence is decidedly an assemblage of disparate desires and constraints, of strategies and relinquishments, of minor untruths and major betrayals, of good and bad conscience—all of which accreted, by various means and toward various ends, until this event was hidden from view. To conclude and to better grasp the historic significance: What if we compared this wall of silence to other analogous cases? What if we dared make use of *analogy*? A risky challenge, but one that can prove "a useful guide in knowledge production," provided it be explicit and smartly deployed, seeking not to establish an *identity* between two objects, but to discern their resemblances and differences, in order to capture each in its respective *singularity*.[8] Twenty years ago at this writing, the author of these lines worked on a study of the 17 October 1961 massacre in Paris—or, to be exact, on a study of one of the rare actors who had attempted to document and denounce that massacre at the time it took place.[9] The proximity in time of the 1961 massacre and the 1967 destruction of the Maghrebi Quarter is what gave rise to the analogy, which goes far beyond mere chronological adjacency.

In Paris on 17 October 1961, following a peaceful demonstration organized by the FLN to protest a curfew imposed on that organization, more than one hundred Algerians were assassinated by French police forces, some shot, others drowned. The next day, the official toll was set at two dead, and the police prefect, Maurice Papon, claimed that those two casualties were the result of a settling of scores between rival Algerian factions. This *state-sponsored* violence—deliberate and unquestionably *illegitimate*, to cite Max Weber's categories of analysis—was coupled with a *state lie*, just as deliberate, which was not dispelled until several decades later, thanks to the work of a few persistent historians: first among them Jean-Luc Einaudi in France, and Jim House and Neil MacMaster in Great Britain.[10]

Does this analogy allow for heightened intelligibility, and therefore a better comprehension of what happened before, during, and after the night of 10–11 June 1967 in Jerusalem? Here also, we are dealing with *state-sponsored violence*, decided at the highest level of government and applied jointly by the Israeli army and the West Jerusalem municipality. This state violence was also blatantly coupled with a *state lie*, deliberately organized to conceal the political responsibility for the operation. The events of 1961 and 1967 share much in common: state violence coupled with a state lie; willingness to attribute the event to a few "blunders" on the part of the French police in one case, and to a few overzealous Israeli entrepreneurs in the other; the same archival void at the highest levels of the state apparatus and decision-making structures; the same abundance of records at the lower levels of the logistical application of the decision;[11] the same asymmetrical colonial-style violence against unarmed civilians; the same unease of the FLN in 1961 and the Algerian government in 1967, each reluctant to somehow showcase "immigrant" nationals as opposed to the "Algerians of Algeria."[12]

The differences are equally numerous, and fundamental: more than one hundred deaths in Paris, between one and three deaths in Jerusalem; no destruction in Paris, an entire neighborhood razed in Jerusalem; violence deployed in an administratively acknowledged capital and outside a war zone in the case of Paris, violence deployed in a scarcely claimed and only recently conquered capital in the case of Jerusalem; eminent responsibility of the police in Paris, eminent responsibility of the army in Jerusalem. . . . Each national narrative harbors grey areas, its "pasts that don't pass," its failure to come to terms with moments of infamy and indignity; and the point here is not to establish some ranking between the two events, some hierarchy based on personal criteria of moral opprobrium or political assessment. If such were the case, according to that gauge, one might spontaneously assume that the massacre of more than one hundred Algerian civilians in Paris in 1961 would be a more "grievous" event than the destruction of some one hundred houses in Jerusalem in June 1967. But that indeed is not the issue, nor is this the role of the historian, whose purpose is to *understand* and not to *judge*; to instruct and establish the facts, and not to qualify them morally or characterize them legally.

The debate that distinguishes the respective roles of judge and historian is old, impassioned, and eminently complex. Marc Bloch laid down the essential terms in his luminous *The Historian's Craft*, written between 1941 and 1943: "There are two ways of being impartial: that of the scholar and that of the judge. They have a common root in their honest submission to the truth. [. . .] However, there comes a time when their paths divide. When the scholar has observed and explained, his task is finished. It yet remains for the judge to pass sentence."[13] No surrendering here, nor renouncing; quite the reverse, for Bloch reminds us how demanding the *mission* of the historian can be, inasmuch as it consists of striving to suspend judgment: "When all is said and done, a single word, 'understanding,' is the beacon light of our studies. [. . .] Even in action, we are far too prone to judge. It is so easy to denounce. We are never sufficiently understanding."[14] Bloch, whose engagement in the resistance movement would cost him his life, is by no means advocating that historians remain in their ivory towers, sheltered from impassioned debate. He argues so that his *historian's craft*, his professional commitment *as historian*, remains separate from his passions, to whatever extent possible.

Bloch thus sheds light on the significance of a historian's inquiry into the destruction of the Maghrebi Quarter and, therefore, into the need to compare this event to better understand it. For beyond their irreducible differences, the two tragedies, "Paris, 17 October 1961" and "Jerusalem, 10 June 1967," are linked by an invisible thread: the place of the historian and the discipline of history "up against the wall" with only the tools of the trade—in frontal position, at the foot of the event, in the face of its violence and brutality—making it more challenging to ensure that judgment does not prevail over understanding, that reprobation does not prevail over discernment. In the face of victimhood and the sensitivities of public opinion, and thus in the face of the obligation to compile incontrovertible documentation, to build a robust narrative, the historian must operate in each case with the same ethical and epistemological rigor, and face the same difficulty to tear down—or, most often, work around—the various walls of silence and skepticism to establish solidly and calmly the factual truth. Here then, thanks to Bloch and to historians as a group, is how one briefly sums up the specific constraints of this inquiry into the life and death of the Maghrebi Quarter of Jerusalem.

Restitution

To finish, to truly finish, a final question remains, the rawest and most cruel: What for? To what end? Why ought we to remember, why should the facts be restored? Why not forget? This question kept arising since the start of this inquiry in 2016: Why stir up a painful past? Why run the risk of reigniting old resentments? Why not let it be, in the end, hidden behind its wall of silence? The answer to this question is tricky. First of all, it has to do with the issue of *acknowledgment*: the facts have to be scientifically established in order to acknowledge the suffering of victims and the responsibility of the protagonists, those who issued orders to subcontractors. If this recognition is then met with an effort to share and instruct, it can establish a *mutual agreement* as to how the event factually unfolded, thereby moving beyond the trauma toward a narrative, whether fortunate or unfortunate, glorious or distressing. This acknowledgment of the facts does not purport to shut down debate over their *interpretation*, their lawfulness or unlawfulness, their legitimacy or illegitimacy, but quite the reverse: to *enable* debate, to build it upon a common base, which fosters and organizes the controversy.

But, for that matter, do we really have the choice? Can the protagonists in this story claim ignorance? This history is little known, poorly understood, but it is not unknown; it *exists*, it cannot be wiped from the record. It exists through individual and family memories, and through the imprint of place-names left behind in the vicinity of the Maghrebi Quarter, but also via crises that episodically reactivate the original trauma, like successive "returns of the repressed." The collapse of the Maghrebi ramp in February 2004, the hostilities that ensued between the Jordanian waqf and the Israeli authorities, Israel's unilateral withdrawal from UNESCO in 2018, the bloody clashes over the opening of the "Western Wall Tunnel" (eighty deaths in 1996), and, more broadly, the violence that resurfaces every time a controversy breaks out over an archaeological find within the perimeter, or over the conditions of respective access to the holy Muslim and Jewish places, controversies that have grown increasingly frequent in recent years with the rising pressure from religious Jewish activists who are agitating to revisit the status quo agreement of 1967[15]—all these episodes, despite their distinctiveness, are also symptoms of this past that hasn't yet passed.

It should be said that the "Western Wall Plaza," which today extends over the perimeter of the former Maghrebi Quarter, carries a particular political and symbolic charge. It is on this plaza that young Israeli soldiers swear their induction oath; where Jews of Israel and the diaspora gather for large annual pilgrimages or to celebrate their young boys' bar mitzvahs; where heads of state, including popes, come to pay tribute to the biblical past of Israel; where tourists pose for pictures and deposit their wishes or prayers on little bits of paper slipped between the stones of the Wall; where proponents of liberal Judaism confront their more orthodox fellow Jews over the issue of women's prayer space; where archaeologists contend with religious authorities for the control of digs and how to proceed.... This empty, open space, the only one within the old city of Jerusalem—and for good reason—is one of the most monitored, most visited, most photographed places in all the world. This only serves to accentuate the pernicious tension between *familiarity* and *ignorance*; the plaza is a place everyone thinks they know, though they are unaware of its most immediate history (figure 70).

FIGURE 70. "**Western Wall Plaza,**" 2013. Source: © Vincent Lemire.

The issue of *acknowledgment*, therefore, is also an issue of *knowledge*. The history of the Maghrebi Quarter not only is necessary to enrich present-day public discourse, but is also a crucial ingredient in our historical knowledge base as pertains to certain fundamental issues. This is why the present inquiry, though not exhaustive, is not confined to the story of a vanished neighborhood, but has attempted to revive it over the *longue durée* since its foundation in the late twelfth century, so that the tragic conditions of its *death* might no longer preclude the history of its *life*. This long history has allowed us to greatly refresh our knowledge of Jerusalem, an object of so many obsessions and misperceptions. It provides a definitive argument that the history of Jerusalem cannot be reduced to the chronicle of the Israeli-Palestinian conflict, a binary confrontation that has only scratched its surface during the most recent period.

If we allow the history of the "Maghrebi" quarter to resonate with those of the so-called Syrian, Serbian, Frankish, Armenian, Ethiopian, Coptic, Greek, or Russian quarters, we conclude that the vision of Jerusalem as a world city is not some empty slogan, but rather a tangible reality experienced by its inhabitants up to the present day. This history also restores rightful place to the Ayyubid and Mamluk period (1187–1516), the foundational period of the

Maghrebi Quarter, which also produced a large share of the architectural patrimony of today's city. It also testifies to the importance of the waqfs, the Muslim religious foundations, which continue today to structure large segments of real estate in the old city. It also sheds new light on the Ottoman history of Jerusalem (1516–1917) by focusing on numerous institutions that, whether on-site or from Damascus and Istanbul, administered and organized the daily life of its inhabitants over the course of three centuries.

The history of the Maghrebi Quarter also compels us to more closely relate the history of Jerusalem to its hinterland. Until 1948, the village of Ein Karem supplied more than half the revenue of the Abu Madyan waqf, thereby feeding, clothing, and caring for the pilgrims of the Maghrebi Quarter. This was no detached shrine city, linked only to transnational pilgrimage routes; rather, Jerusalem is revealed here as having been fully integrated into its *terroir*, at the heart of an intensive network of town-country relations. At the archival level, the history of the Maghrebi Quarter confirms the tremendous value of local administrative sources, notably the judicial and municipal archives, which alone are able to account for the internal dynamics of the city. Finally, at the chronological level, the history of the Maghrebi Quarter highlights the fundamental break caused by the British Mandate, when endogenous institutions were severely weakened and Zionist ambitions were gaining ground. France's support of the Maghrebi Quarter in the 1950s reminds us that "protection of the Holy Places," a notion often considered as outdated, did play a genuine role in the effective history of Jerusalem. Likewise, the final years of the Maghrebi Quarter in the early 1960s shine a light on the Jordanian history of Jerusalem, a history mostly overlooked which still needs to be written. The destruction of the quarter, finally, brings into bold relief the turning point that the Six-Day War represented for Israel, when messianic fervor overtook all the levers of Israeli government, including its most secular institutions.

This history is all the more crucial in that it is still *ongoing*, and far from over. Evictions proceed at a steady pace in East Jerusalem, as witnessed by the clashes in the spring of 2021 over the Sheikh Jarrah or Ras al-Amud neighborhoods; the destruction of houses that has continued unabated since 1967, routinely condemned by Israeli NGOs such as Ir-Amim or B'tselem; and the marginalization of Muslim holy places that remains more than ever a para-mount objective for the Israeli right and far right, as evidenced by heightened mobilization on the Temple Mount / Haram al-Sharif. Here also is why the destruction of the Maghrebi Quarter must not be forgotten: it is no isolated, inconsequential, one-off event whose *memory* is simply entered into the historical record. Quite the contrary, it is an inaugural moment, a particularly dramatic one, of *history* in the making, in the process of being written, in the present and undoubtedly into the future.

The historiographic and heuristic gain is clearly invaluable. The history of the Maghrebi Quarter over the *longue durée* represents an incomparable vantage point for the history of Jerusalem, Israel, Palestine, the Mediterranean, Zionism, the Holy Places, French colonialism, Islamic empires, and Muslim pilgrimages. . . . This history, eight centuries old, remains incomplete and will necessarily be collective. Further input will be required regarding the poorly documented Ayyubid period in particular (1187–1261), as well as further testimony from the 1950s and 1960s, many witnesses of which are still alive today. In order to reflect together on the issues of *knowledge* and *acknowledgment*, we finally need to consider the question of *restitution*: matters pertaining to pedagogy and the availability of historical materials both inside and outside the school setting, aimed in particular at the younger generation, children and grandchildren of the former inhabitants of the quarter, children and grandchildren of the wreckers and the bystanders of the destruction.

So that this untold story might finally be told, earning a *place-name* in its own right, so that the Wall might also become a place of memory of the Maghrebi Quarter, the issue of visibility is crucial. The history of the Maghrebi Quarter has until now remained unspeakable, unmentionable, and finally *invisible*. To render it accessible, not only must it be reconstituted—the classic work of the historian—but we must also find a way to share it among all those who have been its witnesses, as well as among those who, whether on a daily basis or occasionally, tread upon this bit of urban space known unequivocally as the "Western Wall Plaza." For that, virtual reenactments open up fresh possibilities.[16] Because the quarter was not only destroyed but also *erased*, deleted from maps and memory, a three-dimensional reconstruction seems justified both scientifically and ethically, for this *reconstitution* might well be the basis for a genuine *restitution*, by aggregating archaeological and historical data with memories of the former inhabitants, to restore to this buried past a certain density, a certain consistency . . . a certain *presence*. Fifty-five years after the destruction of the Maghrebi Quarter, one can only believe that the time of forgetting is past, and that the time of history is come.

Jerusalem, October 2021

ACKNOWLEDGMENTS

This work on the life and death of the Maghrebi Quarter of Jerusalem is the result of a five-year investigation throughout which I enjoyed endless support and encouragement. The first writing of this text took place between February 2018 and February 2019, during my sister Marie's illness, and was completed at the time of her death. It is, first of all, Marie whom I'm thinking of here, for throughout her ordeal she gave each of us strength and spirit, welcoming her near and dear to be with her, right up to the final hour. I know how much this writing owes to her in terms of commitment and sincerity. Writing and life are always inextricably mingled—and, at times, writing and death as well.

This investigation first took the form of a dissertation for accreditation to direct research in history, which helped shape its framework and methodology to some degree. Deep gratitude to Jean-Pierre Filiu, who saw fit from day one to be its guarantor, and whose hallmark serenity and composure proved utterly contagious. I gratefully acknowledge Gadi Algazi, Denis Charbit, Rashid Khalidi, Henry Laurens, Ann-Laura Stoler, and Sylvie Thénault, who graciously accepted to sit on the jury and thus be early readers of this text, and to then engage with me in a critical and reasoned discussion, the only kind that matters when dealing with such sensitive issues.

In Paris, certain crucial friendships nurtured and reassured me all along this challenging journey. I am thinking first of all of my mentor and friend Patrick Boucheron, he who listens, who guides, who opens, who comforts. I am also thinking of Yann Potin, invaluable partner when it comes to navigating the unruly archipelago of archives and the complexity of long time. I'm thinking of Valérie Hannin, who was interested in the project right away, and who graciously found a place for it in the magazine *L'Histoire*. I am thinking of Séverine Nikel, who welcomed the original text at Seuil Editions; to Caroline Pichon, who turned it into a book; to the whole Seuil team, who have lent it shape and rigor. I am also thinking of Jane Kuntz, who has translated this book into English for Stanford University Press, and who, with her questions and suggestions, contributed in no small measure to improving the text in French. I am thinking of all the colleagues and friends at the University of Paris-Est / Gustave Eiffel, and to the teams at the French Center for Research in Jerusalem (CRFJ), who have partnered with me for over twenty years. And finally, last but not least, I am thinking of Julie Sibony, who accompanied me in this investigation from the very beginning, and whose support was particularly valuable in the final stages of writing and editing.

In Jerusalem I was immediately supported by Haïfa Khalidi, who introduced me to her story one evening, gazing out the windows of her home, and it was that inaugural narrative that bound me irrevocably to the vanished Maghrebi Quarter. Next, Lilach Assaf has been the invaluable mainstay of all my work in the Israeli archives, and a great help in connecting me with certain witnesses. I met certain former inhabitants of the quarter thanks to Cyrille Louis, and then thanks to Valérie Nivelon, during preparation for a program on Radio France Internationale marking the fiftieth anniversary of the June 1967 war. The producer Mariana Otero saw fit to trust me with analyzing and commenting on the photographs that Gilles Caron had taken during the war; thanks to her, Gilles became my guide, shielding me as I entered Jerusalem in his wake, in the midst of the fighting and on the verge of the quarter's disappearance.

Archival holdings are not, in the first instance, the stacks, boxes, and files, but rather the archivists and documentarians who together forge the archive, who catalog it and make it accessible; in short, those who enable its existence. This investigation would have been impossible without the backing of these irreplaceable agents for historical research: Şerife Eroğlu Memiş and Mohamad Safadi (waqf archives in Ankara and in Abu-Dis), Önder Bayir (imperial

Ottoman archives in Istanbul), Simone Shliarter (Central Zionist Archives), Motti Ben-Ari (archives at the Ben-Zvi Institute), Khader Salameh (Khalidi Library), Adel Budeiri (Budeiri Library), Serguey Loktionov (archives of the Custody of the Holy Land), Michaël Mahler and Menahem Levin (archives of the Jerusalem municipality), Bérangère Fourquaux (diplomatic archives in Nantes), Anne Liskenne (archives of the Ministry of Foreign Affairs in Paris), personnel at the Archives Nationales d'Outre-Mer (Archives of the Overseas Territories) in Aix-en-Provence, Jean-Michel de Tarragon (photography collection at the École biblique et archéologique française in Jerusalem), Daniel Palmieri (Red Cross archives in Geneva), Anne Verdure-Mary and Thomas Cazentre (Massignon holdings at the Bibliothèque nationale de France), Debbie Usher (Middle East Center Archives at Oxford), Bahija Simou (Royal Archives at Rabat), and Anthony Krause and Jens Boel (UNESCO archives).

Thanks are also owed to François Bon and his fellow archaeologists Ofer Marder, Khalaily Hamoudi, Shlomit Weksler-Bdolah, Hervé Barbé, Fanny Vitto, Peter Gendelman, and Orgal Chalaf for their help and support with the Israeli Antiquities Authority. And finally, warm thanks to Manon Pignot, Julien Loiseau, Katell Berthelot, Olivier Tourny, Frédéric Moret, Laurence Américi, Frédéric Abécassis, Robert Ilbert, Roberto Mazza, Michelle Campos, Beshara Doumani, Hamid Barrada, Chloé Rosner, Raja Khalidi, Musa Sroor, Randi Deghilem, Eugene L. Rogan, Charles Enderlin, Aurélia Smotriez, Jean-Marc Liling, Irene Salenson, Meron Benvenisti, Andrew Bellisari, Salim Tamari, Marius Schattner, Karen Akoka, and Leila Shahid . . . for they all crossed paths with this investigation and nurtured it with their advice, readings, ideas, invitations, and promptings . . . shared experiences.

This archival quest also enjoyed the support and stimulus of the core team of the European Research Council's Open Jerusalem Project throughout these years. Thanks to Stéphane Ancel, Yasemin Avci, Louise Corvasier, Leyla Dakhli, Angelos Dalachanis, Abdulhameed al-Kayyali, Falestin Naïli, Yann Potin, Maria-Chiara Rioli, and Katerina Stathi. Thanks to them, and to dozens of colleagues around the world today who are committed to this long-haul project. The history of Jerusalem will be increasingly open, collective, fluid, and mobile in the years to come, and we can imagine that the history of the Maghrebi Quarter might be further enriched from this sustained openness.

Yes, in writing, life and death do mingle; and to live the historian's profession with dignity, we must take care to mix "a little life into one's art and a little art into one's life." From Paris to Jerusalem, it is Marius, Adèle, Raoul, and Chloé who have joyously and loudly accompanied this work and who, above all, kept it from taking up all the room . . . thanks be upon them!

NOTES

Introduction: A Place for History

1. Salamon 2004. https://www.emsc-csem.org/Doc/Salamon_11022004.pdf/.

2. "Report of the Technical Mission to the Old City of Jerusalem," UNESCO, WHC-O7/31.COM/INF.7A.2, World Heritage Committee, 31st session, Christchurch, New Zealand, 27 February–2 March 2007; https://www.un.org/unispal/doc ument/auto-insert-206780/.

3. "Address by the Director-General of UNESCO Mr. Koichiro Matsuura," UNESCO, WHC-O7/31.COM/INF.7A.2, World Heritage Committee, 31st session, Christchurch, New Zealand, 19 March 2007.

4. Goetschel, Lemire, and Potin 2018; Anatole-Gabriel 2016.

5. Emek Shaveh, "Why Is the Mughrabi Ramp a Political Issue?" 9 September 2014; http://alt-arch.org/en/why-is-the-Mughrabi-ramp-a-political-issue/.

6. René Maheu (director-general of UNESCO), "Israël et l'UNESCO," *Le Monde*, 21 November 1974, pp. 1–3: "En détruisant un quartier de structure médiévale qui faisait partie intégrante du tissu urbain traditionnel de la vieille cité [. . .], il est certain que l'aspect du site au voisinage de la célèbre porte des Maghrébins a été profondément altéré" (By destroying a neighborhood of medieval structures that made up an integral part of the traditional urban fabric of the old city, [. . .] it is certain that the appearance of the site neighboring the famous Maghrebi Gate has been profoundly altered).

7. Halbwachs 1925.

8. No bibliography is available in French, apart from Lemire and Salenson 2018; and Lemire 2017. In English, there is one largely deficient article: Abowd 2000. In Arabic, monographs focused especially on the administration of religious endowments

present in the quarter include Al-Alami 1981; Civic Coalition for Defending the Palestinian's Rights in Jerusalem 2008; Aramin and Rifai 2011; Al-Maghribi 2014; and Al-Jubeh 2019a. In Hebrew, there is a brief article on the legal framework of the Waqf Abu Madyan in Weigert 1990; and a brief notice devoted to the demolition of the quarter, in Bahat 2016–17.

9. Khalidi 2003.

10. Oren 2003. One of the most striking examples of this odd avoidance is that, out of this book's 460 pages, the destruction of the Maghrebi Quarter is mentioned only incidentally, in two lines (p. 307).

11. Kloetzel 1935; Ben-Dov, Naor, and Avner 1983; Storper-Perez 1989; Saposnik 2008, 2015; Ricca 2010; Cohen-Hattab 2017, 2018.

12. Filiu 2008.

13. Hillenbrand and Auld 2009; Rosen-Ayalon 2002: 101–8; Loiseau 2016: 257–59.

14. Roncayolo 1990: 20.

15. Gilles Paris, "UNESCO: Les raisons du retrait des États-Unis et d'Israël," *Le Monde*, 13 October 2017.

16. Halbwachs 1971: 150.

17. Massignon 1951: 73–120; Yerushalmi 1985: 38–39; Peters 1985: 528–29 ("The Western Wall"). On Jewish Maghrebis in Palestine, see R. Cohen 2005. On the French colonial history of the term "Maghreb," see Hannoum 2021.

18. Algazi 1994.

19. Stoler 2009.

20. Lemire 2016.

21. Lemire 2017.

22. Thénault 2005.

23. Revel 1989.

24. Lemire 2016.

25. Charbit 1998.

26. Laurens 1999–2015.

27. Perec 1974.

28. Perec 1978.

29. Lemire 2016.

30. Hobsbawm 1987.

Prologue: The Legal Foundation of a Jerusalem Neighborhood

1. On current trends in the historiography of the waqfs and the debates surrounding the interpretive methodology, see Deghilem 1995. On the key issue of the Palestine waqfs' adaptability to the political issues of property ownership, see Reiter 1996 (introduction, p. 10: "Consequently, the major issue discussed in this study is to what degree the waqf, as an institution of the old world order, proved capable of adapting itself

to modern socio-economic conditions). The term "waqf," sometimes spelled "wakf," "ouakaf," or "ouakf," has been standardized for ease of reading.

2. *Sijillât Mahkamah Shar'iyya, Jerusalem*, vol. 194, f. 365.

3. Burgoyne and Richards 1987: 223–39 ("Al-Tankiziyya").

4. Sroor 2005b.

5. Doumani 1985.

6. Under the Open Jerusalem Project, whose aim is to facilitate access to the historical archives for the history of Jerusalem between 1840 and 1940, a digitization of microfilms preserved at the University of Haifa has been implemented for the period 1834–1920 (1249 H–1339 H), which corresponds to the registries no. 319 to 418, now accessible online for all students and researchers unable to do on-site consultation of the registries or microfilms. See www.openjerusalem.org/.

7. Vakıflar Genel Müdürlüğü Arşivi, Ankara (hereafter VGMA), registry 583, p. 27, no. 20. Thanks to Şerife Eroğlu Memiş for this input.

8. Massignon 1951.

9. Centre des archives diplomatiques de Nantes (hereafter CADN), Jerusalem 294 PO/2, box 37, folder 1 ("Documents and Translations").

10. Deghilem 1995.

11. CADN, Jerusalem 294 PO/2, 37/1. The name "Abu Madyan," sometimes spelled "Abou Mediane" or Abou Mediene," is standardized here for ease of reading.

12. Marçais 2011 (second edition).

13. The term "Maghrebi," sometimes spelled "Maghrébin," "Moghrabi," "Maughrébin," or "Maghribi," has been standardized here for ease of reading. Various spellings are used for the plural proper noun, reflecting the Arabic. "Maghrebis" will be used here.

14. Kedar 1992; Eddé 2008. A local tradition relates that the hand of Sidi Abu Madyan is still preserved today in a cenotaph inside the zawiya of the Maghrebis, a building adjacent to the quarter which, for this reason, escaped destruction in June 1967.

15. Marçais 1960–2005, 2nd edition; Grill 2016, 3rd edition.

16. Marçais 1960–2005, 2nd edition.

17. Little 1989; Hillenbrand and Auld 2009; Loiseau 2016.

18. Kedar, Weksler-Bdolah, and Da'adli 2012; Burgoyne and Richards 1987.

19. Al-Din 1876.

20. Muhtadi 2007. According to judicial sources uncovered by Abla Muhtadi, Mujir ad-Din's house adjoined the al-Fakhariya zawiya and was therefore located in the immediate vicinity of the Maghrebi Quarter.

21. Faron and Hubert 1995.

22. CADN, Jerusalem 294 PO/2, 37/1; Massignon 1951.

23. Cited in O'Neil 2019.

24. Burgoyne and Richards 1987: 258–69.

25. Nazmi al-Jubeh, based on court archives, was able to identify some twenty judges of Maghrebi origin between the fourteenth and nineteenth centuries. Al-Jubeh 2019a: 154–59.

26. Al-Jubeh 2019a: 153–54. Photographs and detailed description of this Koran by Kader Salameh at the site "Museum with No Frontiers," http://islamicart.museumwnf.org/database_item.php?id=object;ISL;pa;Mus01;26;en.

27. Massignon 1951: 88.

28. Ben-Arieh 1984–86, vol. 2: 47.

29. On the process of peri-urbanization of Ein Karem in the twentieth century, read Kark and Oren-Nordheim 2001: 290–92.

30. On the villages surrounding Ein Karem before 1948, see Khalidi 1997.

31. Lemire 2010.

32. Luke 1:39.

33. Ben-Arieh 1984–86, vol. 2: 48.

34. Massignon 1951: 88. The term "zawiya," sometimes written "zaouïa," "zawiyya," or "zawia," is standardized here for ease of reading.

35. Sroor 2005.

36. Talbi 1960–2005. "Maghariba" in Bearman et al., 2nd edition; Hannoum 2021.

37. Massignon 1951: 89.

38. Massignon 1951: 73–75. Massignon develops this idea a little further on, suggesting that inspiration be drawn from the "judicial resources of old Semitic law, for restoring less implacable and more humane international relations, basing them on the notion of right to asylum, of *amān* [security], *dhimma* [protection] and *ikrām al-dayf* [hospitality], which bestows hospitality upon all unarmed guests, without discrimination, tolerating no exception, absolutely like the International Red Cross."

39. CADN, Jerusalem 294 PO/2, 37/1.

40. Massignon 1951: 90.

41. Massignon 1951: 74.

42. The appointment or replacement of the steward (*mutewalli*), as we will see, would be frequently contested. Massignon 1951: 90.

43. Massignon 1951: 92.

44. This is from the 1902 translation, clearer than Massignon's, in which, probably as the result of a typo, he writes that the plots of land "will be granted for a period of more than two years" (the word "no" is missing).

45. Iogna-Prat 1998.

46. Massignon 1951: 89.

47. Filiu 2008.

Chapter 1: In the Empire of the Sultans

1. CADN, Jerusalem, 294 PO/2, 37/1.

2. For a summary presentation of the archives of the French Consulate General of

Jerusalem brought back to Nantes, see http://www.archives.openjerusalem.org/index
.php/repatriated-documents-from-the-french-consulate-in-jerusalem/.

3. CADN, Jerusalem, 294 PO/2, 37/1.

4. CADN, Jerusalem, 294 PO/2, 37/1. The term mutewalli (steward), sometimes
spelled "metoualli" or "metouali," is standardized here for ease of reading.

5. Başbakanlık Osmanlı Arşivi (hereafter BOA), Istanbul, ŞD.2296.40.20-B, 18
Receb 1318 (11 November 1900). The term "Hajj," sometimes spelled "Hadj" or "Haj,"
is standardized here for ease of reading.

6. Errors and corrections of dates are very frequent in the French consular archives,
due undoubtedly to the confusion between calendar systems for documents from the
Ottoman era.

7. CADN, Jerusalem, 294 PO/2, 37/1.

8. CADN, Jerusalem, 294 PO/2, 37/1.

9. Tamari 2018: 490–509. Salim Tamari notes that prior to World War I, the Waqf
Abu Madyan held possession of over 70 percent of properties in the quarter (506).

10. Al-Jubeh 2019a.

11. CADN, Jerusalem, 294 PO/2, 37/1.

12. The term "Buraq," sometimes spelled "Bourak," "Bouraq," or "Burak," is standardized here for ease of reading.

13. CADN, Jerusalem, 294 PO/2, 37/1, 18 October 1693 (17 Safar 1105).

14. CADN, Jerusalem, 294 PO/2, 37/1, 18 October 1693 (17 Safar 1105). See also
Singer 1994: 71–75.

15. CADN, Jerusalem 294 PO/2, 37/1, 6 November 1696 (10 Rabi'ul Akhar 1108).

16. CADN, Jerusalem 294 PO/2, 37/1, 6 November 1696 (10 Rabi'ul Akhar 1108).

17. Reiter 1996.

18. CADN, Jerusalem, 294 PO/2, 37/1, document numbered 18bis, 7 Safar 1220
(7 May 1805).

19. CADN, Jerusalem, 294 PO/2, 37/1, document numbered 20bis, 26 Rajab 1221
(9 October 1806).

20. CADN, Jerusalem, 294 PO/2, 37/1, document numbered 21bis, 22 Chaabane
1222 (25 October 1807).

21. Weber 2009.

22. Singer 2002; Stephan 1944; Peri 1983; Myres 2000.

23. In the legal file compiled by the French Consulate in 1949, another document
informs us about debt collection procedures with respect to the Ein Karem inhabitants. On 28 January 1862 (27 Rajab 1278), an agreement between the mutewalli of
the Waqf Abu Madyan and the "sheikhs and notables of the village of Ein Karem"
acknowledges that nine "tenant farmers on lands belonging to the waqf have not paid
their rental fees (*hiker*) for five years and ask that an agreement be reached whereby
they can stagger the payment of their arrears." The agreement, accepted and signed
by all parties, stipulates that the debtors "will pay to the waqf steward, every year for

the next five years, the amount of 400 piasters, representing 1,000 piasters of arrears and 1,000 piasters for rent in the current year." CADN, Jerusalem, 294 PO/2, 37/1 document numbered 9bis.

24. Algazi 1994.

25. Rafeq 2000.

26. Archives de la Custodie franciscaine à Jérusalem (hereafter ACFJ), Giudea / Aïn Karem: San Giovanni Battista in Montana / 1 [1762–99]. Thanks to Maria-Chiara Rioli for her invaluable input.

27. ACFJ, Giudea / Aïn Karem: S. Giovanni Battista in Montana / 2 [1678–1818].

28. The fact that Abu Madyan was of Andalusian origin (he was born in Seville) might also have had some bearing, since the Spanish Franciscans who settled in Ein Karem certainly knew the name of the endowment from which they were renting.

29. Sroor 2009.

30. CADN, Jerusalem, 294 PO/2, 37/1, 19 November 1840 (24 Ramadan 1256).

31. CADN, Jerusalem, 294 PO/2, 37/1, 19 November 1840 (24 Ramadan 1256).

32. See chapter 2 of this book.

33. Muhtadi and Naili 2018. This article shows that the official return to Ottoman administration took place, in fact, in late November 1840.

34. CADN, Jerusalem, 294 PO/2, 37/1, 19 November 1840 (24 Ramadan 1256).

35. CADN, Jerusalem, 294 PO/2, 37/1, document numbered 10bis, 6 July 1864 (1 Safar 1281).

36. On this matter, see also the documents cited in Sroor 2009.

37. CADN, Jerusalem, 294 PO/2, 37/1, document numbered 10bis, 6 July 1864 (1 Safar 1281).

38. CADN, Jerusalem, 294 PO/2, 37/1, document numbered 12bis, 23 September 1866 (13 Joumada al-awwal 1283).

39. In the legal file compiled by the French Consulate in 1949, another document informs us about the new patrimonial rivalries brought about by the arrival of religious congregations in Ein Karem and by the embedding of more or less concealed leasing rights. On 12 October 1873 (19 Sha'aban 1290), the Jerusalem tribunal confronts the steward of the Waqf Abu Madyan and "Mr. Yacoub, dragoman of the Archimandrite, religious head of the Russian community" regarding an annual rent payment and confusion among several occupants, "since the Sultan does not authorize Russians to acquire property" (CADN, Jerusalem, 294 PO/2, 37/1, document numbered 14bis).

40. My thanks to Mohamad Safadi for his support, and thanks also to Şerife Eroğlu Memiş for her crucial help during this investigation in the Abu Dis archives. Also noteworthy is Al-Jubeh 2019a: 173, which refers to an account ledger dating from 1663.

41. Balance sheets consulted: 1272 (1855–56); 1275 (1858–59); 1276 (1859–60); 1288 (1871–72); 1292 (1875–76); 1295 (1878); 1316 (1898–99); 1317 (1899–1900); 1318 (1900–1901); 1319 (1901–2); 1325 (1907–8); 1326 (1908–9); 1328 (1910–11); 1331 (1912–13).

42. See, for example, the balance sheet for the year 1318 (1900–1901) at the Islamic Research and Heritage Revival Institute, Abu-Dis (hereafter IRHRI), box 41, file no. 3/5/28/1272/13.

43. See, for example, the balance sheet for the year 1288 (1871–72) at the IRHRI, box 41, file no. 3/5/28/1272/13.

44. See, for example, the balance sheet for the year 1295 (1878) at the IRHRI, box 41, file no. 3/5/28/1272/13.

45. See, for example, the balance sheet for the year 1319 (1901–2), in a preprinted ledger, at the IRHRI, box 41, file no. 3/5/28/1272/13.

46. At the IRHRI, box 41, file no. 3/5/28/1272/13.

47. Lemire 2016: 193–220 ("Les folles journées révolutionnaires de 1908").

48. Lemire 2016: 159–92 ("La revolution municipale"). A concurrent observation was established for the sixteenth century by Nazmi al-Jubeh 2019a: 160–61, which points out that the population of the Maghrebi Quarter rose from about 150 to about 650 between the 1525–26 census and that of 1562–63, at a time when the city was experiencing strong population growth, though to a lesser degree. It is certain, at any rate, that the early Ottoman period was marked by a strong demographic trend in the Maghrebi Quarter.

49. IRHRI, box 7, file no. 7/3/2.0/63/1330/13.

50. IRHRI, box 7, file no. 7/3/2.0/63/1330/13.

51. IRHRI, box 41, file no. 3/5/28/1272/13.

52. This trend is also linked to the development of pilgrimages originating in colonial empires. On this point, see Escande 2012; Chantre 2018. See also, for the modern period, Faroqhi 1994.

53. IRHRI, box 41, file no. 3/5/0/5/1294/13.

54. Lemire 2016: 247–56.

55. Lemire 2016: 31–65.

56. Campos 2011: 224–44 (chapter 7, "Unscrambling the Omelet").

57. Faroqhi 1999.

58. Henssen, Philipp, and Weber 2002.

59. Auld and Hillenbrand 2000; Loiseau 2016: 280–83.

60. See in particular VGMA, registry no. 589, p. 119, no. 332, 10 Şevval 1048 (14 February 1639) ; VGMA, registry no. 589, p. 119, no. 332, 13 Muharrem 1137 (2 October 1724); VGMA, registry no. 589, p. 192, no. 327, 10 Ramazan 1196 (19 August 1782); VGMA, registry no. 589, p. 192, no. 328, 1st Rebiulevvel 1181 (28 July 1767); VGMA, registry no. 589, p. 194, no. 330, 5 Muharrem 1205 (14 September 1790); VGMA, registry no. 589, p. 195, no. 331, 13 Receb 1171 (23 March 1758). Most of these founding acts explicitly specify that the mutewalli of the Waqf Abu Madyan would also be in charge of the new endowment's finances.

61. Büssow 2014; Hitzel 2014; Eroğlu Memiş 2018.

62. Başbakanlık Osmanlı Arşivi (hereafter BOA), Istanbul, C.EV.552.27881, 21 Zilkade 1216 (25 March 1802).

63. BOA, EV.MH.795.179, 26 Rebiulahir 1277 (11 November 1860).

64. Büssow 2011.

65. A. Cohen 2001.

66. BOA, EV.D.13645, Kânûn-i sâni 1264 (January–February 1849); BOA, EV.D.18277, 10 Mart 1280 (22 March 1863); BOA, EV.D.18617, Tesrîn-i evvel 1279 (October–November 1863); BOA, EV.D.19214, Tesrîn-i evvel 1280 (October–November 1864).

67. Faroqhi 1994.

68. BOA, EV.HMK.SR.556, 1113 (1701–92); BOA, EV.HMK.SR.704, 1124 (1712–14); BOA, EV.HMK.SR. 1791, 1177 (1763–64); BOA, EV.HMK.SR.556, 1186 (1772–73); BOA, EV.HMK.SR.556, 1197 (1782–83); BOA, EV.HMK.SR.556, 1207 (1792–93).

69. Vakıflar Genel Müdürlüğü Arşivi, Ankara (hereafter VGMA), ADVNS.AHK.ŞM, registry no. 3, p. 148, 1197 (1783).

70. BOA, I.DH.641–44623, 7 Ramazan 1288 (20 November 1871).

71. BOA, ŞD.2296.40, 19 Safer 1322 (5 May 1904).

72. Avci, Lemire, and Özdemir 2018.

73. BOA, BEO.3235.242552, 21 Zilhicce 1325 (25 January 1908): "Kudus ve Yafa'daki Mağribilerin konsoloslar tarafından gordukleri himayenin mahzurlarına binâen ciddi bir tedbir ittihâzı hakkında mûktezasının i'fâsı."

74. BOA, DH.ID.212.27, 9 Şaban 1331 (5 June 1913).

75. Avci and Lemire 2005. These archives are fully accessible on the website www.openjerusalem.org.

76. Avci, Lemire, and Naïli 2015.

77. Arnon 1992.

78. Lemire 2012: 159–92 (chapter 5, "La révolution municipale").

79. Historical Archives of the Jerusalem Municipality (hereafter HAJM), Registers of Jerusalem Municipality Council during the Ottoman period (hereafter RJMCO), vol. 10, p. 14b, item 71, 25 Agustos 1320 (7 September 1904).

80. HAJM, RJMCO, vol. 6, p. 54a, item 365, 1 Nîsân 1313 (13 April 1897).

81. HAJM, RJMCO, vol. 10, p. 27a, item 141, 14 Kânün Awal 1320 (27 December 1904).

82. HAJM, RJMCO, vol. 3, p. 45b, item 309, 1 Huzayrân 1315 (13 June 1899).

83. HAJM, RJMCO, vol. 3, p. 21a, item 154, 4 Mârt 1315 (16 March 1899).

84. HAJM, RJMCO, vol. 3, p. 49b, item 336, 17 Huzayran 1315 (29 June 1899).

85. HAJM, RJMCO, vol. 5, p. 52a, item 341, 4 Nisan 1318 (23 April 1902).

86. HAJM, RJMCO, vol. 5, p. 14a, item 89, 17 Tamuz 1317 (30 July 1901).

87. HAJM, RJMCO, vol. 10, p. 7a, item 36, 29 Huzayrân 1320 (12 July 1904). Dayr Aban is located about twenty kilometers west of Jerusalem, along the path of the railroad that has connected the Holy City to Jaffa since 1892.

88. Al-Jubeh 2019a: 161, mentions a document issuing from the Islamic Tribunal, dating from 1653, which indicates that "ancient custom provides that the Sheikh of

the Maghrebis be consulted prior to confirming the hire of a market guardian, of a treasurer of the soap producers, a doorman of the khans, a doorman of the al-Aqsa Mosque, or a doorman assigned to guard a large residence."

89. Chateaubriand 1811: 345 (part 4, "Jerusalem").

90. An excerpt of Nazmi al-Jubeh's testimony can be seen at the site http://www .mughrabiquarter.info/. In the rest of the testimony, Nazmi al-Jubeh (born in 1955) returns to his discovery of the demolished quarter:

> We went down the stairs that connect the al-Sharaf quarter to the Gate of the Chain, then we took the Abu Madyan lane that leads to the Maghrebi Quarter. And as we went down the first steps, we were in for a shock, the quarter no longer existed. We saw Israeli soldiers and rabbis on the wreckage of the former quarter. They stopped us and asked to see our ID. I wondered: where is the al-Maslouhi family? Where are their children? Where is my friend Muhammad? I had the feeling that the whole world was collapsing. We all began to cry. We were all crying, from my father to my youngest brother.

91. Avci and Lemire 2005.

92. HAJM, RJMCO, vol. 5, p. 14b, item 94, 19 Tammûz 1317 (1 August 1901).

93. HAJM, RJMCO, vol. 12, p. 13a, item 76, 19 Shubât 1322 (4 March 1907).

94. Lemire 2010.

95. HAJM, RJMCO, vol. 5, p. 39a, item 245, 16 Kanon Awal 1317 (29 January 1902).

96. HAJM, RJMCO, vol. 5, p. 40b, item 254, 4 Shubât 1317 (17 February 1902).

97. HAJM, RJMCO, vol. 9, p. 22a, item 142, 24 Mârt 1316 (6 June 1900). On the Sheikh Eid Mosque: Kedar, Weksler-Bdolah, and Da'adli 2012.

Chapter 2: In the Turmoil of War and the Mandate

1. CADN, Jerusalem, 294 PO/2, 37/1, n.d. ("Le Waqf Abou Mediene"), typed manuscript, 13 pages.

2. Rogan 2015.

3. Naïli 2017.

4. Biger 1994; Aaronsohn, and Trimbur 2008.

5. CADN, Jerusalem 294 PO/2, 37/1, n.d. ("Le Waqf Abou Mediene"), typed manuscript, 13 pages.

6. Mazza 2009; Jacobson 2011; Alem 1982.

7. "The Zionist Central Archives," *American Archivist* 13, no. 4 (1950): 351–56.

8. Charbit 1998.

9. Most research tools are available online at http://www.zionistarchives.org.il/en/.

10. Central Zionist Archives (hereafter CZA), series L.51 (50 linear meters).

11. Antébi mentions the date of 28 February as date of receipt, which is surely a slip of the pen. CZA, L.51/14, 2 February 1913.

12. CZA, A.34/42, 16 February 1913.

13. CZA, L.51/14, 11 May 1913.

14. Among the abundant bibliographical items: Kloetzel 1935; Ben Dov, Naor, and Aner 1983; Storper-Perez 1989; Saposnik 2008; Rica 2010; Saposnik 2015; Cohen-Hattab and Kohn 2017; Cohen-Hattab and Bar 2018.

15. In the French consular archives, there is a hint of these usage conflicts in front of the Western Wall just before World War I: CADN, Jerusalem 294 PO/2, 37/1, "Copy of an Act of the Jerusalem Administrative Council Dated 12 Techrin Seni 1327 (12 November 1910), no. 1680": The Sanjak Administrative Council of Jerusalem (Meclis-i Vala) states on 12 November 1910 that "Mosaic [Jewish] observance has attempted to place tables and chairs at a place located outside the walls of the Omar Mosque, called Buraq, this place being part of the Waqf Abu Madyan," and notes that "it is legally prohibited to place any object there."

16. The accounts of these individual initiatives are sorely lacking any documentary evidence. In Rossof 1998: 186, there is mention of an attempt in the 1830s by Rabbi Shemarya Luria. Montefiore 2011: 428 evokes an attempt by Moses Montefiore in March 1866. In 1914 the local chronicler Abraham Moses Luncz reports on the attempt by the Baron Edmond de Rothschild to purchase the Maghrebi Quarter in 1887. According to Luncz, Edmond de Rothschild is believed to have offered to trade for the perimeter of the Maghrebi Quarter land of equivalent value outside the ramparts, upon which an equivalent number of housing units would be built. The value of the houses in the quarter was said to be assessed at 740,000 francs. Also according to Luncz, the project was reportedly approved at first by Governor Mehmed Raouf Pacha, who later reversed his decision under pressure from the Sheikh al-Islam of Istanbul. In his account, Luncz also points out that "the Muslims never showed any signs of intolerance toward those who come to pray to the one God in whom they believe" (Luncz 1914: 58).

17. Halpern and Reinharz 1998.

18. CZA, A.153/44–45, 13 November 1912.

19. CZA, A.153/44–45, 4 January 1913.

20. CZA, A.34/42, 20 May 1913.

21. CZA, A.34/42, 5 June 1913. Underlined in the text.

22. Traces of this rental project are also found in a letter from Antébi dated 16 February 1913 (CZA, A.34/42, 16 February 1913).

23. CZA, A.58/12, 22 March 1912.

24. Weltmann 1961.

25. Pasha 1922.

26. CZA, Z.3/68. Thanks to Roberto Mazza for alerting me to these documents. See his recent article "The Deal of the Century? The Attempted Sale of the Western Wall by Cemal Pasha in 1916," *Middle Eastern Studies* 57 (2021): 696–711.

27. CZA, Z.3/68, 17 November 1915.

28. CZA, Z.3/68, 17 November 1915. Emphasis in original.

29. Bozarslan 2013.

30. Jacobson to Lichteim, 31 December 1915, CZA, Z.3/68.

31. Jacobson to Brandeis, 31 December 1915, CZA, Z.3/68. Emphasis in original.

32. CZA, Z.3/68, 9 March 1916. This document is corroborated by the direct testimony of Menahem Ussishkin, collected and recorded by the Vaad Leumi during the Mandate years, and preserved today in the J.1/331 series of the Central Zionist Archives (CZA J1/331/6):

> It was in the beginning of the year 1915, while I was the President of Hovevei Zion in Russia and our representative in Eretz Yisrael was Menachem Sheinkin. I received a telegram from Eretz Yisrael through Romania, since during the war it was impossible to send telegrams from Eretz Yisrael directly to Russia. In that telegram, Mr. Sheinkin informed me that they were negotiating with Djemal Pasha regarding the purchase of the Maghrebi area in front of the Western Wall and that it was required for that matter that I would send him immediately an advance payment of 50,000 gold francs. I don't have that telegram because the entire Hovevei-Zion archive remained in Odessa, in the hands of the Bolsheviks. The day I received the telegram I passed a sum of 50,000 francs to Yakobus Cohen, a banker in Haag, who was one of the directors of the treasure of the Jewish settlement. I didn't receive any further information until after the war when I came to Eretz Yisrael. Then, the late Mr. Sheinkin told me that due to complications of the war at the Suez Canal, it was difficult to meet with Djemal Pasha in order to arrange the matter and therefore the negotiation couldn't proceed. This negotiation was managed by Djemal Pasha's people and with his consent."

33. CZA, KKL.10/33, 28 April 1916.

34. CZA, Z.3/68, 13 June 1916.

35. "Dr. Jacob Thon, Founder of Jewish National Council in Palestine, Dies; Was 62," Jewish Telegraphic Agency, 7 March 1950.

36. CZA, Z.3/68, 17 July 1916. Albert Antébi died of typhus in Istanbul in 1919. See Antébi 1996.

37. CZA, Z.3/68, n.d. (July 1916).

38. Dakhli 2014.

39. CZA, Z.3/68, 23 July 1916.

40. Jacobson 2011.

41. William H. McLean, *City of Jerusalem Town Planning Scheme [Prepared for War Office]*, British National Archives (hereafter BNA), Colonial Office, CO.1069/743, 1918.

42. Kendall 1948: 4–10 ("The 1918, 1919 and 1922 Schemes: Short Descriptive Review of the Plans Prepared by Sir William McLean, the Late M. Patrick Geddes and the Late C. R. Ashbee"); Biger 1986; Hyman 1994 (in particular chapter 2, 39–105); Efrat 1993; al-Jubeh 2019b.

43. C. R. Ashbee, interview with the *Observer* in 1919; copy found in the papers of Sir Ronald Storrs (1881–1956), Pembroke College, Cambridge, box 3, file no. 1, 1919 (cited in Wharton 2008: 46). See also Pullan and Kyriacou 2009.

44. Barakat 2016; Mazza 2018.

45. Patrick Geddes, "Jerusalem Actual and Possible: A Preliminary Report to the Chief Administrator of Palestine and the Military Governor of Jerusalem on Town Planning and City Improvements, November 1919," CZA, Z.4/1646/2 (typescript).

46. Geddes, "Jerusalem Actual and Possible," p. 4; emphasis in the original. See Lemire 2016 (chapter 2, "Aux origines de la ville-musée").

47. Geddes, "Jerusalem Actual and Possible," p. 4.

48. Geddes, "Jerusalem Actual and Possible," p. 8.

49. Geddes, "Jerusalem Actual and Possible," pp. 10–11.

50. Hysler Rubin 2011.

51. This is, at any rate, what was posited by Dotan Goren. See Goren 2016.

52. CZA, J.1/71, 5 October 1925. Emphasis in original.

53. David Yellin to Eliezer Friedmann, CZA, A.153/13, March 1927.

54. Avni 1999; Avni et al. 2002.

55. Willis 1928.

56. Nur 2008.

57. Zohar, Rubin, and Salamon 2014.

58. *Milwaukee Journal*, 12 July 1927, p. 2.

59. R. Cohen 2008 (chapter 1, "The Earthquake").

60. Walter 2008.

61. Bahat 2007.

62. Ben-Dov, Naor, and Aner 1983; A. Cohen 1989b. Prior to the sanctuary status conferred upon the Western Wall, the lamentation ritual associated with the destruction of the Temple (Tisha be'av) took place on the Mount of Olives.

63. Sarah Irving, "Donations and Their Destinations in the 1927 Palestine Earthquake," *Revue d'histoire culturelle*, 2021, special issue "Friends, Neighbors and Foes: The Cultural History of Jewish-Arab Relations in Palestine/Israel, 19th–21st centuries," Avner Ben-Amos and Vincent Lemire, eds., https://revues.mshparisnord.fr/rhc/index.php?id=1068.

64. "Frais effectués par les mutewallis des waqfs Abou Mediene à Jérusalem et ailleurs durant l'année 1927" (Costs incurred by the mutewallis of the Waqf Abu Madyan in Jerusalem and elsewhere during the year 1927.) CADN, Jerusalem, 294 PO/2, 37/1, n.d.

65. "Liste des immeubles du waqf maghrébin (Abou Mediene), sis en Palestine" (List of buildings belonging to the Maghrebi Waqf Abu Madyan located in Palestine), CADN, Jerusalem, 294 PO/2, 37/1, n.d. (1927).

66. CADN, Jerusalem, 294 PO/2, 37/1, document numbered 26bis, 13 February 1929.

67. Reiter 1996; Khayat 1962.

68. See chapter 1 of this book.

69. See chapter 1 of this book.

70. "Costs Incurred by the Mutewallis of the Waqfs Abu Madyan in Jerusalem and Elsewhere during the Year 1927," CADN, Jerusalem, 294 PO/2, 37/1, n.d.

71. Ministère des Affaires étrangères, La Courneuve (hereafter MAE), Direction des Affaires Politiques et Commerciales (Foreign Ministry, Department of Political and Commercial Affairs), Palestine, vol. 59, 22 May 1928.

72. MAE, Direction des Affaires Politiques et Commerciales, Palestine, vol. 59, 2 August 1928. In the margin next to the sentence, "It is not possible to consider such a delegation," the Foreign Ministry clerk in charge of handling this letter wrote: "This is a joke."

73. MAE, Direction des Affaires Politiques et Commerciales, Palestine, vol. 59, 5 March 1928. See chapter 3 in this book ("René Neuville, Man of the Hour"), on recalling this exchange of letters in 1949.

74. H. Cohen 2015. See also A. Cohen 2016: 105–7; Barakat 2018.

75. Laurens 1999–2015, vol. 2: 153–89 ("Le Mur des Lamentations").

76. *Davar*, 31 August 1927, p. 2. Thanks to Gadi Algazi and to Jean-Marc Liling for their input on this issue.

77. *Davar*, 1 September 1927, p. 1.

78. *Davar*, 2 September 1927, p. 1

79. *Sawt al-Shaab*, 3 September 1927, p. 2.

80. *Davar*, 5 September 1927, p. 2.

81. *Davar*, 5 September 1927, p. 2.

82. Nir Mann, "He Laid the Foundation for Israel's Army: His Story Was Kept Secret—until His Diary Turned Up." *Haaretz*, 9 May 2020.

83. Schattner 1991: 151.

84. CZA, J.1/71, 14 October 1928.

85. "Le Mur des Lamentations à Jérusalem aurait été profané par la police" (The Wailing Wall said to have been desecrated by the police), *L'Écho d'Alger*, 30 September 1928.

86. Laurens, 1999–2015, vol. 2:159.

87. H. Cohen 2015.

88. Thanks to Eugene L. Rogan (St Antony's College, Oxford) and to Debbie Usher (Middle East Center Archives, Oxford) for their help during this investigation.

89. "Palestine Riots, 1929: Dossier for Chief Secretary; Official Telegrams, Reports, Memoranda, and Press Resumé," Middle East Center Archives, Oxford (hereafter MECA), Sir Harry Luke Papers, box 5/2.

90. Abba Ahimeir, "On Questions of the Moment (from the Journal of a Fascist)," *Do'ar Hayom*, 8 October 1928, cited in H. Cohen 2015: 71.

91. "A Conversation with Chief Rabbi Kook," *Do'ar Hayom*, 18 August 1929, cited in H. Cohen 2015: 74.

92. Eliel Löfgren, Charles Barde, and J. Van Kempen, *Report of the International Commission Appointed by His Majesty's Government in the United Kingdom of Great Britain and Northern Ireland, with the Approval of the Council of the League of Nations, to Determine the Rights and Claims of Moslems and Jews in Connection with the Wailing Wall at Jerusalem*, League of Nations, 1930.

93. Löfgren, Barde, and Van Kempen, *Report of the International Commission*, p. 10.

94. Löfgren, Barde, and Van Kempen, *Report of the International Commission*, p. 44.

95. MAE, Direction des Affaires Politiques et Commerciales, Palestine, vol. 59, 12 October 1929.

96. MAE, Direction des Affaires Politiques et Commerciales, Palestine, vol. 59, 12 October 1929.

97. MAE, Direction des Affaires Politiques et Commerciales, Palestine, vol. 59, 10 October 1929.

98. Consul General Jacques d'Aumale to the MAE, Direction des Affaires Politiques et Commerciales, Palestine, vol. 59, 10 October 1929.

99. MAE, Direction des Affaires Politiques et Commerciales, Palestine, vol. 59, 9 October 1929.

100. MAE, Direction des Affaires Politiques et Commerciales, Palestine, vol. 59, 9 October 1929.

101. Telegram, MAE, Direction des Affaires Politiques et Commerciales, Palestine, vol. 59, 16 October 1929.

102. *Le Progrès de Sidi-Bel-Abbès*, Tuesday 10 September 1929, p. 1.

103. *L'Écho d'Alger*, Friday 30 August 1929, p. 1

104. Laurens 2015.

105. MAE, Direction des Affaires Politiques et Commerciales, Palestine, vol. 59, 21 July 1930.

106. Nicault 2000.

107. CADN, Jerusalem 294 PO/2, 37/1, 9 March 1936.

108. CADN, Jerusalem 294 PO/2, 37/1, 14 March 1936.

109. "Arafat did live in this house for about three years, from 1933 to 1936, from the age four to seven." Rubinstein 1995: 21–23.

110. According to Azzam Abu Saud and other authors, Yasser Arafat is believed to have actually been born in this house, and not in Cairo, as notably asserted by Danny Rubinstein; but in the absence of an evidentiary document, the question remains open. Abu Saud 2004–5.

111. Abu Saud 2004–5.

Chapter 3: Protection and Imperial Ambition

1. CADN, Jerusalem, 294 PO/2, boxes 37 to 40.

2. It is significant that there are no decisive documents pertaining to the Waqf Abu Madyan or the Maghrebi Quarter during World War II, a suspended moment in the history of Jerusalem. On this point, see Lemire and Reichman 2017.

3. "Waqf Abou Mediene: Correspondance 1949–1954," CADN, Jerusalem 294 PO/2, box 37, folder 2, 17 June 1949.

4. Étienne 2012; Stora 1986.

5. Entry by Gilles Morin and Justinien Raymond accessed online at http://maitron -en-ligne.univ-paris1.fr/spip.php?article123669.

6. Rica 2005.

7. Büssow 2014.

8. Rey 2018.

9. CADN, Jerusalem 294 PO/2, 37/2, 17 June 1949.

10. Rota 2003:

In the night of 9 July [1948], renewed commotion, they are firing on the village [. . .]. At 2:00 a.m., more explosions. The Jews are dropping bombs and are occupying Yaqub Mountain which faces our house. During the day, a bomb falls on a little wall of our former chaplaincy [. . .]. Starting in early afternoon, renewed fighting grows fiercer. The cannon fire is relentless. It is then that the Transjordanian commander withdraws with his soldiers and abandons the mountain to the Jews [. . .]. The village is completely empty, all that remains are a few [Arab] volunteers who defend us at the top of the mountain [. . .]. In the evening of the 17th [. . .] the bombing sounds more intense than usual; bombs and grenades rain down [. . .]. [On 18 July] around 8:45 in the morning [. . .] we hear men's voices in our olive grove and they're not speaking Arabic. We don't have time to react emotionally, we leave through the gallery and find ourselves face-to-face with several men armed to the teeth. They had broken through the vineyard gate and onto our property. When they saw us, they asked where are the Arabs, the ammunition, the weapons. [. . .] An officer steps forward and declares proudly: "We have taken Ein Karem [. . .]. Don't be afraid, we will guard you better than the Arabs [. . .]." Starting on 18 July, the date of the occupation, St. Jean was entirely cut off from the surrounding villages.

11. Pappe 2000.

12. Morris 2003.

13. CADN, Jerusalem 294 PO/2, 37/2, 17 June 1949.

14. Sbaï 2018.

15. Schillo 2006.

16. Boyer 1949.

17. Perrot 1952; Neuville 1948.

18. CADN, Jerusalem 294 PO/2, 37/2, 6 July 1949.

19. Neuville 1934.

20. CADN, Jerusalem 294 PO/2, 37/2, 6 July 1949.

21. Schillo 2006.

22. Schillo 2006.

23. CADN, Jerusalem 294 PO/2, 37/2, 6 July 1949.

24. Sroor 2005a.

25. Sroor 2009.

26. CADN, Jerusalem 294 PO/2, 37/2, 6 July 1949.

27. Ulbert 2016.

28. See chapter 2 in this book ("11 July 1927: Earthquake in Jerusalem").

29. Kupferschmidt 1987; Reiter 1996.

30. CADN, Jerusalem 294 PO/2, 37/2, 6 July 1949.

31. CADN, Jerusalem 294 PO/2, 37/2, 6 July 1949.

32. Cited and translated in Tamari 1999: 262–77.

33. CADN, Jerusalem 294 PO/2, 37/2, 6 July 1949.

34. CADN, Jerusalem 294 PO/2, 37/2, 30 July 1949.

35. Letter cited in Scelles 1949: 12.

36. Letter cited in Scelles 1949: 12.

37. Bitan 2008.

38. CADN, Jerusalem 294 PO/2, 37/2, 26 September 1949.

39. CADN, Jerusalem 294 PO/2, 37/2, 26 September 1949.

40. CADN, Jerusalem 294 PO/2, 37/2, 11 November 1949.

41. Michel 2003.

42. Frémeaux 2004.

43. CADN, Jerusalem 294 PO/2, 37/2, 25 December 1949.

44. CADN, Jerusalem 294 PO/2, 37/2, 4 January 1950.

45. For example, in the dossier CADN, Jerusalem 294 PO/2, 37/2: on 11 February 1950, the club secretary Ahmed Madani complains (in Arabic) "that the North African colony was deprived of the distributions of blankets, coal, and flour carried out by the Red Cross after the heavy snowfall." On 25 October 1950, Hajj Ali Nakib points out (in Arabic) that "under the Mandate regime, our poor were paid something either from Social Affairs or from the waqfs; at present, nobody is taking care of them." On 16 November 1950, the same Hajj Ali Nakib writes (in Arabic): "We place in you and in your country all our hopes."

46. CADN, Jerusalem 294 PO/2, 37/2, 15 November 1949.

47. On the analysis of the key items of this dossier, see the prologue and chapter 1 of this book.

48. Penicaud 2020 and 2014. On the genealogy of Louis Massignon's anti-Zionism, see Lazar 2009. See also the new website https://louismassignon.fr.

49. Sbaï 2018.

50. Bibliothèque nationale de France, site Richelieu (hereafter BNF), Department of Manuscripts, collection NAF 28658. Thanks to Anne Verdure-Mary and to Thomas Cazentre for their help in my investigation.

51. Danino 2005.

52. BNF, collection NAF 28658, box 147.

53. Article published in the journal *Pax Christi* no. 9, 1949.

54. Scelles 1949. This article is striking for the number of phrases borrowed directly from the long letter sent by Neuville to Algiers on 6 July 1949, with a copy to Massignon. The circulation of ideas and writings among diplomats and intellectuals does indeed take place in both directions.

55. Massignon 1951: 73.

56. Massignon 1951: 75.

57. Massignon 1951: 76.

58. Goetschel, Lemire, and Potin 2018; Maurel 2010.

59. Louis Massignon to Geuthner Editions, 14 April 1952; BNF, collection NAF 28658, box 149.

60. CADN, Jerusalem 294 PO/2, 37/2, 8 November 1950.

61. CADN, Jerusalem 294 PO/2, 37/2, 4 May 1950.

62. "Egypt and Jordan: 15 December 1950–23 January 1951; Twelfth Annual Cultural Report," CADN, Jerusalem 294 PO/2, 37/2, 18 March 1951, 13 typed pages.

63. "Egypt and Jordan," p. 2.

64. "Egypt and Jordan," p. 8.

65. Blévis 2012.

66. "Egypt and Jordan," p. 11. Emphasis in original..

67. Reiner 2002; Rica 2010. A number of other authors also emphasize the synchronous connection between the Ottoman conquest of Jerusalem and the sanctuary status of the Western Wall. On this point see Vilnay 1973 ("Kotel ha-Maaravi: The Wailing Wall").

68. Albera, Marquette, and Pénicaud 2015. Regarding another case of late "etymological recovery," the toponym "ghetto," see Lemire 2001.

69. Massignon 1951: 84.

70. "Egypt and Jordan" p. 8.

71. "Egypt and Jordan," p. 8.

72. CADN, Jerusalem 294 PO/2, 37/2, 7 January 1951.

73. CADN, Jerusalem 294 PO/2, 37/2, 24 February 1951.

74. CADN, Jerusalem 294 PO/2, 37/2, 26 April 1951.

75. Laurens 1999–2015, vol. 3 ("End of Reign in Jordan").

76. Mbaye 2009.

77. Archives nationales d'Outre-Mer (National Overseas Archive), Aix-en-Provence (hereafter ANOM), box 81.F–844.

78. ANOM, 81.F–844, 25 April 1952.

79. ANOM, 81.F–844, 13 June 1952.

80. ANOM, 81.F–844, 17 June 1952.

81. "Algiers Press Roundup for 1st to 15 September 1952," ANOM, 81.F–844.

82. BNF Department of Manuscripts, collection NAF 28658, box 149, 28 May 1952.

83. ANOM, 81.F–844, 30 August 1952.

84. ANOM, 81.F–844, 2 October 1952.

85. ANOM, 81.F–844, 22 October 1952.

86. ANOM, 81.F–844, 21 October 1952 (unsigned handwritten note).

87. Archives de l'Archevêché d'Alger (Archdiocese of Algiers), serial no. E.216 ("Muslims and Christians"), 8 April 1952. Thanks to Andrew Bellisari for this input.

88. CADN, Jerusalem 294 PO/2, 37/2, 15 October 1952.

89. Madame Jeanne Scelles-Millie, "Trip to North Africa and to Paris by Sheikh Hidoussi Hajj Ali Steward of the Waqf Abu Madyan of Jerusalem," CADN, Jerusalem 294 PO/2, 37/2, 30 October 1952, 18 typed pages.

90. Scelles-Millie, "Trip to North Africa and to Paris," p. 10.

91. "Le Habous d'Abou Mediene en danger" (The Abu Madyan Habous in Danger), *Es Saada*, 23 August 1952.

92. ANOM, 81.F–844, 5 November 1952.

93. ANOM, 81.F–844, 5 November 1952.

94. Maghrebis residing outside Jerusalem are documented several times in the French consular archives. For instance, on 15 September 1951, a certain Khaïr Saïd, "head of the Committee in Charge of French North Africans in Bethlehem and Hebron," had written to the French consul in Jerusalem suggesting that he extend his protection to all the Maghrebi communities of Palestine:

> Would His Excellency consent to send a committee, one from Bethlehem and Hebron, one from Jerusalem and Nablus, one from Amman, one from Damascus, and one from Beirut? This committee is composed of Morrocans, Tunisians, and Algerians to visit France and North Africa, so that they might take pity on their brothers who are in a situation of real destitution and are in need of assistance. This committee must come under French authority [. . .]. I think this idea will prove very useful and important to show the foreign people France's love for the North African people.

CADN, Jerusalem 294 PO/2, 37/2, 15 September 1951.

95. ANOM, 81.F–844, 6 January 1953.

96. CADN, Jerusalem 294 PO/2, 37/2, 23 April 1952.

97. CADN, Jerusalem 294 PO/2, 37/2, 10 November 1952.

98. CADN, Jerusalem 294 PO/2, 37/2, 5 November 1952.

99. "WAM Financial Needs and Morrocan, Tunisian, and Algerian Subsidies 1953–1955," CADN, Jerusalem 294 PO/2, 37/2,

100. ANOM, 81.F–844, 3 October 1953.

101. ANOM, 81.F–844, 3 October 1953.

102. "India, Egypt, and Jordan: 3 January 1953–28 January 1953; Fourteenth Annual Cultural Report," CADN, Jerusalem 294 PO/2, 37/2, 5 March 1953, p. 7.

103. "Hajj Ali Nakib c'est ne pas bon pour peuple de nord africain, par exemple un homme malade il donne pas rien et il ne aide pas, il reste. Et il ne visite pas, parce qu'il Hajj Ali maintenant comme un Lord [. . .] parce qu'il la fête il bien vole." CADN, Jerusalem 294 PO/2, 37/2, 11 August 1953.

104. CADN, Jerusalem 294 PO/2, 37/2, 13 August 1953.

105. CADN, Jerusalem 294 PO/2, 37/2, 9 May 1953.

106. ANOM, 81.F–844, 23 September 1953.

107. ANOM, 81.F–844, 23 September 1953.

108. "Visit to the Waqf Abu Madyn," ANOM, 81.F–844, 26 October 1953, 4 typed pages.

109. ANOM, 81.F–844, 26 October 1953, p. 3.

110. ANOM, 81.F–844, 26 October 1953, p. 4.

111. ANOM, 81.F–844, 21 December 1953.

112. "1954: Visit to M. Kirèche, called Dejdou," CADN, Jerusalem 294 PO/2, 37/3, 11 June 1954.

113. CADN, Jerusalem 294 PO/2, 37/3, 17 June 1954.

114. CADN, Jerusalem 294 PO/2, 37/3, 17 June 1954 (handwritten note).

115. ANOM, 81.F–844, 18 May 1954.

116. BNF, collection NAF 28658, box 149.

117. "Report of Mission Carried Out in Palestine from 24 to 29 August 1954," ANOM, 81.F–844, 29 November 1954, 13 typed pages), citations pp. 2–4.

118. ANOM, 81.F–844, 29 November 1954, p. 4.

119. ANOM, 81.F–844, 29 November 1954, p. 5.

120. ANOM, 81.F–844, 29 November 1954, p. 7.

121. ANOM, 81.F–844, 29 November 1954, p. 8.

122. "Egypt and Hachemite Jordan: 21 December 1954–15 February 1955; Fifteenth Annual Cultural Report," CADN, Jerusalem 294 PO/2, 37/2, 5 March 1955, 9 typed pages, citation p. 6.

Chapter 4: Colonial Contradictions and Geopolitical Upheaval

1. Thénault 2005.

2. Rivet 2002.

3. Ferro 2006.

4. Deluermoz and Singaravelou 2012.

5. CADN, Jerusalem 294 PO/2, 37, n.d. (July 1957).

6. CADN, Jerusalem 294 PO/2, 37/2, 23 June 1954.

7. CADN, Jerusalem 294 PO/2, 37/2, 26 April 1954.

8. CADN, Jerusalem 294 PO/2, 37/2, 10 January 1955.

9. CADN, Jerusalem 294 PO/2, 38, 26 March 1956.

10. ANOM, 81.F–844, 9 May 1955.

11. ANOM, 81.F–844, 9 May 1955.

12. See chapter 1 in this book. It seems that Mr. Pierrestiger is relying on the skills of attorney Hassan Budeiri, as evidenced by the letter Budeiri addressed to the consulate on 10 May 1953: "With reference to your letter no. 213 of the sixth of this month, relating to the Waqf Abu Madyan documents, I requested from the Sharia Tribunal of Jerusalem three copies of each of the solicited documents [. . .]. As for the documents relating to the properties in Ramleh and Lydda, I doubt that they were registered in Jerusalem."

13. CADN, Jerusalem 294 PO/2, 38, 4 February 1953 / 20 August 1953.

14. See the obituary: "Anwar Nuseibeh, 74: Palestinian Moderate." *New York Times*, 24 November 1986, p. 14.

15. ANOM, 81.F–844, 9 May 1955.

16. ANOM, 81.F–844, 9 May 1955.

17. ANOM, 81.F–844, 27 December 1955.

18. Reiter 1997.

19. Reiter 1997.

20. ANOM, 81.F–844, 20 January 1956.

21. ANOM, 81.F–844, 10 February 1956.

22. ANOM, 81.F–844, 24 February 1956.

23. ANOM, 81.F–844, 23 April 1956.

24. ANOM, 81.F–844, 18 March 1956. Qadi Benhoura was one of the eminent notable figures of so-called "moderate" Muslim Algeria. He lived in Paris and consented to head the final mission of the Waqf Abu Madyan in Jerusalem in 1957.

25. ANOM, 81.F–844, 14 March 1956.

26. ANOM, 81.F–844, 15 March 1956. On the positioning of the Algerian ulemas in the context of the war, see Courreyre 2020, chapter 3 ("L'Association des oulémas dans la guerre d'indépendance: Engagements individuels, prudence collective").

27. ANOM, 81.F–844, 10 April 1957. Note that the annual indemnity on offer effectively corresponds to a (rather generous) conversion of the 417 Palestinian pounds of the Mandate period, since a Palestinian pound was then worth 1,000 francs.

28. ANOM, 81.F–844, 10 April 1957.

29. ANOM, 81.F–844, 25 January 1956.

30. BNF, collection NAF 28658, box 149, 21 March 1955.

31. "Report for Mission Carried Out in Palestine from 5 to 12 August 1955 by Mr.≈Lunis Mahfud," CADN, Jerusalem 294 PO/2, box 40, 18 August 1955, 10 typed pages.

32. "Report for Mission," pp. 2–3.

33. "Report for Mission," appendix 1 ("Expenses").

34. "Report for Mission," appendix 2 ("Translation of an Undated Petition").

35. "Financial Needs of the Waqf Abu Madyan and Moroccan, Tunisian, and Algerian Subsidies," CADN, Jerusalem 294 PO/2, 37/2, n.d. (summer 1954).

36. Lemire 2010: 31–56 ("Géographie hydraulique, géographie historique ").

37. IRHRI, dossier no. 45/2/1.19/47/13 (1947).

38. ANOM, 81.F–844, 4 August 1956.

39. ANOM, 81.F—844, notice de renseignement jointe au courrier du 4 août 1956 (information insert attached to letter of 4 August 1956).

40. "Mission Report, Palestine July-August 1956," ANOM, 81.F–844, 18 August 1956, 15 typed pages, citation p. 12.

41. "Mission Report, Palestine July-August 1956," p. 6.

42. "Mission Report, Palestine July-August 1956," p. 12.

43. "Mission Report, Palestine July-August 1956," p. 7.

44. "Mission Report, Palestine July-August 1956," p. 14.

45. Destremeau and Moncelon 2011: 153 ("L'assassinat de Lounis Mahfoud"); Borrmans and De Perett 2014.

46. Laurens 1999–2015, vol. 3: 453–510 ("Suez").

47. Laurens 1999–2015, vol. 3: 527–29 ("Les leçons de la crise de Suez").

48. See chapter 2 in this book.

49. CADN, Jerusalem 294 PO/2, box 40, folder no. 2, 14 July 1956.

50. CADN, Jerusalem 294 PO/2, 40/2, 6 September 1956.

51. ANOM, 81.F–843 ("Pilgrimages 1961"; "Pilgrimages 1962").

52. ANOM, 81.F–843, n.d. ("Pilgrimages 1961").

53. IRHRI, box 983, dossier no. 45/4/12,5/46/13, 18 May 1956.

54. Translation in ANOM, 81.F–844, 3 November 1958 (note from the SDECE).

55. CADN, Jerusalem 294 PO/2, box 40, folder no. 1.

56. ANOM, 81.F–844, 3 November 1958.

57. CADN, Jerusalem 294 PO/2, 40/3, 12 September 1958.

58. Renard 2004.

59. "Mission to Jerusalem: Visit to Waqf Abu Madyan and the North African Colony by Cadi Benhoura," CADN, Jerusalem 294 PO/2, 37/3, 23 September 1957, 42 typed pages, citation p. 4.

60. "Mission to Jerusalem," p. 4.

61. "Mission to Jerusalem," p. 6.

62. "Mission to Jerusalem," p. 10.

63. "Mission to Jerusalem," p. 10.

64. "Mission to Jerusalem," pp. 18–19.

65. "Mission to Jerusalem," pp. 19–20.

66. "Mission to Jerusalem," p. 32.

67. "Mission to Jerusalem," p. 33.

68. "Mission to Jerusalem," pp. 26–27.

69. "Mission to Jerusalem," p. 36.

70. "Mission to Jerusalem," p. 40.

71. ANOM, 81.F–844, 26 January 1959.

72. ANOM, 81.F–844, 15 May 1959.

73. BNF, collection NAF 28658, box 149, 31 March 1957.

74. BNF, collection NAF 28658, box 149, 12 October 1957.

75. "Egypt, Lebanon, Jordan, Syria: 7 January–17 February 1959; Eighteenth Annual Cultural Report," BNF, collection NAF 28658, box 149, February 1959, 21 typed pages, citation p. 12.

76. By late April 1956, the French consul general in Jerusalem had already identified certain press campaigns directed against Hajj Lunis Mahfud as being remote-controlled by the Jordanian authorities, who were thought to be manipulating for this purpose certain Moroccan and Tunisian inhabitants of the Maghrebi Quarter: "The short piece in the newspaper, addressed to Mr. Lunis Mahfud, comes from one of the chief instigators of the trial: Abdul Mukhtar, a rather dim-witted Moroccan who is doing the bidding of El Tunsi, a notorious crook convicted many times in criminal court, who is seeking to utilize the trial to blackmail the mutewalli." ANOM 81F/844, 28 April 1956.

77. Destremeau and Moncelon 2011.

78. ANOM, 81.F–844, 18 August 1959.

79. ANOM, 81.F–844, 18 August 1959.

80. ANOM, 81.F–844, 14 June 1959.

81. ANOM, 81.F–844, 18 August 1959.

82. ANOM, 81.F–844, 14 June 1959.

83. See his biographical notice at https://www.ccomptes.fr/fr/biographies/mafart -michel-jean.

84. ANOM, 81.F–844, 6 November 1959.

85. Audigier 2010.

86. *Ha-Herut*, 29 January 1961, p. 3, refers to an appeal before the Supreme Court regarding "122 lots" located in Ein Karem. An earlier article, again in *Ha-Herut* (7 November 1960), points to proceedings before the "Tribunal of the District of Jerusalem" in the sectors of Ein Karem and Kiryat Yovel.

87. Stoler 2009.

88. ANOM, 81.F–844, 9 February 1961.

89. ANOM, 81.F–844, 9 February 1961.

90. ANOM, 81.F–844, 4 May 1961.

91. ANOM, 81.F–844, 19 May 1961.

92. ANOM, 81.F–844, 10 July 1961.

93. ANOM, 81.F–844, 1 August 1961.

94. ANOM, 81.F–844, 12 February 1962.

95. Dewerpe 2006.

96. ANOM, 81.F–844, 6 November 1962.

97. "Israel Backs Paris Request on Wakf," *Ha-Herut*, 2 November 1962.

98. *Haaretz*, 4 November 1962.

99. Liskenne 2015.

100. ANOM, 81.F–844, 12 December 1962.

101. ANOM, 81.F–844, 18 December 1962.

102. ANOM, 81.F–844, 4 January 1963.

103. ANOM, 81.F–844, 17 January 1963.

104. CADN, Jerusalem 294 PO/2, box 39.

Chapter 5: Expel and Demolish

1. Glueck 1968: 12–13:

On Tuesday, June 13, 1967, Bill Dever, Ezra Spicehandler and I had walked to the Western Wall, which was opened up to the general public on Wednesday, June 14, 1967, when some approximately 200,000 people pilgrimaged to it in celebration of Shavuot. The entrance for them was through the Dung Gate, with police letting several hundred people at a time move forward, before compelling them to move on. The police had the entire pilgrimage beautifully controlled, according to the newspaper, and from what I have heard from people who participated in the mass pilgrimage.

2. On this notion of an event "evading" the archive, see Stoler 2009.

3. Gilli and Guilhembet 2012.

4. Meron Benvenisti died on 20 September 2020. See Ian Black, "Meron Benvenisti Obituary," *Guardian*, 30 September 2020.

5. Islamic Research and Heritage Revival Institute, Abu-Dis (hereafter IRHRI), call no. 0/1959/1.19/2.

6. Lemire 2010: 167–200, chapter 3: "Les citernes et l'eau du ciel."

7. "Scènes et mœurs palestiniennes: Puits et citernes en Palestine." *Jérusalem* 101 (November 1912) : 241–49: "Chaque maison, le plus souvent, a sa citerne; dans les villes et les villages, il y a en outre des citernes publiques. Il arrive fréquemment que, dans les explorations bibliques, quand on recherche l'emplacement d'une ville anéantie, les citernes subsistantes soient les plus fidèles indices." (Most of the time, each house has its cistern; in towns and villages, there are also public cisterns. It frequently happens during biblical excavations, when we are looking for the location of an obliterated city, that the surviving cisterns prove the most faithful clues.)

8. This list is reproduced in its entirety in al-Jubeh 2019a: 194–99.

9. According to the testimony of Ameen Qawasmi, born in 1961 in the Maghrebi Quarter into a family of six children, certain bedrooms were accessible via an interior courtyard. Video excerpt at http://www.mughrabiquarter.info/.

10. There is report footage from 10 January 1964 (15:09 in duration) devoted to Paul VI's visit to the INA site in Jerusalem: https://www.ina.fr/video/CAF89015656/. All speeches delivered by Paul VI during his pilgrimage are searchable online at the Vatican site: http://w2.vatican.va/content/paul-vi/fr/travels/documents/terrasanta.html.

11. Bernard Rouget, "Connaissance du monde," January 1960 (Gaumont Pathé Archives).

12. Correspondence received from Muhammad Ibrahim Abdelhaq and Issa Hashem al-Moghrabi to his Majesty Hassan II, 28 January 1975. Head of Royal Archives, Rabat, Registry of Royal Correspondence. For detailed analysis of this letter, see chapter 6 in this book. Thanks to Bahija Simou, director of Royal Archives, for her input.

13. Warm thanks to Adel Budeiri for his trust and his help. On the Budeiri family, see the article "Budeiri Family" in Mattar 2000: 82.

14. According to Mahmoud al-Maslouhi's testimony, it was this school that was demolished first in June 1967, at the same time as the police station and a shop "belonging to Abdul Fattah." Video clip http://www.mughrabiquarter.info/.

15. The law that launches and regulates the Dome of the Rock renovation project dates to December 1954. *Official Gazette of the Hashemite Kingdom of Jordan* 1205 (16 December 1954): 911.

16. Katz 2005.

17. Dumper 1997: 33; Rubinstein 1980.

18. Katz 2003.

19. Laurens 1999–2015, Vol. 3: 635–37.

20. Abu Saud 2004–5.

21. Katz 2003: 227.

22. Wallach 2020.

23. Kendall 1948.

24. Henry Kendall, *Jerusalem Jordan Regional Planning Proposals*, October 1965.

25. Kendall, *Jerusalem Jordan*, plate 10 ("Gardens and Vistas"), proposals 2 and 10.

26. Kendall, *Jerusalem Jordan*, plate 8 ("Streets and Parking"), proposal 6. This parking lot project was made possible by an enlarging of the passage under the Maghrebi Gate, an enlargement achieved in 1953, according to Jean-Michel de Tarragon, "The Five Modifications of Dung-Gate: Bāb Harat al-Magharibah in Jerusalem," *Jerusalem Quarterly*, forthcoming. In this same article, Jean-Michel de Tarragon shows that the Maghrebi Gate was flanked by an outer tower until the late 1930s.

27. Kendall, *Jerusalem Jordan*, plates 13–26 ("Specific Projects with Generalized Locations"), proposal 49.

28. The archives of the Jordanian municipality of Jerusalem (1948–67) are currently undergoing a process of proofing, indexing, and translation, headed by Haneen Naamneh under the Archival-City Project, to be uploaded to the website www.open-jerusalem.org.

29. Ricca 2007: 22 and 52; Abowd 2000. Abowd's article (p. 9) is based on an interview he conducted with a former mukhtar of the Maghrebi Quarter, Muhammad Abdelhaq, on 26 September 1999.

30. CADN, Jerusalem 294 PO/2, box 29, 29 December 1966.

31. CADN, Jerusalem 294 PO/2, box 48, 6 February 1963.

32. CADN, Jerusalem 294 PO/2, box 59, 17 December 1964.

33. "Mayor Khatib Outlines Projects for the Holy City in 1967," *Jerusalem Star*, 28 December 1966.

34. Correspondence with the author, March 2017.

35. Stinespring 1966.

36. Stinespring 1967.

37. Louis and Shlaim 2012.

38. Segev 2007a.

39. CADN, Jerusalem 294 PO/2, box 48, 10 August 1965. On the sacralization process of Jewish holy places in Jerusalem after 1948, see Bar 2010. See also Dieckhoff 1987: 128–32 ("Organiser l'espace sacré").

40. CADN, Jerusalem 294 PO/2, box 48, 6 October 1966.

41. Rokem 2012: http://journals.openedition.org/bcrfj/6895.

42. Dumper 1997: 97.

43. CADN, Jerusalem 294 PO/3, box 59, 10 November 1966.

44. CADN, Jerusalem 294 PO/3, box 59, 13 November 1966.

45. CADN, Jerusalem 294 PO/3, box 59, 10 June 1973.

46. Laurens 1999–2015, vol. 3: 697–728 ("La crise ultime").

47. CADN, Jerusalem 294 PO/3, box 59, box 21, 31 May 1967.

48. CADN, Jerusalem 294 PO/3, box 59, box 21, 27 May 1967.

49. CADN, Jerusalem 294 PO/3, box 59, box 21, 2 June 1967.

50. Segev 2007a: 409–14.

51. Caron 2012.

52. Poivert 2013.

53. Mariana Otero, *Histoire d'un regard*. Production Archipel 33, 2019.

54. Poivert, Bachelot, and Cohn-Bendit 2018.

55. The exhibit "Gilles Caron: Inner Gaze" (Mishkan Museum of Art, Ein Herod, June-September 2017) also presented a few previously unreleased photographs taken by Gilles Caron during the Six-Day War.

56. "Gilles Caron: Inner Gaze."

57. "Gilles Caron: Inner Gaze."

58. Uzi Narkiss gives a detailed account of the scene in Narkis 1978: 328–29, indicating that he arrived at the Western Wall at 2:00 p.m.

59. Narkis 1978: 328–29.

60. Narkis 1978: 328–29.

61. Narkis 1978: 328–29.

62. Testimony of Arie Avidor, former Israeli ambassador to France, mobilized in the Sinai during the Six-Day War; telephone interview on 18 December 2018.

63. *Paris Match* 949 (17 June 1967) devotes 18 pages to Gilles Caron's coverage.

64. This visit would inspire Enrico Macias to write the song "Noël à Jérusalem," produced in 1968: "Noël à Jérusalem, près d'un mur que l'on croyait perdu […]. Noël à Jérusalem, près d'un mur que l'on a retrouvé." (Christmas in Jerusalem by a wall we thought we'd lost […] Christmas in Jerusalem, by a wall regained.)

65. Poivert 2013.

66. Poivert 2013.

67. The photograph was published in *L'histoire* 436 (June 2017): 39.

68. *Arab World* 8 (November-December 1967): 11. Thanks to Gadi Algazi for sending me this document.

69. *Arab World* 8 (November-December 1967): 9.

70. "Western Wall Area Cleared," *Jerusalem Post*, 12 June 1969, p. 4.

71. "Western Wall Are Cleared," p. 4. The anecdote of Baron de Rothschild's visit is also mentioned in Gilbert 1996: 294–95.

72. Eliezer Zhurabin, a former member of the terrorist group Lehi, according to an article by Aluf Been in *Haaretz*, 1 July 2012.

73. *Jerusalem Post*, 12 June 1967, p. 4. See the article "Chavouot" in Wigoder 1993: 217–20.

74. INA-ORTF Archives, call no. PHD94044239, "Inter Actualités de 13 heures" (the 1 p.m. news on radio France-Inter), 14 June 1967. Thanks to Valérie Nivelon at Radio France Internationale for bringing this to my attention and sending the document along.

75. Certain excerpts from *Inter Actualités* news were used in the program *La Marche du Monde* on 10 June 2017 (producer Valérie Nivelon): http://www.rfi.fr /emission/20171209-israel-jerusalem-1967-secret-esplanade-mur-guerre-six-jours-khalidi -lemire.

76. On the ideological context of France at the time of the Six-Day War, see Charbit 2009; Coulon 2009.

77. The context of urban planning in the 1960s is undoubtedly a further factor explaining the media's indifference, since during the same period, the old urban cores of several large European agglomerations were undergoing large urban renewal and renovation projects, which were often destructive (Les Halles in Paris, the City of London, the Meriadeck neighborhood in Bordeaux, the cathedral neighborhood in Rouen), to "decongest" the cities, but also to clear the plazas in front of certain patrimonial monuments, such as cathedrals, train stations, and theaters. On this point, see Burgel 2012.

78. *Haaretz*, 21 June 1967, p. 4.

79. *Davar*, 23 June 1967.

80. *Davar*, 19 July 1967, p. 6.

81. Notably, a four-page feature on different architects' projects for developing the new plaza. *Davar*, 29 September 1967, p. 27–30.

82. *Haaretz*, 21 July 1967.

83. Interview conducted in Jerusalem on 1 June 2017.

84. Interview conducted in Jerusalem on 1 June 2017.

85. Dakkak 2000. This testimony is corroborated by that of Ahmad Al-Jareedi, an inhabitant of the Maghrebi Quarter of Tunisian origin: "I remember that the Israelis had buses at the Damascus Gate for those who wanted to leave via the bridge that led to Amman. The Israelis were giving out chocolate to those who got on the bus." Testimony accessed at https://vimeo.com/395176943/. Ahmad Al-Jareedi also recounts his memories of the demolition:

> On Saturday, after everyone had gone to bed, I opened the window, and I felt the ground shake, I thought it was an earthquake. My neighbor Abu Ahmad told me, 'No, the Israelis are in the process of tearing down the quarter.' At dawn, we could see all the houses destroyed [. . .]. We had three daughters, Haya, Mona, and Fayrouz, who was just a baby. As we were leaving, my wife asked me where Fayrouz was, and I told her, 'I thought you took her with you.' I went back. I had also forgotten some Jordanian dinars in a cupboard. But an Israeli soldier told me it was forbidden to go back. I told him that there was an infant in the house, so he said OK, go ahead, but don't take anything else. I got Fayrouz out before the house was demolished.

86. Interview conducted in Jerusalem on 31 May 2017.

87. Interview conducted in Jerusalem on 31 May 2017.

88. Interview conducted in Jerusalem on 31 May 2017.

89. Elad Assoulin and Anat Ronko, "The Maghrebi Quarter," 2013 (7:42), accessed at https://vimeo.com/85663970.

90. Interview conducted in Jerusalem on 1 June 2017.

91. Certain of these witnesses were filmed as part of the project www.mughrabi-quarter.info, which makes available for streaming twelve excerpts from interviews conducted with former inhabitants of the quarter: Mahmoud Maslouhi (6:53), Nawal Qasem al-Daraji al-Maslouhi (2:04), Aisha al-Maslouhi (4:02), Mohammed Abed Jalil al-Maloudi (1:51), Fuad Hashem Ahmad Zughayer (5:57), Bassima Zughayer (4:14), Ameen Qawasmi (3:26), Issa Issa Qawasmi (2:24), Nazmi al-Jubeh (8:51), Ahmad Ibn Abdullah al-Jareedi, Maher Abu-Mayyale (1:31), and Isshaq Awaida (3:56).

92. Interview conducted in Jerusalem on 15 February 2018.

93. All the witnesses recall Hajjah Rasmiyyah Ali Tabakhi, the elderly widow who died beneath the rubble of her house. Her name is cited by numerous authors, including Uzi Benzian, the journalist who covered the events for *Haaretz*, in Benziman 1973: 37.

94. Interview conducted in Jerusalem on 15 February 2018.

95. At this writing, a copy of this album is in the library of the Ben-Zvi Institute in Jerusalem, call no. E.114.2/6510.

96. Lea Majaro Mintz, born in 1926 in the Jewish Quarter of old Jerusalem, settled back there after the Six-Day War. Biographical notice accessed at https://museum.imj .org.il/artcenter/newsite/en/.

97. Nir Hasson, "How a Small Group of Israelis Made the Western Wall Jewish Again," *Haaretz*, 31 May 2017. Hasson presents Baruch Barkai as a former member of the Lehi-Stern group.

98. Itamar Ben-Avi, *Shema Yisrael, ha-Kotel Kotlenu, ha-Kotel Ehad* (Jerusalem: Refa'el Hayim ha-Cohen Print House, 1967–68).

99. The information is repeated by Nir Hasson in his article "How a Small Group of Israelis Made the Western Wall Jewish Again," *Haaretz*, 31 May 2017.

100. Eitan Ben Moshe, *Yorshalim*, 26 November 1999 (quoted in Abowd 2000).

101. Ben Moshe, *Yorshalim*.

102. Abraham Rabinovich, "Benvenisti: Kollek's Right-Hand Man Steps Down," *Jerusalem Post Magazine*, 3 March 1972, p. 5. Meron Benvenisti died on 20 September 2020. See Ian Black, "Meron Benvenisti Obituary," *Guardian*, 30 September 2020.

103. Benvenisti 1996.

104. Benvenisti 1976: 307.

105. As part of the Open Jerusalem project, I was authorized by Meron Benvenisti to consult his archives deposited at the Ben-Zvi Institute, not yet sorted or cataloged.

106. Abdul-Hadi 2007, vol, 2: 184; Al-Khatib 1972: 48 (appendix 3, "Décret de dissolution du Conseil Municipal de Jérusalem, 29 juin 1967"); Morzellec 1979: 530. During these three weeks, Meron Benvenisti was working under the joint authority of Mayor Teddy Kollek and the military governor of Jerusalem, Shlomo Lahat, who would serve as mayor of Tel Aviv between 1974 and 1993).

107. These raw data contained in the Meron Benvenisti archives correspond to certain testimonies from that time, notably that of Sister Marie-Thérèse, a nurse at Sainte-Anne and at Lithostrotos during the fighting, published in "Le journal de soeur Marie-Thérèse: La guerre que j'ai vécu à Jérusalem," *Témoignage chrétien* 1203 (Thursday 27 July 1967): 13–20:

> Dozens of people whose houses had just collapsed were fleeing into the streets, screaming.
>
> With the father guiding him, all they could do was witness that the mother and five younger children had been crushed or blown apart by a bomb.
>
> A horrible smell was coming from who knows where; I opened a door and recoiled, horrified: a mountain of corpses. I closed the door and waited on the threshold. I kept repeating to the Jewish soldiers: "This is a hospital here."
>
> The Indian hospice near Herod's Gate. It's the inn for Muslim pilgrims

from Pakistan. Bombs ripped through the low part of the hospice and set it on fire. In three vaulted rooms were lying a dozen seriously injured persons, burnt in an odd way, bellies slashed open, arms torn off. It was horrendous. There were too few of us to take them all at once. We had to make several trips, carrying the wounded on metallic bedframes through the alleyways.

There are two dead in front of the door, one of whom is naked, his clothing burnt, the body opened up. We take one of the wounded.

We rush to the hospital to bury the dead that are piling up at the entrance, but we don't have a vehicle [. . .]. So, one by one, we carry them away. We have to be very careful because their limbs were falling off. For me, along with three nurses, I carried once again in the green cart the mother and the five children [. . .]. We entered the Muslim cemetery where a man was burying his wife and his daughter. We went over to the mass grave amidst a pestilential stench. I passed one of the babies whose head opened up. My dress was drenched in blood.

108. Ben-Zvi Institute, Benvenisti Archives, handwritten note, n.d.

109. Ben-Zvi Institute, Benvenisti Archives, typescript, 24 June 1967.

110. "Discussion at Meeting with Mayor Teddy Kollek at the Jerusalem Municipality Office, Sunday, August 27, 1967, 10:00 to 12:00 a.m." Ben-Zvi Institute, Benvenisti Archives, typescript, p. 7.

111. Historical Archives of the Jerusalem Municipality (hereafter HAJM), box 1210, dossier call no. 2/22/6.

112. Segev 2007a: 401.

113. HAJM, box 1210, dossier call no. 2/22/6, 9 June 1967.

114. HAJM, box 1210, dossier call no. 2/22/6, 9 June 1967.

115. Narkiss 1978. Narkiss openly expresses this spirit of revenge: "In 1965, General Yitzhak Rabin, Chief of Staff, appointed me commander of the central region. During the two years that followed, I devoted all my time and thought to that misshapen border that cut the city in two, and that I hoped with all my heart to see disappear" (pp. 18–19).

116. HAJM, box 1210, dossier call no. 2/22/6, 9 June 1967.

117. HAJM, box 1210, dossier call no. 2/22/6, 9 June 1967.

118. Israel State Archives (hereafter ISA), GL-3847/4, National Park Authority, p. 116, 10 June 1967. There is also a reproduction of this map in Nitzan-Shiftan and Silkof 2017: 172.

119. Thanks to Lilach Assaf and to Fadi Algazi for identifying the five signatures. We can also refer to Nitzan-Shiftan and Wilkof 2017.

120. Arieh Sharon was notably the architect of the "Hall of Remembrance" at the Yad Vashem, inaugurated in 1961; of the headquarters of the central bank of Israel, inaugurated in 1965; of the headquarters of the Jewish Agency in Tel Aviv, inaugurated

in 1965; of the Israeli pavilion at Expo 67 in Montreal; of the Ben-Gurion Institute and Archives at Sde-Boker, inaugurated in 1969; and of the cable car at Massada, inaugurated in 1971.

121. Sharon 1973. See https://www.ariehsharon.org/PlanningJerusalem.

122. Avi-Yonah and Stern 1976–79; Yuval Baruch and Rachel Kudish Vashdi, "From the Israel Department of Antiquities to the Founding of the Israel Antiquities Authority," accessed at http://www.antiquities.org.il/article_eng.aspx?sec_id=38&subj_id=154.

123. Turner 1984; Rica 2007: 148.

124. Rica 2007: 88.

125. Yannai and Pearlman 1964; Friling and Peschanski 2012: 367; Ohana 2017: 172.

126. Kedar, Weksler-Bdolah, and Da'adli 2012.

127. Shiller and Yaffe 2007.

128. Bahat 2016–17.

129. Research conducted in January 2018 by Lilach Assaf in the Israeli military archives located on the Tel-Hashomer base.

130. Uzi Narkiss would assume his share of responsibility in what he called the "clearing" of the plaza in the memoir he would publish ten years later: "J'ai autorisé le nettoyage de l'esplanade devant le Mur pour que des milliers de personnes s'y rendent et puissent y trouver de la place, lors de la fête de la Pentecôte." (I authorized the clearing of the plaza in front of the Wall so that thousands of people could go there and find enough room during the feast of Shavuot.) Narkiss 1978: 341.

131. Kollek, T. and Kollek A. 1978: 197, cited in Hiltermann 1993:

> Something had to be done about the small slum houses that crowded close to the Western Wall, the Moghrabi quarter. The one area that should have been spacious and bright was cramped and dark [. . .]. When we decided to allow the first pilgrimage in 19 years [. . .] we expected hundreds of thousands of people to take part [. . .]. But how would these hundreds of thousands of people reach the Wall through the dangerous, narrow alleyways? The only answer was to do away with the slim hovels of the Moghrabi quarter [. . .]. My overpowering feeling was: do it now, it may be impossible to do it later and it must be done [. . .]. Then the archaeologists and other experts went to the Wall and drew a map of exactly what should be torn down.

Anne-Marie Goichon, in Goichon 1976, publishes a photograph of Kollek taking Simone de Beauvoir to visit the plaza. Also noteworthy is a thank-you note from Kollek to the contractor Zalman Broshi, dated 31 July 1967—written on ordinary paper, not municipality stationery—in which Kollek stresses the "pro bono" nature of the operation: "Thank you for volunteering to enlarge the Kotel and for how efficiently and quickly you accomplished this voluntary and unpaid work. Our reward, for all of us, will be the restoration of the glory of Jerusalem." HAJM, box 2059, dossier 10, document 45, cited in O'Neil 2019: note 26.

132. Benziman 1973: 37. In 1980, Benziman's account was translated into English and published, with a few changes, in Tibawi 1980.

133. The photograph is inserted in the gallery devoted to Micha Bar-Am's reporting during the Six-Day War, at the Agence Magnum site: https://pro.magnumphotos.com /Catalogue/Micha-Bar-Am/1967/ISRAEL-The-Six-Day-War-1967-NN140460.html.

134. Morris 1988; Pappe 2006.

135. In his journal, for the date of 8 June, David Ben-Gurion speaks of the great emotion he felt upon visiting the Western Wall, dwells upon the means for "consolidating" the conquest of Jerusalem and Hebron, and refers explicitly to the need for an intensive demographic colonization, but makes no mention of the whole issue of the Maghrebi Quarter; https://bengurionarchive.bgu.ac.il/en/.

136. ISA, minutes of the government meeting of 11 June 1967, accessed at https:// www.archives.gov.il/archives/Archive/0b0717068031be30/File/0b07170680348bd6 /Item/0907170680348cfe. Document cited in Marius Schattner and Frédérique Schillo, *Sous tes pierres Jérusalem, ou les ruses de l'archéologie* (Paris: Plon, forthcoming).

137. ISA, HZ–4089/14, Foreign Ministry, 9 June 1967.

138. Laskier 2001.

139. "Israeli Diplomat is a Woman," Jewish Telegraphic Agency 183 (21 September 1979): 3. A few months before being appointed ambassador to UNESCO, Yael Vered would be mobilized to defend the Israeli position targeted by the UNESCO resolution regarding the excavations underway at the Maghrebi Gate. UNESCO, Executive Board, 107th Session, "Jérusalem et l'application de la résolution 20 C/4/7.6/13."

140. ISA, HZ–4089/14, Foreign Ministry, 9 June 1967.

141. ISA, HZ–4089/14, Foreign Ministry, 9 June 1967.

142. Abdul-Hadi 2007, vol. 4:171.

143. HAJM, carton 4960–5994, binder 5994/4, 26 September 1967.

144. ISA, P.4793–9, Cabinet of the Prime Minister, from Teddy Kollek to Levi Eshkol, 26 September 1967.

145. ISA, P.4793–9, Ministry of Finance, from D. Kanterovitz (Department of the Budget) to Aharon Bidan (Cabinet of the Prime Minister), ref. 20/1/11/1, 27 February 1968.

Chapter 6: After the Catastrophe

1. All the documents identified within the Royal Archives of Rabat were shared with me on-site by archive director Ms. Bahija Simou, to whom I extend my warm gratitude.

2. A biography of the former mayor of Jerusalem was recently published in Amman: Ra'ûf Abû Jâber, *Sîrât hayâ wa sijil injâz: Muhammad Rûhî Al Khatîb* (Amman: self-published), 2006.

3. In the Palestinian historiography and memory, the Six-Day War is considered as a "relapse" (*naksa*) of the grand inaugural "catastrophe" (*nakba*) of 1948, even though Nasser and King Hussein of Jordan also used the term to distinguish the two episodes and to understate the scope of the June 1967 defeat. On this point, see Laurens 1999–2015, vol. 4: 28.

4. Thanks to Ms. Bahija Simou for the translation of these two letters.

5. Benjamin 447.

6. Patrick Boucheron, "Encore la trace, encore l'aura: Walter Benjamin et l'obsession de l'historien." Colloquium: Enfance: Autour de Walter Benjamin, University of Lille III, 15 February 2013.

7. Boucheron 2010: 28–29. Boucheron takes up this distinction again in his qualifying dissertation, Boucheron 2019: 369: "And what is to be done, then, if not history, which, because it is or should be an art of emancipation, sides with traces against aura?"

8. CADN, Jerusalem 294 PO/3, box 27, 23 June 1967.

9. CADN, Jerusalem 294 PO/3, box 21, 14 June 1967.

10. CADN, Jerusalem 294 PO/3, box 21, 14 June 1967.

11. "Western Wall Area Cleared," *Jerusalem Post*, 12 June 1967, p. 4.

12. CADN, Jerusalem 294 PO/3, box 64, 7 August 1968.

13. CADN, Jerusalem 294 PO/3, box 64, 11 July 1967.

14. Laurens 1999–2015, vol. 4: 36; Segev 2007a: 413. Segev mentions specifically that Moshe Dayan had the flag removed following a remark by the chief military prosecutor, Meir Shamgar.

15. CADN, Jerusalem 294 PO/3, box 17, 25 August 1967, p. 413.

16. CADN, Jerusalem 294 PO/3, box 21, 21 June 1967.

17. CADN, Jerusalem 294 PO/3, box 21, 26 June 1967.

18. Palestinian Academic Society for the Study of International Affairs (hereafter PASSIA), *Documents on Jerusalem*, 4 vols., 2007.

19. PASSIA, *Documents on Jerusalem*, vol. 2:4. Ruhi al-Khatib's memorandum is published as an appendix, along with other documents, in the report submitted by Ernesto Thalmann to the UN secretary-general on 12 September 1967, accessed online at https://www.unispal.un.org.

20. PASSIA, *Documents on Jerusalem*, vol. 2: 15:

One hundred and thirty-five houses in the Maghrebi Quarter adjoining the Wailing Wall and adjacent to the two Mosques of Omar and Aksa which are Muslim Holy Places, have been dynamited and razed by bulldozers. Because of this, 650 Muslims, all of them poor and pious persons living near the Muslim Holy Place, were removed from their homes and driven away after having been allowed no more than three hours to evacuate their homes, which they had to do while the curfew was in effect. One can easily imagine the consternation of these families, who had to see to the removal of their property and take care of their children and their aged. One part of these buildings, comprising some houses and two small mosques, belongs to the Muslim Waqf. The other part was private property over which the Jews had no rights. They razed these buildings in order to make room for a Jewish religious institution.

21. PASSIA, *Documents on Jerusalem*, vol. 4:182.

22. ISA, HZ 4293-2, pp. 112–21, December 1967.

23. ISA, HZ 4293-2, pp. 88–100, 6 November 1968.

24. UNESCO, 15th General Assembly, Paris, 20 November 1968, resolution no. 3.343. Accessed online at https://unesdoc.UNESCO.org/ark:/48223/pf0000114047.

25. Regarding the Geddes Plan of 1919 and its contents, see chapter 2 in this book.

26. ISA, HZ 4293-2, Uri Gordon (deputy manager of UN Dept. 2) to Mr. Farran (UN Dept. 1), 18 November 1968.

27. ISA, HZ 4293-2, Zvi Rafiah (manager of the UN Department), Ministry of Foreign Affairs, to the legal counselor to the Ministry of Foreign Affairs, 9 December 1968.

28. On this point, see Rica 2007: 127–53 (chapter 5: "UNESCO and Jerusalem"). See also Goetschel, Lemire, and Potin 2018.

29. Maurel 2010. To push this inquiry even further, the UNESCO archives in Paris could be engaged, with particular analysis of dossier 87-EX-31 (7 May 1971) and of dossier CAB/7/8 (1971), which notably contains Raymond Lemaire's summary report regarding the Maghrebi ramp (available for consultation with special waiver). Thanks to Anthony Krause (UNESCO) and to Jens Boel (director of UNESCO archives) for their input. See also the op-ed by the director-general of UNESCO, René Maheu, "Israel et l'UNESCO," which appeared on page 1 of *Le Monde* on 21 November 1974, and which focused on recalling the destruction carried out by the Israel authorities while also making the case for integrating Israel into the UNESCO apparatus:

> Is the severity of the draft resolution [...] justified? Is halting aid to Israel the best way in this case to increase the effectiveness of the organization's action? [...] From summer 1967 to summer 1969, the part of the western wall of the holy enclosure (Haram-esh-Sharif) called the Wailing Wall was cleared along 140 meters, twice as long as what was previously accessible, and a vast plaza was opened up in front of the Wall by demolishing a neighborhood whose medieval structure made up an integral part of the traditional urban fabric of the old city. Apart from the fact that this quarter included a few buildings of architectural value or indisputable cultural character, such as the Zaouiah-Al-Kakhrya [*sic*], it is undeniable that the aspect of the site in the vicinity of the famous Maghrebi Gate was profoundly altered [...]. What is appropriate here is the active presence of UNESCO. There is reason to believe that, in spite of the practical difficulties, not to mention cost, of a literal application of the res-

olution, the general conference will make a decision along those lines. But how to adopt for Jerusalem a sanction policy that would, by force of circumstance, amount to a policy of absence?

30. Awaiting future publications, we can consult the text of one of his lectures: Andrew Bellisari, "Les revendications patrimoniales de la décolonisation: Cas de la Grande Mosquée de Paris et de la Cathédrale d'Alger," Centre d'Études Maghrébines en Algérie (Oran, Algeria), November 2015, accessed at his personal page: https://www .academia.edu/19596698/.

31. *Algérie Actualité* 87 (Sunday 18 June 1967): 8.

32. *Algérie Actualité* 87 (Sunday 18 June 1967): 8.

33. "Algeria Claims Wailing Wall," *Jerusalem Post*, 20 June 1967, p. 5.

34. It is also symptomatic that nothing is said in the *Algérie Actualité* concerning the affective ties between Houari Boumédiène and the founder of the Maghrebi Quarter of Jerusalem, Sidi Abu Madyan. Boumédiène, who symbolically engaged his troops on the side of Nasser's in June 1967, did not react publicly to the destruction of the Maghrebi Quarter in various speeches delivered in the immediate aftermath of the war to glorify the solidarity between the "nation of Algerian martyrs" and the "Arab nation," which had not lost the war "so long as all possible weapons had not been exhausted" (thanks to Leyla Kakhli for this information). Boumédiène's silence with regard to the Maghrebi Quarter is all the more striking in that, after the fire at the al-Aqsa Mosque in August 1969, he wrote to the UN secretary-general to denounce a "barbarous act" that recalled "the darkest days that Europe experienced under Nazi occupation." PASSIA, *Documents on Jerusalem*, 2007, vol. 3, p. 21. Regarding Algeria's military engagement during the Six-Day War, see Belkaid 2017.

35. The UNRWA archives, based in Amman, are to this day difficult to access, for both logistical and political reasons. A dissertation, however, has been devoted to the history of the organization, with unprecedented access to the archives: Kjersti Gravelsæter Berg, "The Unending Temporary: United Nations Relief and Works Agency (UNRWA) and the Politics of Humanitarian Assistance to Palestinian Refugee Camps 1949–2012," University of Bergen, 2012. In it, there are some data on the former inhabitants of the Maghrebi Quarter living as refugees in the Shuafat camp. There is also indirect information concerning UNRWA's action in archive files that I was able to consult at the ICRC.

36. Royal Archives of Rabat, "Waqf Abu Madyan," 28 April 1930.

37. According to Tom Abowd (Abowd 2000), based upon an interview conducted with Muhammad Abdelhaq on 14 July 1999, the latter purportedly confirmed the reality of this visit, during which he is said to have asked King Hassan II to register the inhabitants of the Maghrebi Quarter of Jerusalem in the registry of the Ministry of Religious Affairs.

38. Schattner and Schillo 2013. The expulsion of these families can also be linked to the position taken by the UNESCO General Assembly a few days earlier; see René

Maheu, "Israel et l'UNESCO," *Le Monde*, 21 November 1974, pp. 1–3.

39. Royal Archives of Rabat, 28 January 1975.

40. "Moroccan Minority Living in Jerusalem: Complaint by the Moroccan Red Crescent of 30 January 1975," International Committee of the Red Cross, Geneva (hereafter ICRC) Archives, B-AG-202-139-143.02, 25 February 1975.

41. This is the case in particular for Tom Abowd (Abowd 2000).

42. The archives site offers a good overview of the collection (https://www.icrc .org/fr/archives), and the catalogs are accessible online at http://www.icrc.org/fr/doc /resources/documents/misc/archives-inventory-b.htm/. Thanks to Daniel Palmieri for his warm welcome and guidance.

43. "Moroccan Minority," 25 February 1975.

44. "Moroccan Minority," 5 June 1975.

45. "List of Demolished Houses, Drawn Up by Mr. Aref el-Aref, 1 July 1969–1 July 1970," ICRC Archives, B-AG-202-139-073.

46. Entry "al-Arif, Arif (1892–1973)" in Mattar 2000: 66–67; el-Aref 1951 and 1975.

47. "List of Demolished Houses," 1 July 1969.

48. "Moroccan Minority," 3 July 1975.

49. "Moroccan Minority," 22 September 1967.

50. "Moroccan Minority," 5 December 1967.

51. We can note here that the intervention of the Moroccan Red Crescent and the International Red Cross is concurrent with the creation of the "Al-Quds Committee," at the sixth Islamic Conference (Jeddah, 12–15 July 1975), notably at the initiative of Morocco, chair of the organization since 1979.

52. ICRC Archives, CICR, B-AG-202-139-002* ("General correspondence concerning Middle East conflict, part one, 5 June 1967–27 December 1968").

53. ICRC Archives, CICR, B-AG-202-139-002*, ("General correspondence concerning Middle East conflict, part one, 5 June 1967–27 December 1968").

54. Laurens 1995–2000, vol. 4: 52–58 ("The Fate of the Occupied Territories").

55. "General Correspondence and Reports on the Indigenous Population (Ex-Palestine, Territories Occupied by Israel), 1967, part 1, 15 June 1967–31 August 1967," ICRC Archives, B-AG-231-156-001.

56. ("Relief in the Territories Occupied by Israel, 16 June 1967–27 April 1969," ICRC Archives, B-AG-280-156-002.

57. Geneva Convention Relative to the Protection of Civilian Persons in Time of War (12 August 1949), Article 53: "Any destruction by the Occupying Power of real or personal property belonging individually or collectively to private persons, or to the State, or to other public authorities, or to social or cooperative organizations, is prohibited, except where such destruction is rendered absolutely necessary by military operations."

58. "ICRC Protests Concerning the Destruction of Houses by the Israeli Army, 24 July 1967–15 January 1969," ICRC Archives, B-AG-202-139-075. Excerpt of the report

submitted by Dr. Hans Bernath, ICRC delegate in Jerusalem, 24 July 1967:

> Visit by the mukhtars (village chiefs) of Yalu, Beit Nuba and Imwas [...]. "On 6 June 1967, around 03:00, the Israeli armed forces entered the three villages, the Jordanian army having deserted its position near the convent around midnight. There wasn't a single Jordanian soldier in the villages, and for this reason, there was no fighting ahead of the occupation. The inhabitants were asked to exit their homes without bringing anything with them, and to leave the doors open. Gathered on the outskirts of the village, they received orders to head into the mountains. Anyone who attempted to return to their house would be killed, they were told. They then set off, many barefoot, the women unveiled, with no food or water, everyone, children and the elderly, except the very old and those who could not walk. Around 10:00, they arrived in Ramallah, around 7,000 persons in all [...]. On 12 June 1967, they asked the military governor of Ramallah to let them return to their villages to at least gather their fruits and vegetables. But the refusal was categorical: closed military zone [...]. The UNRWA began distributing food rations to this dispossessed population. They demanded tents and lands where they could settle." The ICRC delegation did not question the veracity of the three mukhtars' testimony.

59. ICRC Archives, B-AG-202-139-153.03 (26 December 1974).

60. Historical Archives of the Jerusalem Municipality (hereafter HAJM), box 4960–5994.

61. On the projects and worksites of the reconquest of the old city, the most thorough and accomplished summary is Ricca 2007.

62. HAJM, box 4960–5994, binder 5994/4, list from 13 November 1968 (88 names) augmented on 1 February 1969 (92 names).

63. HAJM, 5994/4, 4 September 1968.

64. HAJM, 5994/4, 21 October 1968.

65. Fares Ayub to Myassar Abdallah al-Jareedi, HAJM, 5994/4, 12 November 1968.

66. HAJM, 5994/4, 20 May 1969.

67. Treasury reporting rates of exchange as of 31 March 1967: 1 US dollar = 3,000 Israeli pounds; 1 US dollar = 0.3564 Jordanian dinar. Treasury reporting rates of exchange as of 31 December 1967: 1 US dollar = 3.5 Israeli pounds; 1 US dollar = 0.3559 Jordanian dinar. Therefore, in March 1967, 1 JOD = 8.5 IL; in December 1967, 1 JOD = 10 IL. During the 1970s, Israeli inflation coupled with the stability of the Jordanian currency led to a worsening of this exchange rate. According to a report of the ICRC delegation in Jerusalem in September 1975 ("Moroccan Minority," 22 September 1975), "36,550 Jordanian dinars equivalent to about 720,000 Israeli pounds." Therefore, at this date, 1 JOD = 19.70 IL.

68. HAJM, 5994/4, 15 November 1967.

69. HAJM, 5994/4, 15 November 1967.

70. HAJM, 5994/4, n.d. (November 1967).

71. HAJM, 5994/4, 30 July 1968.

72. HAJM, 5994/4, n.d. (September 1968).

73. HAJM, 5994/4, 15 November 1967.

74. A chess tournament in Jerusalem bears his name today. A biographical notice is available at the tournament site: http://www.jeruchess.com/GideonJaphet2016/About.aspx.

75. HAJM, 5994/4, 10 January 1968.

76. HAJM, 5994/4, 10 January 1968.

77. HAJM, 5994/4, 10 January 1968.

78. HAJM, 5994/4, 10 January 1968.

79. HAJM, 5994/4, 4 February 1968.

80. HAJM, 5994/4, 4 February 1968.

81. "List of Demolished Houses Drawn Up by Mr. Aref el-Aref, 1 July 1969–1 July 1970," ICRC Archives, B-AG-202-139-073.

82. A few examples among many others: Veinstein 1981; Cornette 1989; Bourquin 1989.

83. HAJM, 5994/4, 1 March 1968.

84. HAJM, 5994/4, 11 May 1968.

85. HAJM, 5994/4, 6 May 1968.

86. HAJM, 5994/4, 8 September 1968.

87. HAJM, 5994/4, 27 June 1968.

88. HAJM, 5994/4, 13 November 1968.

89. HAJM, 5994/4, 22 December 1967.

90. HAJM, 5994/4, 25 October 1967.

91. At the time of the second disbursement of 200,000 IL., Kollek complained in the press that it had taken more than six months for the Housing Ministry to confirm the payment for the reparations budget.

92. Fares Ayub to Myassar Abdallah al-Jareedi, 12 November 1968. HAJM 5994/4.

93. HAJM, 5994/4, 12 February 1969.

94. HAJM, 5994/4, 17 March 1969.

95. HAJM, 5994/4, 17 February 1969.

96. HAJM, 5994/4, 14 June 1968.

97. HAJM, 5994/4, 4 September 1968.

98. HAJM, 5994/4, 25 August 1968.

99. HAJM, 5994/4, 17 February 1969.

100. "Moroccan Minority," 22 September 1967.

101. Cohen-Hattab and Bar 2018; Lemire and Salenson 2018; Coon 2001.

102. In April 2016, when it was announced that the reading room would be closed and access to the paper archives suspended, historians and users of Israel's national

archives sprang into action. The Institute for Israeli-Palestinian Conflict Research (AKEVOT) was one of the most active organizations on this issue, which is still under discussion. See https://www.akevot.org.il/en/news-item/state-archive-ends-access-to -paper/.

103. *Jerusalem Post*, 8 August 1967. The manipulation of discussions over users of the Western Wall, be they religious or secular, orthodox or liberal, male or female, is still part of the strategic toolbox meant to justify expansion projects.

104. Benziman 1973.

105. HAJM, box 1210, dossier call no. 2/22/6.

106. Durkheim 1912.

107. Institut Ben-Zvi, Archives Benvenisti, 17 July 1968.

108. Institut Ben-Zvi, Archives Benvenisti, 31 July 1968.

109. Institut Ben-Zvi, Archives Benvenisti, 23 August 1968.

110. Institut Ben-Zvi, Archives Benvenisti, 23 August 1968.

111. HAJM 5994/4, 6 February 1969.

112. Meron Benvenisti to Rabbi Dov Perl, 11 March 1969. ISA, HZ 4293–2.

113. Institut Ben-Zvi, Archives Benvenisti, 16 March 1969.

114. ISA, HZ 4293–2, typescript, 30 March 1969.

115. The composition of the fourteenth government of the sixth Knesset is detailed at https://www.knesset.gov.il/.

116. ISA, HZ 4293–2, typescript, 30 March 1969.

117. ISA, HZ 4293–2, handwritten, n.d.

118. ISA, HZ 4293–2, handwritten, n.d. 930 March 1969). The original text in Hebrew, personal translation with the help of Lilach Assaf. The dashes are transcribed here with slashes. To facilitate reading, the names of the speakers are in bold.

119. ISA, HZ 4293–2, 7 May 1969.

120. Institut Ben-Zvi, Archives Benvenisti, 19 May 1969.

121. Dieckhoff 1993; Attias and Benbassa 1998.

122. Cohen-Hattab and Bar 2017.

123. ISA, HZ 4293–2, 13 June 1969.

124. ISA, HZ 4293–2, 15 June 1969.

125. ISA, HZ 4293–2, 15 June 1969 (2).

126. *Jerusalem Post*, 16 June 1969, p. 8.

127. *Jerusalem Post*, 20 June 1969, p. 3.

128. Yosef Algazi, "A Blasphemy," *Zo Haderekh*, 25 June 1969 (published in Hebrew).

Epilogue: The Archives in the Ground

1. Israel Antiquities Authority, "The National Treasures Storerooms," accessed at http://www.antiquities.org.il/. Thanks to François Bon for his help during this phase of the inquiry.

2. Raz Kletter, "Beit Strauss: Antiquities in the Toilets," *Emek Shaveh*, October 2015. Report accessed at https://emekshaveh.org/en/wp-content/uploads/2015/01/Beit-Strauss-Eng-Web-.pdf.

3. Barbé, Vitto, and Greenwald 2014.

4. Barbé, Vitto, and Greenwald 2014: 41–42.

5. See chapter 5 in this book.

6. Thanks to Hervé Barbé and to Fanny Vitto for their welcome and their advice within the IAA collections.

7. Weksler-Bdolah et al. 2009.

8. Emek Shaveh, "High Court Petition: The Jerusalem Planning and Building Committee Will Hear Objections to Beit Haliba," 2 September 2015. Accessed at https://emekshaveh.org/en/objections-to-beit-haliba-sept-2015-eng/.

9. Weksler-Bdolah et al. 2009: 2.

10. Weksler-Bdolah et al. 2009: 19.

11. See chapter 1 in this book ("Maghrebis in the City: The Oblique Light of the Municipal Archives").

12. Weksler-Bdolah et al. 2009: 13.

13. See prologue in this book.

14. Kedar, Weksler-Bdolah, and Da'adli 2012.

15. Weksler-Bdolah et al. 2009: 14.

16. Leroi-Gourhan 1950.

17. Nir Hasson, "Rare Photograph Reveals Ancient Jerusalem Mosque Destroyed in 1967," *Haaretz*, 15 June 2012.

18. Al-Jubeh 2019a.

19. Ben-Amos 2010.

20. Nir Hasson, "Rare Photograph," 15 June 2012.

21. Salenson 2014 ("Conserver le patrimoine pour sauvegarder l'identité").

Conclusion: A Wall of Silence

1. Yoel Cohen, 1999.

2. T. Kollek and A. Kollek 1978, 197.

3. Noiriel 1991.

4. Deluermoz 2021.

5. "Secours dans les territoires occupés par Israël, 16 juin 1967–27 avril 1969" (Relief in the territories occupied by Israel, 16 June 1967–27 April 1969), ICRC Archives, CICR, B-AG-280-156-002.

6. ICRC Archives, CICR, International Humanitarian Law, chapter 50 ("Destruction and Seizure of Property of an Adversary"), https://ihl-databases.icrc.org/customary-ihl/fre/docs/v1_rul_rule50; Gilli and Guilhembet 2012.

7. On this point, see Salenson 2014.

8. Lahire 2007. See chapter 3, "Sociologie et analogie," p. 66.

9. Lemire and Potin 2002.

10. Einaudi 1991; House and MacMaster 2008.

11. Dewerpe 2006. The author makes exactly the same observation: "Plus on monte de l'administratif au politique, de l'exécution à la décision, moins on trouve d'archives." (The higher you climb from administration into politics, from execution to decision-making, the less archival material you find.")

12. Thénault 2008.

13. Bloch 1962: 138–139.

14. Bloch 1962: 143.

15. Tatarsky 2021.

16. This virtual 3D reconstitution project has been developed in partnership between the Archival-City Project (Gustave Eiffel University) and the Virtual Illès Relief Initiative led by Maryvelma Smith O'Neil and Webster University in Geneva (see www.mughrabiquarter.info). Other resources are available online, notably http://www.moghrabi-jerusalem.com, which includes, for example, a directory of some one hundred currently identified members of the Maghrebi community of Jerusalem.

BIBLIOGRAPHY

Aaronsohn, R., and D. Trimbur, eds. 2008. *De Balfour à Ben-Gourion: Les puissances européennes et la Palestine, 1917–1948.* Paris: CNRS Éditions.

Abdul-Hadi, M., ed. 2007. *Documents on Jerusalem,* 4 vols. PASSIA.

Abel, F.-M. and L.-H. Vincent. 1914. *Jérusalem: Recherches de topographie, d'archéologie et d'histoire. Volume 2: Jérusalem nouvelle.* Paris: J. Gabalda.

Abowd, T. 2000. "The Moroccan Quarter: A History of the Present." *Jerusalem Quarterly* 7:6–16.

Abu Jaber, R. 2006. *Sîrât hayâ wa sijil injâz: Muhammad Rûhî Al Khatîb.* Amman: self-published.

Abu Saud, A. 2004–5. "Yasser Arafat, the Early Years: A Personal Recollection of Arafat's Childhood and Formative Years." *Palestine-Israel Journal* 11, no. 3–4.

Adler Elkan, N. 1930. *Jewish Travellers.* London: Routledge.

Al-Alami, A. 1981. *Waqfiyyât al-Maghariba.* Dairatu al-Awqaf al-Âmma.

Albera, D., I. Marquette, and M. Pénicaud, eds. 2015. *Lieux saints partagés.* Arles, France: Actes Sud.

Al-Din, M. 1876. *Histoire de Jérusalem et d'Hébron,* trans. H. Sauvaire. Paris: Ernest Leroux.

Alem, J-P. 1982. *La déclaration Balfour: Aux sources de l'État d'Israël.* Brussels: Éditions Complexe.

Algazi, G. 1994. "Violence, mémoire et pouvoir seigneurial à la fin du Moyen Âge." *Actes de la recherche en sciences sociales* 105 (December): 26–28.

Al-Jubeh, N. 2001. "Jewish Settlement in the Old City of Jerusalem after 1967." *Palestine-Israel Journal* 8, no. 1.

———. 2010. "1917 to the Present: Basic Changes, but Not Dramatic; Al-Haram al-Sharif in the Aftermath of 1967." In O. Grabar and B. Z. Kedar, *Where Heaven and Earth Meet: Jerusalem's Sacred Esplanade*, 275–89. Jerusalem and Austin: Yad Ben-Zvi Press and University of Texas Press.

———. 2019a. *Harat al-yahud wa harat al-maghariba fi al-Quds al-qadima: Al-tarikh wa al-masir ma bayna al-tadmir wa al-tahwid* (The Jewish Quarter and the Maghrebi Quarter in the old city of Jerusalem: History and destiny, between destruction and Judaization). Beirut: Institute of Palestine Studies.

———. 2019b. "Patrick Geddes: Luminary or Prophet of Demonic Planning." *Jerusalem Quarterly* 80:23–40.

Amir-Moezzi, M. A., ed. 2007. *Dictionnaire du Coran*. Paris: Robert Laffont.

Anatole-Gabriel, I. 2016. *La fabrique du patrimoine de l'humanité: L'UNESCO et la protection patrimoniale (1945–1992)*. Paris: Publications de la Sorbonne.

Antébi, E. 1996. *L'homme du Sérail*. Paris: Nil Éditions.

Arnon, A. 1992. "The Quarters of Jerusalem in the Ottoman Period." *Middle Eastern Studies* 28, no. 1 (January): 1–65.

Asali, K. J., ed. 1990. *Jerusalem in History*. New York: Olive Branch Press.

Attias, J.-C. and E. Benbassa. 1998. *Israël imaginaire*. Paris: Flammarion.

Audigier, F. 2010. "Les gaullistes face au discours gaullien sur l'autodétermination de l'Algérie (16 septembre 1959)." *Histoire@Politique: Politique, culture, société* 12, September-December.

Auld, S. and R. Hillenbrand, eds. 2000. *Ottoman Jerusalem: The Living City, 1517–1917*. London: Fox Communications and Publications.

Avci, Y. and V. Lemire. 2005. "De la modernité administrative à la modernisation urbaine: Une réévaluation de la municipalité ottomane de Jérusalem (1867–1917)." In N. Lafi, ed., *Municipalités méditerranéennes: Les réformes urbaines ottomanes au miroir d'une histoire comparée*, 73–138. Berlin: Klaus Schwarz Verlag.

Avci, Y., V. Lemire, and Falestin Naïli. 2015. "Publishing Jerusalem's Ottoman Municipal Archives (1892–1917): A Turning Point for the City's Historiography." *Jerusalem Quarterly* 60:110–19.

Avci, Y., V. Lemire, and Ö. Yazici Özdemi. 2018. "Collective Petitions as a Reflective Archival Source for Jerusalem's Networks of *Citadinité* in the Late 19th Century." In A. Dalachanis and V. Lemire, eds., *Ordinary Jerusalem, 1840–1940: Opening New Archives, Revisiting a Global City*, 161–85. Leiden, Netherlands: Brill.

Avi-Yonah, M., and E. Stern. 1976–79. *Encyclopedia of Archaeological Excavations in the Holy Land*, 4 vols. Oxford, UK: Oxford University Press.

Avni, R. 1999. "The 1927 Jericho Earthquake: Comprehensive Macroseismic Analysis Based on Contemporary Sources." PhD dissertation, Ben-Gurion University of the Negev, Beer Sheva. In Hebrew.

Avni, R., D. Bowman, A. Shapira, and A. Nur. 2002. "Erroneous Interpretation of Historical Documents Related to the Epicenter of the 1927 Jericho Earthquake in the Holy Land." *Journal of Seismology* 4, no. 6: 469–76.

Bahat, D. 2007. "History of the Kotel." *Ariel* 180–181 July: 38. Published in Hebrew.

———. 1996. *The Illustrated Atlas of Jerusalem*. Jerusalem: Carta.

Bahat, S., 2016–17. "Ha-Shekhuna She'amda Lifney Kotlenu" (The Neighborhood That Stood in Front of Our Kotel). *Et-Mol* 250:1–4. Published in Hebrew.

Bar, D. 2010. "War and Sacred Space: The Influence of the 1948 War on Sacred Space in the State of Israel." In M. Breger, Y. Reiter, and L. Hammer, eds., *Holy Places in the Israeli-Palestinian Conflict: Confrontation and Coexistence*, 67–91. London and New York: Routledge.

Bar, D. and R. Rubin. 2011. "The Jewish Quarter after 1967: A Case Study on the Creation of an Ideological-Cultural Landscape in Jerusalem's Old City." *Journal of Urban History* 37, no. 5: 775–92.

Barakat, R. 2018. "Criminals or Martyrs? Let the Courts Decide! British Colonial Legacy in Palestine and the Criminalization of Resistance." *Al-Muntaqa* 1:84–97.

Barbé, H., F. Vitto, and R, Greenwald. 2014. "When, Why and by Whom the Mughrabi Gate Was Opened? Excavations at the Mughrabi Gate in the Old City of Jerusalem (2007, 2012–2014)." In G. Stiebel, O. Peleg-Barakat, D. Ben-Ami, and Y. Gadot, eds., *New Studies in the Archaeology Jerusalem and Its Region Vol. 8*, 32–44. Jerusalem: Tel Aviv University, Israel Antiquities Authority, and Hebrew University.

Baruch, Y. 2017. "The Real Story." Israel Antiquities Authority, https://www.antiquities.org.il/article_eng.aspx?sec_id=17&sub_subj_id=468.

Belkaid, A. 2017. "L'Algérie de Houari Boumediène au secours de l'Égypte de Nasser." *Orient XXI*, 26 September.

Ben-Amos, A. 2010. *Israël: La fabrique de l'identité nationale*. Paris: CNRS Éditions.

Ben-Arieh, Yehoshua. 1984–86. *Jerusalem in the 19th Century*, 2 vols. Jerusalem and New York: St. Martin's Press and Yad Ishad Ben-Zvi.

Ben-Bassat, Y. and E. Ginio, eds. 2011. *Late Ottoman Palestine: The Period of Young Turk Rule*. London: I. B. Tauris.

Ben-Dov, M., M. Naor, and Z. Avner. 1983. *The Western Wall*. Tel Aviv: Ministry of Defense Publishing House.

Benjamin, W. 1999. *The Arcades Project*. Cambridge, MA, and London: Belknap Press of Harvard University Press.

Benvenisti, M. 1996. *Jérusalem: Une histoire politique*. Arles, France: Actes Sud/Solin.

———. 1976. *Jerusalem: The Torn City*. Minneapolis: University of Minnesota Press.

———. 2007. *Sons of the Cypresses: Memories, Reflections and Regrets from a Political Life*. Berkeley: University of California Press.

Benziman, U. 1973. *Jerusalem: Unwalled City*. Tel Aviv: Schocken Editions.

Biger, G. 1986. "Urban Planning and the Garden Suburbs of Jerusalem, 1918–1925." *Studies in Zionism* 7, no. 1: 1–9.

———. 1994. *An Empire in the Holy Land: Historical Geography of the British Administration in Palestine, 1917–1929*. Jerusalem: Magnes Press.

Bitan, D. 2008. "L'UNSCOP et l'internationalisation de Jérusalem en 1947: Un plan pour préserver l'hégémonie occidentale en Palestine?" In R. Aaronsohn and D. Trimbur, eds., *De Balfour à Ben Gourion: Les puissances européennes et la Palestine 1917-1948*, 435–86. Paris: CNRS Éditions.

Blevis, L. 2012. "Quelle citoyenneté pour les Algériens?" In A. Bouchene, J.-P. Peyroulou, O. Siari Tengour, and S. Thénault, *Histoire de l'Algérie à la période coloniale: 1830–1962*, 352–58. Paris: Éditions. La Découverte / Barzakh.

Bloch, M. 1962. *The Historian's Craft.* New York: Knopf.

Borrmans, M., and A. De Peretti. 2014. *Louis Massignon et le Comité Chrétien d'Entente France-Islam (1947–1962).* Paris: Karthala.

Boucheron, P. 2010. *Faire profession d'historien.* Paris: Publications de la Sorbonne.

———. 2019. *La trace et l'aura: Vies posthumes d'Ambroise de Milan (IVe–XVIe siècles).* Paris: Le Seuil.

Boucheron, P., ed. 2017. *Histoire mondiale de la France.* Paris: Le Seuil.

Bourquin, Laurent. 1989. "Les objets de la vie quotidienne dans la première moitié du XVIe siècle à travers cent inventaires après décès parisiens." *Revue d'histoire moderne et contemporaine* 36, no. 3 (July-September): 464–75.

Boyer, N. 1949. "L'expérience d'une médiation: L'intervention des Nations Unies en Palestine." *Politique étrangère* 14, no. 4: 365–78.

Bozarslan, H. 2013. *Histoire de la Turquie: De l'empire à nos jours.* Paris: Tallandier.

Breger, M., Y. Reiter, and L. Hammer. 2010. *Holy Places in the Israeli-Palestinian Conflict: Confrontation and Coexistence.* London and New York: Routledge.

Buhis Aramin, M., and N. D. Rifai. 2011. *Al-Maghariba wa âit al-Burâq al-sharîf: Haqâʾiq wa abâtîl* (The Maghrebis and the Holy Wall of al-Buraq: Truths and Untruths). Manshurât al-Arshif al-Watani al-Falistini.

Burgel, G. 2012. *La ville contemporaine après 1945.* In J.-L. Pinol, ed., *Histoire de l'Europe urbaine*, vol. 6. Paris: Le Seuil.

Burgoyne, M. H., and D. S. Richards. 1987. *Mamluk Jerusalem: An Architectural Study.* Jerusalem: British School of Archaeology in Jerusalem / World of Islam Festival Trust.

———. 2010. "1187–1260: The Furthest Mosque (al-Masjid al-Aqsa) under Ayyubid Rule." In O. Grabar and B. Z. Kedar, eds., *Where Heaven and Earth Meet: Jerusalem's Sacred Esplanade.* Jerusalem and Austin: Yad Ben-Zvi Press and University of Texas Press.

Busse, H. 1991. "Jerusalem in the Story of Muhammad's Night Journey and Ascension." *Jerusalem Studies in Arabic and Islam* 14:1–40.

Büssow, J. 2011. *Hamidian Palestine: Politics and Society in the District of Jerusalem 1872–1908.* Leiden, Netherlands: Brill.

———. 2014. "Ottoman Reform and Urban Government in the District of Jerusalem, 1867–1917." In N. Lafi and U. Freitag, eds., *Urban Governance under the Ottomans: Between Cosmopolitanism and Conflict.* London: Routledge.

Campos, M. U. 2011. *Ottoman Brothers: Muslims, Christians and Jews in Early Twentieth-Century Palestine.* Stanford, CA: Stanford University Press.

Canaan, T. 1932. "The Palestinian Arab House: Its Architecture and Folklore." *Journal of the Palestine Oriental Society* 12:223–47.

Caron, G. 2012. *J'ai voulu voir: Lettres d'Algérie.* Paris: Calmann-Levy.

Chantre, L. 2018. *Pèlerinages d'empire: Une histoire européenne du pèlerinage à la Mecque.* Paris: Publications de la Sorbonne.

Charbit, D. 1998. *Sionismes: Textes fondamentaux.* Paris: Albin Michel.

Charbit, D., ed. 2009. *Les intellectuels français et Israël.* Paris: Éditions de l'éclat.

Chateaubriand, F.-R. de. 1811. *Itinéraire de Paris à Jérusalem.*

Civic Coalition for Defending the Palestinians' Rights in Jerusalem. 2008. *Hârat al-maghariba: Dirâsatu hâlihi* (Maghrebi Quarter: Current Status Report). Jerusalem.

Cohen, A. 1989a. *Economic Life in Ottoman Jerusalem.* Cambridge, UK: Cambridge University Press.

———. 1989b. "The Walls of Jerusalem." In C. E. Bosworth, C. Issawi, R. Savory, and A. L. Udovitch, eds., *Essays in Honour of Bernard Lewis: The Islamic World from Classical to Modern Times,* 467–78. Princeton, NJ: Darwin Press.

———. 2001. *The Guilds of Ottoman Jerusalem.* Leiden, Netherlands: Brill.

———. 2010. "Haram-i-Serif: The Temple Mount under Ottoman Rule." In O. Grabar and B. Z. Kedar, eds., *Where Heaven and Earth Meet: Jerusalem's Sacred Esplanade,* 211–29. Jerusalem and Austin: Yad Ben-Zvi Press and University of Texas Press.

———. 2011. *Studies on Ottoman Palestine.* Farnham, UK and Burlington, VT: Ashgate.

———. 2016. *Juifs et Musulmans en Palestine et en Israël des origines à nos jours.* Paris: Tallandier.

Cohen, A., and B. Lewis. 1978. *Population and Revenue in the Towns of Palestine in the Sixteenth Century.* Princeton, NJ: Princeton University Press.

Cohen, H. 2015. *Year Zero of the Arab-Israeli Conflict: 1929.* Waltham, MA: Brandeis University Press.

Cohen, Raymond. 2008. *Saving the Holy Sepulchre: How Rival Christians Came Together to Rescue Their Holiest Shrine.* Oxford, UK: Oxford University Press.

Cohen, Rina. 2005. "Les Juifs 'Moghrabi' en Palestine (1830–1903): Les enjeux de la protection française." *Archives Juives* 38:28–46.

Cohen, Y. 1999. "The Political Role of the Israeli Chief Rabbinate in the Temple Mount Question." *Jewish Political Studies Review* 11, no. 1–2 (Spring): 101–26.

Cohen-Hattab, K., and D. Bar. 2017. "Can the Two Go Together? Archaeology and Sanctity at the Western Wall and Surrounding Area, 1967–1977." *Journal of Modern Jewish Studies* 16:395–415.

———. 2018. "From Wailing to Rebirth: The Development of the Western Wall as an Israeli National Symbol after the Six-Day War." *Contemporary Jewry* 38:281–300.

———. 2020. *The Western Wall: The Dispute over Israel's Holiest Jewish Site, 1967–2000.* Leiden, Netherlands: Brill.

Cohen-Hattab, K., and A. Kohn. 2017. "The Nationalization of Holy Sites: Yishuv-Era Visual Representations of the Western Wall and Rachel's Tomb." *Jewish Quarterly Review* 107:66–89.

Coon, A. 2001. "The Urban Transformation of Jerusalem, 1967–2001." *Islamic Studies* 40, no. 3–4: 463–73.

Cornette, J. 1989. "La révolution des objets: Le Paris des inventaires après-décès (XVIIe–XVIIIe siècles)." *Revue d'histoire moderne et contemporaine* 36, no. 3 (July-September): 476–86.

Coulon, L. 2009. *L'opinion française, Israël et le conflit israélo-arabe (1947–1987).* Paris: Honoré Champion.

Courreyre, C. 2020. *L'Algérie des Oulémas: Une histoire de l'Algérie contemporaine (1931–1991).* Paris: Éditions de la Sorbonne.

Dakhli, L. 2014. "Comment la Première Guerre mondiale a transformé le Proche-Orient: Nationalisme arabe et souffrances indicibles." *Orient XXI,* November.

Dakkak, I. 2000. "Juin 1967, la résistance au quotidien." In F. Mardam-Bey and E. Sanbar, eds., *Jérusalem: Le sacré et le politique,* 243–72. Arles, France: Actes Sud/ Sindbad.

Dalachanis, A., and V. Lemire, eds. 2018. *Ordinary Jerusalem, 1840–1940: Opening New Archives, Revisiting a Global City.* Leiden, Netherlands: Brill.

Danino, O. 2005. "La France et la question de Jérusalem, 3 avril 1949–7 juin 1967." *Relations internationales* 122, no. 2: 47–62.

Deghilem, R., ed. 1995. *Le waqf dans l'espace islamique: Outil de pouvoir sociopolitique.* Damascus: IFEAD.

Deluermoz, Q., ed. 2021. *D'ici et d'ailleurs: Histoires globales de la France contemporaine.* Paris: La Découverte.

Deluermoz, Q., and P. Singaravelou. 2012. "Explorer le champ des possibles: Approches contrefactuelles et futurs non advenus en histoire." *Revue d'histoire moderne et contemporaine* 59, no. 3 (July-September): 118–43.

Destremeau, C., and J. Moncelon. 2011. *Louis Massignon.* Paris: Perrin.

Dewerpe, A. 2006. *Charonne, 8 février 1962: Anthropologie historique d'un massacre d'État.* Paris: Gallimard.

Dieckhoff, A. 1987. *Les espaces d'Israël: Essai sur la stratégie territoriale israélienne.* Paris: Gallimard.

———. 1993. *L'invention d'une nation: Israël et la modernité politique.* Paris: Gallimard.

Doumani, B. 1985. "Palestinian Islamic Court Records: A Source for Socioeconomic History." *MESA Bulletin* 19:155–72.

Dumper, M., 1997. *The Politics of Jerusalem since 1967.* New York: Columbia University Press.

———. 2014. *Jerusalem Unbound: Geography, History and the Future of the Holy City.* New York: Columbia University Press.

Durkheim, É. 1912. *Les Formes élémentaires de la vie religieuse.* Paris: PUF.

Edde, A.-M. 2008. *Saladin.* Paris: Flammarion.

Efrat, E. 1993. "British Town Planning Perspectives of Jerusalem in Transition." *Planning Perspectives* 8, no. 4: 377–93.

Einaudi, J.-L. 1991. *La bataille de Paris (17 octobre 1961).* Paris: Le Seuil.

El-Aref, A. 1951. *Tarikh al-Quds* (The history of Jerusalem). Cairo.

———. 1975. "The Closing Phase of Ottoman Rule in Jerusalem." In M. Ma'oz, *Studies on Palestine during the Ottoman Period*, 334–40. Jerusalem: Hebrew University Magnes Press.

Elad, A. 1995. *Medieval Jerusalem and Islamic Worship: Holy Places, Ceremonies, Pilgrimage.* Leiden, Netherlands: Brill.

Eroğlu Memiş, Ş. 2018. "Between Ottomanization and Local Networks: Appointment Registers as Archival Sources for Waqf Studies; The Case of Jerusalem's Maghariba Neighborhood." In A. Dalachanis and V. Lemire, eds., *Ordinary Jerusalem, 1840–1940: Opening New Archives, Revisiting a Global City*, 75–99. Leiden, Netherlands: Brill.

Escande, L. ed. 2012. *Avec les pèlerins de La Mecque: Le voyage du docteur Carbonell en 1908.* Aix-en-Provence, France: Presses universitaires de Provence / Maison méditerranéenne des sciences de l'Homme.

Étienne, B. 2012. *Abdelkader.* Paris: Fayard.

Faron, O., and E. Hubert, eds. 1995. *Le sol et l'immeuble: Les formes dissociées de la propriété immobilière dans les villes de France et d'Italie, 12e–19e siècles.* Rome: EFR.

Faroqhi, S. 1994. *Pilgrims and Sultans: The Hajj under the Ottomans, 1517–1683.* London and New York: I. B. Tauris.

———. 1999. *Approaching Ottoman History: An Introduction to the Sources.* New York: Cambridge University Press.

Ferro, M. 2006. *1956, Suez: Naissance d'un tiers-monde.* Paris: Complexe.

Filiu, J.-P. 2008. *L'apocalypse dans l'Islam.* Paris: Fayard.

Freitag, U., M. Fuhrmann, N. Lafi, and F. Riedler, eds. 2011. *The City in the Ottoman Empire: Migration and the Making of Urban Modernity.* New York: Routledge.

Fremeaux, Jacques. 2004. "L'union française: Le rêve d'une France unie?" In P/ Blanchard et al., *Culture impériale 1931–1961*, 163–73. Paris: Éditions Autrement.

Friling, T., and D. Peschanski, 2012. *David Ben Gourion: Les secrets de la création de l'État d'Israël, journal 1947–1948.* Paris: La Martinière.

Georgeon, F., and F. Hitzel, eds. 2012. *Les Ottomans et le temps.* Leiden, Netherlands: Brill.

Gerber, H. 1985. *Ottoman Rule in Jerusalem, 1890–1914.* Berlin: K. Schwarz.

Geva, H., B. Mazar, Y. Shiloh, et al. 1993. "Jerusalem." In E. Stern et al., eds., *The New Encyclopedia of Archaeological Excavations in the Holy Land*, vol. 2, 698–804. Jerusalem: Carta-Israel Exploration Society.

Gilbert, M. 1996. *Jerusalem in the Twentieth Century*. New York: J. Wiley & Sons.

Gilli, P., and J.-P. Guilhembet, eds., 2012. *Le châtiment des villes dans les espaces méditerranéens (Antiquité, Moyen Âge, Époque moderne)*. Studies in European Urban History 26. Turnhout, Belgium: Brepols.

Goetschel, P., V. Lemire, and Y. Potin, eds. 2018. "Patrimoine, une histoire politique." *Vingtième siècle* 137 (special issue).

Goichon, A.-M. 1976. *Jérusalem: Fin de la ville universelle?* Paris: Maisonneuve & Larose.

Goitein, S. D. 1986. Entry "Al-Quds." In *Encyclopédie de l'Islam*, 2nd edition, vol. 5, 322–34.

Goren, D. 2016. "Shutaf Amin l'rhishat ha-Kotel ha-Maʿaravi: Haj Amin al-Husseini b'Sherut Vaʿad ha-Tsirim 1918–1920" (A Reliable Partner for Purchasing the Western Wall. Hajj Amin al-Husseini in the Service of the Zionist Commission 1918–1920). *Et-Mol* 243:18–20.

Goren, H., and R. Rubin. 1996. "Schick's Models of Jerusalem and Its Monuments." *Palestine Exploration Quarterly* 128 (July-December): 103–24.

Grabar, O., and B. Z. Kedar. 2010. *Where Heaven and Earth Meet: Jerusalem's Sacred Esplanade*. Jerusalem and Austin: Yad Ben-Zvi Press and University of Texas Press.

Gribetz, J. M. 2014. *Religion, Race, and the Early Zionist-Arab Encounter*. Princeton, NJ: Princeton University Press.

Gril, D. 2016. "Abū Madyan." In K. Fleet, G. Krämer, D. Matringe, J. Nawas, and E. Rowson, eds., *Encyclopedia of Islam, 3rd edition*. Leiden, Netherlands: Brill.

Gutmann, J., ed. 1976. *The Temple of Solomon: Archaeological Fact and Medieval Tradition in Christian, Islamic and Jewish Art*. Missoula, MT: Scholars Press.

Halbwachs, M. 1925. *Les cadres sociaux de la mémoire*. Paris: Alcan, 1925 (republished: Paris, Albin Michel, 1994).

——, 1971 (1st edition 1941). *La topographie légendaire des évangiles en Terre sainte*. Paris: PUF.

Halpern, B., and J. Reinharz. 1998. *Zionism and the Creation of a New Society*. Oxford, UK: Oxford University Press.

Hannoum, Abdelmajid. 2021. *The Invention of the Maghreb: Between Africa and the Middle East*. Cambridge, UK: Cambridge University Press.

Hanssen, J., T. Philipp, and S. Weber, eds. 2002. *The Empire in the City: Arab Provincial Capitals in the Late Ottoman Empire*. Würzburg, Germany: Ergon in Kommission.

Heyd, U. 1960. *Ottoman Documents on Palestine, 1552–1615*. Oxford, UK: Clarendon Press.

Hillenbrand, R., and S. Auld. 2009. *Ayyubid Jerusalem: The Holy City in Context, 1187–1250*. London: Altajir Trust.

Hiltermann, J. R. 1993. "Teddy Kollek and the Native Question." *Middle East Report* 182:24–27.

Hitzel, F. 2014. *Le dernier siècle de l'empire ottoman (1789–1923)*. Paris: Les Belles Lettres.

Hobsbawm, E. 1987. *The Age of Empire (1875–1914)*. London: Weidenfeld & Nicolson.

House, J., and N. MacMaster. 2008. *Paris 1961, Les Algériens, la République et la terreur d'État*. Paris: Tallendier.

Hyman, B. 1994. "British Planners in Palestine, 1918–1936." PhD thesis, London School of Economics and Political Science.

Hysler Rubin, N. E. 2011. "Geography, Colonialism and Town Planning: Patrick Geddes' Plan for Mandatory Jerusalem." *Cultural Geographies* 18, no. 2: 231–48.

Iogna-Prat, D. 1998. *Ordonner et exclure: Cluny et la société chrétienne face à l'hérésie, au judaïsme et à l'islam, 1000–1150*. Paris: Aubier.

Irving, S. 2021. "Donations and Their Destinations in the 1927 Palestine Earthquake." *Revue d'histoire culturelle*, http://revues.mshparisnord.fr/rhc/index.php?id=1068.

Jacobson, A. 2011. *From Empire to Empire: Jerusalem between Ottoman and British Rule*. Syracuse, NY: Syracuse University Press.

Jayyusi, L. 2014. *Interrupted: Modernity and Colonial Transformation 1917–present*. Northampton, MA: Interlink Books.

Kaplony, A., 2010. "635/638–1099: The Mosque of Jerusalem (*Masjid Bayt al-Maqdis*)." In O. Grabar and B. Z. Kedar, eds., *Where Heaven and Earth Meet: Jerusalem's Sacred Esplanade*, 100–131. Jerusalem and Austin: Yad Ben-Zvi Press and University of Texas Press.

Kark, R., and M. Oren-Nordheim. 2001. *Jerusalem and Its Environs, Quarters, Neighborhoods, Villages, 1800–1948*. Jerusalem and Detroit: Hebrew University Magnes Press and Wayne State University Press.

Katz, K. 2003. "Building Jordanian Legitimacy: Renovating Jerusalem's Holy Places." *The Muslim World* 93:211–32.

———. 2005. *Holy Places and National Places: Jerusalem under Jordanian Rule*. Gainesville: University Press of Florida.

Kedar, B. Z. 1992. "The Battle of Hattin Revisited." In B. Z. Kedar, ed., *The Horns of Hattin: Proceedings of the 2nd Conference of the Society for the Study of the Crusades and the Latin East*, 190–207. Jerusalem: Yad Izhak Ben-Zvi.

Kedar, B. Z., S. Weksler-Bdolah, and T. Da'adli. 2012. "The Madrasa Afdaliyya / Maqâm Al-Shaykh 'Id: An Example of Ayyubid Architecture in Jerusalem." *Revue biblique* 119, no. 2: 271–87.

Kendall, H. 1948. *The City Plan: Preservation and Development during the British Mandate, 1918–1948*. London: H. M. Stationery Office.

Khalidi, R. 2003. *L'identité palestinienne: La construction d'une conscience nationale moderne*. Paris: La Fabrique. Originally published New York: Columbia University Press, 1997.

———. 2020. *The Hundred Years' War on Palestine: A History of Settler Colonial Conquest and Resistance*. New York: Metropolitan Books.

Khalidi, W., ed. 1997. *All That Remains: The Palestinian Villages Occupied and Depopulated by Israel in 1948.* Washington: Institute for Palestine Studies.

Khayat, H. A. 1962. "Waqfs in Palestine and Israel, from the Ottoman Reforms to the Present." PhD dissertation, American University (Washington, DC).

Klein, M. 2014. *Lives in Common: Arabs and Jews in Jerusalem, Jaffa and Hebron.* London: Hurst & Company.

Kloetzel, C. Z. 1935. *The Way to the Wailing Wall.* Jerusalem: Azriel Press.

Kollek, T., and A. Kollek, A. 1978. *For Jerusalem: A Life.* New York: Random House.

Krämer, G. 2008. *A History of Palestine: From the Ottoman Conquest to the Founding of the State of Israel.* Princeton, NJ, and Oxford, UK: Princeton University Press.

Kupferschmidt, U. M. 1987. *The Supreme Muslim Council: Islam under the British Mandate for Palestine.* Leiden, Netherlands: Brill.

Kushner, D., ed. 1986. *Palestine in the Late Ottoman Period: Political, Social and Economic Transformation.* Jerusalem: Yad Izhak Ben-Zvi.

Lafi, N. 2011. "Petitions and Accommodating Urban Change in the Ottoman Empire." In E. Özdalgi, M. S. Özervarli, and F. Tansug, eds., *Istanbul as Seen from a Distance: Centre and Provinces in the Ottoman Empire,* 73–82. Istanbul: Swedish Research Institute.

Lahire, B. 2007. *L'esprit sociologique.* Paris: La Découverte.

Laskier, M. M. 2001. "Israel and Algeria amid French Colonialism and the Arab-Israeli Conflict, 1954–1978." *Israel Studies* 6, no. 2: 1–32.

Laurens, H. 2015. *L'Orient arabe: Arabisme et islamisme de 1798 à 1945.* Paris: Arman Colin.

———. 1999–2015. *La question de Palestine.* 5 vols. Paris: Fayard.

Lazar, D. 2009. "Louis Massignon, le sionisme et l'État d'Israël." In D. Charbit, ed., *Les intellectuels français et Israël,* 83–96. Paris: Éditions de l'éclat.

Le Morzellec, J. 1979. *La question de Jérusalem devant l'Organisation des Nations Unies.* Brussels: Bruylant Éditions.

Lemire, V. 2001. "Les puits du Ghetto: Conflits de mémoire et logiques d'appropriation (Venise, 1450–1650)." *Histoire urbaine* 4:105–26.

———. 2010. *La soif de Jérusalem: Essai d'hydrohistoire (1840–1940).* Paris: Publications de la Sorbonne.

———. 2012. *Jérusalem 1900, la ville sainte à l'âge des possibles.* Paris: Armand Colin (reprint Points-Seuil, 2016). English version at https://press.uchicago.edu/ucp/books/book/chicago/J/bo19585779.html.

———. 2017. "1962: Le crépuscule de l'Algérie française à Jérusalem." In P. Boucheron, ed., *Histoire mondiale de la France,* 683–87. Paris: Le Seuil.

Lemire, V., ed. 2016. *Histoire d'une ville monde.* Paris: Flammarion. English version at https://www.ucpress.edu/book/9780520299900/jerusalem.

Lemire, V., and Y. Potin. 2002. "'Ici on noie les Algériens': Fabriques documentaires, avatars politiques et mémoires partagées d'une icône militante (1961–2001)." *Genèses* 49:140–62.

Lemire, V., and A. Reichman. 2017. "Jérusalem 1939–1945: Une ville en paix?" *Études arméniennes contemporaines* 9:133–55.

Lemire, V., and I. Salenson. 2018. "La destruction du quartier des Maghrébins: Entre histoire, urbanisme et archéologie (1967–2007)." *Les cahiers de l'Orient* 130:129–46.

Leroi-Gourhan, A. 1950. *Les fouilles préhistoriques: Techniques et methodes*. Paris: Éditions Picard et Cie.

Liskenne, A. 2015. *L'Algérie indépendante: L'ambassade de Jean-Marcel Jeanneney (juillet 1962–janvier 1963)*. Paris: Armand Colin.

Little, D. P. 1989. "Jerusalem under the Ayyubids and Mamluks, 1187–1516 AD." In K. J. Asali, ed., *Jerusalem in History: 3000 BC to the Present Day*, 177–99. London and New York: Kegan Paul International.

Loiseau, J. 2014. *Les Mamelouks (XIIIᵉ-XVIᵉ siècle): Une expérience du pouvoir dans l'Islam médiéval*. Paris: Le Seuil.

———. 2016. "Faire de Jérusalem une ville islamique: Le peuplement" and "Couronner Jérusalem: La construction de l'enceinte de Soliman." In Vincent Lemire, ed., *Jérusalem: Histoire d'une ville monde*, 257–59 and 280–83. Paris: Flammarion.

Louis, R., and A. Shlaim. 2012. *The 1967 Arab-Israeli War: Origins and Consequences*. Cambridge, UK: Cambridge University Press.

Luncz, A. M. 1914. *Jerusalem Almanach*, vol. 10.

Ma'oz, M. 1975. *Studies on Palestine during the Ottoman Period*. Jerusalem: Hebrew University Magnes Press.

Malherbe, M. 2008. *Quand l'histoire change les noms de lieux: Les lieux à dénominations multiples*. Paris: L'Harmattan.

Maraval, P. 1985. *Lieux saints et pèlerinages d'Orient*. Paris: Le Cerf.

Marçais, G. 1960–2005. "Abu Madyan, Shu'ayb ben al-Husayn al-Andalusi." In P. J. Bearman, T. Bianquis, C. E. Bosworth, E. Van Donzel, and W. P. Heinrichs, eds., *Encyclopaedia of Islam, 2nd Edition, 2011*. Leiden, Netherlands: Brill.

Mardam-Bey, F., and E. Sanbar. 2000. *Jérusalem, le sacré et le politique*. Arles, France: Actes Sud.

Masalha, N. 1992. *Expulsion of the Palestinians: The Concept of "Transfer" in Zionist Political Thought, 1882–1948*. Beirut: Institute for Palestine Studies.

———. 2003. *The Politics of Denial: Israel and the Palestinian Refugee Problem*. London: Pluto Press.

Massignon, L. 1951. "Documents sur certains waqfs des Lieux saints de l'Islam: Principalement sur le waqf Tamimi à Hébron et sur le waqf tlemcénien Abu Madyan à Jérusalem." *Revue des études islamiques* 19:73–120.

Mattar, P., ed. 2000. *Encyclopedia of the Palestinians*. New York: Facts on File.

Maurel, C. 2010. *Histoire de l'UNESCO: Les trente premières années*. Paris: L'Harmattan.

Mazza, R., 2009. *Jerusalem from the Ottomans to the British.* London and New York: Tauris Academic Studies.

———. 2013. "Missing Voices in Rediscovering Late Ottoman and Early British Jerusalem," *Jerusalem Quarterly* 53:61–71.

———. 2018. "The Preservation and Safeguarding of the Amenities of the Holy City without Favour or Prejudice to Race or Creed: The Pro-Jerusalem Society and Ronald Storrs, 1917–1926." In Dalachanis and Lemire, eds., *Ordinary Jerusalem, 1840–1940. Opening New Archives, Revisiting a Global City*, 403–22. Leiden, Netherlands: Brill.

———. 2021. "The Deal of the Century? The Attempted Sale of the Western Wall by Cemal Pasha in 1916." *Middle Eastern Studies* 57:696–711.

Mbaye, O. 2009. "Le CAOM: Un centre d'archives partagées?" *Afrique & histoire* 7, no. 1: 291–99.

Meddeb, A., ed. 1996. *Multiple Jérusalem.* Paris: Maisonneuve & Larose.

Meddeb, A., and B. Stora, eds. 2013. *A History of Jewish-Muslim Relations from the Origins to the Present Day*, trans. J. M. Todd and M. Smith. Princeton, NJ: Princeton University Press.

Michel, M. 2003. *Les Africains et la Grande Guerre: L'appel à l'Afrique (1914–1918).* Paris: Karthala.

Montefiore, S. S. 2011. *Jérusalem:. Biographie.* Paris: Calmann-Lévy.

Morris, B. 1988. *The Birth of the Palestinian Refugee Problem Revisited.* Cambridge, UK: Cambridge University Press.

Muhtadi, A. 2007. *Registres du tribunal islamique de Jérusalem, catalogue analytique.* Amman: University of Amman in Jordan.

Muhtadi, A., and F. Naili. 2018. "Back into the Imperial Fold: The End of Egyptian Rule through the Court Records of Jerusalem, 1839–1840." In A. Dalachanis and V. Lemire, eds., *Ordinary Jerusalem, 1840–1940: Opening New Archives, Revisiting a Global City*, 186–99. Leiden, Netherlands: Brill.

Myres, D. 2000. "Al-'Imara al-'Amira: The Charitable Foundation of Khassaki Sultan (959/1552)." In S. Auld and R. Hillenbrand, eds., *Ottoman Jerusalem: The Living City; 1517–1917, Vol. 1*, 539–81. London: Fox Communications and Publications.

Naamneh, H. 2021. "Navigating the Time of Arab Jerusalem: A Perspective from Within." *Journal of Palestine Studies* 50, no. 3: 52–55.

Naïli, F. 2017. "Chronique d'une mort annoncée? La municipalité ottomane de Jérusalem dans la tourmente de la Première Guerre mondiale." *Revue des mondes musulmans et de la Méditerranée* 141:171–90.

Narkiss, U. 1978. *La bataille pour Jérusalem (juin 1967).* Paris: Hachette.

Nassar, I. 2008. "Jerusalem in the Late Ottoman Period: Historical Writing and the Native Voice." In T. Mayer and S. Mourad, eds., *Jerusalem Idea and Reality*, 205–23. London: Routledge.

Neuville, R. 1934. "Le préhistorique de Palestine." *Revue biblique* 43, no. 2 (April): 237–59.

———. 1948. *Heurs et malheurs des consuls de France à Jérusalem.* Jerusalem: Ariel Printing Works.

Nicault, C. 2000. "Diplomatie et violence politique: Autour des troubles palestiniens de 1929." *Revue d'histoire moderne et contemporaine* 47, no. 1 January-March): 159–76.

———. 2008. *Une histoire de Jérusalem, 1850–1967.* Paris: CNRS Éditions.

Nitzan-Shiftan, A. and S. Wilkof. 2017. " 'A Historical Opportunity': Landscape, Statism, and Competition in the Making of the Walls of Jerusalem National Park, 1967–1970." *Cathedra* 163:163–90. Published in Hebrew.

Noiriel, G. 1991. *La tyrannie du national: Le droit d'asile en Europe (1793–1993).* Paris: Calmann-Lévy.

Nur, A. 2008. *Apocalypse: Earthquakes, Archaeology, and the Wrath of God.* Princeton, NJ: Princeton University Press.

Ohana, D. 2017. *Nationalizing Judaism: Zionism as a Theological Ideology.* Lanham, MD: Lexington Books.

O'Neil, M. S. 2019. "The Maghrebi Quarter Digital Archive and the Virtual Illés Relief Initiative." *Jerusalem Quarterly* 81.

Oren, M. B. 2003. *Six Days of War: June 1967 and the Making of the Modern Middle-East.* New York: Presidio Press Books.

Pappe, I. 2000. *La guerre de 1948 en Palestine.* Paris: La Fabrique.

———. 2006. *The Ethnic Cleansing of Palestine.* London and New York: One World Publications.

Pasha, D. 1922. *Memories of a Turkish Statesman, 1913–1919.* London: Hutchinson.

Penicaud, M. 2014. *Le réveil des Sept Dormants: Un pèlerinage islamo-chrétien en Bretagne.* Paris: Éditions du Cerf.

———. 2020. *Louis Massignon: Le "catholique musulman."* Paris: Bayard.

Perec, G. 1974. *Espèces d'espaces.* Paris: Galilée.

———. 1978. *La vie mode d'emploi.* Paris: Hachette.

Peri, O., 1983. "The Waqf as an Instrument to Increase and Consolidate Political Power: The Case of Khasseki Sultan Waqf in Late 18th-Cent. Ottoman Jerusalem." *Asian and African Studies* 17: 47–62.

Perrot, J. 1952. "René Neuville: Nécrologie." *Syria* 29, no. 3-4: 40941.

Peters, F. E. 1985. *Jerusalem: The Holy City in the Eyes of Chroniclers, Visitors, Pilgrims and Prophets, from the Days of Abraham to the Beginnings of Modern Times.* Princeton, NJ: Princeton University Press.

Poivert, M. 2013. *Gilles Caron: Le conflit intérieur.* Paris: Photosynthèses.

Poivert, M., W. Bachelot, and D. Cohn-Bendit. 2018. *Gilles Caron: Paris 1968.* Paris: Flammarion.

Pullan, W., and L. Kyriacou. 2009. "The Work of Charles Ashbee: Ideological Urban Visions with Everyday City Spaces." *Jerusalem Quarterly* 39:51–61.

Purvis, J. D. 1991. *Jerusalem, the Holy City: A Bibliography, Vol. 2*. Chicago: American Theological Library Association.

Rafeq, A.-K. 2000. "Ownership of Real Property by Foreigners in Syria, 1869–1873." In R. Owen, ed., *New Perspectives on Property and Land in the Middle East*, 175–240. Cambridge, MA: Harvard University Center for Middle Eastern Studies.

Rana, B. 2016. "Urban Planning, Colonialism, and the Pro-Jerusalem Society." *Jerusalem Quarterly* 65:22–34.

Reiner, E. 2002. "Traditions of Holy Places in Medieval Palestine: Oral versus Written." In R. Sarfati et al., eds., *Offerings from Jerusalem: Portrayals of Holy Places by Jewish Artists*, 9–19. Jerusalem: Israel Museum.

Reiter, Y., 1996. *Islamic Endowments in Jerusalem under British Mandate*. London: Routledge.

———. 1997. *Islamic Institutions in Jerusalem Palestinian Muslim Organization under Jordanian and Israeli Rule*. London: Kluwer Law International Editions.

Reiter, Y., and J. Seligman. 2010. "1917 to the Present: Al-Haram al-Sharif / Temple Mount (Har Ha-Bayit) and the Western Wall." In O. Grabar and B. Z. Kedar, eds., *Where Heaven and Earth Meet: Jerusalem's Sacred Esplanade*, 231–73. Jerusalem and Austin: Yad Ben-Zvi Press, University of Texas Press.

Renard, M. 2004. "L'impossible séparation: Administrations coloniales, élus et religieux musulmans face à 'l'indépendance du culte musulman en Algérie' (1947–1959)." In *La guerre d'Algérie au miroir des décolonisations françaises: Actes du Colloque en l'honneur de Charles-Robert Ageron*. Paris: SFHOM.

Revel, J. 1989. "L'histoire au ras du sol." Preface to the French edition of Giovanni Levi, *Le pouvoir au village: Histoire d'un exorciste dans le Piémont du XVIIᵉ siècle*, i–xxxii. Paris: Gallimard.

Rey, M. 2018. *Histoire de la Syrie (XIXᵉ–XXIᵉ siècles)*. Paris: Fayard.

Ricca, S. 2007. *Reinventing Jerusalem: Israel's Reconstruction of the Jewish Quarter after 1967*. London and New York: I. B. Tauris.

———. 2010. "Heritage, Nationalism and the Shifting Symbolism of the Wailing Wall." *Archives de Sciences sociales de religions* 51 (July–September): 169–88.

Rioli, M.C. 2020. *A Liminal Church: Refugees, Conversions and the Latin Diocese of Jerusalem, 1946–1956*. Leiden, Netherlands: Brill.

Rivet, D. 2002. *Le Maghreb à l'épreuve de la colonisation*. Paris: Hachette Littératures.

Rogan, E. L. 2015. *The Fall of the Ottomans: The Great War in the Middle East*. New York: Basic Books.

Rokem, J. 2012. "Politics and Conflict in a Contested City." *Bulletin du Centre de recherche français à Jérusalem* 23.

Roncayolo, M. 1990. *La ville et ses territoires*. Paris: Gallimard.

Rosen-Ayalon, M. 2002. *Art et archéologie islamiques en Palestine*. Paris: Presses universitaires de France.

Rossoff, D. 1998. *Where Heaven Touches Earth*, Jerusalem: Guardian Press.

Rota, O. 2003. "L'exode arabe d'Eïn-Kerem en 1948: La relation des événements par les sœurs de Notre-Dame de Sion, St. Jean in Montana." *Tsafon* 46 (Winter): 179–98.

Rubinstein, D. 1980. "The Jerusalem Municipality under the Ottomans, British and Jordanians." In J. Kraemer, ed., *Jerusalem, Problems and Prospects*. New York: Praeger.

Rubinstein, Danny. 1995. *The Mystery of Arafat*. Lebanon, NH: Steerforth Press.

Salah al-Maghribi, A. 2014. *Min Jarjara ila al-karmal: Tajribat 'â'ilatu al-Maghribi fil-hijra wal-hawiyya* (From Jarjara to Carmel: A Maghrebi Family's experience of exile and identity).

Salamon, A., ed. 2004. "Seismically Induced Ground Effects of the February 11, 2004, ML 5.2, Northeastern Dead Sea Earthquake." *Geological Survey of Israel*. Jerusalem. https://www.isprambiente.gov.it/files/progetti/inqua/report-final.pdf.

Salenson, I. 2014. *Jérusalem: Bâtir deux villes en une*. Paris: Éditions de l'Aube.

Sanbar, E., ed. 2013. *Jérusalem et la Palestine: Le fonds photographique de École biblique de Jérusalem*. Paris: Hazan.

Saposnik, Arieh Bruce, 2008. *Becoming Hebrew: The Creation of a Jewish National Culture in Ottoman Palestine*. Oxford, UK: Oxford University Press.

———. 2015. "Wailing Walls and Iron Walls: The Western Wall as Sacred Symbol in Zionist National Iconography." *American Historical Review* 120, no. 5 (December): 1653–81.

Sbaï, J. 2018. *La politique musulmane de la France: Un projet chrétien pour l'Islam ? (1911–1954)*. Paris: CNRS Éditions.

Scelles, J. 1949. "Du Mur des Lamentations au Wakf Algérien." *Revue de la Méditerranée* 6:12.

Schattner, M. 1991. *Histoire de la droite israélienne: De Jabotinsky à Shamir*. Paris: Éditions Complexe.

Schattner, M., and F. Schillo. 2013. *La Guerre du Kippour n'aura pas lieu: Comment Israël s'est fait surprendre*. Paris: André Versaille.

———. 2022. *Sous tes pierres Jérusalem, ou les ruses de l'archéologie*. Paris: Plon.

Schillo, F. 2006. "La France et le règlement onusien de la première guerre israélo-arabe (May 1948–July 1949). *Relations Internationales* 3, no. 127: 25–45.

Schmelz, U. O. 1987. *Modern Jerusalem's Demographic Evolutions*. Jerusalem: Jerusalem Institute for Israel Studies.

Schnapp, A., N. Schlanger, S. Lévin, and N. Coye. 2007. "Archives de l'archéologie européenne." *Les nouvelles de l'archéologie*, no. 110.

Schwake, N. 2001. "Le développement du réseau hospitalier en Palestine." In D. Trimbur and R. Aaronsohn, eds., *De Bonaparte à Balfour, la France, l'Europe occidentale et la Palestine 1779–1917*, 109–0. Paris: CNRS Éditions.

Segev, T. 2007a. *1967: Israel, the War, and the Year That Transformed the Middle-East*. London: Metropolitan Books.

———. 2007b. "The June 1967 War and the Palestinian Refugee Problem." *Journal of Palestine Studies* 36, no. 3: 6–22.

————. 2007c. *1967: Six jours qui ont changé le monde*. Paris: Hachette.

Sharon, A. 1973. *Planning Jérusalem: The Master Plan for the Old City of Jerusalem and Its Environs*. Jerusalem and London: Weidenfeld & Nicolson.

Sharon, M. 1977. "The Ayyubid Walls of Jerusalem: A New Inscription from the Time of Al-Mu'azzam 'Isa." In M. Rosen-Ayalon, ed., *Studies in Memory of Gaston Wiet*, 179–93. Jerusalem: Institute of Asian and African Studies / Hebrew University of Jerusalem.

Shiller, E., and A. Yaffe. 2007. "The Demolition of the Mughrabi Neighborhood after the Release of Jerusalem and the Founding of the Kotel Order." *Ariel* 180–81: 121–24. Published in Hebrew.

Singer, A. 1994. *Palestinian Peasants and Ottoman Officials: Rural Administration around Sixteenth-Century Jerusalem*, 71–75. Cambridge, UK: Cambridge University Press.

————. 2002. *Constructing Ottoman Beneficence: An Imperial Soup Kitchen in Jerusalem*. Albany: State University of New York Press.

Sivan, E. 1967. "Le caractère sacré de Jérusalem dans l'Islam aux XIIe–XIIIe siècles." *Studia Islamica* 27:149–82.

————. 1971. "The Beginnings of the 'Fada'il al-Quds' Literature." *Der Islam* 48:100–110.

Sroor, M. 2005a. *Fondations pieuses en mouvement: De la transformation du statut de propriété des biens waqfs à Jérusalem 1858–1917*. Aix-en-Provence, France: IREMAM; and Damascus: IFPO.

————. 2005b. "Jerusalem's Islamic Archives: Sources for the Question of the Waqf in the Ottoman Period." *Jerusalem Quarterly* 22–23: 80–86.

————. 2009. "La transformation des biens waqfs en propriété privée (jérusalemite et étrangère) à Jérusalem, 1858–1917." In Roger Heacok, ed., *Temps et espaces en Palestine: Flux et résistances identitaires*, 97–128. Beirut: Presses de l'IFP.

Stephan, S. H. 1944. "An Endowment Deed of Khasseki Sultan, Dated 24th May 1552." *Quarterly of the Department of Antiquities in Palestine* 10:170–94.

Stinespring, W. 1966. "Wilson's Arch Revisited." *Biblical Archaeologist* 29, no. 1 (February): 27–36.

————. 1967. "Wilson's Arch and the Masonic Hall." *Biblical Archaeologist* 30, no. 1 (February): 27–31.

Stoler, A,-L. 2009. *Along the Archival Grain: Epistemic Anxieties and Colonial Common Sense*. Princeton, NJ: Princeton University Press.

Stora, B. 1986. *Messali Hadj*. Paris: L'Harmattan.

Storper-Perez, D. 1989. *Au pied du mur de Jérusalem*. Paris: Éditions du Cerf.

Talbi, M. 1960–2005. "Maghariba." In P. J. Bearman, T. Bianquis, C. E. Bosworth, E. Van Donzel, and W. P. Heinrichs, eds. *Encyclopaedia of Islam*, 2nd edition. Leiden, Netherlands: Brill.

Tamari, S. 1999. *Jerusalem 1948. The Arab Neighbourhoods and Their Fate in the War*. Bethlehem: Institute of Jerusalem Studies.

———. 2018. "Waqf Endowments in the Old City of Jerusalem: Changing Status and Archival Sources." In A. Dalachanis and V. Lemire, eds., *Ordinary Jerusalem, 1840–1940: Opening New Archives, Revisiting a Global City*, 490–509. Leiden, Netherlands: Brill.

Tarragon, Jean-Michel de. 2022. "The Five Modifications of Dung-Gate: Bāb Harat al-Magharibah in Jerusalem." *Jerusalem Quarterly*, forthcoming.

Tatarsky, Aviv. 2021. "Israeli Court Is Rubber Stamping Temple Mount Zealots." *Haaretz*, 17 October.

Thénault, S. 2005. *Histoire de la guerre d'indépendance algérienne*. Paris: Flammarion.

———. 2008. "17 octobre 1961: Terreur d'État et violence 'coloniale.'" *La vie des idées*, 7 February.

Tibawi, A. L. 1980. "Special Report: The Destruction of an Islamic Heritage in Jerusalem." *Arab Studies Quarterly* 2, no. 2: 180–89.

Trimbur, D., ed. 2001. *De Bonaparte à Balfour: La France, l'Europe occidentale et la Palestine (1779 1917)*. Paris: CNRS Éditions.

Turner, M. 1984. "Conservation in Jerusalem: The Heritage List." *Kidma: Israel Journal of Development* 28:22–29.

Ulbert, J. 2016. "Qu'est-ce qu'un chancelier de consulat? Une approche par les textes de droit français." *Mélanges de l'École française de Rome: Italie et Méditerranée modernes et contemporaines* 128, no. 2.

Valensi, L. 1998. "Anthropologie comparée des pratiques de dévotion: Le pèlerinage en Terre Sainte au temps des Ottomans." In J. Dakhlia, ed., *Urbanité arabe: Hommage à Bernard Lepetit*, 33–75. Paris: Sindbad-Actes Sud.

Veinstein, Gilles. 1981. "Les pèlerins de La Mecque à travers quelques inventaires après décès ottomans (XVIIᵉ–XVIIIᵉ siècles)." *Revue de l'Occident musulman et de la Méditerranée* 31:63–71.

Vilnay, Z. 1973. *Legends of Jerusalem*. Philadelphia: Jewish Publication Society in America.

Wallach, Y. 2020. *A City in Fragments: Urban Text in Modern Jerusalem*. Stanford, CA: Stanford University Press.

Walter, F. 2008. *Catastrophes: Une histoire culturelle (XVIᵉ–XXIᵉ siècles)*. Paris: Le Seuil.

Weber, S. 2009. *Damascus: Ottoman Modernity and Urban Trans-formation (1808–1918)*. Aarhus, Denmark: Aarhus University Press.

Weigert, G. 1990. "A Maghrebi Religious Endowment in Fourteenth-Century Jerusalem." *Cathedra* 8:25–34.

Weinstock, N. 2011. *Terre promise, trop promise: Genèse du conflit israélo-palestinien, 1882–1948*. Paris: Odile Jacob.

Weksler-Bdolah, S., A. Onn, B. Ouahnouna, and S. Kisilevitz. 2009. "Jerusalem, the Western Wall Plaza Excavations, 2005–2009." *Hadashot Arkheologiyot* 121.

Weltmann, S. E. 1961. "Germany, Turkey, and the Zionist Movement, 1914–1918." *Review of Politics* 23 (April): 246–69.

Wharton, A. 2008. "Jerusalem Remade." In S. Isenstadt and K. Rizvi, eds., *Modernism and the Middle-East: Architecture and Politics in the Twentieth Century.* Seattle: University of Washington Press.

Wigoder, G., ed. 1993. *Dictionnaire encyclopédique du judaïsme.* Paris: Editions du Cerf.

Willis, B. 1928. "Earthquakes in the Holy Land." *Bulletin of the Seismological Society of America* 18, no. 2 (June).

Yannai, Y., and M. Pearlman. 1964. *Historical Sites in Israel.* With preface by Yigael Yadin. London: W. H. Allen.

Yerushalmi, Y. H. 1984. *Zakhor: Histoire juive et mémoire juive.* Paris: Gallimard.

Zipperstein, S. E. 2020. *Law and the Arab–Israeli Conflict: The Trials of Palestine.* London: Routledge.

Zohar, M., R. Rubin, and A. Salamon. 2014. "Earthquake Damage and Repair: New Evidence from Jerusalem on the 1927 Jericho Earthquake." *Seismological Research Letters* 85, no. 4: 912–22.

INDEX

Note: page numbers in italics refer to figures. Those followed by n refer to notes, with note number.

Abd al-Daïm al-Maghribi, 63

Abdallah I (king of Jordan): assassination of, 123; plan to assimilate Arab Palestine, 123

Abdelhaq, Muhammad Ibrahim: collection of data on destroyed Maghrebi Quarter homes, 240; description of destroyed home of, 241; installation as steward of Waqf Abu Madyan, 155–57, 167, 168; refusal to sign compensation disclaimer/renunciation letter, 262; replacement as steward of Waqf Abu Madyan, 206; request to Morocco for Waqf Abu Madyan aid, 229–30, 239, 246; visit to Rabat, 239

Abd-el-Kader (Sheikh), 40

Abd el-Kader El-Jazairi, Saïd, 98–99

Abdelkassem Moghrab, Muhammad, 45–46

Abdin Khalifa Khalif, Abdin (Caïd of Oued), 128

Abd el-Kader, Emir, 105

Abdul-Hadi, Amin, 122–23

Abed Jalil al-Maloudi, Mohammed (Abu Munir), 206

Abowd, Tom, 340n37

Abu Gosh, Musa Sadat, 253, 255–56, 259

"The Abu Madyan Hubus in Danger" (Es-Saada), 128

Abu Madyan Shu'ayb: and establishment of waqfs in Jerusalem, 6, 7; and founding act of Waqf Abu Madyan, 22–23; hand of, preserved in zawiya of Maghrebis, 309n14; life of, 23

Abu Saud, Azzam, 185

Abu Saud, Salim Khalil, 100

Abu Saud, Tawfiq, 275

Abu Saud, Waja, 274–75

Abu Saud, Zahwa, 100

Abu Shaker, Issa Musa, 253, 255, 259

ad-Din, Mujir, 24–25

al-Afdal Ali, 6, 19–22, 23